American Flying Boats
and Amphibious Aircraft

American Flying Boats and Amphibious Aircraft

An Illustrated History

E.R. JOHNSON

McFarland & Company, Inc., Publishers

Jefferson, North Carolina, and London

All three-view illustrations are by Lloyd S. Jones.
All photographs are courtesy David W. Ostrowski,
unless otherwise noted.

LIBRARY OF CONGRESS CATALOGUING-IN-PUBLICATION DATA

Johnson, E.R., 1948–
American flying boats and amphibious aircraft :
an illustrated history / E.R. Johnson.
p.   cm.
Includes bibliographical references and index.

ISBN 978-0-7864-3974-4
softcover : 50# alkaline paper

1. Seaplanes—United States—History.
2. Amphibian planes—History.   I. Title.

TL684.J65   2010   629.133'3480973—dc22   2009039619

British Library cataloguing data are available

Front cover, from top: Front profile of Boeing 314 Clipper;
side profile of Consolidated OA-10; top profile of Martin
P6M-1 SeaMaster *(bottom left)*; top profile of Curtiss E Boat

Manufactured in the United States of America

*McFarland & Company, Inc., Publishers
Box 611, Jefferson, North Carolina 28640
www.mcfarlandpub.com*

Acknowledgments

Bringing this book from a bare outline to a finished manuscript was very much a collaborative effort.

I am especially indebted to Lloyd S. Jones and David W. Ostrowski for their unswerving support over the entire course of this project. Lloyd, in order to create a number of the book's three-view drawings, was forced to work from only photographs and reported dimensions; Dave spent an untold number of hours searching for photographic images, which, in turn, he had to identify, reproduce, and format.

I owe special thanks to K.O. Eckland of Aerofiles and Rick Leisenring of the Curtiss Museum for their assistance with some of the hard-to-find photographs, and also I thank Walt Boyne for helping me make connections with some of my research sources.

Fellow aviation history buff and friend Bob Patmore generously loaned me the use of many of the references found in the book's bibliography.

I extend heartfelt appreciation to all of the contributors to the Aerofiles website (see http://www.aerofiles.com/hom.html) for placing a storehouse of priceless aviation data right at my fingertips.

Finally, the 5.9 hours spent with Steve Robinson, CFII, in the left seat of his Lake LA4-200 on Grand Lake near Tulsa, Oklahoma, provided firsthand experience in the unique problems of water flying.

Contents

Preface

    This book was written to provide a concise and comprehensive historical survey of the many different types of flying boats and amphibious aircraft designed and built in the United States over a 96-year period. In terms of scope, a flying boat or amphibious aircraft includes any type of seaplane which uses a boat-type hull for its primary buoyancy, as opposed to detachable floats. While the book does not claim to cover every type of American flying boat or amphibious aircraft ever conceived, a serious attempt has been made to include those which can be documented, minimally at least, by some type of visual record.

    The book is divided into three chronological periods—Part I: The Early Era, 1912–1928; Part II: The Golden Era, 1928–1945; and Part III: The Post-War Era, 1945–Present—and within each, individual aircraft types are reported in alpha-numeric order by manufacturer or builder. In addition to historical background, each aircraft report includes technical specifications, drawings, and one or more photographs. A historical overview, at the beginning of each part, summarizes the considerations that shaped flying boat and amphibious aircraft design relevant to that period, such as advances in aeronautical technology, military procurement, and civilian applications.

    Supplementing the three main parts of the book are three appendices featuring (A) lesser known flying boat and amphibious aircraft types, (B) design concepts that never achieved the flying stage, and (C) three glossaries (aeronautical, military, and aircraft nomenclature) of terms and abbreviations used throughout the book.

PART I

The Early Era, 1912–1928

HISTORICAL OVERVIEW

"Our greatest weakness lies in giving up. The most certain way to succeed is always to try just one more time." — *Thomas A. Edison*

Flying Boat and Amphibious Aircraft Origins

American aviation pioneer and inventor Glenn Hammond Curtiss is generally acknowledged as the "father" of the flying boat and also developed the first amphibian. But his earliest attempt to fly an aircraft off the water—the float-equipped "Loon" in 1908—ended in a dismal failure. The first successful water takeoff (under power) was made by Henri Fabre at Martigues, France, on March 28, 1910, in a float-equipped aircraft named *Le Canard*. Glenn Curtiss did subsequently become the first American airman to accomplish both a water takeoff and landing when he flew his D "Hydro-Aeroplane" from San Diego Bay on January 26, 1911. The D Hydro was a standard, Curtiss-designed 60-hp Type D pusher landplane fitted with a single, flat-bottomed spruce float built locally by Baker Machine Co. Then a year later, in San Diego again, he tried to expand the hydro concept into a true flying boat, adapting a beamy, flat-bottomed hull to the Type D wings and tailplane, then mounting the 60-hp engine within the hull as a chain-driven tractor; however, the resulting aircraft (see Flying Boat No. 1, page 30) turned out to be incapable of flight.

Unwilling to give up, Curtiss built another flying boat (see Flying Boat No. 2, page 32) at Hammondsport, New York, during the summer of 1912. While keeping the flat-bottomed scow configuration, he extended the hull afterbody out far enough to support a cruciform tailplane; wing loading was reduced with the larger Type E wings and power-to-weight ratio improved by mounting a 75-hp O engine as a pusher. But during early testing, despite the improvements, the aircraft resisted all efforts to "unstick" from the water. Through a determined process of trial and error, Curtiss recognized two interrelated problems associated with the displacement of the boat hull: (1) hydrodynamic drag induced along the hull's entire length was exceeding aerodynamic lift; and (2) longitudinal stiffness was limiting the aircraft's ability to pitch up to a flying angle of attack. The solution he finally hit upon was to incorporate a traverse "step" between the fore and afterbodies of the hull, just behind the center of gravity. With the step, the hull afterbody would lift out of the water as the aircraft gathered speed, decreasing drag forces by almost half, and once "on the step," at flying speed, the aircraft could raise its nose and thus fly itself off.

Much the same as the Wright Brother's quest for heavier-than-air, powered flight, Glenn Curtiss shifted the paradigm as to waterborne flight, and every flying boat, amphibian, and seaplane that has flown since, is an heir to his efforts. In 1913, Curtiss initiated the first amphibious experiments with a variation of his A-2 pusher (see Curtiss OWL in Appendix A), and although the first truly useful amphibians did not appear for almost another decade, Curtiss nonetheless paved the way.

Aeronautical Progress

As early aviation pioneers discovered, creating a flying boat was not a simple matter of grafting part of an airplane onto a boat hull. In order to achieve flight from the water and land on it again, a flying boat demanded a unique mixture of design characteristics: it had to combine all of the aerodynamic features of a landplane (i.e., lift + thrust over weight + drag) with a planing hull that would permit it to accelerate to flying speed. At the same time, the hull needed to be seaworthy, maneuverable, and stable on the water. The invention of the hull step demonstrated that hydrodynamic lift could be used to reduce drag to the point where flight was possible. Early experience gained by Curtiss and others generated many improvements in hull design, the step becoming progressively deeper and a V-chine being added to the hull planing surfaces for improved stability and handling. Sponsons—buoyant extensions to the sides of the hull forebody—began appearing on larger flying boats to offset the increased weight and tophamper of larger wings, multiple powerplants, and fuel.

Given the fact that the science of aeronautics was still in its infancy, would-be flying boat designers faced immense obstacles during the earliest years of development. Water-cooled aero engines like the Curtiss O or the Roberts Six produced such low power-to-weight ratios (i.e., 1 hp for 3½ to 4 lbs.), that the aircraft were barely flyable, and even then, under only the most favorable conditions of water and wind. Evidence of this was seen recently in the protracted flight trials—the aircraft flew on September 13, 2008, a year after initial attempts—encountered with the Curtiss Museum's "America" replica, which is powered by a pair of original 100-hp Curtiss OXX-6 engines (for more information see http://curtiss-flying-boat.com/index.html). Construction material in those days was necessarily restricted to light varieties of wood like spruce (note that marine and aircraft grades of plywood did not appear until the 1930s), and the need to keep wing-loading as low as possible tended to produce large, heavily-braced structures, which, as a result of drag, seriously limited overall performance in terms of speed, climb, and range.

The advent of new engines like the 400-hp Liberty 12 in 1917 ushered in major improvements in flying boat performance. Their much better power-to-weight ratios (e.g., 1 hp for 2 lbs.) could be directly translated to higher useful loads and longer range, even if parasite drag only allowed smaller increases in speed and climb. While the duration of the earliest flights was measured in feet, flying boats like the Naval Aircraft Factory (Curtiss) F-5L were routinely patrolling 800-mile stretches of ocean by the end of World War I. The decade of the 1920s saw even more progress in American flying boat development. Air-cooled radial engines (e.g., Wright *Whirlwind* [300 hp] and *Cyclone* [525 hp]; Pratt & Whitney *Wasp* [425 hp] and *Hornet* [525 hp]), which made their debut during the late 1920s, brought new levels of reliability and even better power-to-weight efficiency. Much of the parasite drag normally associated with flying boats was considerably reduced by better streamlining techniques and breakthroughs in airfoil and structural design allowing wings of reduced area that required less external bracing. Lighter but more durable hulls fabricated from riveted aluminum, the first example of which appeared in 1923 (see Aeromarine AMC, below), became a standard feature of flying boats in the mid–1920s. And by the end of the decade, innovators like Sikorsky and Consolidated (see Part II) were in the process of developing new designs for monoplane flying boats that would set the stage for the military and commercial expansion of the 1930s. Availability of better powerplants as well as advances in aerodynamic and structural design also brought about a renewed interest in amphibious capability, and by the late 1920s, new types of single- and multi-engine amphibians had established themselves in both military and civilian markets.

Military Procurement

In terms of financial impetus, it is probably safe to say the prospect of military funding has been the single most influential factor underlying aircraft design and development, with civilian aviation taking second place behind it. Glenn Curtiss, for example, was as much a businessman as he was an inventor, and the lure of potential U.S. Navy contracts (and the Army to a lesser extent) became a driving factor in his desire to produce the first float-equipped seaplanes and flying boats. Initially, the Navy envisaged flying boats in the role of "scouts" that could launched and recovered from warships, and with the delivery of its first Curtiss C-1 (see page 32) in late 1912, began a series of trials designed to test the concept. As it continued to experiment between 1913 and 1916, the Navy acquired at least twelve more flying boats, mainly Curtiss F models (see below), and within a similar timeframe, a smaller number of Curtiss boats were evaluated by the Army Signal Corps.

But the most significant military interest in American flying boats at that time came not from the U.S. government but the British Admiralty. In late 1914, after the start of World War I in Europe, Curtiss received the first of a series of contracts to deliver military derivatives of his twin-engine America to the Royal Naval Air Service, which, after engine upgrades and a redesign of the hull, began entering service in 1915 as the Felixstowe F.1. Operations with the RNAS F.1s marked the early stages of what was to become the flying boat's most important military mission; namely, maritime patrol, including long-range reconnaissance, convoy escort, and antisubmarine duties. The working partnership between Glenn Curtiss and John Cyril Porte, who headed RNAS operations at Felixstowe, England, helped set the stage for mass-production of newer flying boat types like the Curtiss H-16 and HS, along with the Naval Aircraft Factory F-5.

U.S. Navy interest in acquiring more flying boats grew exponentially after America entered World War I on April 6, 1917. In fact, the indiscriminate sinking of U.S.-flagged merchant vessels by German U-Boats had been a major factor leading to the nation's declaration of war, and flying boats were perceived as a potential means of dealing with the menace. As deliveries proceeded, flying boats became the most numerous type of combat aircraft in the Navy's arsenal, and increasing demand for them led to establishment of the Naval Aircraft Factory (NAF) at Philadelphia in late 1917 for the purpose of augmenting civilian production. Wartime production of Curtiss flying boats was also subcontracted to other manufacturers such as Standard, LWF, Gallaudet, Boeing, and Loughead. By the time hostilities ended in November 1918, the Navy had accepted delivery of over 1,600 flying boats of different types.

Even after the war, the Navy continued to maintain a sizeable fleet of flying boats for the maritime patrol function, consisting mainly of Curtiss H-16s and HS-1L/2Ls and NAF F-5Ls procured under wartime contracts. Continuing naval development of the Curtiss NC series (see page 46) culminated in the first crossing of the Atlantic Ocean by an aircraft on May 31, 1919. The establishment of the U.S. Naval Bureau of Aeronautics (BuAer) in 1921 proved to have a lasting impact on procurement of all naval aircraft, flying boats and amphibians included, and under BuAer's guidance, NAF's role became more important with regard to the formulation and testing of new ideas. This was no more apparent than during the late 1920s, when the Navy replaced its World War I-era flying boats with new types of biplanes that were based on virtually identical NAF designs (see Douglas PD, Hall PH, Keystone PK, and Martin PM in Part II). But even while doing this, BuAer was simultaneously pursuing long-range plans to replace the biplanes with the Navy's first generation of monoplane flying boats (see Consolidated PY and Martin P2M, P3M in Part II).

Although the U.S. military services had expressed some interest in aircraft having amphibious capability even before World War I, the extra weight and drag associated with landing gear was deemed to impose unacceptable limits on useful load and range. But a fresh approach to the problem during the early 1920s resulted in the creation of a new category of military aircraft—the utility and observation amphibian. The first example, Grover Loening's single-engine OL-1/OA-1 (see page 55), appeared in 1923, and was subsequently acquired by the Navy, Marine Corps, Army, and Coast Guard. Instead of trying to adapt wheels to a flying boat, Loening designed his aircraft from the ground up as an amphibian, devising a novel "shoehorn" tractor layout that combined elements of flying boats and floatplanes with an effective manual gear retraction system. Although taken into Navy service in 1927 under a patrol designation (i.e., PS-1), the Sikorsky S-36 (see page 71) can be regarded as the forerunner of the various types of twin-engine, general-purpose military amphibians (e.g., Sikorsky S-38, Douglas Dolphin, Grumman Goose, etc.) that would see such widespread use in the 1930s and 1940s by all services, including the Coast Guard.

Civil Developments

Although commercial air travel in America did not really start gaining momentum until the late 1920s, the earliest passenger-carrying services in the nation actually began operations with flying boats on inland waterways and relatively short coastal routes. The first, the St. Peterburg–Tampa Airboat Line, commenced service across Tampa Bay in January 1914 with two Benoist Type XIV flying boats (see page 21), though its operations ceased after only four months due to financial difficulties. Silas Christofferson was reported to have operated a single-engine flying boat of his own design (see Christofferson Hydro in Appendix A, page 298) as the San Francisco–Oakland Aerial Ferry sometime in 1914. Another short-lived venture, Chaplin Air Line, flew passengers in a Curtiss MF (see page 45) between Los Angeles and Catalina Island for a brief time in 1919. More ambitious was Aeromarine Airways, which used modified Curtiss HS-2s and NAF F-5Ls (see page 11) to fly passengers between Southern Florida, Cuba, and the Bahamas from 1919 to 1923. Pacific Marine Airways operated two Curtiss HS-2s between Los Angeles and Catalina Island from 1920 until 1928, when it was taken over by Western Air Express. In 1922, under the sponsorship of Loening Aircraft, using three of its Flying Yachts (see page 54), the New York-Newport Air Service carried passengers between New York City and Newport, Rhode Island until a crash in 1923 caused it to discontinue operations. At least as significant as the Ford 4-AT/5-AT Tri-Motor's role in the expansion of U.S. air routes over land during the mid– and late 1920s, Sikorsky's S-38 (see page 73) established the precedent for an analogous expansion of international routes over water when the first examples began entering service in 1928 with newly-established airlines such as the New York, Rio & Buenos Aires Line and Pan American Airways.

Small numbers of flying boats were also employed to establish the first international Air Mail routes. Edward Hubbard (Victoria Air Service) inaugurated mail service between Seattle and Vancouver, British Columbia, in 1919 with a Boeing B-1 flying boat (see page 25) and maintained the route until 1927. Air Mail service to the Caribbean was started in 1923 with Curtiss HS-2s operated by Gulf Coast Air Line, which flew the mail from New Orleans to Pilottown, Louisiana, where it would be transferred to ships bound for Caribbean ports. Gulf Coast ceased operations in 1927 when its franchise was taken over by Pan American Airways. Although small numbers of privately owned flying boats existed as early as 1913, efforts to market them for personal or business transportation were generally unsuccessful until the late 1920s, when more up-to-date amphibians like the Loening Air Yacht (see page 60) began selling to wealthy executives, mainly on the Eastern Seaboard.

THE EARLY ERA • 1912–1928

Aircraft Manufacturer	Model	First Flight
Aeromarine Plane and Motor Corp.:	A40	1919
	A50, A52, A55 Limousine Flying Boat	1919
	A75	1919
	AMC	1923
American Aeronautical Co. (Savoia-Marchetti):	S-55	1927
	S-56	1926
	S-62	1928
Benoist Aeroplane Co.:	Type 13, 14, and 16	1913
	Type 15	1915
Boeing Airplane Co.:	B-1	1919
	PB-1, -2	1925
	B204 Courier	1928

Aircraft Manufacturer	*Model*	*First Flight*
Curtiss Aeroplane Co.:	D (Flying Boat No. 1)	1912
	E (Flying Boat No. 2)	1912
	F	1912
	H-1 to H-4 Small America	1914
	K	1915
	H-8, H-12, and H-16 Large America	1915
	T Triplane (Model 3)	1916
	HS	1917
	MF and Seagull (Model 18)	1918
	NC-1 to NC-10	1918
Eastman Aircraft Corp.:	E-2 Sea Rover/Sea Pirate	1928
Ireland Aircraft, Inc.:	N-1/-2 Neptune	1927
Leoning Aeronautical Engr. Co.:	Flying Yacht (S-1)	1922
	OL, HL (OA-1, -2)	1923
	C-1, C-2 Air Yacht	1928
Lewis and Vought Corp.:	VE-10 Batboat	1919
Naval Aircraft Factory:	F-5L (PN-5, PN-6)	1918
	TF	1920
	PN-7, PN-8, PN-9, PN-10, and PN-12	1924
Sikorsky Mfg. Co.:	S-34	1926
	S-36 (PS-1)	1927
	S-38 (PS-2, C-6)	1928
Sperry Aircraft Co.:	Land and Sea Triplane	1918

Aeromarine Plane & Motor Co.

Derived originally from the Aeromarine Corp., the Aeromarine Plane & Motor Co. was organized in 1917 in Keyport, New Jersey, and manufactured its first aircraft the same year. In 1920, it established Aeromarine West Indies Airways based in Key West, Florida, and in 1921, became a distributing agent for surplus U.S. Navy aircraft and aero engines. The company ceased all aircraft and airline operations in 1924 and reorganized as the Healey-Aeromarine Bus Co.; rights to aircraft production were transferred to Boland Aeroplane Co.

Aeromarine 40 (1919)

TECHNICAL SPECIFICATIONS (40F)

Type: 2-place U.S. Navy trainer; civil sport aircraft
Total produced: 50 U.S. Navy; 6 civil versions (est.)
Powerplant: one 100-hp Curtiss OXX-6 8-cylinder water-cooled engine driving a two-bladed wooden fixed-pitch propeller.
Performance: max. speed 71 mph at s.l.; ceiling 3,500 ft.; range 250 mi. (est.).
Weights: 2,061 lbs. empty, 2,592 lbs. loaded.
Dimensions: span (upper) 48 ft. 6 in., length 28 ft. 11 in., wing area (not reported).

The model 40, following the model 39 landplane trainer, was designed and built in response to a 1918 Navy Department order for a two-seat seaplane trainer. Very similar in general design to the Curtiss model MF trainer (see page 45), which it was intended to augment, the model 40 was a two-bay biplane of all wood construction having upper and lower wings of unequal span. The wooden hull was of a single-step, V-chine design that extended to and incorporated the tailplane, and the horizontal tail surfaces were mounted atop the vertical fin to keep them out of the spray. The engine was strut-mounted in the wing center-section in a pusher configuration. Side-by-side seating was provided for the instructor and student in the nose section of the hull.

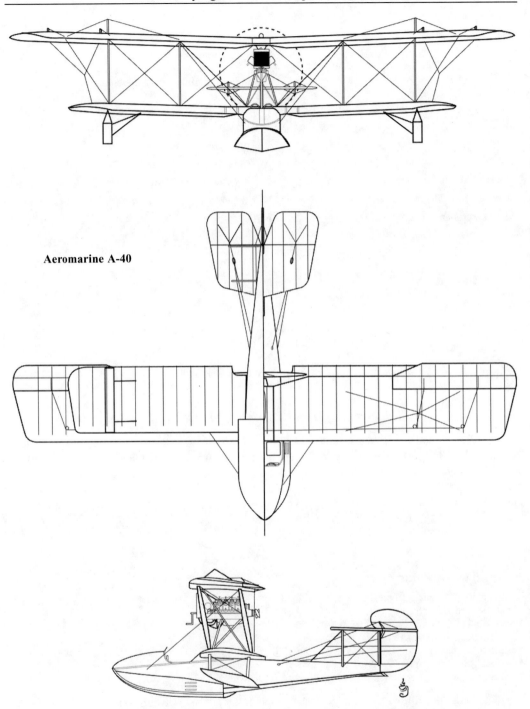

Aeromarine A-40

Although the first civil model 40 may have flown in 1918 with a 150-hp Aeromarine U-8 engine, the first documented flight of the Navy model 40F occurred in 1919. When World War I ended, the original Navy order for 200 aircraft was reduced to 50, and all examples were delivered after the armistice. The type remained active with the Navy through the early 1920s until replaced by newer aircraft. During service, some model 40Fs were reportedly refitted with 150-hp Hispano-Suiza engines to improve performance and payload. The civil versions (40 and 40B, 140-hp Hispano-Suiza

Aeromarine's A-40 was intended to augment Curtiss Fs and MFs in the training of Navy pilots, but its contract was cut short by the end of World War I.

engine; 40 C, 150-hp Aeromarine engine; 40L, 130-hp Aeromarine L engine; 40T, 100-hp Curtiss OXX-6 engine; and 40U, 100-hp Aeromarine U-6 engine) were produced in 1919 and sold for around $9,000 each.

Aeromarine 50, 52, and 55 Limousine Flying Boat (1919)

TECHNICAL SPECIFICATIONS (50C)

Type: 3 or 4-place civil transport.
Total produced: 4–5 (est.).

Aeromarine Model 50B shown in late 1919 with enclosed cockpit. The models 50, 52, and 55 represented an ultimately unsuccessful attempt to offer improved civil versions utilizing components of the Navy A40 trainer.

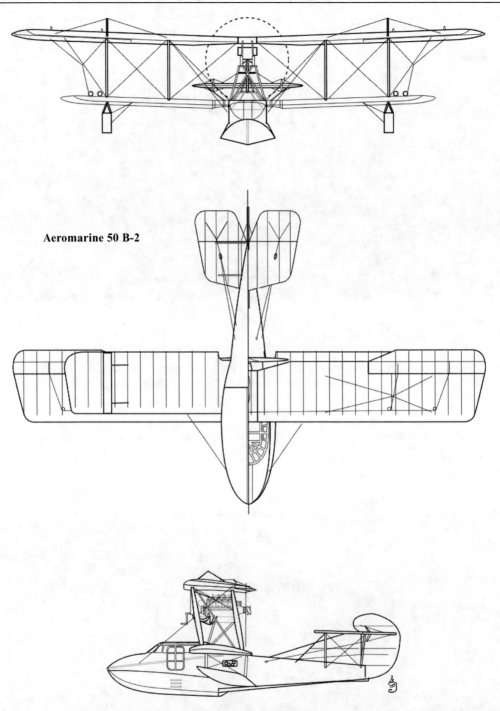

Aeromarine 50 B-2

Powerplant: one 150-hp or 180-hp Aeromarine U-8 8-cylinder water-cooled engine driving a two-bladed wooden fixed-pitch propeller.
Performance: max. speed 75 mph at s.l.; ceiling (not reported); range 300 mi.
Weights: empty (not reported), 3,276 lbs. loaded.
Dimensions: as 40F, above.

The models 50, 52, and 55 Limousine Flying Boat represented an attempt by Aeromarine to offer a more powerful civil design utilizing the wings, tailplane, and general hull structure of the model 40F. The models 50 and 50C were flown in 1919 with open cockpits for the pilot and passengers; the model 50B of 1919, 52 of 1921, and 55 of 1922 all featured enclosed cockpits. At least one model 50 is reported to have operated with Aero, Ltd. during 1919 over the 100-mile route between New York City and Atlantic City, New Jersey, ostensibly as a passenger carrier, but more likely for the purpose of moving alcoholic beverages following the passage of the Prohibition Act earlier the same year. In 1923, an enlarged model 60 with two 180-hp pusher engines was planned, but no flying example was ever completed.

Aeromarine 75 (1920)

TECHNICAL SPECIFICATIONS

Type: 12–14 passenger civil transport.
Total produced: 4–5 (est.).
Powerplant: two 420-hp Liberty 12A 12-cylinder water-cooled engines driving two-bladed wooden fixed-
 pitch propellers.
Performance: max. speed 82 mph, cruise 75 mph; ceiling 5,000 ft.; range 830 mi.
Weights: empty 9,000 lbs. (est.), 13,600 lbs. loaded.
Dimensions: span (upper) 103 ft. 9 in., length 49 ft. 4 in., wing area 1,397 sq. ft.

The model 75, also referred to as the Flying Cruiser, was not an original Aeromarine design but a modification of ex-Navy Curtiss F-5Ls which the company had acquired surplus. The conversion involved moving the two-place cockpit back to the trailing edge of the wings and installing passenger accommodations with side windows in the forward half of the hull. Completed in late 1920, the first two model 75s began operating in 1921 with Aeromarine's subsidiary, Aeromarine East Indies Airways, where they commenced scheduled operations between New York City and Havana, Cuba, via Atlantic City, Beaufort, South Carolina, Miami, and Key West. The two-day air journey took only half the time required by train and boat. In 1922, as more model 75s came into service, the carrier opened a new a route across Lake Erie between Detroit and Cleveland and extended southern services to include Nassau and Bimini islands. In late 1923, after three years of regular flights, Aeromarine Airways ceased operations due to financial difficulties.

A fairly straightforward adaptation of the NAF/Curtiss F-5L, Aeromarine 75 "Nina" as operated by Aeromarine Airways on Caribbean routes during the early 1920s.

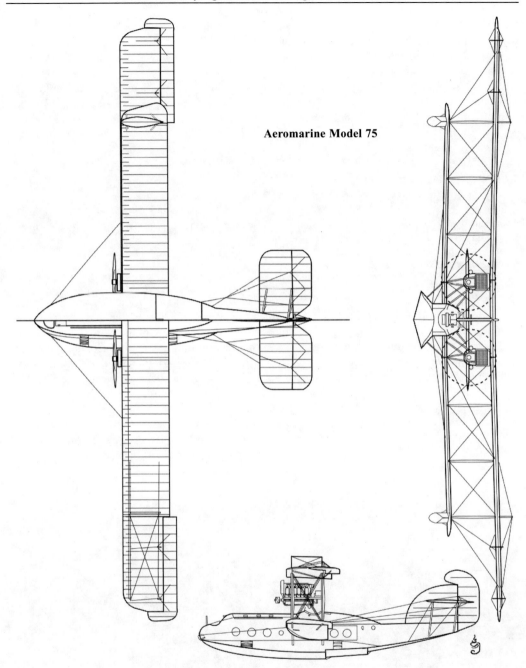

Aeromarine Model 75

Aeromarine AMC (1923)

TECHNICAL SPECIFICATIONS

Type: 6-passenger civil transport.
Total produced: 1
Powerplant: one 400-hp Liberty 12 12-cylinder water-cooled engine driving a two-bladed wooden fixed-pitch
      propeller.
Performance: max. speed 97 mph, cruise 80 mph; ceiling 14,000 ft.; range (not reported).
Weights: empty (not reported), 2,440 lbs. loaded.
Dimensions: span (upper) 65 ft. 0 in., length 32 ft. 10 in., wing area (not reported).

Similar in configuration to the Curtiss HS series, the AMC (Aeromarine Metal Commercial) was an effort to introduce a civil flying boat of conventional two-bay biplane design that possessed a more modern airframe, most notably an all-duraluminum hull and a dural-framed empennage. Once operational, the company had hoped to put them in service as replacements for Aeromarine Airway's aging fleet of wooden-hulled model 75s. The AMC flew for the first time in June 1923 and soon afterward commenced a trial route between New York and San Juan, Puerto Rico, however, Aeromarine and its airline subsidiary ceased operations in late 1923, and no more AMCs were completed. While not a commercial success, the AMC did nonetheless establish a new standard for flying boats with more durable metal hulls.

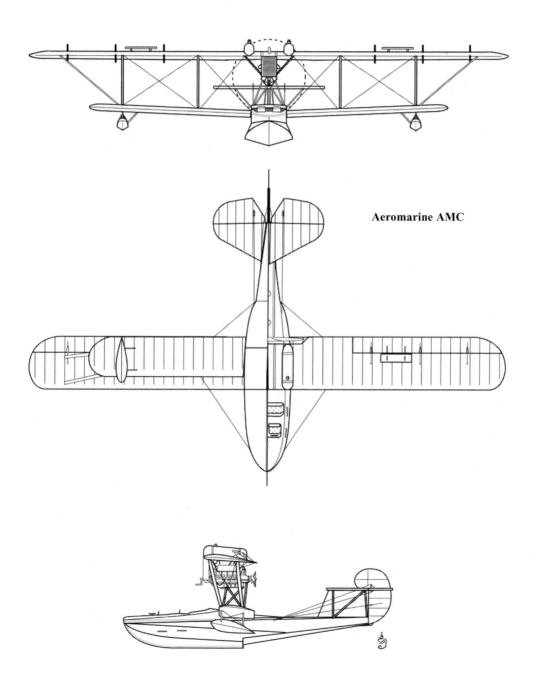

Aeromarine AMC

The sole Aeromarine AMC as shown in Canadian registration after being sold to Fairchild Air Transport. Though the AMC was not a commercial success, its all-aluminum hull helped establish new standards for flying boat construction.

American Aeronautical Corp.

The American Aeronautical Corp. of Port Washington, New York, was established in 1926 to license-build and market aircraft in the U.S. which had been designed and manufactured by the well-known Italian firm of Savoia-Marchetti. A plane built in the American plant was often referred to as an "American Marchetti" to downplay its foreign origins. The parent Italian company was founded in 1915 by Umberto Savoia and the name Marchetti was added in 1922 when Allessandro Marchetti joined the company as chief designer.

American Marchetti S-55 (1927)

TECHNICAL SPECIFICATIONS (U.S. VERSION)

Type: 4- to 6-passenger civil transport.
Total produced: 3 in U.S.; 200 in Italy.
Powerplant: two 515-hp Isotta-Fraschina 12-cylinder water-cooled engines driving two-bladed wooden fixed-pitch propellers.
Performance: max. speed 128 mph, cruise 110 mph; ceiling 16,400 ft.; range 2,175 mi.
Weights: 12,677 lbs. empty, 18,210 lbs. loaded.
Dimensions: span 78 ft. 9 in., length 54 ft. 11 in., wing area 1,001 sq. ft.

When the first Italian-made S-55 prototype flew in 1925, it represented an epoch-making advance in flying boat design. Its unorthodox planform employed a cantilever monoplane wing that was shoulder-mounted to twin boat hulls, with a triple-fin tailplane supported by two booms extending from the hulls. The two engines, arranged in tandem, were supported by struts on top of the wing center section, which also housed the two-man cockpit. During the late 1920s and early 1930s,

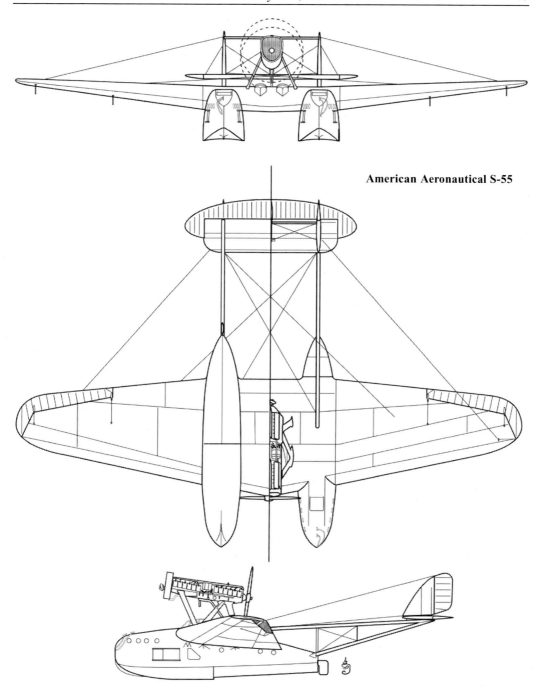

American Aeronautical S-55

S-55s made a number of record-breaking breaking flights, the best remembered of which was the 24-plane formation led by Air Marshall Italo Balbo from Orbetello, Italy, to Chicago, Illinois, in 1933. Most of the S-55s manufactured in Italy served with the *Regia Aeronautica* as maritime patrol boats, and the final examples were retired in 1939. Three S-55s were completed in the U.S. by American Aeronautical in 1927 and 1928 under civil registrations NC20K, NC105H, and NC175M. They sold for $57,000 each, and buyers had the option of specifying either Isotta-Fraschini, Wright *Cyclone*, or Curtiss *Conqueror* engines, although the three S-55s completed in the U.S. all apparently came with Issota-Fraschini engines.

One of three S-55s built in the U.S. by American Aeronautical, NC20K is shown in the markings of Alaska Airways, Inc., which operated it until 1932.

American Marchetti S-56, BB-1 (1926)

TECHNICAL SPECIFICATIONS (S-56B)

Type: 2 or 3-seat civil transport/trainer.
Total produced: 36–40 in U.S.
Powerplant: one 125-hp Kinner 5-cylinder air-cooled radial engine driving a two-bladed wooden fixed-pitch propeller.
Performance: max. speed 95 mph, cruise 80 mph; ceiling 7,000 ft.; range 280 mi.
Weights: 1,350 lbs. empty, 2,150 lbs. loaded.
Dimensions: span 34 ft. 1 in., length 25 ft. 7 in., wing area 285 sq. ft.

Introduced in Italy in 1924, powered by a 90-hp Anzani engine, the first American S-56 was manufactured in 1926 with a 90-hp Kinner K-5. Unlike the S-55, the S-56A was a fairly conventional one-bay, strut and wire-braced biplane having a hull and wings of mostly wooden construction. The A model came with amphibious landing gear retracted by means of a manual hand crank. American Aeronautical marketed them primarily to civil users at a base price of $7,375. The S-56B, which appeared in 1931, differed in having a 125-hp Kinner B-5 which upped the useful load and made carrying a third passenger more practical. The out-of-sequence S-56C (also listed as S-56-31) was sold as a two-seater with a 100-hp Kinner engine. One S-56C later converted to a single seat configuration and given extra fuel capacity, was used on an around-the-world flight by Zachary Reynolds. In 1931, S-56 production rights were transferred to the Edward G. Budd Mfg. Co., a firm specializing in fabrication of stainless steel, under the designation BB-1. A single example was completed in 1932 with a stainless steel hull plus a wing and tailplane framework of the same material. Two S-56s are said to exist today, though their status is not known.

American Marchetti S-62 (1928)

TECHNICAL SPECIFICATIONS

Type: 3-seat armed scout.
Total produced: 1 in U.S.
Powerplant: one 500-hp Isotta-Fraschina V-type 12-cylinder water-cooled engine driving a two-bladed wooden fixed-pitch propeller.
Armament: One .30-calibre Lewis machine gun in the nose and two .30-calibre Lewis machine guns amidships.
Performance: max. speed 137 mph, cruise 118 mph; ceiling 16,100 ft.; range 1,243 mi.
Weights: 5,798 lbs. empty, 11,089 lbs. loaded.
Dimensions: span 54 ft. 8 in., length 40 ft. 3 in., wing area 748 sq. ft.

Having entered service with the *Regia Aeronautica* in 1926 as a small reconnaissance flying boat, the S-62 represented an attempt by American Aeronautical to interest the U.S. Navy with a domestically-built version. The single U.S.–made example, manufactured in 1928, received ATC certification in 1931; however, the Navy had by that time established a fairly set pattern of procuring its flying boats and floatplanes from established naval contractors (e.g., Consolidated, Douglas, Martin, etc.), so that no military sales of the S-62 were forthcoming.

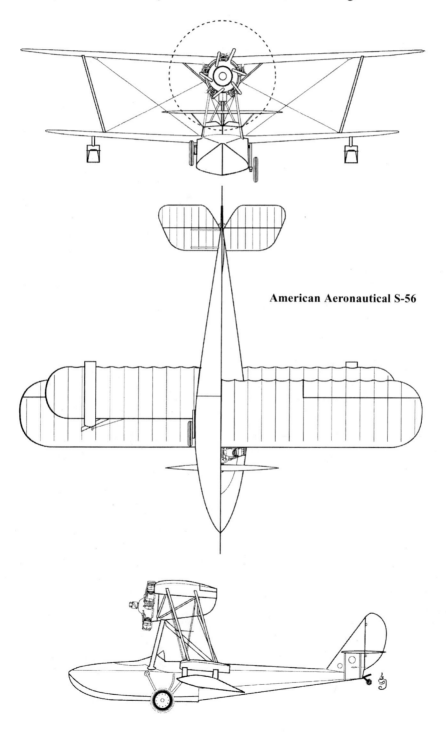

American Aeronautical S-56

One of the more successful pre–Depression civil amphibian designs, this S-56A is shown moored with its wheels retracted.

The entire BB-1 airframe was fabricated from stainless steel parts. Only one was built in 1932.

Italian-made S-62. Efforts to interest the Navy in the license-built U.S. version were unsuccessful.

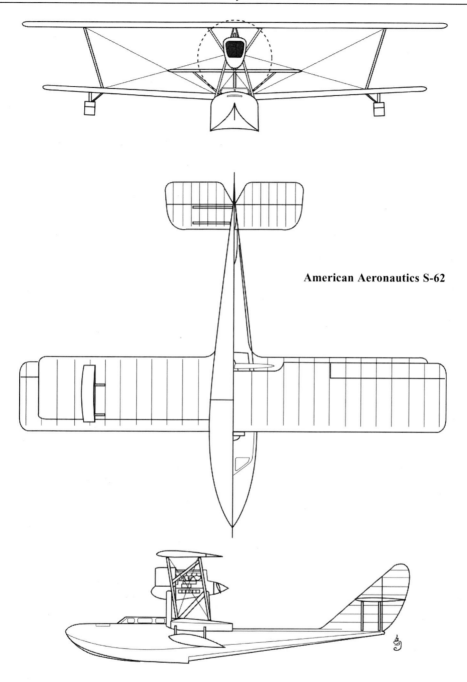

American Aeronautics S-62

Benoist Aeroplane Co.

Founded in 1908 by Thomas Benoist as Benoist Aircraft Co. in St. Louis, Missouri, it was reorganized as Benoist Aeroplane Co. in 1915 and moved to Chicago, Illinois, then moved again in 1917 to Sandusky, Ohio. Benoist's interest in water-borne flight began in 1912 when he began experiments with one of his Type XII landplanes equipped with a single center float. The potential of this pioneering company was foreshortened by Thomas Benoist's untimely death in an aircraft accident in 1917. All operations were suspended soon afterward, at which point a total of 106 aircraft (of all types) had reportedly been completed.

Type XIV shown flying low over Tampa Bay in early 1914. The St. Petersburg-Tampa Airboat Line was the first air carrier in the world to offer scheduled daily service. The venture lasted only four months.

Benoist Type 13, 14, and 16 (1913)

TECHNICAL SPECIFICATIONS (TYPE 14)

Type: 2-place civil transport.
Total produced: 14.
Powerplant: One 75-hp Roberts 6-cylinder water-cooled engine or 80-hp Sturtevant 6-cylinder water-cooled engine driving a two-bladed wooden fixed-pitch propeller.
Performance: Max. speed 64 mph; ceiling (not reported).; range 175 mi.
Weights: empty 1,250 lbs., 2,600 lbs. loaded (est.).
Dimensions: span 44 ft. 0 in., length 26 ft. 10 in., wing area (not reported).

Using the three-bay biplane wings and the empennage of a Type XII landplane, Benoist's Type XIII featured a boat hull fuselage with side-by-side seating for the pilot and one passenger. The Roberts engine was buried in the hull behind the cockpit with the propeller driven via a chain and sprocket. Intended as a trainer and demonstrator, the Type XIII made its first flight in the summer of 1913. The first two of ten essentially similar Type XIV's were completed later the same year and delivered to the St. Petersburg-Tampa (Florida) Airboat Line, which holds the distinction of being the first passenger-carrying airline in the United States. Service was inaugurated in January 1914 with two scheduled round trips per day across Tampa Bay, and by the end of March, the company had carried 1,204 passengers without serious mishap—a truly remarkable achievement for this era of aviation. Service was discontinued in April, however, due to a decline in the local economy, and the two Type XIV's were sold to private owners. Type XIVs were thereafter a common sight at many exhibition flights around the country during 1914 and 1915. Though not mentioned in the sources, the ability to carry only one fare-paying passenger at a time appears to have been a serious financial drawback. The three Type 16s built in 1916 for the Staten Island School of Aeronautics were identical to the Type 14s except for having a canted tail boom made of formed metal.

Benoist Type 15 (Type C) (1915)

TECHNICAL SPECIFICATIONS

Type: 6-place civil transport.
Total produced: 1
Powerplant: two 100-hp Roberts 6-cylinder water-cooled engines driving two-bladed wooden fixed-pitch propellers.
Performance: max. speed 75–80 mph (est.); ceiling (not reported).; range 300 mi. (est.).
Weights: empty 4,000 lbs. (est.), 5,900 lbs. loaded (est.).
Dimensions: span 65 ft. 0 in., length 38 ft. 10 in., wing area (not reported).

Also known as the type C, the Benoist Type 15 was originally conceived to compete for the $50,000 prize offered by the *London Daily Mail* in 1914 for the first transatlantic flight. It was basically an enlarged Type 14 with a four-bay wing layout and upper and lower wings of equal span. The two direct-drive engines were strut-mounted beneath the upper wing. When the onset of World War I prevented any attempt at a transatlantic flight, Benoist sought to interest the British government in purchasing the aircraft for use in antisubmarine patrol and went so far as to make arrangements to have the type mass-produced at a plant owned by the St. Louis Car (rail) Company. By this time, however, the British were already committed to flying boat contracts with Curtiss, and no orders for the Type 15 were forthcoming.

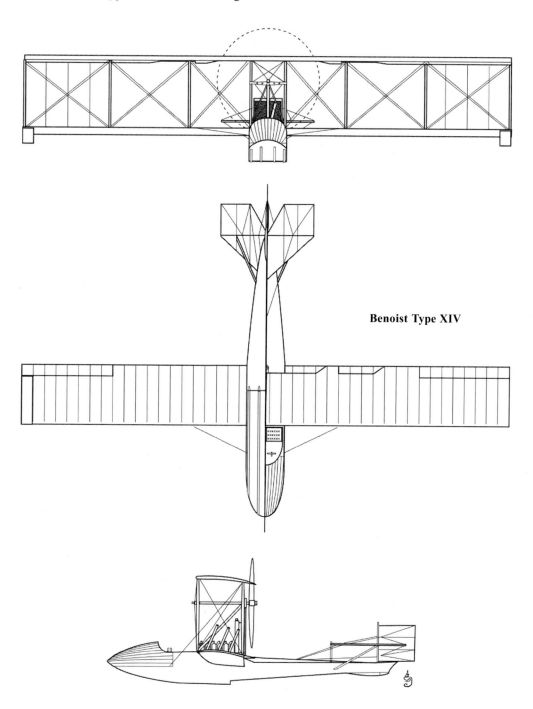

Benoist Type XIV

Benoist hoped to mass-produce the Type 15 for the British Royal Naval Air Service, but the company ceased operations soon after Benoist's untimely death in 1917.

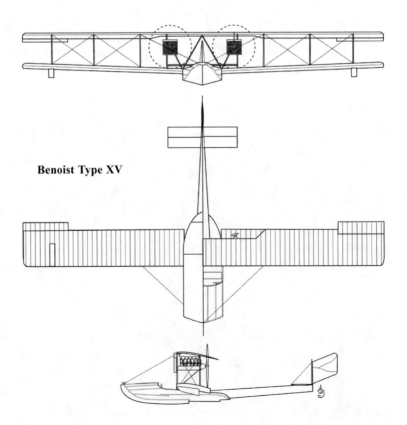

Benoist Type XV

Boeing Airplane Co.

Certainly one of the best known names in American aviation, the company was founded by William E. (Bill) Boeing in 1916 as Pacific Aero Products Co. in Seattle, Washington, then renamed Boeing Airplane Co. in 1917. Boeing's first airplane, a twin-float seaplane named the B & W, flew for the first time in mid–1916. The company secured the first of the many military contracts that would follow in June 1918, when it received an order from the Navy Department to build 50 Curtiss HS-2L flying boats.

Boeing B-1 Seaplane (1919)

TECHNICAL SPECIFICATIONS (LIBERTY VERSION)

Type: 3-place civil transport.
Total produced: 1
Powerplant: one 200-hp Hall-Scott 6-cylinder water-cooled engine; later refitted with a 400-hp Liberty 12-cylinder water-cooled engine driving a four-bladed wooden fixed-pitch propeller.
Performance: max. speed 90 mph, cruise 80 mph; ceiling 13,300 ft.; range 400 mi.
Weights: empty 2,500 lbs. (est.), 3,850 lbs. loaded.
Dimensions: span 50 ft. 3 in., length 31 ft. 3 in., wing area (not reported).

The B-1 is said to have been Boeing's first attempt to sell an aircraft to purely commercial buyers, primarily for the purpose of carrying mail along coastal regions such as Seattle. Its design emerged as a two-bay biplane that looked much like a scaled down HS-2 in general configuration. The hull was constructed of a laminated wood veneer, and the Hall-Scott engine initially used was pusher mounted on struts right below the upper wing center-section. Not too long after making its first flight on December 27, 1919, the B-1 commenced flying the mail between Seattle and Victoria, British Columbia, a 150-mile roundtrip across the Strait of Juan de Fuca. Although no commercial sales of the aircraft ever materialized, the single B-1 continued the fly the Seattle-Victoria mail route until 1927, wearing out six engines in the process and covering 350,000 miles. The aircraft was reportedly removed from storage and restored in 1951.

The single B-1 produced, shown in Canadian registration in the 1920s. This aircraft covered 350,000 miles and wore out six engines during its eight-year career.

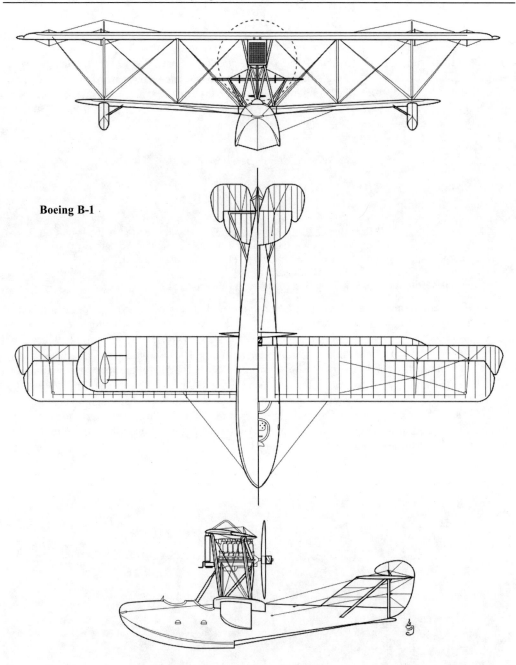

Boeing B-1

Boeing PB (1925)

TECHNICAL SPECIFICATIONS (XPB-1)

Type: 5-place naval maritime patrol.

Total produced: 1.

Powerplant: two 800-hp Packard 2A-2540 12-cylinder water-cooled engines driving four-bladed wooden fixed-pitch propellers.

Armament: none fitted.

Performance: max. speed 125 mph, cruise 80 mph; ceiling 3,300 ft.; range 2,230 mi.

Weights: empty 12,742 lbs., 26,822 lbs. loaded.

Dimensions: span 87 ft. 6 in., length 59 ft. 5 in., wing area 1,823 sq. ft.

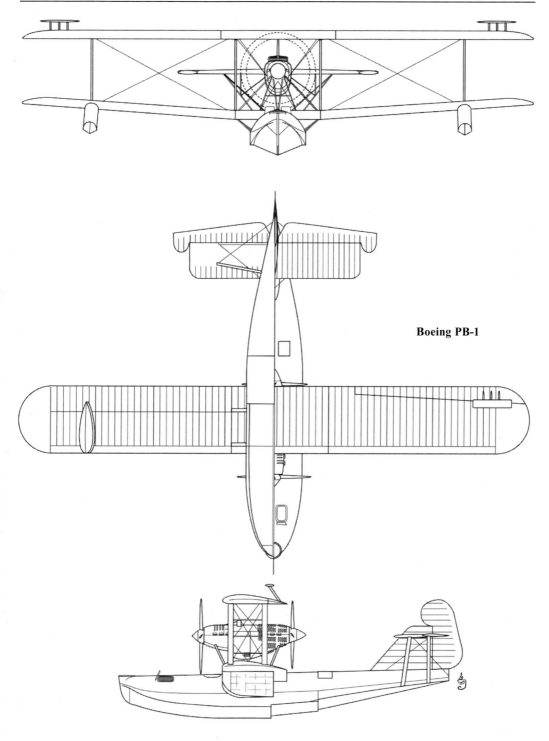

Boeing PB-1

Ordered by the Naval Bureau of Aeronautics (BuAer) in 1925, the XPB-1 was essentially an enlarged Naval Aircraft Factory (NAF) PN-7 (see page 67) which incorporated an all-metal two-step, aluminum hull together with a unique tandem arrangement for its two Packard engines. Originally, the Navy had contemplated using the XPB-1 to lead two NAF PN-9s on the first flight attempt between the California coast and the Hawaiian Islands. While the XPB-1 made it first flight on

The PB-1, when it appeared in mid–1925, was the first type of naval patrol boat to be built with an all-metal hull. The single prototype spent most of its career with NAF as a flying testbed.

August 31, 1925, problems with the Packard engines caused its participation in the California-Hawaii trip to be cancelled. The XPB-1 was thereafter retained by NAF as a testbed, and during 1928, once BuAer had officially switched to a preference for air-cooled engines in Navy aircraft, it was re-designated XPB-2 after being modified and tested with 500-hp Pratt & Whitney R-1690 *Hornet* radial engines, also mounted in tandem, but no production was undertaken.

Boeing 204 Courier (1928)

TECHNICAL SPECIFICATIONS

Type: 4-place civil transport.
Total produced: 10 (est.)
Powerplant: one 410-hp Pratt & Whitney R-1340 *Wasp* 9-cylinder air-cooled radial engine driving a two-bladed ground-adjustable metal propeller.
Performance: max. speed 115 mph, cruise 95 mph; ceiling 9,000 ft.; range 350 mi.
Weights: not reported; useful load listed as 1,630 lbs.
Dimensions: span 39 ft. 8 in., length 32 ft. 7 in., wing area (not reported).

Sometimes referred to as a development of the B-1 of 1919, the Model 204, flown for the first time on March 4, 1928, was actually an entirely different airframe. The 204 originated as a single-bay biplane having its pusher engine mounted on struts between the fuselage and the wing center-

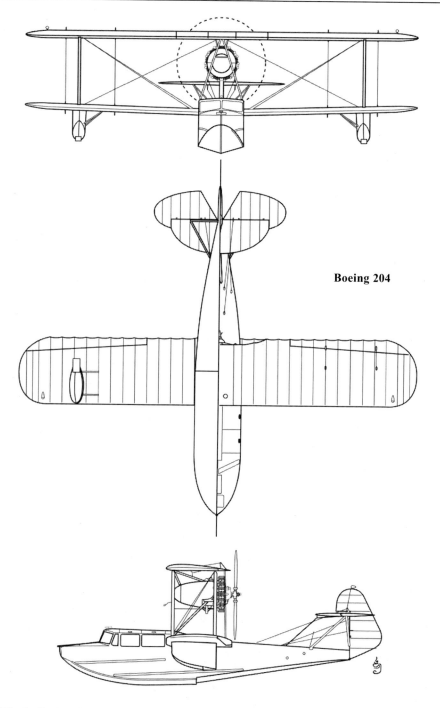

Boeing 204

section. The hull was constructed entirely of wood and featured an enclosed cabin. Five 204s are listed as having been built by Boeing in Seattle during 1928 and 1929, one of which was delivered to William E. Boeing as a personal transport, and four are thought to have been completed by Boeing Aircraft of Canada in Vancouver. One 204 was purchased by Western Air Express to be used on its Catalina Island route and an at least one other was employed by Western Canada Airways on over-water routes. One Canadian-built example, known as the C-204 Totem, was completed with monoplane wings and operated under Canadian registration.

One of five 204s completed by Boeing in Seattle. The diagonal pattern of the wood veneer on the hull is clearly visible. Another four or five 204s were built by Boeing of Canada in Vancouver, B.C.

Curtiss Aeroplane & Motor Co.

Founded by Glenn H. Curtiss and Augustus M. Herring in 1908 at Hammondsport, New York, as the Curtiss-Herring Aeroplane & Motor Co., it was reorganized as the Curtiss Aeroplane Co. in 1910 and renamed Curtiss Aeroplane & Motor Co. in 1916. Glenn Curtiss is commonly acknowledged as having been the "father" of the flying boat. His company, from 1911 to 1919, was at the forefront of most flying boat development, to wit: making the first documented flight of a flying boat in 1912; introducing the first practical flying boat trainers in 1913; producing (in collaboration with British pioneer Cyril Porte) the most successful naval flying boats of the world War I-era; and designing the first aircraft (i.e., NC-4) to cross the Atlantic Ocean. Curtiss Aeroplane and Motor merged with Wright Aeronautical in 1929 and subsequently reappeared as the Curtiss-Wright Airplane Co. Glenn Curtiss died unexpectedly in 1930 at age 52.

Curtiss Model D (Flying Boat No. 1) (1912)

TECHNICAL SPECIFICATIONS

Type: 1 or 2-place civil trainer.
Total produced: 1
Powerplant: one 60-hp Curtiss 8-cylinder water-cooled engine driving two two-bladed wooden fixed-pitch propellers via a chain drive.
Performance: none.
Weights: not reported.
Dimensions: span 26 ft. 3 in., length 20 ft. (est.), wing area 236 sq. ft. (est.).

Following successful hydroplane (floatplane) experiments in 1911, Glenn Curtiss sought to move water-borne flight a step further by adapting a set of the four-bay biplane wings and boom empen-

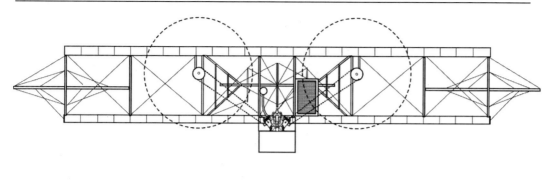

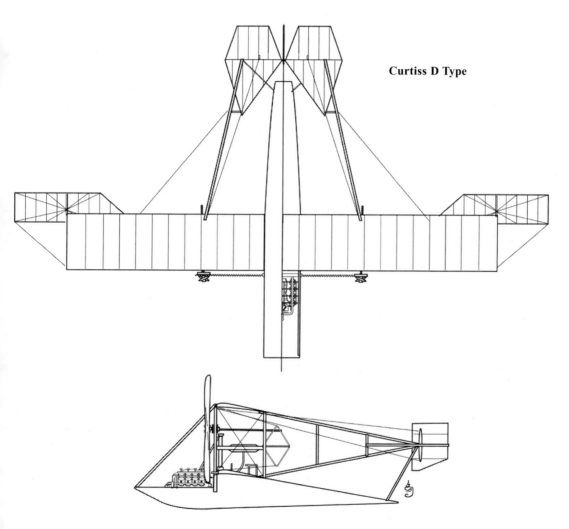

Curtiss D Type

nage from the model D landplane to a boat hull. The flat-bottomed wooden hull was essentially a lengthened and widened hydroplane pontoon to which the lower wings were directly attached. To overcome the tail-heaviness inherent to a pusher configuration, the engine was mounted in the hull, right in front of the wing, with two chain-driven tractor propellers fitted to shafts on the first bay of interplane struts. The cockpit was positioned behind the engine, between the lower wings. Trials with this aircraft, later referred to as Flying Boat No. 1, were carried out in San Diego during early January 1912. As later admitted by Curtiss himself and other witnesses present, this aircraft

Curtiss' first flying boat attempt, the Model D. A combination of factors—hull shape, insufficient power and wing area—prevented it from flying.

never left the water. Undeterred, Curtiss left San Diego in the spring of 1912 to return to Hammondsport, where he commenced work on Flying Boat No. 2.

Curtiss Model E (Flying Boat No. 2 [C-1/AB-1]) (1912)

TECHNICAL SPECIFICATIONS

Type: 2 or 3-place naval/civil trainer.
Total produced: 6–10 (est.)
Powerplant: one 75–100-hp Curtiss OX 8-cylinder water-cooled engine driving a two-bladed wooden fixed-pitch propeller.
Performance: max. speed 60 mph (est.); ceiling (not reported); range (not reported).
Weights: empty 1,490 lbs., 2,500 lbs. loaded (est.).
Dimensions: span 37 ft. 0 in. (40 ft. 0 in. on some), length 27 ft. 2 in., wing area 350 sq. ft. (est.).

Though not the first flying boat built, the model E, sometimes known as Flying Boat No. 2, did in fact make the world's first flight of a flying boat during the month of July in 1912. Taking the experience of prior experiments, Glenn Curtiss started work on a second flying boat during the spring of 1912, which, in its original configuration, utilized standard components of the 1911 model E land and hydro (float) plane, including twenty-eight-foot, eight-inch single-surface, equal-span wings and a pusher-mounted 75-hp Curtiss O V-8 engine. Its flat-bottomed, scow-type hull, unlike Boat No. 1, extended all the way aft to support an empennage consisting of a long-chord fin and rudder with cruciform horizontal surfaces. To reduce the danger of sinking after hard landings, the hull was constructed with six watertight compartments.

Initial trials were not successful, as Flying Boat No. 2 could not be made to "unstick" from the water at takeoff speed. After observing numerous attempts, Curtiss modified the hull to incorporate a "step" just behind the center-of gravity. The step, which became a standard feature on virtually all flying boats, produced a large reduction in hydrodynamic drag by lifting almost half of the hull free of the water and increased lift by permitting the nose of the aircraft to be rotated up to a positive angle of attack. Other changes made included standpipes that bled air into the cavity behind the step, a secondary canard elevator on the nose (later removed due to control problems), and triangular extensions to the upper wing to increase lift. By the fall of 1912 Curtiss had made sufficient progress with the design to sell the Navy it first boat-hulled aircraft, entering service in

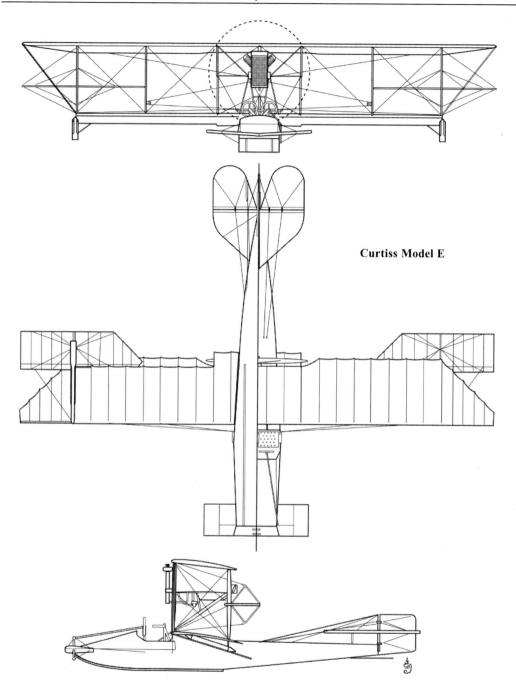

Curtiss Model E

late November as the C-1 (changed to AB-1 in 1914). This aircraft (identified variously as the "Freak Boat" in later Curtiss records) made the first catapult launch by a flying boat in December 1912.

Later model E flying boats featured deepened, V-bottom hulls with a more pronounced step, as well as more powerful engines, a larger rudder, and a diagonal strut in front of the motor mount to prevent the engine from leaving its mounts in hard landings. Besides the Navy's C-1, a number of E boats were built for the Army and the Curtiss Flying School, plus two or three more to civilian purchasers, one of which was used by Lawrence Sperry during 1914 to conduct the first experiments of an airborne gyroscope.

The first E boat, shown here in mid–1912, with front stabilizer that was later removed. The introduction of the hull step and other improvements made it the world's first flying boat.

The Army's S.C. 15 in 1913. Although this aircraft is thought to have F-type wings, it is identified as an E Boat in some texts.

Curtiss Model F (1912)

TECHNICAL SPECIFICATIONS (1917 NAVY VERSION)

Type: 2 place naval/civil trainer.
Total produced: 200 (est.)
Powerplant: one 100-hp Curtiss OXX-3 8-cylinder water-cooled engine driving a two-bladed wooden fixed-pitch propeller.
Performance: max. speed 69 mph; ceiling 4,500 ft.; range 390 mi.

Weights: empty 1,860 lbs., 2,460 lbs. loaded.
Dimensions: span 45 ft. 1 in., length 27 ft. 10 in., wing area 387 sq. ft.

Appearing soon after the model E, the Curtiss model F or "F Boat" was the first type of flying boat to be ordered into quantity production and eventually became the U.S. Navy's standard seaplane trainer through the World War I-era and afterward. One of the chief differences between the early F boats and the E was the internal construction of the wings: the E wing was made up of separate five foot panels between which the spars were hinged, whereas on Fs, the spars ran continu-

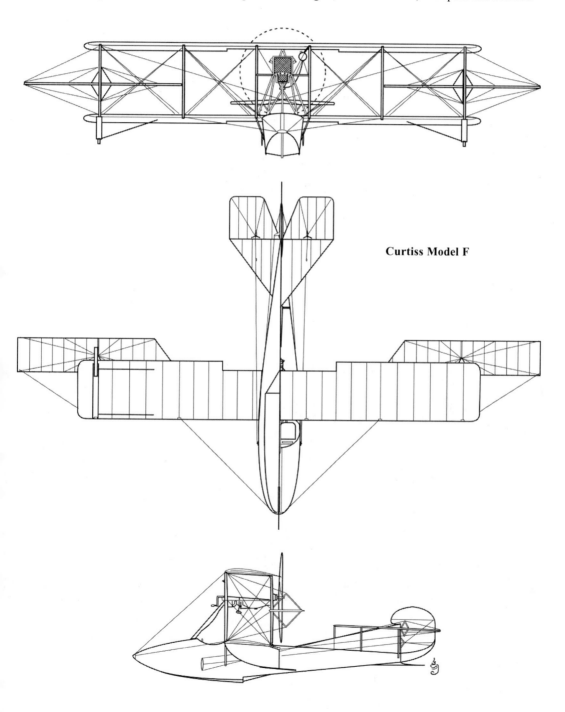

Curtiss Model F

ously from root to tip. The first F to fly had been ordered by the U.S. Army in June 1912 originally as a landplane scout, then, following a change order issued in October, was reconfigured as a flying boat—the Army's first. Delivered and test flown in late November 1912, it retained the two-bay, thirty-eight-foot, four-inch equal span wings, interplane ailerons, and 75-hp pusher engine of the standard F landplane, but possessed a boat hull similar to the Navy's C-1. After taking it into service as the SC-15, the Army used the aircraft as a trainer until it was destroyed in a crash in April 1913.

The F Boats that followed in 1913 and 1914 differed considerably according to who purchased them. Known as the "Spoonbill" F due to the shape of its forward hull, one built in 1913 for businessman Harold McCormick (International Harvester) retained the standard F wings, but featured a 90-hp engine that was tractor-mounted forward of the raised cockpit enclosure. Later, in 1914, the aircraft was rebuilt to a pusher configuration similar to the Army's SC-15. In late 1913 four F Boats were procured by the Navy under the designations C-2 through C-5 (later AB-2 through AB-5). These differed from previous Fs in having unequal span wings (thirty-nine-foot upper, thirty-foot lower), but retained the interplane ailerons. The Navy used them mainly to test and evaluate seaplane operations from ships, and AB-3 became the first Navy aircraft to see military action in April 1914 when it was launched from the U.S.S. *Birmingham* to scout over Veracruz, Mexico, during the French intervention. Another F built for demonstration in 1914, listed as the "English Boat," shared the unequal wing layout of Navy types but featured trailing-edge ailerons in the upper span. Three F Boats built for the Italian Navy in 1914 were delivered with the standard equal span wings, interplane ailerons, and improvements to the hull; five more identical aircraft were later manufactured in Italy under license.

During 1915 and 1916, the Navy took delivery of eight more F Boats, which were completed in the equal-span configuration with interplane ailerons, and four very similar aircraft were acquired by the Army Signal Corps during the same time. In April 1917, as a consequence of U.S. entry into World War I, the Navy placed an order for a further 144 F Boats to be used as standard flying boat trainers. The aircraft delivered under this contract were completed with 100-hp OXX-3 engines and a four-foot, nine-inch increase in the span of the upper wing, and some late production models came with trailing-edge ailerons instead of the interplane type. After World War I ended, many F boats were subsequently declared surplus and sold to private owners.

The first Navy F Boat, the C-2, probably in 1913. Early Fs were outwardly similar to Es, but possessed new wings with continuous rather than hinged spars.

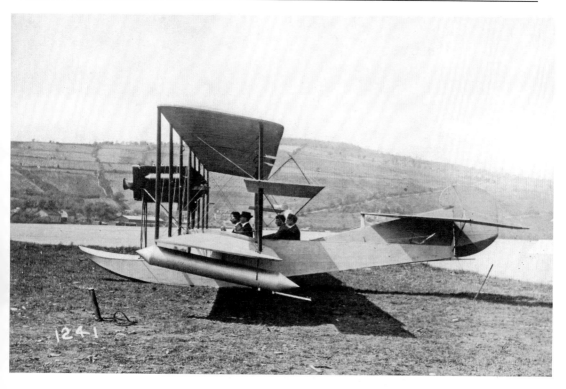

The tractor engine F boat, known as the "Spoonbill," built for businessman Harold McCormick in 1913.

Later F Boat with equal span wings serving with the Navy as a trainer during World War I.

Curtiss H-1 to H-4 Small America (1914)

TECHNICAL SPECIFICATIONS

Type: 5-place civil transport, naval patrol boat.
Total produced: 63.
Powerplant: two 90-hp Curtiss OX-5 8-cylinder water-cooled engines driving two-bladed wooden fixed-pitch
    propellers.
Performance: max. speed 60 mph; ceiling (not reported) ft.; 390 mi.
Weights: empty 3,000 lbs., 5,000 lbs. loaded (est.).
Dimensions: span (upper) 74 ft. 0 in., length 38 ft. 0 in., wing area (not reported).

Making its first flight on June 23, 1914, the Curtiss H-1 America was originally built for department
store mogul Rodman Wanamaker to compete for a $50,000 prize offered by the *London Daily*

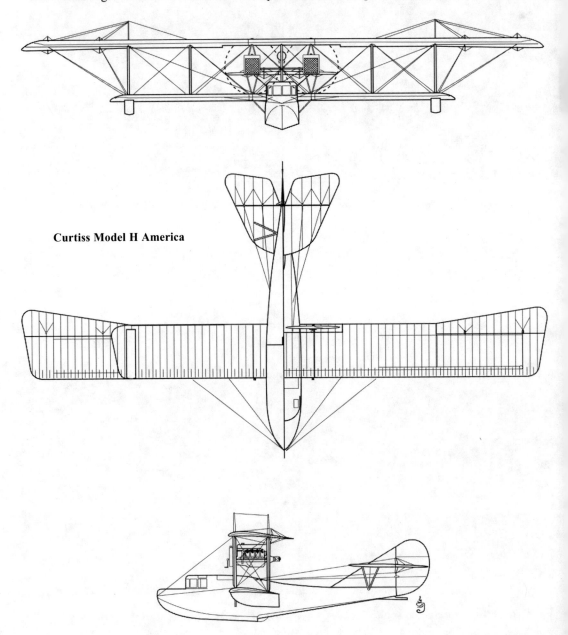

Curtiss Model H America

The H-1 America as it appeared in 1914 with the third engine added. After modifications to the hull and installation of more powerful engines, the H series became the most successful maritime patrol boats of World War I.

Mail for completing the first transatlantic flight. The H-1 employed a one-step hull similar to that of the F, but went to a three-bay biplane wing arrangement with trailing edge ailerons on the upper span. Once trials revealed that the aircraft was seriously underpowered in terms of useful load, a third OX-5 was fitted atop the upper wing center section but was subsequently removed when its added weight and drag negated any gain in performance. After the transatlantic flight was made impossible by the onset of World War I, Curtiss sought to interest the British Admiralty in military versions of the America, and one H-2 and eleven H-4s (no H-3s) were exported during 1914 and 1915. The first two delivered to the Royal Naval Air Service (RNAS) in late 1914 were evaluated at the RNAS base at Felixstowe. Shortcomings encountered with the type during RNAS trials led to a complete redesign of the hull by John Cyril Porte and the substitution of 100-hp Anzani engines. As modified, the H-4 was designated the Felixstowe F.1 in RNAS service, and the remaining fifty H-4s delivered in 1915 were subsequently rebuilt to F.1 standards.

Curtiss K (1915)

TECHNICAL SPECIFICATIONS

Type: 3-place naval trainer or small patrol boat.
Total produced: 56
Powerplant: one 160-hp Curtiss V-X 8-cylinder water-cooled engine driving a two-bladed wooden fixed-pitch propeller.
Performance: max. speed 74 mph; ceiling (not reported); range 364 mi.
Weights: empty 2,700 lbs., 3,900 lbs. loaded.
Dimensions: span (upper) 55 ft. 10 in., length 31 ft. 5 in., wing area 592 sq. ft.

Essentially a twenty percent enlargement of the model F, the K was reported to have been the largest single-engine flying boat in the world when it flew in early 1915. Other notable differences were the slight amount of sweepback added to the wings, inset ailerons in the upper span rather than the interplane type, and a more pronounced V in the bottom hull shape. Construction of the first K airframe was completed by late 1914 but difficulties with the V-X engine delayed the first flight until the following January. In October 1915, one of the factory Ks established a seaplane record of flying 183 miles nonstop in two hours twenty-seven minutes at an average speed of 74.7 mph. No Ks were ordered by the U.S. Navy, but the Russian government gave Curtiss a contract in late 1915 for 54 examples to be delivered in 1916. The shipment to Russia, by way of Vancouver and

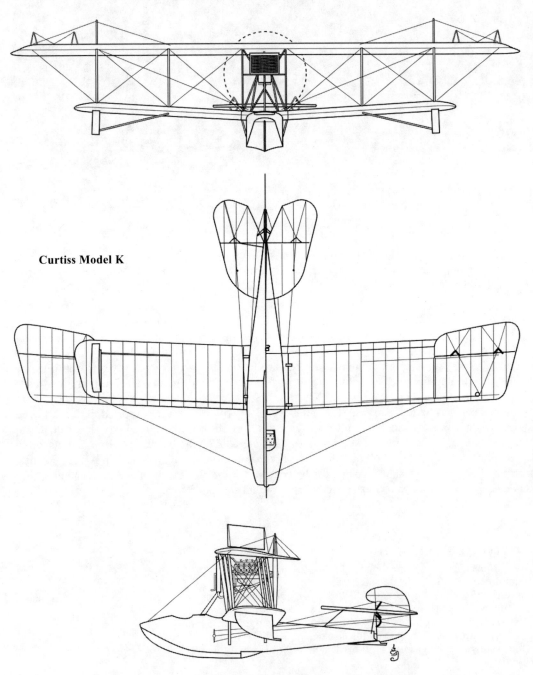

Curtiss Model K

Twenty percent larger than the F boat, the model K, at 3,900 lbs. loaded, was the largest single-engine flying boat in the world when it flew in 1915.

Vladisvostok, was plagued with delays and problems on arrival of such extent that many of the wooden hulls were rendered unserviceable due to exposure to the elements.

Curtiss H-8, H-12, and H-16 Large America (1915)

TECHNICAL SPECIFICATIONS (H-16)

Type: 4 to 5-place naval patrol boat.
Total produced: 421 (all versions)
Powerplant: two 400-hp Liberty 12-cylinder water-cooled engines driving four-bladed wooden fixed-pitch propellers.
Performance: max. speed 95 mph; ceiling 9,950-ft.; range 378 mi.
Armament: two .30-calibre Lewis machine guns in the bow, one .30-calibre Lewis machine gun on each

One of 20 Curtiss-built Felistowe F.2s acquired in late 1917 and taken into U.S. Navy service as the H-12. The first was powered by 250-hp Rolls-Royce engines, but the remainder came with 350-hp American-made Liberty 12s.

side in waist positions, and one .30-calibre Lewis machine gun in the rear cockpit; and one 230-lb. bomb carried under each wing.

Weights: empty 7,400 lbs., 10,900 lbs. loaded.

Dimensions: span (upper) 95 ft. 1 in., length 46 ft. 2 in., wing area 1,164 sq. ft.

The Curtiss Large Americas claim the distinction of being the first type of combat-capable aircraft to be produced in the United Stated during World War I. In an attempt to overcome the shortcomings of the H-4 series, Curtiss introduced the H-8 in late 1915, featuring a larger, four-bay wing of twenty-five percent greater area along with 160-hp Curtiss V-X pusher engines. However, as a result of RNAS trials conducted at Felixstowe during the spring of 1916, the type was found to be lacking in both power and hull strength. To correct these problems, the H-8 was subjected to wide-

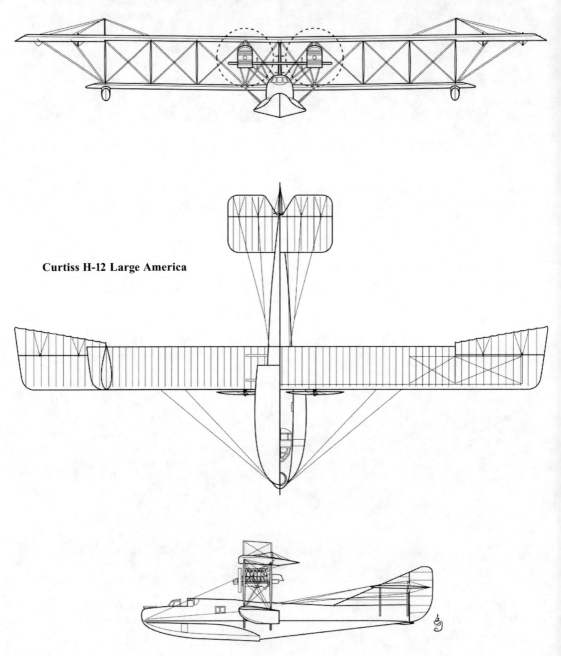

Curtiss H-12 Large America

spread improvements that included installation of tractor-mounted 250-hp Rolls-Royce Eagle V-12 engines and a hull redesign known as the Porte II, and as modified, taken into RNAS service as the Felixstowe F.2. Of the seventy-one F.2s completed (less engines) by Curtiss to the new RNAS specifications, twenty examples were acquired by the U.S. Navy during late 1917 and early 1918 under the designation H-12. The first H-12 was powered by Roll-Royce engines, but the remainder were delivered with the newly-available, American-made 350-hp Liberty 12s.

Introduced in late 1917 with increased wingspan, the Porte two-step sponson hull, and heavier armament, the first H-16 was accepted by the Navy in February 1918, and 199 production models

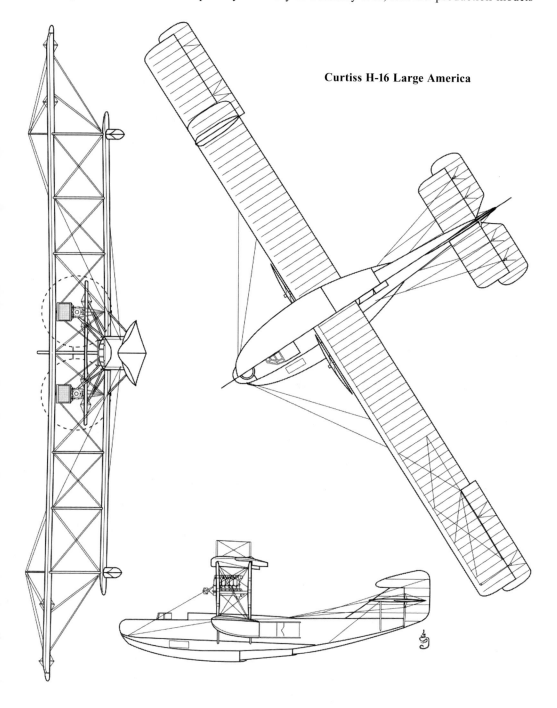

Curtiss H-16 Large America

The H-16, along with the NAF F-5L, remained in service as the Navy's standard maritime patrol type from 1918 up through the mid–1920s.

followed, of which 72 were allocated to the RNAS. U.S. versions were equipped with 400-hp Liberty engines, whereas RNAS types, designated Felixstowe F.2As, were powered by 345-hp Rolls-Royce Eagles. Wartime demand for H-16s grew to such a great extent that license-production was awarded to the new Naval Aircraft Factory (NAF) at Philadelphia, which completed a further 150 examples between March and October 1918. Curtiss tested an H-16 reconfigured with pusher engines and wing sweep to compensate for the change in center of gravity, but no production of the type resulted. After the armistice, many H-16s continued in Navy service, and the final examples were not withdrawn until 1928.

Curtiss HS (1917)

TECHNICAL SPECIFICATIONS (HS-2L)

Type: 3-place naval patrol boat.
Total produced: 1,151 (all versions)
Powerplant: one 350-hp Liberty 12 12-cylinder water-cooled engine driving a four-bladed wooden fixed-pitch propeller.
Performance: max. speed 83 mph; ceiling 5,200- ft.; range 517 mi.
Armament: one flexible .30-calibre Lewis machine gun in the bow; and one 230-lb. bomb under each bottom wing.
Weights: 4,300 lbs. empty, 6,432 lbs. loaded.
Dimensions: span (upper) 74 ft. ½ in., length 39 ft. 0 in., wing area 803 sq. ft.

Designed in response to a Navy requirement for a smaller coastal patrol flying boat, the HS-1 (initially tested with twin engines as the H-14) appeared in early 1917 as a one-third scale-down of the H-16 having a single pusher-mounted powerplant. The HS-1 was conceived as a 3-bay biplane, and like the H-16, incorporated the refinements of the Porte-type hull. The first HS-1 proved to be underpowered with the original 200-hp Curtiss VXX V-8 engine, but performance dramatically improved when the aircraft was refitted with a 350-hp Liberty V-12 in October 1917. Designated the HS-1L, the Liberty-powered type was ordered into large-scale production in such great numbers that, in addition to the Curtiss order for 664 examples, license contracts were given to Standard Aircraft Corp. (250), Lowe, Willard and Fowler Co. (200), Gallaudet Aircraft Corp. (60), Boeing Airplane Co. (50), and Loughead Aircraft Co. (2), for 1,226 aircraft total. When the war ended, however, these orders were cut back to 1,101 aircraft, while another twenty to

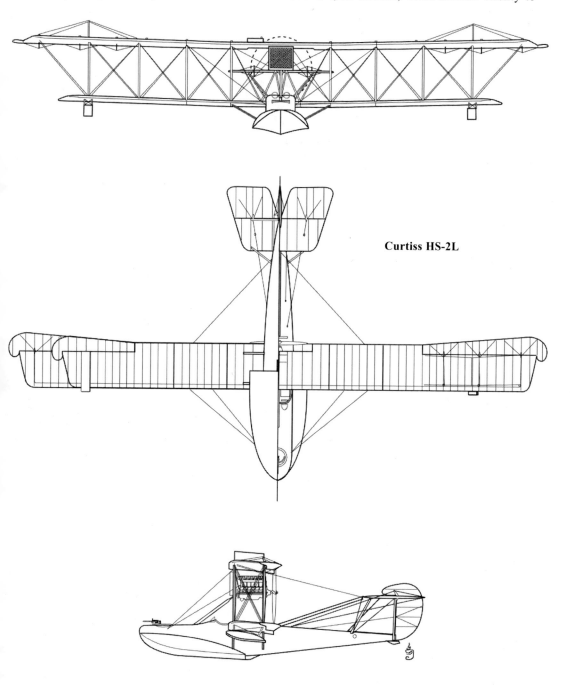

Curtiss HS-2L

The HS-2L shown in World War I–era markings. In May 1918, the HS became the first type of U.S.-made combat aircraft to enter service in France. It remained in Navy service until 1926.

twenty-five were reportedly assembled at various naval stations from spare parts available. To boost armament payload, the HS-2L appeared in mid–1918 with an eleven foot one inch increase in wingspan and an additional bay of struts, and all pending HS production was thereafter bought up to the 2L standard. The final version, the HS-3L featuring an improved hull design, did not fly until 1919, and only five had been completed by Curtiss and two by NAF when all HS production ceased.

The HS claimed the honor of being the first type of American-designed and built aircraft to be received by U.S. forces in France, when, in late May 1918, the first eight HS-1Ls were taken into service by the Navy station at Pauillac and, as deliveries proceeded, another 174 HS-1Ls and 2Ls equipped nine more stations in France by the time of the armistice in November. After the war, the HS-2L remained the Navy's standard single-engine patrol and flying boat trainer until the last examples were retired in 1926. A number of surplus HS-2Ls were later purchased by civilian operators who used them to carry passengers and mail up through the early 1930s.

Curtiss MF and Seagull (Models 18 and 20) (1918)

TECHNICAL SPECIFICATIONS (MF)

Type: 2-place naval trainer.
Total produced: 96
Powerplant: one 100-hp Curtiss OXX-3 8-cylinder water-cooled engine driving a two-bladed wooden fixed-pitch propeller.
Performance: max. speed 72 mph; ceiling 4,100-ft.; range 345 mi.
Weights: 1,850 lbs. empty, 2,488 lbs. loaded.
Dimensions: span (upper) 49 ft. 9 in., length 28 ft. 10 in., wing area 402 sq. ft.

The MF was introduced in 1918 as the replacement for the Navy's F Boat trainers. Although listed as a Modified F, it was actually an entirely new design that utilized the sponson-type hull of the H-16, a new wing with trailing-edge ailerons on the upper span, along with a reshaped fin and balanced rudder. Curtiss received an order for forty-seven aircraft, however, only sixteen MFs had been delivered when the contract was cancelled following the armistice. Eighty more examples built by NAF were delivered to the Navy after the war.

Surplus MFs re-acquired by Curtiss, refurbished and upgraded with 160-hp Curtiss C-6 engines, were offered to the civilian market as model 18 Seagulls, but the effort was generally unsuccessful, and only sixteen Seagulls were sold. Other firms like Cox-Klemin Aircraft Co. also acquired surplus MFs for resale to the civilian market. Another Seagull variation, known simply as the Crane Amphibian, was introduced in 1924 with amphibious landing gear.

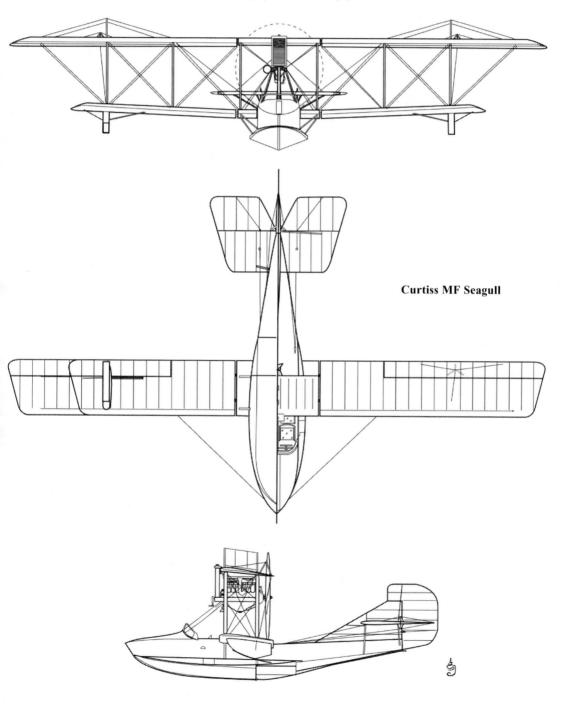

Curtiss MF Seagull

Production of the MF was foreshortened by the end of World War I. Eighty of ninety-six built were completed by the Naval Air Factory after the war. Efforts to market civilian versions met with limited success.

Curtiss NC-1 to NC-10 (1918)

TECHNICAL SPECIFICATIONS (NC-4)

Type: 5-place naval patrol boat.
Total produced: 10
Powerplant: four 420-hp Liberty 12A 12-cylinder water-cooled engines driving two-bladed wooden fixed-pitch propellers.
Performance: max. speed 90 mph; ceiling 4,500- ft.; range 1,470 mi.
Armament: proposed but none installed.
Weights: 15,874 lbs. empty, 28,000 lbs. loaded.
Dimensions: span (upper) 126 ft. 0 in., length 68 ft. 3 in., wing area 2,380 sq. ft.

    The NC-4 completed the first crossing of the Atlantic Ocean by any aircraft when it reached England on May 31, 1919, following a 51-hour, 31-minute flight which had originated from Rockaway Beach, New York. Popularly known as "Nancy Boats," the NC (Navy-Curtiss) class stemmed from a mid–1917 Navy requirement for a flying boat that possessed transatlantic range for extended submarine patrols. The initial development contract was issued to Curtiss in November 1917, and following a study of several different design concepts by naval officials, a three-engine layout was adopted. Because the NCs were classified as a research and development project, the four aircraft ordered were not to be built at Curtiss' main plant in Buffalo but sub-contracted out to eight different companies for various parts and sub-assemblies.

    The NC-1 was completed in late September 1918 and made its first flight on October 4. Despite lifting a record payload of 51 passengers and crew in November, the three-engine layout was determined insufficient to lift the takeoff weight (i.e., 28,000 lbs.) to carry enough fuel for transatlantic range, as a result of which the NC-2 was completed in April 1918 with four engines mounted in a tandem configuration. But when performance with the tandem engines proved to be unsatisfactory, the NC-3 and -4, which both flew in early 1919, were completed with two engines mounted in tandem between the wings on the centerline and two tractor engines mounted outboard; the NC-2 was thereafter cannibalized so that the NC-1 could be modified to the NC-3/-4 standard. The NC transatlantic flight plan called for 3,875-mile, five-leg journey from Rockaway Beach: 540 miles to Halifax, Nova Scotia; 460 miles to Trepassey Bay, Newfoundland; 1,300 miles to the Azores; 800 miles to Lisbon, Portugal; and finally, 775 miles to Plymouth, England. After departing on May 8, 1919, the NC-1 and -3 both were subsequently damaged upon landing in the Azores, the NC-1 being abandoned, while the NC-3 jury-rigged sails to make it as far as Sao Miguel Island. The NC-4 was left to ultimately complete its journey twenty-three days after departing the U.S. coast.

Six more aircraft, NC-5 through -10, were built by NAF during 1918 and 1919, the NC-5 and -6 being completed in a three-engine configuration and NC-7, -8, -9, and -10 in the four-engine NC-4 pattern. The NCs still in service in 1922 were re-designated P2N. Upon completion of a publicity tour in 1919, the hull of the NC-4 was placed on display by the Smithsonian Institution. After obtaining the remaining components from storage, a total restoration of the NC-4 was completed as a joint Navy-Smithsonian project in 1969, and it was loaned to the Navy in 1974 for exhibition in the Naval Aviation Museum in Pensacola, Florida, where it remains today.

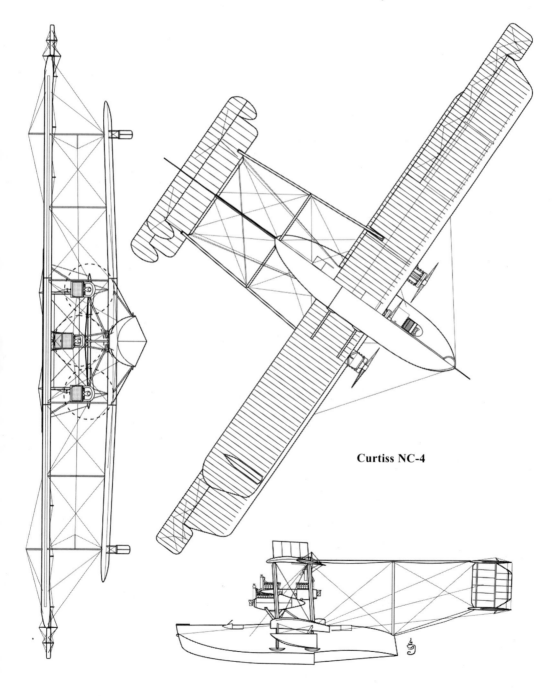

Curtiss NC-4

The NC-4, shown here, became the most famous of the series when it completed the first flight across the Atlantic Ocean on May 31, 1919. It is preserved today at the Naval Aviation Museum in Pensacola, Florida.

Eastman Aircraft Corp.

Starting as part of Eastman Laboratories (i.e., Eastman-Kodak) in 1928, it became the Eastman Aircraft Corp. of Detroit, Michigan in 1929 under the leadership of James Eastman, P. R. Beasley, and Thomas Towle. The company was acquired by Detroit Aircraft Co. in 1930.

Eastman E-2 Sea Rover/Sea Pirate (1928)

TECHNICAL SPECIFICATIONS (E-2)

Type: 2 to 3-place civil transport.
Total produced: 18
Powerplant: one 120-hp Warner *Scarab* 7-cylinder air-cooled radial engine driving a two-bladed metal fixed-pitch propeller.
Performance: max. speed 110 mph, cruise 90 mph; ceiling (not reported); range 360 mi.
Weights: not reported; useful load listed as 980 lbs.
Dimensions: span (upper) 36 ft. 0 in., length 26 ft. 3 in., wing area (not reported).

One of 18 Warner-powered E-2s built between 1928 and 1930. The use of V-type struts instead of rigging wires is clearly visible in this photograph. The hull's frame was wooden and clad in aluminum.

Known also as the Beasley-Eastman, the first E-2 Sea Rover was flown in 1928, initially with a 90-hp Anzani engine but later retrofitted with a 120-hp Warner. The design emerged as a sesquiplane (i.e., much smaller lower wings in proportion to span and chord) having the upper wing braced by diagonal V-struts rather than wires. The engine was neatly faired into a nacelle in the upper wing center section and the hull was a wooden structure clad in metal of a single-step, deep V-chine pattern. Marketed to private and commercial users, the E-2 was originally offered for a price of $6,750, and a total of eighteen were produced between 1928 and 1930. At least one was known to have operated with Gorst Air Transport in the Seattle area in 1929 and 1930 and five were used as bush planes

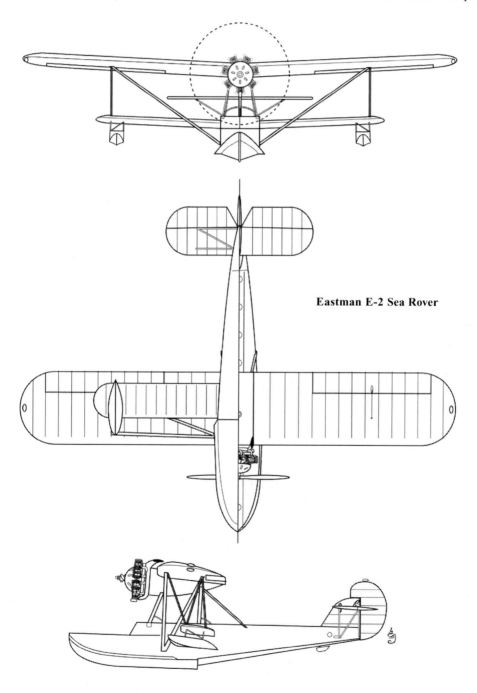

Eastman E-2 Sea Rover

in Vancouver, British Columbia. In 1930 three E-2s were converted to an amphibious configuration, two fitted with 185-hp Curtiss R-600 Challenger water-cooled engines as E-2A Sea Pirates and a third equipped with a Packard 225-hp diesel as the E-2D. The only known surviving E-2, restored from the remains of two of the Canadian aircraft, is presently on display at the British Columbia Air Museum in Vancouver.

Ireland Aircraft, Inc.

Although this company is reputed to have manufactured over fifty aircraft between 1925 and 1930, there is surprisingly little information to be found about its activities. It was formed in 1926 by G. Sumner at Curtiss Field in Garden City, New York. In 1931 it was reorganized as Amphibions, Inc. (an old spelling of the term), and continued to produce aircraft at the same location until 1933, when it apparently ceased operations.

Ireland N-1 and -2 Neptune (1927)

TECHNICAL SPECIFICATIONS (N-2B)

Type: 4 to 5-place civil amphibian.
Total produced: 46 (est.)
Powerplant: one 300-hp Wright R-975 J-6 *Whirlwind* 9-cylinder air-cooled radial engine driving a three-bladed metal fixed-pitch propeller.
Performance: max. speed 115 mph, cruise 90 mph; ceiling (not reported); range 400 mi.
Weights: 2,949 lbs. empty, 4,400 lbs. gross.
Dimensions: span 40 ft. 0 in., length 30 ft. 0 in., wing area (not reported).

N-2B with enclosed cockpit. Neptunes gained popularity with commercial operators in coastal and lake regions, and 46 examples are believed to have been sold before production ceased in 1930.

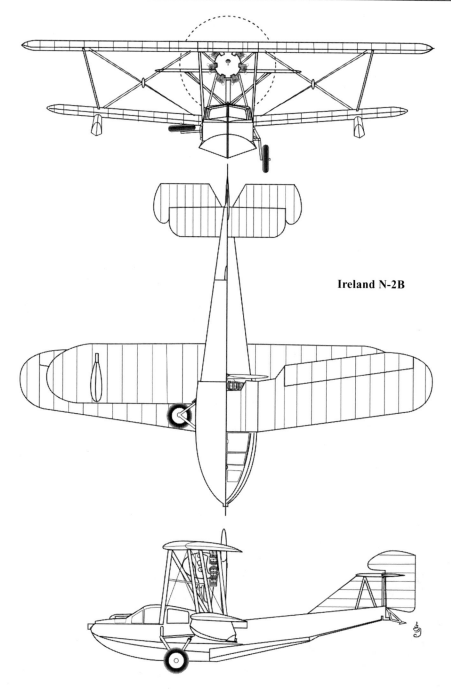

Ireland N-2B

Also referred to as the "Amphibiplane," the Ireland Neptune was a single-bay, wire-braced biplane with a pusher engine mounted between the cabanes. Construction of the two-step hull consisted of a steel tube framework covered in Alclad, while the wing and tail groups were conventional fabric-covered wooden structures. For water operations, the landing gear could be manually cranked-up, perpendicular to the hull. The 4-place N-1B Neptune (no N-1A mentioned) was first flown in 1927 with a 220-hp Wright J-5 engine and open cockpits for the pilot and passengers. While six N-1Bs are estimated to have been sold in 1927-1928 in the $14,600 price range, they were considered underpowered for their weight, and most were later refitted with more powerful engines.

The most numerous variant, the N-2B of 1928, featured a Wright J-6 engine and provision for an extra passenger, and forty examples were reportedly sold in 1928 and 1929. Curtiss Flying Service (a subsidiary of Curtiss Aeroplane and Motor Co.), operated N-2Bs out of Boston to Hyannis, Martha's Vineyard, and Nantucket, and to Portland, Rockland, and Bar Harbor, Maine; Curtiss Flying Service of the Middle West also operated at least one N-2B from Lake Michigan on a route known as the Chicago Loop. The final Neptune versions, produced in 1929 and 1930, were ten N-2Cs powered by 450-hp Pratt & Whitney R-1340 *Wasp* engines that came with a fully-enclosed cabin for the pilot and four passengers.

Lewis and Vought Corp.

Destined to become one of the best-known manufacturers of naval aircraft, Lewis and Vought Corp. was formed in 1917 at Astoria, New York, by Birdseye B. Lewis and Chance M. Vought and in 1922, when Lewis withdrew, became the Chance Vought Corp. In 1929 the company merged with United Aircraft and Transport Co. as the Chance Vought Aircraft Division and moved to East Hartford, Connecticut; a year later, in 1930, founder Chance Vought unexpectedly died of an infection stemming from dental surgery.

Vought VE-10 Batboat (1919)

TECHNICAL SPECIFICATIONS

Type: 3-place Navy scout/trainer.
Total produced: 1
Powerplant: one 90-hp Curtiss OX-5 6-cylinder water-cooled engine driving a two-bladed wooden fixed-pitch propeller.
Performance: max. speed 90 mph, cruise 80 mph; ceiling (not reported); range 200 mi.
Weights: 1,330 lbs. empty, 1,950 lbs. loaded.
Dimensions: span (upper) 36 ft. 6 in., length 27 ft. 0 in., wing area (not reported).

After experiencing initial success with the VE-7 land and floatplane, Vought sought to interest the Navy in a small flying boat, presumably as a scout or a trainer that would serve a function

Intended to compete against the Aeromarine A40 and Curtiss MF for potential Navy contracts, the VE-10 was the only flying boat to be built by Vought. The company went on to become a major Navy contractor in the design and production of land-based and float-equipped aircraft.

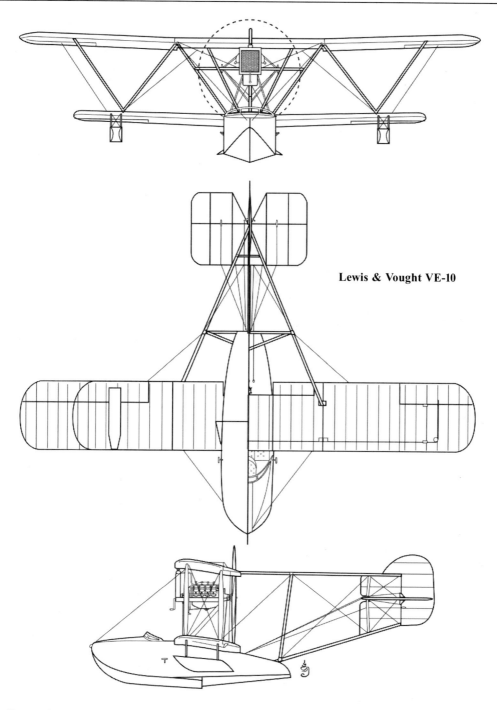

Lewis & Vought VE-10

similar to that of the Aeromarine 40F or Curtiss MF. The VE-10 emerged as short-hulled biplane of wooden construction with a tailplane supported by booms extending from the rear of the hull. The sesquiplane wing layout featured an interesting one-bay configuration of W-struts that dispensed with rigging wires. When flown in mid–1919, general performance was impressive for such low horsepower, but the type's erratic water handling characteristics caused it to be judged unsatisfactory. The Navy expressed little interest in the VE-10 and efforts to sell it commercially were unsuccessful. This would be Vought's one and only flying boat venture.

Loening Aeronautical Engineering Co.

Grover C. Loening, one of the great pioneers of water-borne flight, became America's first formally educated aeronautical engineer upon receiving his Master's Degree in Aeronautics from Columbia University in 1911. After working for other firms, he formed the Loening Aeronautical Engineering Co. located in New York City in 1917. The company merged with Keystone Aircraft Co. in 1928, functioning afterward as the Loening Aeronautical Division until ceasing all operations in 1938.

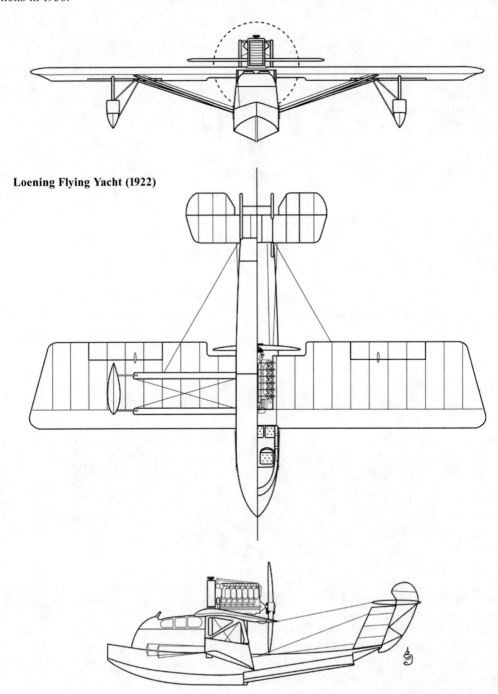

Loening Flying Yacht (1922)

Soon after it flew in 1921, the Flying Yacht established a new seaplane speed record of 141 mph and an altitude record of 19,500 feet. Loening received the Collier Trophy for his efforts.

Loening Flying Yacht (S-1) (1921)

TECHNICAL SPECIFICATIONS

Type: 5-place civil transport; Army scout.
Total·produced: 16
Powerplant: one 400-hp Liberty 12 12-cylinder water-cooled engine driving a four-bladed wooden fixed-pitch propeller.
Performance: max. speed 141 mph, cruise 110 mph; ceiling 19,500 ft.; range (not reported).
Weights: not reported.
Dimensions: span 45 ft. 0 in., length 30 ft. 0 in., wing area (not reported).

After making a start in flying boats with the small Duckling in 1918 (see Appendix A, page 310), Loening began work on a considerably more complex design known as the Flying Yacht, which, when it flew in 1921, became the second monoplane flying boat to fly (after the Curtiss model M of 1913, see Appendix A, page 321). The design incorporated a wing planform similar to that used on Loening's M series of Navy land and floatplanes. Its cockpit enclosure, in front of the wing-mounted pusher engine, was built up onto a main hull float that extended backward to support the tall empennage, a configuration that would be seen years later on the Spencer Air Car (see Part II, page 210) and the Republic Seabee (see Part III, page 276). The tailplane consisted of twin fins and rudders with high-mounted horizontal control surfaces. During 1921 this aircraft established a sea-plane speed record of 141 mph and an altitude record of 19,500 feet, for which Loening received the Collier Trophy. Nine were delivered to the Army as the S-1 and three went into commercial service with New York-Newport Air Service until a crash ended further operations in 1923.

Loening OL, HL (OA-1, -2) (1923)

TECHNICAL SPECIFICATIONS (OL-2 [OL-9])

Type: 3-place military observation amphibian.
Total produced: 160 (all versions)
Powerplant: one 400-hp Liberty 12 12-cylinder water-cooled engine driving a four-bladed wooden fixed-pitch propeller [one 450-hp Pratt & Whitney R-1340-4 9-cylinder air-cooled radial engine driving a three-bladed ground-adjustable propeller].

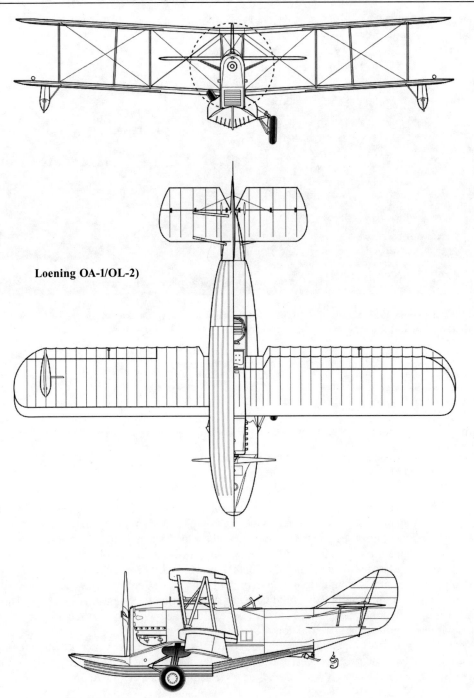

Loening OA-1/OL-2)

Armament: one flexible .30-calibre Lewis machine gun in the rear cockpit, [one fixed .30-calibre machine in the upper wing; and four 114-lb. bombs on wing racks].
Performance: max. speed 121 mph [122 mph]; ceiling 12,100 ft. [14,300 ft.]; range 405 mi. [625 mi.].
Weights: 3,540 lbs. [3,469 lbs.] empty, 5,010 lbs. [5,404] loaded.
Dimensions: span 45 ft. 0 in., length 33 ft. 10 in. [34 ft. 19 in.], wing area 500 sq. ft. [502 sq. ft].

When the first examples appeared in 1923, Loening's "shoehorn" series of military observation planes were really flying boat-floatplane hybrids in which the upper fuselage was faired entirely

The five OL-2s acquired by the Navy in 1925 were identical to the Army model OA-1. Many aircraft of this era were required to use Liberty engines because of War Department surplus inventories.

The OL-6 introduced a third cockpit and a 475-hp Packard engine driving a three-bladed propeller. The Army procured a similar version as the OA-1A.

into a main float that extended all the way rearwards to support the tail group. This novel configuration, similar in many respects to that of the Flying Yacht reported above, was conceived by Loening out of an desire to design an amphibian that would match the performance of a landplane having an engine of similar horsepower. The manually operated landing was retracted via a series of sprockets and chains into recesses in the main float. The original prototype was delivered to the

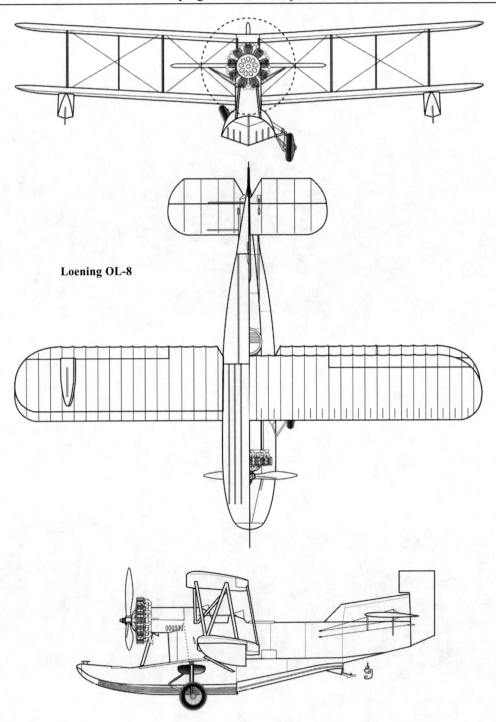

Loening OL-8

Army in 1923 as the XCOA-1 (the C was later dropped) and nine production models followed in 1924. A Navy prototype powered by a 440-hp Packard engine and having a third cockpit was delivered in 1925 as the XOL-1. The same year, the Navy acquired five Liberty-powered OA-1s, placing them in service as OL-2s to be used in the 1925 Artic Expedition, and four essentially identical aircraft were purchased from Loening as OL-3s. The first of six OL-4s, which differed in having a reshaped balanced rudder, revised cowling, and three-bladed metal propeller, was delivered in early

The OL-9 was the final version of the series and the first to be equipped with bomb racks. All -9s were built between 1931 and 1932 after Loening had been acquired by Keystone.

1926. These were followed by three very similar OL-5s, which bore the distinction of being the first aircraft ordered specifically for the U.S. Coast Guard. The USCG OL-5s served until 1935.

Flown in late 1926, the OL-6 came with a 475-hp Packard V-12 engine and a third cockpit, and twenty-six production examples were delivered to the Navy by mid–1927. During the same timeframe, twenty-four very similar OA-1As and Bs were also produced for Army, followed by ten OA-1Cs with reshaped tails. As the wingspan of the OLs was too large to enable them fit onto the deck elevators of the Navy's new aircraft carriers, one OL-6 modified in mid–1927 with a smaller wing and a thicker airfoil section was tested in mid–1927 as the XOL-7, but its performance proved to be disappointing and no production resulted. In late 1927, following an announcement by BuAer that all future naval aircraft would be equipped with air-cooled engines, Loening modified the Last OL-6 to accept installation of an R-1340 radial engine and delivered it as the XOL-8. After trials, twenty production models were delivered during 1928 as the OL-8, followed in 1929 by twenty nearly identical OL-8As. Eight OA-2s, similar to OL-8As except for their 480-hp Wright V-1640 V-12 water-cooled engines, were delivered to the Army the same year. The final version, the OL-9, which differed from the OL-8 in having a fixed .30-calibre machine in the upper wing and under-wing racks for four 114-lb. bombs, was produced during 1931 and 1932 after Loening had been acquired by Keystone, and the last of 26 built was accepted by the Navy in March 1932. Two airframes similar to the OL-8, completed as ambulance planes with a cabin occupying the space behind the pilot's cockpit, were delivered to the Navy in 1930 as XHL-1s. As newer Grumman JF Ducks began arriving during the mid–1930s, OL-8s and 9s were phased out of active service, with the final OL-9 being withdrawn by the end of 1937.

Loening C-1 and -2 Air Yacht (1928)

TECHNICAL SPECIFICATIONS (C-2C)

Type: 9-place civil transport.
Total produced: 43 (all versions)
Powerplant: one 525-hp Wright R-1820 *Cyclone* 9-cylinder air-cooled engine driving a three-bladed metal ground-adjustable propeller.

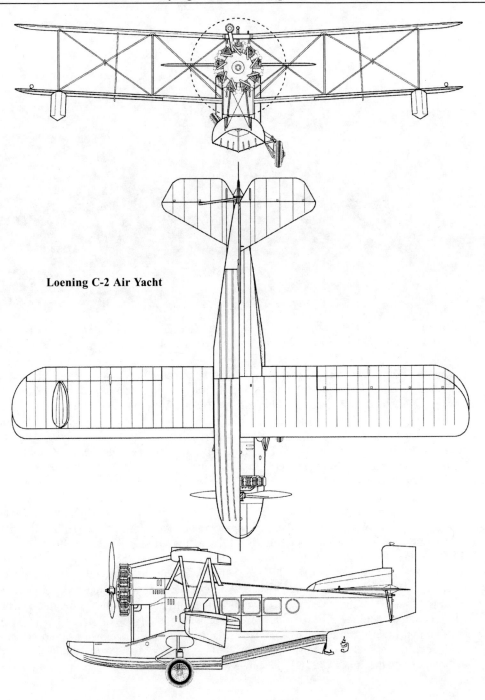

Loening C-2 Air Yacht

Performance: max. speed 124 mph, cruise 102 mph; ceiling 14,500 ft.; range 550 mi.
Weights: 3,500 lbs. empty, 5,900 lbs. loaded.
Dimensions: span 46 ft. 8 in., length 34 ft. 8 in., wing area 525 sq. ft.

The Air Yacht symbolized an effort by Loening to offer a civil amphibian that shared the general layout its successful Navy OL-8. Virtually identical to the XHL-1 military ambulance, the Air Yacht featured a cabin seating up to eight passengers in the fuselage behind the cockpit. The first eight C-1Ws appeared in 1928 with 410-hp Pratt & Whitney R-1340 *Wasp* engines, followed by

Wright *Cyclone*-powered C-2C, built in 1928. Based largely on the design of the Navy OL-8, C-1s and -2s saw wide use in commercial operations in the U.S. and abroad.

twenty-three C-2Cs powered by Wright *Cyclones,* and finally, in 1930, fourteen C-2Hs with Pratt & Whitney R-1690 *Hornets.* A number of Air Yachts were exported overseas for survey and exploration work and through the 1930s, many others served with commercial operators such as Air Ferries, Ltd. (San Francisco), Gorst Air Transport (Seattle), Alaska Southern (Juneau), Pan American Airways (Central and South America), and Western Air Express (Los Angeles).

Naval Aircraft Factory

Created in October 1917 and located at the Navy Yard in Philadelphia, Pennsylvania, the government-owned Naval Aircraft Factory (NAF) functioned under the auspices of the Navy Department, and from 1921, acted as an agency of the Naval Bureau of Aeronautics (BuAer). Although originally established during World War I to supplement production of Navy aircraft by private manufacturers, the organization became a clearing-house for naval aircraft design during the 1920s and 1930s.

Naval Aircraft Factory/Curtiss F-5L (PN-5 and -6) (1918)

TECHNICAL SPECIFICATIONS

Type: 4 to 5-place Navy patrol boat.
Total produced: 227
Powerplant: Two 420-hp Liberty A 12-cylinder water-cooled engines driving four-bladed wooden fixed-pitch propellers.
Armament: two .30-calibre Lewis machine guns in the bow, one .30-calibre Lewis machine gun on each side in waist positions, and one .30-calibre Lewis machine gun in the rear cockpit; and one 230-lb. bomb carried under each wing.
Performance: max. speed 90 mph; ceiling 5,500 ft; range 830 mi.
Weights: 8,720 lbs. empty, 13,600 lbs. loaded.
Dimensions: span (upper) 103 ft. 9 in., length 49 ft. 4 in., wing area 1,397 sq. ft.

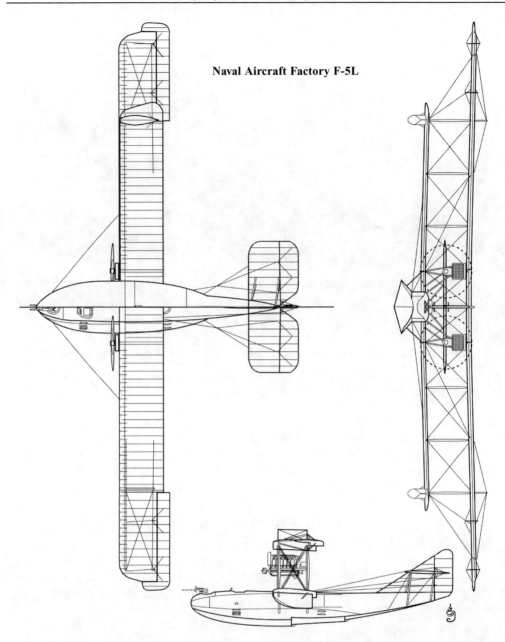

Naval Aircraft Factory F-5L

Coming as the ultimate evolution of the Curtiss Large Americas that began with the H-8, the F-5L incorporated improvements of the Felixstowe F.5 such as removal of the enclosed cockpit, increased fuel capacity, enlarged wing area, more powerful engines, straight-balanced ailerons, and a taller, balanced rudder. Though slightly slower than the H-16, the F-5 enjoyed a significant improvement in range. Powered by Liberty uprated 12A engines, the first F-5L, which had been built by NAF, was delivered to the Navy for trials in September 1918, too late to see action. Production continued after the war, however, with 136 more F-5Ls being completed by NAF, 60 by Curtiss, and 30 by Canadian Aeroplanes, Ltd. The last two, completed by NAF as F-6Ls, featured improvements to the hull and a reshaped fin and balanced rudder, and most F-5Ls remaining in service during the early 1920s were subsequently brought up to this standard. When the Navy adopted a standardized designation system in 1922, the F-5Ls became PN-5s and the two F-6Ls became PN-6s. PN-5s/-6s,

An NAF-built F-5L shown in postwar markings. Derived from the Curtiss H-16, the F-5L incorporated the increased wing area and greater fuel capacity of the Royal Navy's Felixstowe F.5.

together with H-16s, continued to form the mainstay of the Navy's flying patrol boat force until replaced by newer types during the late 1920s.

Naval Aircraft Factory TF (1920)

TECHNICAL SPECIFICATIONS

Type: 3-place Navy escort fighter.
Total produced: 4
Powerplant: Two 300-hp Wright-Hispano H-3 8-cylinder water-cooled engines driving four-bladed wooden fixed-pitch propellers.
Armament: two flexible Lewis .30-calibre machine guns in the bow and one flexible Lewis .30-calibre machine gun in the rear cockpit.
Performance: max. speed 95 mph, cruise 72 mph; ceiling 13,000 ft; range 650 mi.
Weights: 5,575 lbs. empty, 8,846 lbs. loaded.
Dimensions: span (upper) 60 ft. 0 in., length 44 ft. 0 in., wing area 930 sq. ft.

One of four TFs seen at the NAF facility in Philadelphia. The type was originally envisaged as escorting larger flying boats like the H-16 and F-5L on maritime patrol.

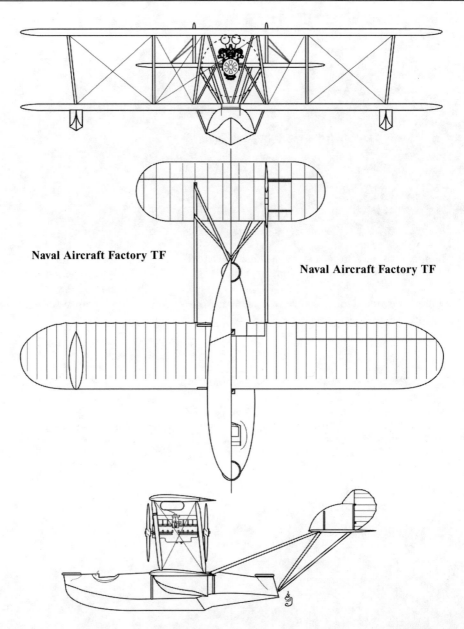

Naval Aircraft Factory TF

Naval Aircraft Factory TF

The origins of the TF (Tandem Fighter) can be traced to a 1918 requirement issued by the British Technical Committee for a long-range sea-borne fighter to escort patrol aircraft (H-16s, F-5s, etc.) on maritime sorties. After the armistice, Navy officials retained sufficient interest in the idea to authorize NAF to proceed with design proposals. After reviewing various options, the Navy approved a twin-tandem engine design that incorporated a hull and tailplane boom arrangement nearly identical to the larger NC series and authorized construction of four prototypes. Originally, the TF was to have been powered by Curtiss-built 400-hp Kirkham powerplants, however, mechanical problems with the Kirkham engines led to a decision to substitute the less powerful Wright-Hispanos. Construction of the first prototype commenced in August 1919 and the first flight took place on October 1, 1920. Testing revealed poor handling characteristics plus a marked tendency of the engines to overheat at high RPM settings. Although three more prototypes were completed and testing during 1921 and 1922, results were still rated as unsatisfactory, and the program was formally cancelled in January 1923. The fourth prototype was reportedly completed with 400-hp Packard 1-A V-12 engines, but no performance data on it is available.

Naval Aircraft Factory PN-7, -8, -9, -10, and -12 (1924)

TECHNICAL SPECIFICATIONS (PN-7 [PN-12])

Type: 5 to 6-place Navy patrol boat.
Total produced: 8
Powerplant: Two 525-hp Wright T-2 12-cylinder water-cooled engines driving two-bladed wooden fixed-pitch propellers [two 525-hp Wright R-1750D 9-cylinder air-cooled engines driving three-bladed ground-adjustable metal propellers].
Armament: one flexible .30-calibre machine gun in the bow, one flexible .30-calibre machine gun amidships, and up to four 230-lb. bombs carried under lower wing.
Performance: max. speed 105 mph [114 mph]; ceiling 9,200 ft. [10,900 ft.]; range 655 mi. [1,310 mi.].
Weights: 9,637 lbs. [7,699 lbs.] empty, 14,203 lbs. [14,122 lbs.] loaded.
Dimensions: span (upper) 72 ft. 10 in., length 49 ft. 1 in. [49 ft. 2in.], wing area 1,217 sq. ft.

The PN series represented a cumulative effort on the part of NAF and BuAer from 1924 to 1928 to develop and test concepts for a new type of patrol flying boat that would replace the Navy's World War I-era fleet of wooden-hulled PN-5s and PN-6s. Construction of the first of the series, the PN-7, was begun during 1923, the first being completed in January 1924 and the second in June. While it retained the wooden hull of the PN-5, the PN-7 incorporated an entirely new set of single-bay biplane wings of fabric-covered, metal construction that utilized a much thicker section USA 27 airfoil in place of the RAF 6 of the PN-5. The increase in lift permitted a significant reduction in both wingspan and area, plus the strength resulting from the deeper wing spars required only one bay of struts outboard the engines. In place of the old Liberty engines, experimental Wright T-2 powerplants were tractor-mounted in neat, streamlined nacelles with the water radiators slung under the upper wing center section. Trials conducted during 1924 indicated vastly improved per-

Although the hull was similar to H-16/F-5L, the PN-7 introduced a shorter span, single-bay wing having a much thicker airfoil section and new engines producing 25 percent more power.

formance over the PN-5; however, the Wright engines proved to be unreliable, and BuAer officials expressed concerns over the long-term durability of the wooden hull.

Based upon experience gained with the PN-7, the first of two PN-8s ordered was delivered in January 1924 with a duraluminum hull identical in shape to the Porte-type sponson hull and was flown with Wright T-3 engines. Other changes included a longer-chord fin and rudder, plus hori-

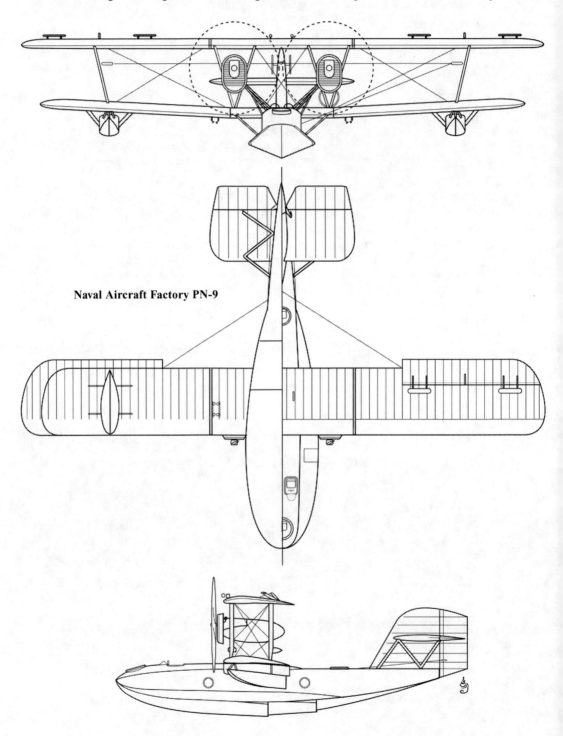

Naval Aircraft Factory PN-9

The Wright *Cyclone*-powered, metal-hulled PN-12 depicted in this photograph became the patrol boat pattern for the Douglas PD, Hall PH, Keystone PK, and Martin PM.

zontal tail surfaces possessing a thicker airfoil section. The second example, delivered in May 1925 as the PN-9, was tested with 480-hp geared Packard 1A-2500 V-12 engines behind large water radiators; soon afterward, the PN-8 was converted to the Packard engines and re-designated PN-9. In company with the metal-hulled Boeing XPB-1 (see page 26), the Navy planned to use both PN-9s to attempt the first flight from the California coast to Hawaii. As events turned out, however, only the second PN-9 was deemed ready for the 2,410-mile flight, and it departed San Francisco on August 31, 1925. Twenty-eight and a half hours and 1,841 miles into the flight, the PN-9 was forced to land in the ocean approximately 560 miles from Hawaii due to fuel exhaustion. The seaworthiness of its metal hull was aptly demonstrated after the crew, using fabric panels detached from the lower wings, sailed the aircraft the remaining distance to the islands. Despite the shortfall, the flight still attained recognition for a new seaplane distance record.

Given the success of the PN-9s, BuAer ordered four essentially identical PN-10s, two of which were delivered in late 1926. During trials carried out during 1927, the two PN-10s went on to establish new seaplane records for distance, speed, and payload. Due to the air-cooled engine policy implemented by BuAer in 1927, NAF was directed to complete the other two PN-10s with different radial engine types under the new designation PN-12. The first, equipped with Wright R-1750 *Cyclone* engines, was delivered in December 1927 and the second, with Pratt & Whitney R-1690 *Hornets*, arrived in June 1928. In May 1928 the first PN-12 set a new seaplane record when it carried a payload of 2,205 lbs. (1,000 kg) over a distance of 1,242 miles (2000 km) at an average speed of 80.5 mph (130 kph). Once BuAer settled on the Wright-powered PN-12 as the pattern for the Navy's new generation of patrol boats, aircraft companies were invited to submit proposals and, over a two year interval, contracts awarded to four different airframe contractors. (See Douglas PD,

PN-9 number one, shown here after being forced to land at sea between California and Hawaii due to fuel exhaustion in August 1925, used fabric from the wings and sailed the remaining 560 miles to Pearl Harbor over a 10-day period.

Hall PH, Martin PM, and Keystone PK in Part II; the out-of-order PN-11 is also reported in Part II, as the P4N.)

Sikorsky Manufacturing Co.

Having previously established himself as an aeronautical engineer in his native Russia, Igor I. Sikorsky immigrated to the United States in 1919 and with the financial backing of other Russian émigrés in 1923, established the Sikorsky Aero Engineering Co. at Bridgeport, Connecticut. After being renamed Sikorsky Manufacturing Co. in 1925, the company merged with United Aircraft and Transport Corp. in 1929, thereafter operating as the Sikorsky Aviation Division. Though best known for his outstanding accomplishments in helicopter development, most of Sikorsky's early commercial success in the U.S. was actually derived from the flying boats he designed during the 1920s and 1930s.

Sikorsky S-34 (1926)

TECHNICAL SPECIFICATIONS

Type: 6-place civil transport.
Total produced: 1
Powerplant: Two 200-hp Wright J-4 9-cylinder water-cooled engines driving two-bladed ground-adjustable
    metal propellers.
Performance: max. speed 111 mph, cruise 90 mph; ceiling 15,000 ft; range 360 mi.
Weights: not reported; useful load listed as 1,600 lbs.
Dimensions: span 50 ft. 5 in., length 34 ft. 0 in., wing area (not reported).

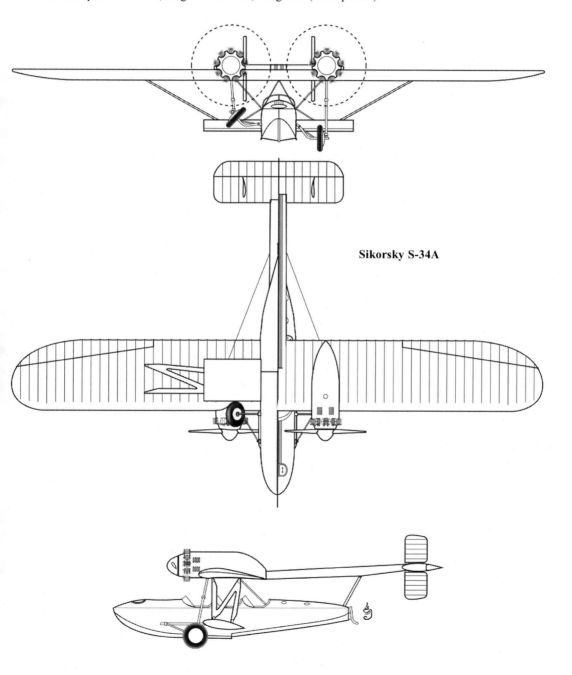

Sikorsky S-34A

Sikorsky's first amphibian, the S-34, seen undergoing engine tests before its first flight. Though not itself a success, many of the S-34's design features were incorporated into the S-36, S-38, S-40, and S-41.

Completed in November 1926 under civil registration X883, the S-34 was Sikorsky's first endeavor to design and fly an amphibian. At a time when most flying boats were still biplanes, the S-34 evolved with a parasol monoplane wing, braced atop the fuselage with cabane and V-struts. Other novel features were airfoil-shaped sponsons on either side of the hull in place of wing floats and amphibious landing gear that retracted upward against the hull. Its two Wright engines were mounted on the upper surface of the wing, and the tail group, which would become characteristic of the early Sikorsky boats, consisted a boom extending from the wing, supported by struts off the rear hull. Unfortunately, the S-34 was lost on its first flight when it developed engine trouble and sank after a hard forced-landing.

Sikorsky S-36 (PS-1) (1927)

TECHNICAL SPECIFICATIONS

Type: 8-place amphibious civil transport; Navy patrol boat.
Total produced: 5
Powerplant: Two 200-hp or 225-hp Wright J-4 9-cylinder water-cooled engines driving two-bladed ground-adjustable metal propellers.
Performance: max. speed 110 mph (est.), cruise 90 mph; ceiling 15,000 ft. (est.); range 200 mi.
Weights: empty (not reported); 6,000 lbs. loaded.
Dimensions: span 56 ft. 0 in., length 34 ft. 0 in., wing area (not reported).

Sikorsky's second flying boat design, the S-36, was flown and tested during 1927 with better success. It shared the general aerodynamic and amphibious characteristics of the S-34 but possessed

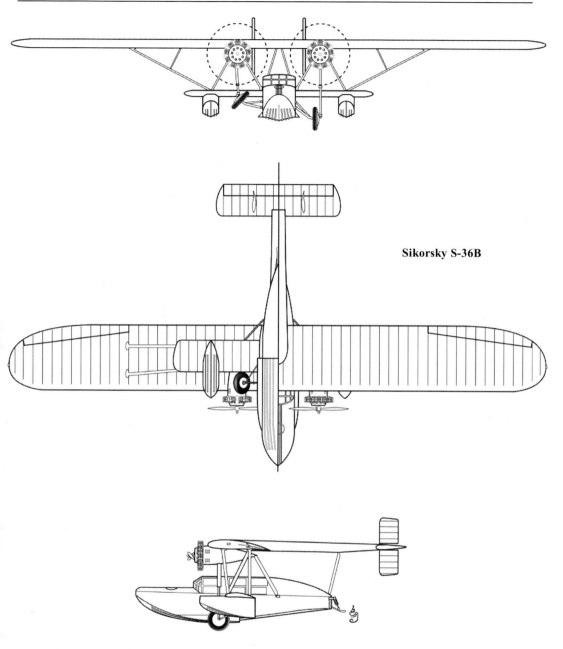

Sikorsky S-36B

more wing area and featured a sesquiplane layout with the wing floats mounted below the bottom wings. Another difference was an upper wing positioned higher over the fuselage to permit the engines and nacelles to be mounted below it. The first S-36 was flown with open cockpits for the pilot and passengers, but subsequent versions came with a raised cockpit enclosure and cabin that blended into the rear of the hull. Of five S-36s known to have been produced, one was delivered to the Andean National Corporation and another to Pan American Airways to perform survey flights in the Caribbean. The single S-36 sold to the Navy was evaluated as XPS-1. Another S-36, christened "Dawn," was purchased in late 1927 by Frances Grayson, a niece of Woodrow Wilson, who intended to be the first woman to fly across the Atlantic Ocean. After departing on December 23, 1927, the Dawn, with Grayson and two pilots on board, disappeared over the ocean.

Frances Grayson, who hoped to be the first women pilot to fly across the Atlantic, disappeared somewhere over the ocean in December 1927, in the S-36 shown here.

Sikorsky S-38 (PS/RS-2 and, C-6) (1928)

TECHNICAL SPECIFICATIONS (S-38B)

Type: 10 to 12-passenger amphibious civil transport; Navy patrol boat.
Total produced: 120 (all versions)
Powerplant: Two 420-hp Pratt & Whitney R-1340 *Wasp* 9-cylinder water-cooled engines driving two-bladed ground-adjustable metal propellers.
Performance: max. speed 124 mph, cruise 109 mph; ceiling 18,000 ft.; range 600 mi.
Weights: 6,548 lbs. empty, 10,479 lbs. loaded.
Dimensions: span 71 ft. 8 in., length 40 ft. 5 in., wing area 720 sq. ft.

Sikorsky's first real commercial success, the amphibious S-38, made its first flight on June 25, 1928. Sometimes referred to as a collection of parts flying in formation, the S-38 was a thirty percent scale-up of the S-36 having twice the horsepower and three times the range. In order to maintain similar proportions, the engines were suspended from the upper wing on struts and the wing floats were lowered. The elegantly contoured hull was built up of a wooden structural framework skinned in duraluminum. Sikorsky received eleven orders for S-38As, the first production version, which were delivered to the New York, Rio, & Buenos Aires Line (NYRBA) for South American routes, Pan American Airways for Caribbean routes, and Western Air Express for Catalina Island, plus two to Navy as the PS-2, one to the Army as the XC-6, and one special luxury model as a private transport for John H. Whitney.

The major production variant, the S-38B, was introduced in late 1928 with slightly more powerful Wasp engines and greater fuel capacity. Approximately 100 S-38Bs had been delivered by 1932, with a majority being sold to scheduled airlines such as NYRBA, Pan American, Western Air Express, Northwest Airways, and Curtiss Flying Service. Four were also accepted by the Navy between 1929 and 1932 under the designation PS-3. Pan American was the largest single purchaser,

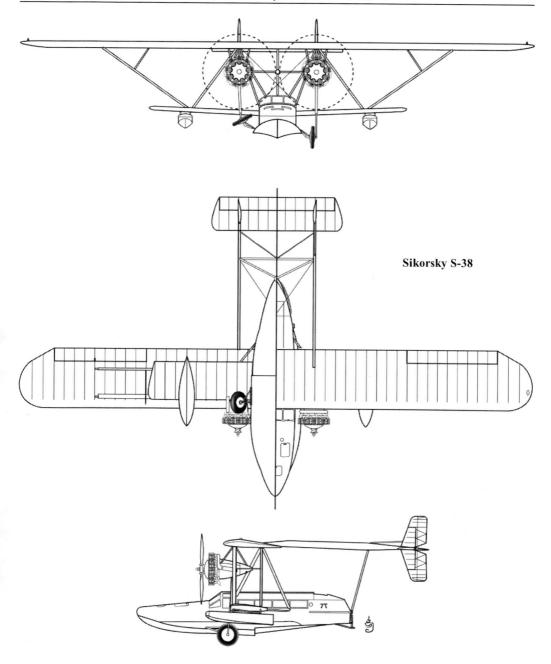

Sikorsky S-38

having as many as 30 S-38s in service at one time, and others were widely used in South America, the Dutch East Indies, and West Africa for both transportation and survey work. The final version, the S-38C, of which nine or ten were produced, was offered in 1929 for shorter haul routes and came with two extra seats and reduced fuel capacity. The principal operators were Inter-Island Airways, with routes linking the four Hawaiian Islands, and Colonial Western Airways, serving the Greats Lakes area. After taking delivery of the PS-2s and -3s with gun positions in the bow and stern, the Navy thereafter removed all armament and reclassified them as transports under the designation RS-2 and -3; one was assigned to the Marine Corps where it was used at Quantico and in Nicaragua. The Navy and Marine types were phased-out during the mid–1930s, but many civil S-38s continued in service through the early 1940s.

The S-38-A used by Western Air Express on its Los Angeles–Catalina Island run during the late 1920s. Western Air Express later merged with Transcontinental Air Transport to form TWA.

This RS-3, assigned to the Marine Corps in 1931, was based in Quantico and saw service with expeditionary forces in Nicaragua.

Sperry Aircraft Co.

The Sperry Aircraft Co. was launched at Farmingdale, New York, in 1918 by Lawrence B. Sperry, son of well-known inventor and entrepreneur Elmer Sperry. When the younger Sperry decided to go into the business of producing aircraft of his own design, he had already established himself as a pilot and aeronautical trendsetter. The company's most successful product was the M-1 Messenger utility biplane (designed by Alfred Verville), twenty-two of which were sold to the Army during the early 1920s. Sperry Aircraft discontinued operations after Lawrence Sperry disappeared over the English Channel in December 1923.

Sperry Land and Sea Triplane (1918)

TECHNICAL SPECIFICATIONS
Type: 3-seat amphibious Navy patrol boat/bomber.
Total produced: 1
Powerplant: one 360-hp Liberty 12-cylinder water-cooled engine driving a four-bladed fixed wooden propeller.
Armament: four 250-lb. bombs carried beneath the lower wings.
Performance: max. speed 85 mph; ceiling (not reported); range (not reported).
Weights: 5,000 lbs. empty (est.), 7,044 lbs. loaded.
Dimensions: span 48 ft. ¾ in., length 31 ft. 6 in., wing area 731 sq. ft.

Though not built to any known naval specification, Sperry's Land and Sea Triplane was presumably intended to fulfill a function similar to the Curtiss HS series but with the added capability of operating from land bases. In all likelihood, the design was conceived by Alfred Verville, who worked closely with Sperry during this time period. The all-wood triplane emerged with two

With the Land and Sea Triplane, Sperry hoped to interest the Navy with an aircraft that could fulfill the mission of the Curtiss HS, with the added capability of operating from land.

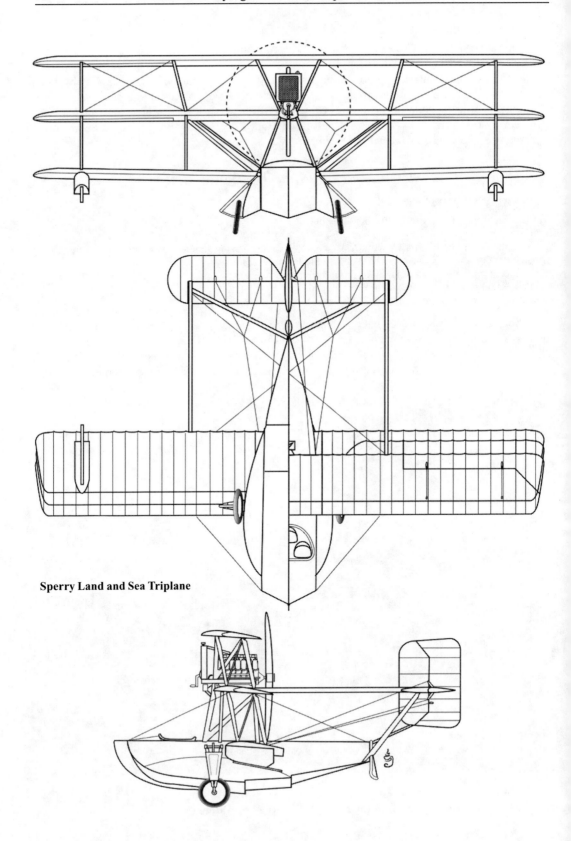

Sperry Land and Sea Triplane

bays of equal span wings very similar in shape and conformation to those of the Airco (de Havilland) DH-4 and a boom-mounted tailplane having a single large fin and rudder. Mounted to the sides of the wide hull, the hand-operated landing gear was designed to pivot upwards for water takeoffs and landings. The aircraft was flown and tested sometime close to the date of the armistice in November 1918. Although the Navy had shown some interest in Sperry's triplane initially, no orders were forthcoming.

PART II

The Golden Era, 1928–1945

HISTORICAL OVERVIEW

> "The work of the individual still remains the spark
> that moves mankind ahead."—*Igor I. Sikorsky*

Aeronautical Progress

In the United States between 1928 and 1945, flying boats and amphibians were built in greater numbers—an estimated 5,913 or more—than during any other period, and the underlying reasons were essentially practical. Since flying boats were not necessarily limited by the distance of take-off runs, they could be designed to operate at appreciably higher takeoff weights than landplanes, and higher takeoff weights corresponded directly to heavier payloads and longer range. For example, comparing the Douglas DC-2 and the Sikorsky S-42, both of which entered commercial service in 1934, the S-42, though cruising 35 mph slower, could lift twice the load (i.e., 38,000 lbs.) and carry it 200 miles further. When the Martin M130 commenced service two years later in 1936, it was the first passenger-carrying aircraft in the world to possess truly transoceanic range and could lift a payload exceeding its empty weight. And a similar rationale applied to military flying boats: a Consolidated PBY-3 possessed over twice the normal range of the contemporaneous Douglas B-18 twin-engine bomber (i.e., 2,175 miles versus 1,082 miles) and had the added capability of operating from widely dispersed sea bases.

In terms of the aeronautical state-of-the-art, flying boat and amphibian designs of this era advanced at a rate at least comparable to landplanes. The early 1930s saw the introduction of new engines that yielded better than a 1:1 power-to-weight ratio (e.g., the Pratt & Whitney R-1830 *Twin Wasp* of 1932 produced 825 hp and weighed 653 lbs.), and within five years, available horsepower had nearly doubled (e.g., 1,500-hp Wright R-2600 *Twin Cyclone* in 1937). An important development led by flying boats in the 1930s was the use of four engines in commercial transports, starting in 1931 with the Sikorsky S-40. Earlier concerns over asymmetric thrust (i.e., the yawing and rolling forces caused by the drag of a dead engine) were largely alleviated by the greater reliability of modern radial engines and lower drag airframe designs.

The leading factor in aerodynamic design, especially in regard to drag reduction, was the fairly rapid transition from strut and wire-braced biplane planforms to monoplanes having semi- or fully-cantilevered wings and tailplanes. As flying boat and amphibian designers continued to innovate, engines received drag rings or NACA-type cowlings and moved up to the leading edge of wings; use of streamlined pylons dispensed with the need for a multiplicity of struts. Of almost equal importance was a trend toward all-metal construction which lent itself to better streamlining. Except for fabric covering on some flying surfaces, aluminum alloy (i.e., dural) became the most common material for fabricating both airframes and skin. Metal construction was not only stronger but more susceptible to modern methods of mass production, as demonstrated by the fact that close to 5,000 of the 5,913 flying boats and amphibians listed here in Part II were manufactured between 1939 and 1945. However, attempts to introduce new construction materials like stainless steel (see Fleetwings Sea Bird, page 127) never gained general acceptance.

More powerful engines allowed dramatic increases in wing-loading factors (e.g., compare 12.9 lbs./sq. ft. of the Douglas PD-1 [1929] with 29.4 lbs./sq. ft of the Martin PBM-1 [1939]), and higher wing-loading meant less wing area and thus less induced drag needed to lift a specified load. The greatest performance gains were in payloads and range, so that by 1935, a flying boat like the Martin M130 could carry 25,000 lbs. over a distance of 3,200 miles, compared to 6,800 lbs. and 2,125 miles for the Douglas DC-3. The 1930s, due in large part to Depression-era economics, was characterized by fierce competition between leading companies—Boeing, Consolidated, Douglas, Grumman, Martin, and Sikorsky—in both the military and commercial sectors. Pressure placed on competing manufacturers to produce new designs resulted in an enormous leaps of progress within a comparatively brief span of time, e.g., 1934—Sikorsky S-42 and Martin M130; 1935—Consolidated PBY; 1936—Douglas DF; 1937—Grumman G-21, Consolidated PB2Y, and Sikorsky PBS; 1938—Boeing 314; and 1939—Martin PBM and Consolidated Model 31.

Military Procurement

From the late 1920s onward, the Navy's desire to increase its reach in two oceans kept flying boat procurement at the forefront. At the same time, however, cutbacks in appropriations due to the Depression caused BuAer to shift design and development emphasis from government-sponsored NAF programs to private contractors. The 122 aircraft ordered between 1927 and 1929, which were all derived from the NAF PN-12 program (see Douglas PD, Hall PH, Keystone PK, and Martin PM), would be the Navy's last true biplane patrol boats, and the nine Martin P3M monoplanes and 47 Consolidated P2Y sesquiplanes, placed in service between 1931 and 1935, augmented rather than replaced them. BuAer moved effectively to upgrade the entire patrol force in 1936 and 1937 when it ordered 199 Consolidated PBYs, the single largest flying boat acquisition since World War I.

In the mid–1930s the Navy began testing an idea that resulted in some of the biggest military flying boats ever constructed. Very large four-engine flying boats, known unofficially as "Sky Dreadnaughts," were envisaged delivering bomb loads equivalent or greater than those of the USAAC's land-based heavy bombers (e.g., Boeing YB-17). The ability to launch such missions from the sea was seen as a strategic hedge in the event the United States found itself cutoff from access to overseas land bases. Three development contracts were awarded: Sikorsky in 1935 for the XPBS-1, Consolidated in 1936 for the XPB2Y-1, and Martin in 1938 for the significantly larger XPB2M-1. The XPBS and XPB2Y both flew in 1937, and following a year of trials, Sikorsky's contract was cancelled and Consolidated authorized to build six PB2Y-2s for further evaluation. Although Consolidated did eventually receive a full-scale production contract in 1941 (for details, see PB2Y, page 102), the Sky Dreadnaught concept was overtaken by wartime priorities in 1942. In the interval, naval planners had concluded that aircraft carriers were better offensive weapons and far more territory could be covered by significantly increased numbers of twin-engine patrol boats (e.g., PBYs and PBMs); the PB2Ys and the sole XPB2M (flown in mid–1942) ultimately served as long-range, over-ocean transports.

The general naval expansion of the 1930s generated a need for smaller transport and utility aircraft capable of operating from shore bases or from ships to shore bases, and from 1932 to 1939, BuAer procured 135 single-engine amphibians (see Grumman JF/J2F) and 40 twin-engine amphibians (see Douglas RD, Grumman JRF, and Sikorsky RS and JRS) to fulfill this function. A similar but smaller expansion of Coast Guard air rescue services during the 1930s accounted for acquisition of another 35 military amphibians (see Douglas RD and Grumman JF,) and 18 flying boats (see Fokker PJ, Hall PH, and Viking OO). During the same timeframe, the Army also maintained a small fleet of amphibians as utility transports around coastal and island bases, purchasing one Sikorsky Y1C-28 (S-39) in 1931, 16 Douglas OA-3s/-4s (Dolphin) in 1932-1933, and 26 Grumman OA-9s (Goose) in 1938.

Between 1939 and 1945, the onset of World War Two led to unparalleled increases in production of flying boats and amphibians alike: 2,382 Consolidated PBYs and NAF PBNs, 210 Consolidated PB2Ys, 474 Grumman and Columbia J2Fs, 238 Grumman JRFs, 216 Grumman J4Fs, seven Hall PH-3s (Coast Guard only), and 1,332 Martin PBMs. For specific production allocations among U.S. and foreign military services, refer to reports on individual aircraft types, below. New flying boat and amphibian designs (as well as most other military aircraft) were effectively 'frozen' after 1940 so that manufacturers could concentrate upon mass-production of existing designs. One exception to the design freeze was the "Sky Freighter" concept—enormous, transoceanic flying boats massing from 125 to 200 tons loaded—which arose in 1942 in response to the U-Boat threat to Allied shipping. Two aircraft were ultimately considered, the six-engine Martin M193 (see Appendix B) and the eight-engine Hughes H-4 (see Part III, page 243), with three H-4 prototypes being authorized in late 1942. However, by the time construction started on the first H-4 in mid–1944, the U-Boat danger had diminished to the point that the project was reduced to one prototype.

Civil Developments

The era between 1928 and 1945 witnessed the rise, the peak, and finally, the fall of flying boats as over-ocean commercial transports. The rise was spearheaded by two organizations: The Aviation Corporation of the Americas, formed by Juan Terry Trippe in 1928 with Pan American Airways as an operating subsidiary, and the New York, Rio and Buenos Aires Line (NYRBA), formed by Ralph O'Neill in 1929. Both companies started business with strong financial backing. Pan American, getting a small head start, commenced a passenger and mail-carrying Caribbean network in October 1928 using Sikorsky S-38s; NYRBA followed in February 1930 with service from Miami to Brazil using newly acquired Consolidated Model 16 Commodores. Then in September 1930, in a swift turn of events—both political and financial—Pan American acquired NYRBA and its assets (including the nine Commodores delivered and four on order), and for the next ten years, expanded its overseas routes virtually without competition.

Pan American introduced the first four-engine *Clippers*, three Sikorsky S-40s, in 1931, inaugurating service on the 600-mile route between Jamaica and Panama and augmenting its Commodores on South American routes. The same year, with a view toward future expansion, Pan American invited Martin and Sikorsky both to design new flying boats that would have transatlantic range; however, in 1933, before any aircraft had been built, Pan American changed Sikorsky's route requirement to South America and Martin's to the Pacific area. Initial deliveries of six new Sikorsky S-42s began in August 1934, followed by four S-42As in 1935 and 1936; and the first of three Martin M130s began flying the first transpacific route (San Francisco to Manila, Philippines) in November 1935. But even as the Pacific service was starting, Pan American turned its eyes again to Atlantic routes and asked aircraft manufacturers to propose a new flying boat design having even better range and payload than the M130. In December 1936, Pan American selected Boeing's proposal, the model 314, with plans to acquire six. The world's first transatlantic passenger service commenced in June 1939, and Pan American ordered six new 314As the following September—the same month World War Two started in Europe. American Export Airlines (AEA), which hoped to break Pan American's monopoly on Atlantic routes, emerged in late 1939 with plans to operate three Sikorsky VS-44As, a demilitarized version of the XPBS-1, and its first scheduled flight took place in January 1942. Wartime priorities finally intervened against AEA and Pan American both, and from early 1942 to late 1945 their aircraft were either impressed into military service or operated under government control. As World War Two was drawing to a close, Pan American and other carriers like TWA and American Export Airlines began making definite moves to establish new overseas routes, but this time with new four-engine landplanes like the Douglas DC-4, the Lockheed

Constellation, and the Boeing Stratocruiser. The era of the transoceanic flying boat came to an end when Pan American retired it last 314 from scheduled service in 1946.

While the big flying boats were opening routes over the oceans during the 1930s, smaller amphibians like the Douglas Dolphin, Grumman Goose, Fairchild F91, and Sikorsky S-41 and S-43 were being acquired by airlines for shorter over-water operations. Pan American and it subsidiaries was the largest single user, employing at the peak 40 amphibians that served primarily on intermediate Caribbean and South American routes. Smaller operations like the Wilmington-Catalina Airline in southern California, Gorst Air Transport in the San Francisco Bay area, Curtiss Flying Service out of Boston and Chicago, and Inter-Island Airways in Hawaii operated single- or and twin-engine amphibians in coastal and island regions. Private ownership of either flying boats or amphibians was generally limited to corporations or wealthy executives (see Loening C-6/K-84 and Grumman G-21) and in some instances to international explorers (see Fairchild F91 and Sikorsky S-39). Attempts during this period to market small amphibians as lightplanes (see Amphibions P-1/-3 Privateer and Curtiss Teal, CW-3 and CA-1; and also see, Applegate Amphibian and Argonaut H-20/-24 Pirate in Appendix A) were generally unsuccessful, and other than one-of-a-kind homebuilts (see Booth Flying Boat in Appendix A), amounted to only about 30 aircraft produced. Percival Spencer sold his S-12 Air Car design (see page 208) to Republic in 1943, which ultimately resulted in mass production of the Seabee (see Part III, page 273) during the post-war era.

THE GOLDEN ERA • 1928–1945

Aircraft Manufacturer	*Model*	*First Flight*
Amphibions, Inc. (Ireland Aircraft, Inc.):	P-1/-3 Privateer	1931
Boeing Airplane Co.:	B314 (PAA Clippers)	1938
	PBB Sea Ranger	1942
Consolidated Aircraft Co.:	PY (Commodore 16)	1929
	P2Y	1932
	PBY (P3Y) Catalina	1935
	PB2Y Coronado	1937
	P4Y Corregidor	1939
Curtiss-Wright Airplane Co.:	A-1, B-1 Teal	1929
	CW-3 Duckling	1934
	CA-1 (Courtney)	1935
Douglas Aircraft Co.:	PD	1929
	Dolphin (RD, C-21, C-26, C-29)	1931
	P3D (OA-5, O-44)	1935
	DF	1936
Fairchild Aircraft Corp.:	F91 Baby Clipper	1935
Fleetwings, Inc.:	F-4, -5 Sea Bird	1936
Fokker Aircraft Corp. of America– General Aviation Mfg. Corp.:	F-11 Flying Yacht	1929
	PJ Flying Life Boat	1933
Goodyear Aircraft Corp.:	GA-1, -2 Duck	1944
Great Lakes Aircraft Corp.:	SG	1933
Grumman Aircraft Engr. Corp.:	JF/J2F Duck	1933
	G-21 (JRF) Goose	1937
	G-44 (J4F) Widgeon	1941

Aircraft Manufacturer	Model	First Flight
Hall Aluminum Aircraft Corp.:	PH	1929
	P2H	1932
Keystone Aircraft Corp.:	PK	1930
Loening Aeronautical Div. of Keystone Aircraft Corp.:	C-4 (K-85) Air yacht	1928
	C-6 (K-84) Commuter	1929
	O2L	1932
	SL	1931
	S2L	1933
Glenn L. Martin Co.:	PM	1929
	P2M, P3M	1931
	M130	1935
	M156	1938
	M162A Tadpole	1937
	PBM Mariner	1939
	PB2M Mars	1942
Naval Aircraft Factory:	P4N (PN-11)	1929
Sikorsky Div., United Aircraft Corp. (Vought-Sikorsky):	S-39 (C-28)	1929
	S-40	1930
	S-41 (RS)	1930
	P2S	1932
	SS	1933
	S-42	1934
	S-43 (JRS, OA-8, OA-11)	1935
	S/VS-44 (PBS)	1937
P. H. Spencer (Larsen Aircraft Co.):	S-12 Air Car	1941
Viking Flying Boat Co. (Stearman-Varney, Inc.):	OO (V-2)	1930

Amphibions, Inc.

After doing business for five years as Ireland Aircraft, Inc. (see Part I), the company was reorganized in 1931 as Amphibions, Inc. (an old spelling of the term) at the same Garden City, New York, location. It apparently ceased manufacturing operations sometime in 1933.

Amphibions P-1, -2, and -3 Privateer (1931)

TECHNICAL SPECIFICATIONS (P-3)

Type: 2 to 3-place civil amphibian.
Total produced: 18
Powerplant: one 165-hp Continental R-670 7-cylinder air-cooled radial engines driving a two-bladed, fixed-pitch wooden propeller.
Performance: max. speed 108 mph, cruise 90 mph; ceiling (not reported); range 300 mi.
Weights: not reported: useful load listed 650 lbs.
Dimensions: span 42 ft. 5 in., length 30 ft. 0 in., wing area 200 sq. ft. (est.)

The P-1 Privateer of 1931, and the fourteen P-2s which followed it in production, appeared as a monoplane having a single-boom empennage, powered by a 110-hp Warner *Scarab* seven-cylinder engine. Hull construction was metal with fabric-covered wing and tail surfaces, and the pusher engine was mounted on a tripod of struts directly above the open cockpit. The P-3, introduced in 1932, featured an enclosed cockpit, a four-and-one-half-foot increase in wingspan, a two-foot lengthening of the hull, and a 165-hp Continental engine. Only one P-3 was built, but five P-2s were

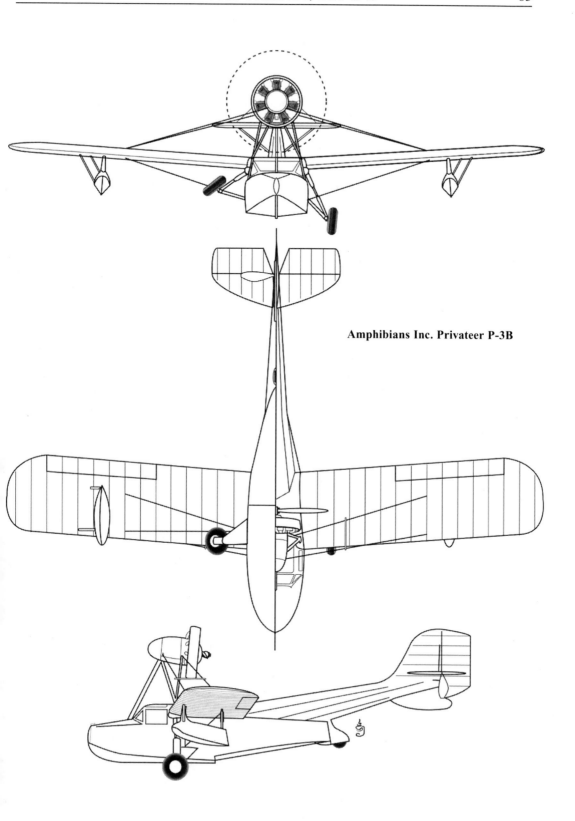

Amphibians Inc. Privateer P-3B

First P-3 with enclosed cockpit (NX773N), probably in 1932. This was also the first of the series to shift from a Warner *Scarab* powerplant to the Continental R-670.

reported to have been upgraded to the P-3 standard. The last examples, four 3-place P-3Bs with 210-hp Continental engines, were built in 1933.

Boeing Airplane Co.

In 1929 Boeing Airplane Co. was acquired by United Aircraft and Transport Corp. and thereafter operated as Boeing Aircraft Division. As a direct result of the Air Mail Act of 1934, airline and aircraft manufacturing companies like United were ordered to break up and reorganize themselves as wholly distinct entities, as a consequence of which Boeing became an independent corporate subsidiary of the newly reorganized United Aircraft Corp. the same year. Founder William E. Boeing liquidated his interests in the company shortly after the reorganization. During the decade of the 1930s, Boeing began focusing nearly all of its creative efforts towards the design and development of very large, multi-engine aircraft, so that by late 1935, when the company was making a bid to enter the commercial flying boat market, it had already established a new standard for four-engine aircraft with its Model 299 (XB-17) and was at an advanced stage of development with the significantly larger Model 297 (XB-15).

Boeing 314 (1938)

TECHNICAL SPECIFICATIONS (314A)

Type: 40 to 74-passenger long-range civil transport.
Total produced: 12
Powerplant: four 1,600-hp Wright R-2600 *Twin Cyclone* 14-cylinder, twin-row air-cooled radial engines driving three-bladed constant-speed metal propellers.
Performance: max. speed 199 mph, cruise 183 mph; ceiling 13,400 ft.; range 3,685 mi.
Weights: 50,268 lbs. empty, 82,500 lbs. max. takeoff.
Dimensions: span 152 ft. 0 in., length 106 ft. 0 in., wing area 2,867 sq. ft.

As a passenger-carrying flying boat, most airline historians acknowledge the Boeing 314 as having been in a class by itself. In overall terms of performance, payload, efficiency, and comfort, it clearly surpassed every other type of commercial flying boat that had flown before it. The origins of the 314 can be traced to specifications drawn up by Pan American Airways in 1935 for a new type of flying boat specifically intended for transatlantic operations. In order to undertake the North Atlantic route between the U.S. coast and England, via Newfoundland and Ireland, Pan American determined that it would need an aircraft capable of carrying a much higher payload than that

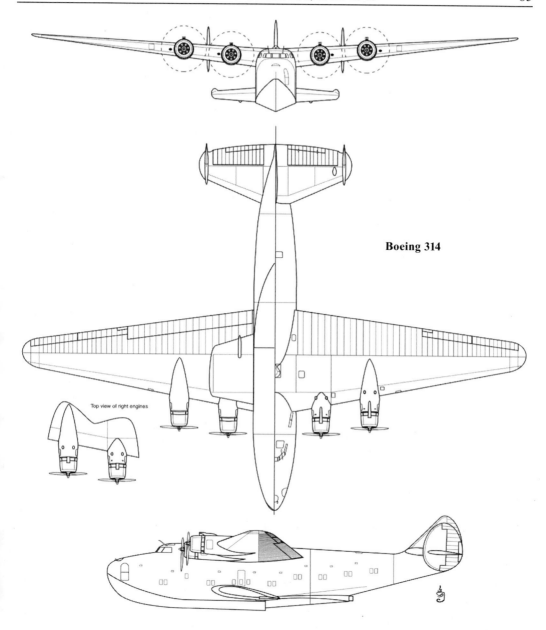

Boeing 314

Top view of right engines

of the Martin 130s (see page 170) currently employed on its Pacific routes. In December 1936, after considering design proposals received from various manufacturers, Pan American selected Boeing to proceed with the development of its proposed model 314, with delivery of the first aircraft expected within one year.

Boeing's engineering staff began laying down a blueprint that borrowed much of the wing design and engine nacelle arrangement from the XB-15 and incorporated a similar light-alloy structure having stressed aluminum skin. The design of the hull was made deep enough to permit an upper deck containing the flight deck, navigation and radio rooms, engineering spaces, accommodations for ten crewmembers, and baggage holds, leaving the entire lower deck with space for up to 74 passengers in day seating or 40 in sleeper berths. The empennage comprised a twin fin and rudder arrangement on a raised horizontal stabilizer that would be clear of the spray. Rather than the more typical wing floats, the 314 featured two-spar fuselage sponsons, both holding 3,525 gal-

Atlantic Clipper, the fourth 314 delivered during the spring of 1939, shown moored with starboard entry door opened. This aircraft operated on transatlantic routes until being commandeered into military service in 1942.

lons of fuel and serving as an entry ramp for passengers. The Wright R-2600s used were the most powerful American-made aircraft engines available at the time the 314 was being planned.

Although the project fell five months behind schedule, it was nonetheless a remarkable engineering achievement for Boeing to have completed an aircraft of such size and complexity in the span of only seventeen months. Taxiing tests in Puget Sound were commenced on May 31, 1938, and the 314 lifted-off on its first flight on June 7. Early testing revealed that the twin fins lacked sufficient area for directional stability, with the result the a third fabric-covered fin was added to the center of the horizontal stabilizer, thus giving the type its characteristic triple-tailed appearance. The first 314, christened *Honolulu Clipper*, was delivered to Pan American's west coast base in late January 1939, where it was placed in service on the San Francisco–Hong Kong route to replace the Martin 130 (i.e., *Hawaii Clipper*) lost the previous year. The remaining five 314s, *California Clipper, Yankee Clipper, Atlantic Clipper, Dixie Clipper*, and *American Clipper*, were thereafter delivered in monthly intervals, the last in mid–June 1939. The first two were allocated Pacific routes, the other four to Atlantic service.

The *Yankee Clipper* departed Baltimore on a North Atlantic survey flight on March 26, 1939, that encompassed both of Pan American's planned routes (southern to Lisbon and Marseilles via the Azores; and northern to Southampton [England] via Shediac [New Brunswick], Botswood [Newfoundland], and Foynes [Ireland]), with a stop in Bermuda. With the *Yankee Clipper* again, Pan American initiated transatlantic mail service over the southern route on May 20, 1939, then a month later over the northern route. The first transatlantic passenger service by any type of heavier-than-air aircraft took place on June 28, 1939, when the *Dixie Clipper* departed New York across the southern route; the *Yankee Clipper* inaugurated northern service the following July 8. Unfortunately, the outbreak of World War II in Europe in September 1939 caused this service to be decidedly brief, transatlantic flights being cancelled with regard to both original routes on October 3. Pan American continued to operate 314s in the Atlantic, but operations were limited to central routes via Brazil and West Africa; others were diverted to new Pacific routes. Despite the setback, six more 314s were ordered from Boeing in late September 1939, and deliveries of the improved 314As commenced in April 1941. The 314A featured many improvements gleaned from recent experience, the

Unidentified 314 shown prior to December 1941. Note neutrality flags on nose, starboard wing, and bottoms of both sponsons.

One of six 314As, *Capetown Clipper*, shown just prior to landing. This aircraft was impressed into Navy service during World War II.

most important of which was uprated R-2600 engines, larger hydromatic propellers, and greater fuel capacity. The first three went to Pan American as the *Pacific Clipper, Anzac Clipper*, and *Capetown Clipper*, however, the remaining three, per agreement with Pan American, were sold to the British Purchasing Commission and thereafter allocated to British Overseas Airways Corp. (BOAC). Upon entering BOAC service, the three aircraft were named *Bristol, Bangor*, and *Berwick*.

One of the more famous Clipper flights occurred between December 2, 1941, and January 6, 1942, when the *Pacific Clipper* was en route from Noumea, New Caledonia to Auckland, New Zealand at the time the Japanese attacked Pearl Harbor. Upon receiving instructions from Pan American to proceed to New York by the much longer westward route, Captain Robert Ford thereafter completed the 8,500-mile return flight via Australia, Java (Indonesia), Ceylon (Sri Lanka), India, Bahrain, Sudan, Belgian Congo, Brazil, and Trinidad. After the U.S. entered the war, four of the 314s were pressed into military service with the U.S. Army Air Forces Air Transport Command as the C-98 and one with the Navy, apparently under the same designation. The militarized 314s were used primarily to ferry personnel on long distance routes all over the world. One was used to carry President Franklin D. Roosevelt to the Casablanca Conference in 1943, and the BOAC 314As were

Bristol, **one of three 314As transferred to British Overseas Airways Corporation (BOAC). After the war, this aircraft was sold to General Phoenix Corporation, based in Baltimore, Maryland, but apparently never used commercially.**

used on several occasions to transport Prime Minister Winston Churchill. In military service, one C-98 was destroyed in a crash near Lisbon, Portugal in February 1943 and two others were later damaged beyond repair; the two remaining were returned to Pan American soon after the war ended.

While Pan American continued to operate its four remaining 314s throughout the war, they were removed from service in early 1946, to be replaced on scheduled operations by Douglas DC-4s and Lockheed L.049 *Constellations*. Five 314s and 314As ended up with World Airways where they were used during the late 1940s for charter services until finally being scrapped in 1950. Another 314A, the *Anzac Clipper*, was sold by World to a private owner but destroyed in 1951. The sole Navy 314, sold to American International Airways, another charter company, was damaged beyond repair in late 1947. The three ex–BOAC 314As were sold to General Phoenix Corp. in Baltimore, Maryland, but apparently never used in commercial operations. Unfortunately, none of these historic aircraft are known to exist today.

Boeing PBB Sea Ranger (1942)

TECHNICAL SPECIFICATIONS (XPBB-1)

Type: 8 to 10-place long-range patrol boat
Total produced: 1
Powerplant: two 2,300-hp Wright R-3350-8 *Double Cyclone* 18-cylinder, twin-row air-cooled radial engines driving three-bladed electric, constant-speed metal propellers.
Armament: six .50-caliber machine guns in two-gun, power-operated turrets in bow, dorsal positions, one flexible .50-caliber machine gun in each waist position, and up to 20,000 lbs. of bombs.
Performance: max. speed 219 mph, cruise 158 mph; ceiling 18,900 ft.; range 4,245 mi. (normal), 6,300 mi. (max.).
Weights: 41,531 lbs. empty, 62,006 lbs. normal gross, 101,130 lbs. max. takeoff.
Dimensions: span 139 ft. 8 in., length 94 ft. 9 in., wing area 1,826 sq. ft.

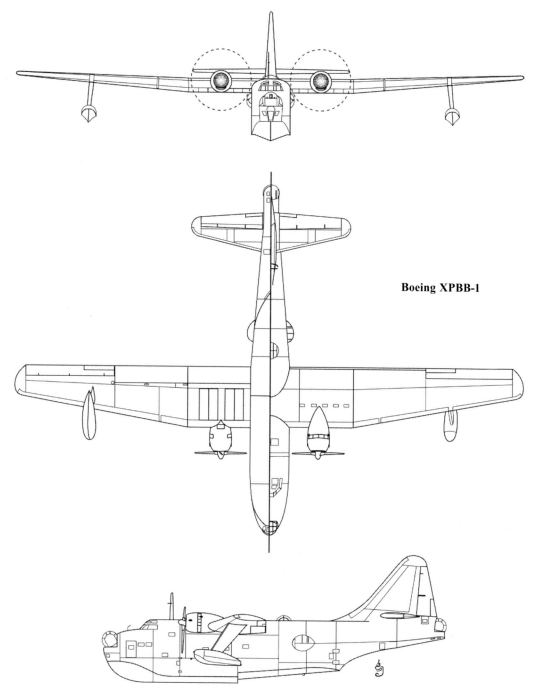

Boeing XPBB-1

Distinguished as the largest twin-engine flying boat to be built by any combatant during World War II, the Boeing model 344 was originally ordered by the Navy in June 1940 as the XPBB-1. At the time, the United States saw itself threatened on both oceans by German and Japanese submarines and surface raiders, leading BuAer to issue a specification for a very long-range, heavily-armed patrol boat that could loiter for a long periods of time over large distances. Even before the prototype flew, Boeing received a provisional order for fifty-seven production models and proceeded with construction of a new plant at Renton, Washington that would be dedicated to manufacturing the PBB-1.

The sole XPBB-1, known unofficially as the "Lone Ranger," seen right after touchdown. Due to the priority of the B-29 program, plans to mass-produce the PBB-1 were cancelled.

Much of the aeronautical technology applied to the design of the XPBB-1 was derived from Boeing's contemporaneous model 340, the XB-29, in particular a high-aspect ratio wing utilizing very large Fowler-type flaps to decrease takeoff and landing speeds. The long hull was very deep in section and employed a two-step planning surface. Each stabilizing float was attached to the wing with a single airfoil-shaped strut of sufficient strength to dispense with the normal diagonal bracing. In order to minimize fuel consumption during long, maximum weight takeoff runs, the XPBB-1 was stressed for boosted takeoffs from large barges designed specially for that purpose. Following its first flight on July 5, 1942, early testing of the XPBB-1, dubbed *Sea Ranger* by the factory, revealed excellent flying characteristics and performance that met or exceeded its military specifications. However, a change in wartime priorities, unrelated to the aircraft itself, dictated that the type would never be placed into production: first, the new Boeing plant at Renton was to be wholly allocated to B-29 production and second, all R-3350 engines were likewise earmarked for the B-29 program. Later nicknamed the "Lone Ranger," the XPBB-1 was delivered to the Navy in October 1943, where it was used for a variety of duties at San Diego. After the war, the aircraft was placed in storage at NAS Norfolk, Virginia.

Consolidated Aircraft Co.

Formed in Buffalo, New York by Reuben H. Fleet in 1923, the Consolidated Aircraft Corp. was destined to become one of the greatest names in flying boats. During the Golden Era (1929-1945), Consolidated produced more flying boats (five major types totaling 2,678 aircraft) than all other American aircraft manufacturers combined. In 1935 the company moved its operations to San Diego, California, to take advantage of more favorable weather conditions, and in 1941, merged with Vultee Aircraft Corp. as Consolidated-Vultee Aircraft Corp. Fleet stepped down from active management of the company soon after the merger and served throughout World War II as an advisor to industry and government.

Consolidated PY and Model 16 Commodore (1929)

TECHNICAL SPECIFICATIONS (XPY-1)

Type: 4 to 5-place naval patrol boat; 20/32-passenger civil transport.
Total produced: 15
Powerplant: two (or three) 450-hp Pratt & Whitney R-1340-38 *Wasp* 9-cylinder air-cooled radial engines
    driving two-bladed, ground-adjustable metal propellers.
Armament: one flexible .30-caliber machine gun in the bow and one flexible .30-caliber machine gun in the
    waist position.
Performance: max. speed 118 mph, cruise 110 mph; ceiling 15,300 ft.; range 1,716 mi. (normal), 2,629 mi. (max.).
Weights: 8,369 lbs. empty, 13,734 lbs. normal gross, 16,492 lbs. max. takeoff.
Dimensions: span 100 ft. 0 in., length 61 ft. 9 in., wing area 1,110 sq. ft.

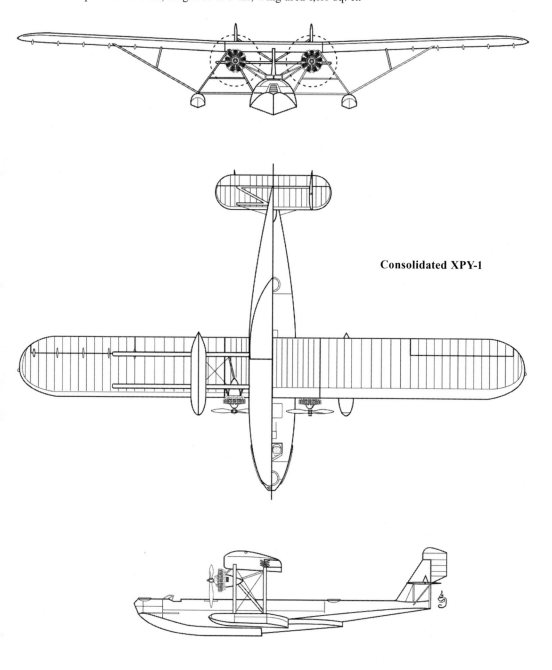

Consolidated XPY-1

The first of Isaac Laddon's famous flying boat designs, the XPY-1 is shown here in 1929 on beaching gear. The type was ultimately produced by Martin as the P2M and P3M.

Ordered in early 1928 as the Navy's first monoplane flying boat, the Consolidated XPY-1 was designed to a BuAer specification calling for a twin-engine aircraft having a single, parasol-mounted wing, mated to a metal hull and empennage similar to that of the NAF PN-11 (see P4N). The task of developing the design was given to Consolidated's Isaac M. " Mac" Laddon, who served as the firm's chief engineer on large aircraft projects. In order to create the aerodynamic proportions dictated by the larger monoplane wing, Laddon and his team first lengthened the PN-11 hull by seven feet nine inches, then positioned the wing overhead with W-struts from which the two engines were suspended. Horizontal spars below the W-struts were used to brace the wing structure and also served as outriggers for the stabilizing floats. As with the earlier PN series, the wings and tail surfaces were of fabric-covered metal construction, and the cockpit and crew accommodations were left open. According to standard naval procurement practices of the day, once the design was fixed, production rights were assigned to BuAer.

Construction of the XPY-1 was completed over a ten-month period and its first flight made on January 10, 1929. Consolidated assigned the factory name "Admiral" to the project, but it was never adopted by the Navy. While testing was underway, to boost speed and climb performance, BuAer ordered Consolidated to add a third R-1340 engine above the wing center-section. In early 1929, BuAer invited manufacturers to submit proposals for production of the new design and, ironically, the Glenn L. Martin Co., which came in as low bidder, received a contract June to build nine examples (see Martin P2M, P3M). Consolidated then turned to the civil market, developing the Model 16 Commodore for the newly formed New York, Rio and Buenos Aires Line (NYRBA). NYRBA, having already commenced local airline operations in South America with Ford Tri-motors, planned to use the Commodores on long, over-water routes originating from Miami, Florida.

The first of fourteen Model 16s ordered by NYRBA was completed and flown during the fall of 1929. In addition to hull cabins that accommodated up to twenty passengers, the Model 16 differed from the XPY-1 in having a fully-enclosed cockpit and being powered by a pair of 575-hp

Havana, **one of 14 Commodores ordered by the New York, Rio and Buenos Aires Line prior to the takeover by Pan American Airways in September 1930.**

Pratt & Whitney R-1690 *Hornet* engines. The first Model 16, christened *Buenos Aires*, commenced regular service on NYRBA's new route from Miami to Brazil in mid–February 1930. Starting with the fifth Commodore produced, listed as the Model 16-1, the hull was lengthened six feet three inches to provide space for twelve additional passengers or cargo, and the final versions, Model 16-2s, came with ring cowls on the engines. Consolidated had delivered nine more Commodores at the time of NYRBA's take-over by Pan American Airways in September 1930, and the remaining four were delivered directly to Pan American. Under a subsidiary named Panair do Brasil, Pan American operated the Commodores on major South American routes until newer types replaced them during 1935. They were afterward used on shorter routes and for crew training, and a small number are known to have been operating in the Caribbean with Bahamas Airways, Ltd., a Pan American affiliate, as late as 1946.

Consolidated P2Y (1932)

TECHNICAL SPECIFICATIONS (P2Y-3)

Type: 5-place naval patrol boat.
Total produced: 47
Powerplant: two 750-hp Wright R-1820-90 Cyclone 9-cylinder air-cooled radial engines driving three-bladed, ground-adjustable metal propellers.
Armament: one flexible .30-caliber machine gun in the bow, two flexible .30-caliber machine guns in the waist positions, and up to 2,000 lbs. of bombs carried on underwing racks.
Performance: max. speed 139 mph, cruise 117 mph; ceiling 16,100 ft.; range 1,180 mi. (normal loaded), 2,050 mi. (max.).
Weights: 12,769 lbs. empty, 21,291 lbs. normal gross, 25,266 lbs. max. takeoff.
Dimensions: span 100 ft. 0 in., length 61 ft. 9 in., wing area 1,514 sq. ft.

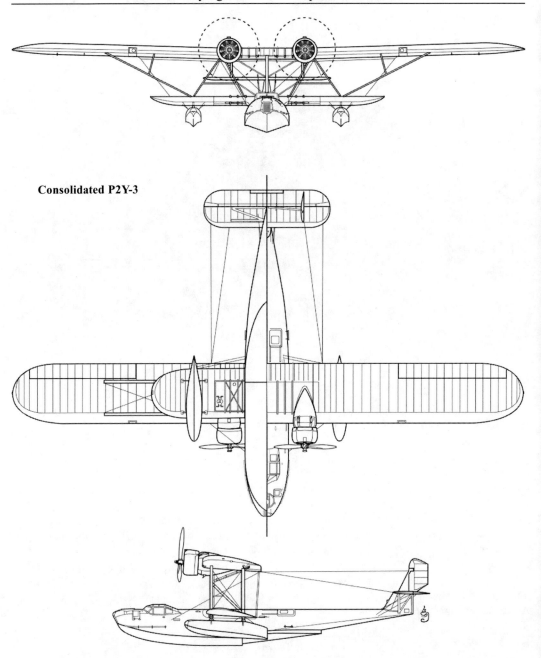

Consolidated P2Y-3

In May 1931 BuAer gave Consolidated a development contract for the XP2Y-1, a redesign of the XPY-1 which involved the addition of sesquiplane wings to the upper hull. The sesquiplane lay-out, adding 404 square feet of wing area, not only reduced wing loading and improved payload but also supplied additional space for fuel storage and bomb racks. Other enhancements included a fully-enclosed cockpit and more powerful R-1820 engines equipped with ring cowlings. In June 1931, after reviewing competitive proposals, BuAer awarded Consolidated a contract to produce a further twenty-three examples as the P2Y-1, with deliveries scheduled to start in early 1933. The XP2Y-1 made its first flight on March 26, 1932, in the three-engine configuration originally specified, but following two months of trials, the third engine was removed, and a two-engine layout was adopted as the production standard.

Consolidated P2Y-1 Long Range Patrol Flying Boat
24 of this type used by U. S. Navy

Naval Air Service flew 6 of this type non-stop from Norfolk, Va.,
to Coco Solo, C. Z. (2059 miles), thence to Acapulco, Mexico
(1677 miles), thence to San Diego, Cal. (1616 miles).

Consolidated Aircraft Corporation
Buffalo, N. Y.

NO. 2093   SEPT.-OCT. 1933

P2Y-1 serving with VP-10 over Norfolk, Virginia, in late 1933. Lower sesquiplane wing not only pro-vided extra lift, but also added space for fuel tankage and weapons storage.

The first production P2Y-1s began entering service with VP-10 at Naval Air Station Norfolk, Virginia, in February 1933, and by the end of the year were also equipping VP-5 in the Panama Canal Zone. Demonstrating the capabilities of their new aircraft, these two units made some notable long-distance flights: non-stop from Norfolk to Coco Solo, Canal Zone in late 1933; then non-stop from San Francisco to Pearl Harbor in mid–1934. The last P2Y-1 on the production line became the XP2Y-2 in August 1933 when modified to have its engines re-mounted on the upper wing in nacelles, together with full-chord engine cowlings having moveable cowl-flaps. In December 1933, follow-ing trials of the XP2Y-2, Consolidated received a contract to manufacture twenty-three more air-craft to be delivered as the P2Y-3. San Diego-based VP-7 received its first P2Y-3 in January 1935, and all had been delivered to Navy units by the end of May. Starting in 1936, at least twenty-one P2Y-1s underwent modifications that brought them up to the P2Y-3 standard and were thereafter returned to service as the P2Y-2. While on active service, P2Y-1s, -2s and -3s also served at vari-ous times with VP-4, VP-14, VP-15, VP-19, VP-20, and VP-21. The Navy began the process of replacing P2Ys with newer equipment during the late 1930s, and all had been withdrawn from front-line units by the end of 1941. A number of P2Y-2s and -3s were thereafter assigned to NAS Pen-sacola as flying boat trainers. Foreign sales included two P2Y-1s, one to Colombia and one to Japan, plus six P2Y-3s to Argentina, the last being delivered in 1937.

One of 23 P2Y-3s, shown here in 1935. Twenty-one P2Y-1s were subsequently modified to incorporate the P2Y-3 improvements and returned to service as P2Y-2s. The P2Y-3s were used as trainers during World War II.

Consolidated PBY (P3Y, OA-10, PBN) Catalina (1935)

TECHNICAL SPECIFICATIONS (PBY-1 [PBY-5A])

Type: 7 to 9-place naval patrol [amphibious] boat.
Total produced: 2,554 (all U.S.-built versions)
Powerplant: two 900-hp [1,200-hp] Pratt & Whitney R-1830-64 [-92] *Twin Wasp* 14-cylinder, twin-row air-cooled radial engines driving three-bladed, variable-pitch [constant-speed] metal propellers.
Armament: one [two] .30-caliber machine guns in a nose turret, two flexible .30-caliber [.50-calibre] machine guns in the waist [blister] positions, [one flexible .30-calibre machine gun in the tunnel], and up to 4,000 lbs. of bombs, depth charges, or torpedoes carried on underwing racks.
Performance: max. speed 177 mph [179 mph], cruise 105 mph [117 mph]; ceiling 20,900 ft. [14,700]; range 2,125 mi. [1,660 mi.] (normal loaded), 4,042 mi. [2,545 mi.] (max.).
Weights: 14,576 lbs. [20,910 lbs.] empty, 22,336 lbs. [33,975 lbs.] normal gross, 28,447 lbs. [35,300 lbs.] max. takeoff.
Dimensions: span 104 ft. 0 in., length 65 ft. 2 in. [63 ft. 10 in.], wing area 1,514 sq. ft.

In terms of sheer numbers, longevity, and versatility, the Consolidated PBY Catalina was destined to become the most famous and most widely used flying boat in the history of aviation. The origins of the PBY can be traced to a requirement issued by BuAer during 1933 soliciting proposals for a new type of patrol boat that would eventually replace the Navy's existing fleet of P2Ys and P3Ms. Consolidated received a development contract in October 1933 to build a flying prototype of its proposed Model 28 under the designation XP3Y-1, and a similar contract was given to Douglas in February 1934 to build the rival XP3D-1 (see P3D, below). Both aircraft were scheduled to be delivered to the Navy for competitive trials in early 1935.

Taking the experience accumulated with the PY and P2Y, Isaac M. Laddon and Consolidated's engineering staff evolved the design of the XP3Y-1 as an all-metal monoplane to be powered by newly available 850-hp Pratt & Whitney *Twin Wasp* engines. Special emphasis was placed on drag-reducing features such as a streamlined pylon supporting a broad, semi-cantilevered wing that dispensed with all but a pair of diagonal lift struts on each side, together with stabilizing floats that

PBY-1 shown serving with Pearl Harbor-based VP-6 in 1937. The order of 100 PBY-1s and 2s in 1935 and 1936 represented an across the fleet upgrade of the Navy's patrol boat force.

The most numerous Catalina variant, 1,533 PBY-5s were built by Consolidated before and during World War II. Another 240 were completed by Boeing of Canada as the PB2B-1.

retracted flush into the wings to form the tips and a fully-cantilevered cruciform tailplane. The entire airframe was to be clad in metal except for fabric-covered control surfaces and wing section aft of the main spar.

Construction of the prototype was completed at Consolidated's Buffalo plant in early 1935 just prior to the company's move en masse to San Diego. On March 21, 1935, after being shipped by rail to Naval Air Station Anacostia, the XP3Y-1 made its first flight. Trials carried out afterward demonstrated a significant improvement in performance over earlier patrol boat types, and while the Douglas XP3D-1 compared favorably, Consolidated bid a lower unit cost ($90,000 each) and consequently received a contract to produce sixty aircraft as the P3Y-1. During the fall of 1935, the prototype was returned to the factory for changes that included lengthening the nose eighteen inches to accommodate an enclosed gun turret, redesigned vertical tail surfaces, and installation of 900-hp R-1830-64 engines. In the interval, the designation was changed to PBY-1, denoting new naval emphasis on the bombing role of the overall patrol mission.

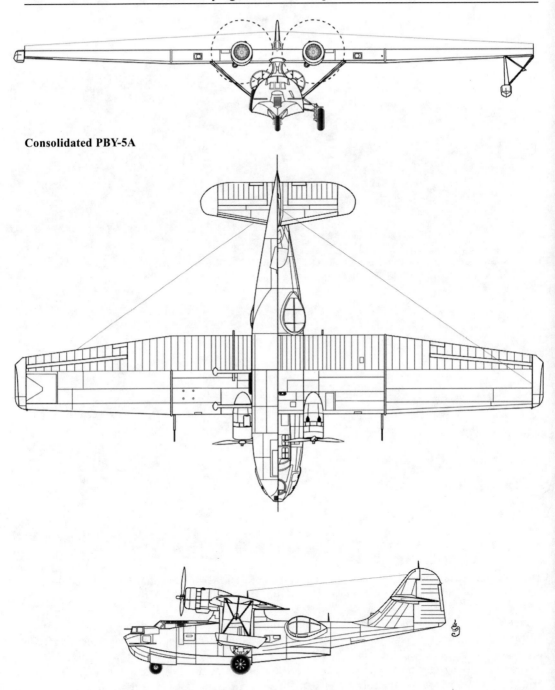

Consolidated PBY-5A

Shortly after being redelivered and test flown on May 19, 1936, the revised XPBY-1 posted a record non-stop flight of 3,443 miles. As deliveries of production aircraft proceeded, PBY-1s began entering service with Pearl Harbor squadrons during the fall of 1936, initially with VP-11, then with VP-12. In mid–1936, BuAer held yet a second competition between the XPBY-1 and the substantially modified Douglas XP3D-2, with the result that Consolidated prevailed again, receiving a contract in July 1936 to manufacture fifty more aircraft as the PBY-2, which differed from the PBY-1 only in small details. Five civil Model 28s were sold in 1937 and 1938: one Model 28-1 to an American explorer who re-sold it to the Soviet Union for an Arctic rescue mission; three Model 28-2s

Identical to the Navy PBY-5A, an OA-10 is depicted in postwar markings of the USAF Air Rescue Service.

This PBY-6A is shown in wartime colors during the last year of the war. Seventy-five went to the USAAF as the OA-10B and another 48 were lend-leased to the Soviet Union.

to the Soviet Union, powered by Wright R-1820 *Cyclone* engines, along with the license to build the type in Russia; and one Model 28-3 to the same explorer who, naming the aircraft *Guba*, subsequently operated it in New Guinea, then re-sold it to Great Britain in 1940. As Navy production continued, the first PBY-2s reached VP units in mid–1937, with the last being delivered by February 1938.

In a move designed to upgrade substantially all of the Navy's old patrol boat fleet, BuAer awarded Consolidated another contract in November 1936 to manufacture sixty-six PBY-3s, which would be powered by 1,000-hp R-1830-66 engines. PBY-3s began entering service in late 1937, and by August 1938, when the last -3 had been delivered, fourteen Navy patrol squadron were equipped with PBY-1s, -2s, and -3s, including five based at Pearl Harbor and two in the Panama Canal Zone. In December 1937, as part its plan to replace older aircraft, BuAer ordered thirty-three PBY-4s to be powered by 1,050-hp R-1830-72 engines, with the first examples reaching operational service during 1938. The last three PBY-4s were competed with blister-type enclosures over the waist gunner's position, a feature that became standard on future models. In March 1939 a civil Model 28-4 was delivered to American Export Airlines and in July 1939, a Model 28-5 sold to Great Britain became the first American military aircraft to be delivered by transatlantic flight. In order to expand the type's mission versatility, BuAer directed that the last PBY-4 be returned to the factory and converted to an amphibian having tricycle retractable landing gear. This aircraft was flown on November 22, 1939, as the XPBY-5A.

In December 1939, in connection with a general expansion of naval aviation prompted by the start of World War II in Europe and increasing tensions with Japan in the Far East, BuAer ordered 200 PBY-5s, the largest Navy procurement of a single type of aircraft since World War I. PBY-5s featured a squared off rudder, 1,200-hp R-1830-82 engines (using 100-octane fuel), plus an upgrade to .50-calibre guns in the waist blisters. During the same time period, Consolidated received additional orders for 174 essentially similar Model 28-5Ms to be delivered to Great Britain, France, Australia, and Canada, the French order, following the German conquest, being eventually absorbed by Great Britain. The first Navy PBY-5 was accepted in September 1940 and the second delivered to the Coast Guard shortly afterward. Taken into RAF service as the Catalina I, the British Model 28-5Ms differed in having R-1830-S1C3G engines, six .303-calibre guns with twin mounts in the blisters, self-sealing fuel tanks, and 225 lbs. of extra armor plating around the gunner's positions. By December 1941, 167 PBY-5s had been delivered to the Navy, together with a further 33 examples completed as amphibious PBY-5As.

Wartime contracts resulted in orders being placed with Consolidated for an additional 1,533 PBY-5 variants: 516 PBY-5s and 710 PBY-5As for the U.S. Navy; 225 PBY-5Bs (non-amphibious Catalina IB) and 70 Catalina IVAs (amphibious) supplied to Great Britain under Lend Lease; and 12 PBY-5As to Dutch forces in the East Indies. To keep pace with PBY demand, Consolidated opened a second assembly line in 1943 at a new plant located in New Orleans, Louisiana. Improvements incorporated to -5 variants during their production life included a twenty percent increase in fuel capacity, self-sealing fuel tanks, engine upgrades, addition of one more .30-calibre gun to the nose turret, and from mid–1942, radar. A proposed redesign of the hull (lengthened eighteen inches with a more pointed bow and a longer rear step), and a taller fin and rudder resulted in the Naval Aircraft Factory PBN-1 Nomad. In July 1941, in order not to disrupt PBY-5/-5A production, the Navy ordered NAF to manufacture 156 PBN-1s; but, as events turned out, only seventeen PBN-1s had been delivered to the Navy by early 1943, when remaining production of the type was allocated to the Soviet Union under Lend Lease.

Besides American production by Consolidated and NAF, 731 PBY-derivatives were built in Canada in 1944 and 1945. Canadian-Vickers (later Canadair) completed 369 PBY-5As (BuAer designation PBV-1), of which 139 went to the RCAF as the Canso A and 230 to the U.S. Army Air Force as the OA-10A. The USAAF had previously acquired fifty-four PBY-5As that were taken into service as OA-10s and used for search and rescue. Boeing of Canada manufactured another 362 examples: 240 as the PB2B-1/Catalina IVB (PBY-5), 55 as the PB2B-1A/Catalina V (PBY-5A), and 67 as the PB2B-2A/Catalina VI (PBY-6A). Most PB2B variants were allocated to the Britain, Canada, Australia, and New Zealand. PBY-5/-5A production in the U.S. terminated in January 1945, and the final Consolidated variant, 167 PBY-6As, were produced at New Orleans from January to September 1945, at which point all PBY production ceased. The PBY-6A differed in having the taller PBN-1 tail, two .50-calibre guns in the bow turret, and radar over the cockpit. Seventy-five PBY-6As were redirected to the U.S. Army Air Force as the OA-10B, plus another 48 went to the Soviet Union. From 1939 to possibly as late as 1948, between 400 and 1,000 Model 28-2s (PBY-2) were license-produced in Russia as the Amtorg GST (*Gidro Samolyet Transportnyi* = hydro aircraft transport). Soviet versions were powered by either Milukin M-62 or Shvetsov ASh-62IR 14-cylinder radial engines having a horsepower rating from 900 hp to 1,000 hp.

The exact distribution of PBY variants among U.S. and Allied combatants during World War II is made difficult by the fact that aircraft originally delivered to the U.S. Navy or the RAF were frequently re-allocated to other users. Between 1942 and 1945, 114 Navy PBY-5 variants were transferred to various Coast Guard units. Approximately 700 were delivered to the RAF as the Catalina

Naval Aircraft Factory PBN-1 shown in dappled paint scheme. The taller fin, more pointed bow, and lengthened hull afterbody are evident. Production was shifted to NAF to prevent Consolidated from retooling the PBY-5 production line.

Modified ex-military PBY-5A operating with Alaska Airlines in the 1960s. Note addition of side windows plus airstair door at the rear.

I and IA (Model 28-5), IB, II, III, and IVB (Canadian-built PB2B-1), and IV (PB2B-2A), all Catalina Vs (PB2B-1A) going directly to Canada. By the end of the war, Australia (RAAF) was operating 168 Catalinas of various marks and New Zealand (RNZAF) had acquired fifty-six. In addition to 185 Canadian-built examples, the RCAF received ten Catalina Is, eight IBs, and fourteen IIs. As previously mentioned, 138 PBN-1s (one destroyed prior to delivery) and forty-eight PBY-6As were supplied to the Soviet Union.

The wartime record of PBYs and Catalinas was legendary. They saw extensive use in both the Pacific and Atlantic theaters in a variety of roles that encompassed maritime reconnaissance, surface attack, antisubmarine warfare (ASW), search and rescue, and even transportation when the need arose. On March 26, 1941, an RAF Coastal Command Catalina located the German battleship *Bismarck* as it was attempting to evade the Royal Navy; on April 4, 1942, an RCAF Catalina spotted a Japanese carrier task force on its way to attack the Royal Navy's Indian Ocean Fleet; and on June 4, 1942, a Navy PBY-5 discovered the Japanese carrier force en route to Midway Island. In the Atlantic ASW campaign, Navy PBYs and RAF Catalinas were credited with sinking forty German U-Boats. Known as the "Black Cat Raiders," several squadrons of Navy PBYs based in the Pacific were specially outfitted to operate as night convoy raiders. These aircraft, painted flat black and fitted with new magnetic anomaly detection (MAD) equipment, accounted for the sinking of 112,700 tons of Japanese merchant shipping and significant damage to at least ten Japanese warships. While PBYs were renowned for picking up downed fliers in the water, specialized Navy Air-Sea Rescue squadrons were first formed in the Pacific in April 1944, operating with USAAF OA-10s organized for the same function. During the early Pacific war especially, Navy PBYs, due to their range, were frequently used to ferry personnel and supplies.

Once World War II ended, non-amphibious PBY-5s were rapidly phased-out of Navy and Coast Guard service, while many PBY-5As and -6As continued in post-war units, primarily in the air-sea-rescue role, some being configured especially to carry droppable life boats. The very last PBY-6As were retired from the Coast Guard in 1954 and from the Navy in 1957. After World War II, many ex–Navy PBYs and ex–RAF Catalinas were transferred to foreign air forces and navies around the world, including Brazil, Chile, Columbia, Denmark, Dominican Republic, Ecuador, Iceland, Indonesia, Israel, Mexico, Norway, Peru, Philippines, South Africa, Sweden, and Uruguay, some reportedly remaining in service until the 1970s.

Many surplus PBYs also found their way into civilian hands during the post-war period. In the 1950s and 1960s, Northern Consolidated Airlines of Alaska operated a number of PBYs out of Fairbanks, carrying passengers, mail and freight. Starting in 1951, Transocean Airlines, based in Oakland, California, maintained a fleet of four PBY-5As to serve its routes in Micronesia (i.e., Marshall, Caroline, and Mariana Islands). Antilles Air Boats used PBY amphibians for charter work in the Caribbean through the 1970s. PBYs were employed by government agencies in geological surveys, and many U.S. Forest Service contractors (e.g., Johnson Flying Service, Inc.) flew PBYs in the aerial fire-bombing role. Flying boats were particularly suited to fire-bombing because they could be fitted with scoops that allowed them to skim over lakes to refill their water tanks. At the time of this writing, there was only one active fire-bomber still in service: PBY-6A, civil registration N95U, operated by Fireman, Inc. in Washington state. A half dozen or so PBYs owned by private individuals and organizations are reported to still be in airworthy condition.

Consolidated PB2Y Coronado (1937)

TECHNICAL SPECIFICATIONS (PB2Y-3)

Type: 10-place naval patrol boat; long-range military transport.

Total produced: 217 (all versions)

Powerplant: four 1,200-hp Pratt & Whitney R-1830-88 *Twin Wasp* 14-cylinder, twin-row air-cooled radial engines driving three-bladed, constant-speed metal propellers outboard and four-bladed, fully-reversible propellers inboard.

Armament: two .50-caliber machine guns in a powered nose turret, two .50-caliber machine guns in a powered dorsal turret, one flexible .50-calibre machine gun in each waist position, and two .50-caliber machine guns in a powered tail turret, plus up to 8,000 lbs. of bombs, depth charges, and/or torpedoes carried in wing bays.

Performance: max. speed 223 mph, cruise 141 mph; ceiling 20,500 ft.; range 1,370 mi. (normal loaded), 2,370 mi. (max.).

Weights: 40,495 lbs. empty, 68,000 lbs. normal gross, max takeoff (not listed).

Dimensions: span 115 ft. 0 in., length 79 ft. 3 in., wing area 1,780 sq. ft.

The Consolidated PB2Y was one of several large, four-engine flying boats (see Sikorsky PBS and Martin PB2M) conceived to fulfill the Navy's "Sky Dreadnought" concept, discussed in detail in the Historical Overview to Part II. In a nutshell, aircraft like the PB2Y were envisaged as not only serving a traditional maritime patrol function, but to also operate as long-range bombers from widely dispersed sea bases. Originally proposed to BuAer as the company Model 29, Consolidated

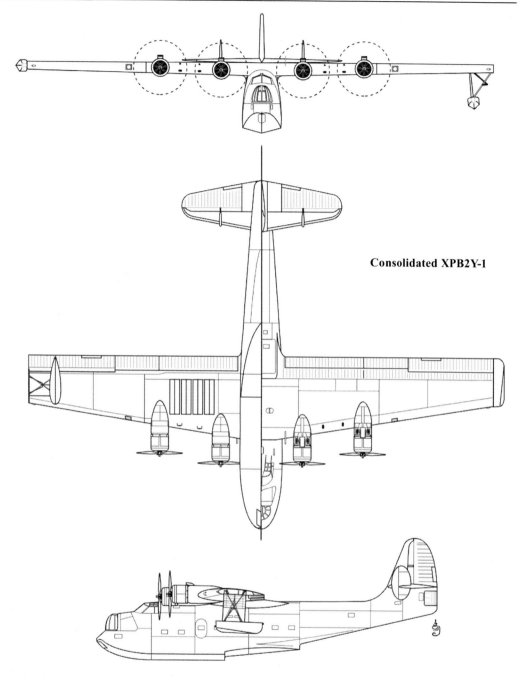

Consolidated XPB2Y-1

received a contract on July 27, 1936, to built one flying prototype under the designation XPB2Y-1. While sharing some characteristics in common with its PBY predecessor such as folding wing floats, a cruciform tail group with a single fin and rudder, and a bow projecting in front of the nose turret, the design of the XPB2Y-1, by comparison, offered a much deeper hull having a fully-cantilevered wing mounted directly atop the fuselage without any supporting pylon. Its higher aspect-ratio wing, swept from the leading edge, carried a load factor (i.e., 30 lbs. per sq. ft.) that was approximately thirty percent higher than that of the contemporaneous PBY-2. Except for moveable control surfaces, the entire structure was skinned in stressed aluminum. A very clean overall configuration was achieved by housing all droppable munitions in flush bays under the wings.

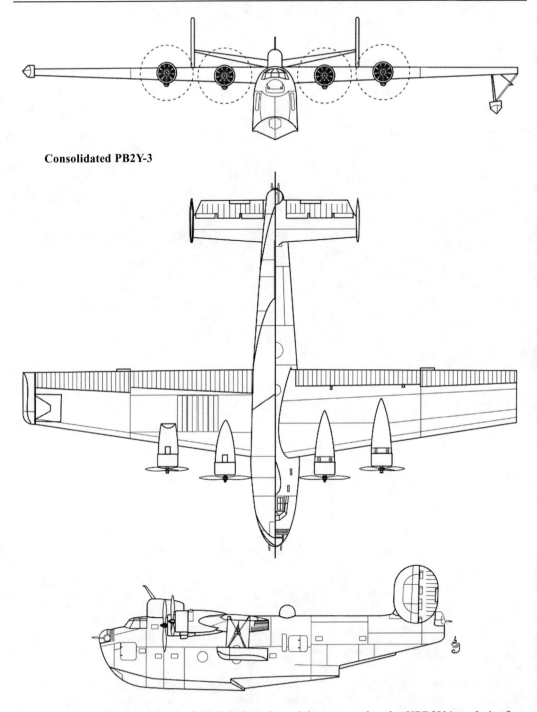

Consolidated PB2Y-3

After a construction period of slightly less than eighteen months, the XPB2Y-1 made its first flight from San Diego on December 17, 1937. Serious problems with directional stability were immediately encountered, with the result that finlets were added to the horizontal stabilizers after the third flight. Further testing revealed continuing stability problems together with the need to improve the hydrodynamic characteristics of the hull planing surfaces. The prototype returned to the factory and emerged in mid–1938 with totally redesigned empennage in which twin circular fins and rudders had been end-mounted to a new horizontal stabilizer that possessed about six degrees of

XPB2Y-1 shown in original configuration in front of Consolidated's plant in San Diego, California, in late 1937. Directional control problems resulted in the addition of finlets and, later, twin fins.

One of 177 PB2Y-3 patrol bomber variants delivered to the Navy in 1942 and 1943. Thirty-three more went to Great Britain as the PB2Y-2B, but were stripped of armament and used as transports.

dihedral. To enhance hull performance, the rear step had been lengthened to extend nearly halfway to the tail. The Navy accepted the XPB2Y-1 following suitability trials, but no production was ordered at that time. The aircraft was thereafter assigned to the Aircraft Scouting Force as the admiral's "flagship."

In March 1939, after what amounted to a virtual redesign of the hull, BuAer authorized Consolidated to proceed with the construction of six PB2Y-2s. The hull of the -2 was deepened to such an extent that the wing was moved down to a shoulder position on the fuselage. Both streamlining and hydrodynamics were improved by fairing the bow smoothly into a reshaped nose turret. Enlarged fins and rudders now resembled those of the Model 31 (see P4Y), and available horsepower was boosted fifteen percent by an upgrade to R-1830-78 engines. New gunner's positions appeared as a dorsal blister behind the wing and circular windows on each side in the waist. Named "Coronado" by the factory, the first PB2Y-2 was delivered to the Navy on December 31, 1940, and four more had been accepted by mid–1941. While empty weight had risen 7,500 lbs., top speed of the new variant increased to 255 mph at 19,000 feet (the fastest of the series) and normal range was nearly twice that of the PBY-5. Following delivery, the Navy used the five PB2Y-2s mainly for operational training and evaluation. The sixth PB2Y-2, modified to the revised production standard, flew in December 1941 as the XPB2Y-3; another PB2Y-2, after being fitted with Wright R-2600 *Twin Cyclone* engines, later reappeared as the XPB2Y-4. The Navy's chief concern over production of the type was not performance but cost: three PBYs could be procured for the price of one PB2Y (approx. $300,000), and naval planners believed larger numbers of twin-engine patrol aircraft spread over a greater area of ocean formed a better long-term military strategy, especially in the Pacific.

In November 1940, even before the first PB2Y-2 had been accepted, Consolidated received a contract for 210 production aircraft, 177 to be delivered to the Navy as the PB2Y-3 and thirty-three to Great Britain as the PB2Y-3B. Heavier by 5,700 lbs., the PB2Y-3 featured self-sealing fuel tanks, 2,000 lbs. of armor protection in vital areas, twin-gun power-operated turrets in the bow, dorsal, and tail positions, plus two flexible waist guns. Production PB2Y-3s began reaching patrol squadrons during the summer of 1942, but by that time, the Sky Dreadnought concept had been overtaken by Navy plans to build up a fleet of fast carriers using smaller aircraft to bomb targets; and as events turned out, it appeared that the PB2Ys, with their capacious hulls and superior range, could be better utilized as over-ocean transports. In October 1943, when 136 PB2Y-3s had been delivered, the 41 remaining airframes were consigned to Rohr Aircraft Corp. to be completed as unarmed PB2Y-3R transports. The -3Rs, weighing 8,000 lbs. less, could be configured to carry up to forty-four passengers or 16,000 lbs. of cargo. Only ten PB2Y-3Bs were ultimately delivered to Britain, where they were stripped of armament and used exclusively as transatlantic transports. And as more Navy land-based aircraft (e.g., PB4Y Liberators) came into service to assume the maritime patrol role, most PB2Y-3s were withdrawn from patrol units and subsequently modified to serve as transports. PB2Y-3s refitted with low-altitude R-1830-92 engines (single-stage superchargers) returned to service as PB2Y-5Rs; and those also receiving a new cabin arrangement for twenty-five medical litters became the PB2Y-5H. All PB2Ys were withdrawn from Navy service soon after the war ended. Since there was very little commercial need for large flying boats in the immediate post-war period, surplus demand for the PB2Ys was practically non-existent. One was sold to billionaire Howard Hughes. The only known surviving example, a PB2Y-5R, now resides at the Naval Aviation Museum in Pensacola, Florida.

The last 41 PB2Y-3s were completed by Rohr Aircraft Corporation and returned to service as PB2Y-3R long-range transports. PB2Y-3s modified as transports returned to service as the PB2Y-5R.

Consolidated P4Y (Model 31) Corregidor (1939)

TECHNICAL SPECIFICATIONS (XP4Y-1)

Type: 52-passenger commercial transport; 10-place naval patrol boat.

Total produced: 1

Powerplant: two 2,300-hp Wright R-3350-8 *Double Cyclone* 18-cylinder, twin-row air-cooled radial engines driving three-bladed, constant-speed metal propellers.

Armament: one 37-mm cannon in a nose turret, two .50-caliber machine guns in a powered dorsal turret, two .50-caliber machine guns in a powered tail turret, plus up to 4,000 lbs. of bombs, depth charges, and/or torpedoes carried externally.

Performance: max. speed 247 mph, cruise 136 mph; ceiling 21,400 ft.; range 2,300 mi. (normal loaded), 3,280 mi. (max.).

Weights: 29,334 lbs. empty, 46,000 lbs. normal gross, 48,000 lbs. max takeoff.

Dimensions: span 110 ft. 0 in., length 74 ft. 1 in., wing area 1,048 sq. ft.

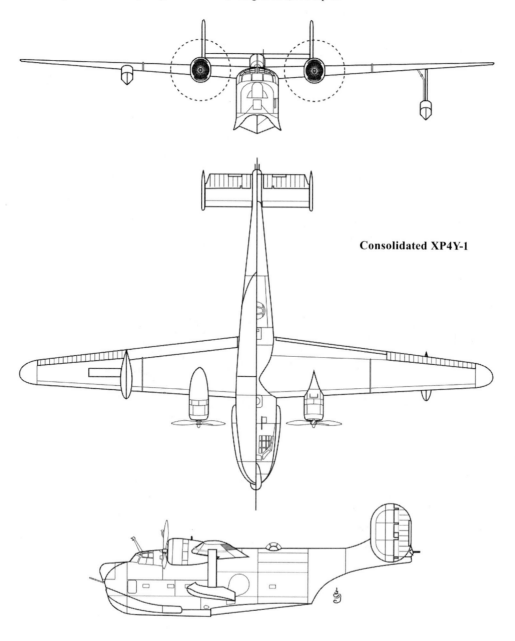

Consolidated XP4Y-1

The origins of the Consolidated Model 31 can be traced to mid–1937, when aeronautical engineer David R. Davis approached Reuben H. Fleet, company president, and Isaac M. Laddon, chief engineer, with the idea of incorporating his patented wing design (i.e., the "Davis wing") to large flying boats. In general, the wing comprised a narrow-chord, high-aspect-ratio planform utilizing a relatively thick airfoil section at the center of pressure. Davis claimed that his design would generate lift at very low angles of attack and thereby eliminate much of the induced drag of the wing. A series of wind tunnel tests (financed by Consolidated) conducted afterward at Cal Tech exceeded even the most optimistic expectations, demonstrating that the Davis wing produced greater aerodynamic efficiency that any wing yet tested.

In 1938, with the aim of producing an experimental demonstrator that could potentially be offered to the commercial market, Fleet authorized Laddon to proceed with a new flying boat design that would integrate the Davis wing with a hull similar in configuration to that of the PB2Y. The structure utilized the advanced technique of flush-riveting the aluminum skins to the metal framework of the wings and fuselage. Moveable control surfaces were of fabric-covered metal construction. To accommodate the narrow chord of the wings, the floats were made to fold inward against the wing undersurfaces. The engines selected, experimental Wright R-3350s, were the most powerful American-made aircraft engines in existence but had yet to be tested on a flying aircraft. Though not built to a military specification, the decision to adopt a twin-engine (instead of a four-engine) layout was undoubtedly influenced by BuAer's recent procurement of the Martin PBM (see below). The shape and arrangement of the Model 31's twin fin tail group benefited from Consoli-

The Model 31 prototype, shown here, incorporated the Davis and was the first type of aircraft to fly with Wright R-3350 engines.

XP4Y-1 depicted in wartime colors. The retractable tip floats and bow skirt are evident in this photograph. Allocation of all R-3350 engine production to the B-29 program caused P4Y production to be cancelled.

dated's previous experience with the PB2Y, and together with the Davis wing, would be seen again in the design of the Model 32 (XB-24). Soon after making its first flight on May 5, 1939 under civil registration number NX21731, the Model 31 established itself as the fastest flying boat in the world, and was also the first aircraft to fly with R-3350 engines.

After no commercial orders for the Model 31 materialized, Consolidated embarked upon a campaign to sell the Navy a military variant that would be revised to a patrol-bomber specification. Although BuAer evinced no interest in the project at the start, Consolidated nonetheless continued the test program at its own expense. Revisions to the prototype during almost two years of testing included raising the empennage to accommodate a tail turret, adding a cuff that widened the planing surfaces of the forward hull, and installation of dummy gun turrets. In April 1942, the Navy finally purchased the Model 31 under the designation XP4Y-1, and soon afterward, ordered the type placed into production as the P4Y-1 at a new plant to be established in New Orleans, Louisiana. The factory name Corregidor was assigned but never officially adopted. In mid–1943, before the P4Y-1 assembly line had been tooled-up, production was cancelled due to the fact that all R-3350 engines were being allocated to the B-29 program for an indefinite time. The New Orleans plant was instead used to open a second assembly line of PBYs.

Curtiss-Wright Airplane Co.

Although Curtiss commanded a leading position in American flying boat design and development from 1912 through the end of the World War I, the company's creative focus after 1920 shifted to other types of aircraft, namely, single-engine military fighters, observation, and attack aircraft, and to a lesser extent, twin-engine landplanes and lightplanes. Although, after re-organization as Curtiss-Wright Corp., the company was very active in Navy floatplane design from 1934 to 1945 (i.e., SOC, SO3C, and SC), it made no effort to reenter the military or commercial market with large flying boats.

Curtiss A-1, B-1 Teal (1930)

TECHNICAL SPECIFICATIONS (A-1)
Type: 3 to 4-seat civil amphibian.
Total produced: 2
Powerplant: one l65-hp Wright J-6-5 *Whirlwind* 5-cylinder air-cooled radial engine driving two-bladed fixed
    metal propeller.
Performance: max. speed 100 mph, cruise 85 mph; ceiling 10,400 ft.; range 450 mi.
Weights: 2,135 lbs. empty; 2,959 lbs. loaded.
Dimensions: span 45 ft. 6 in., length 30 ft. 3 in., wing area 249 sq. ft.

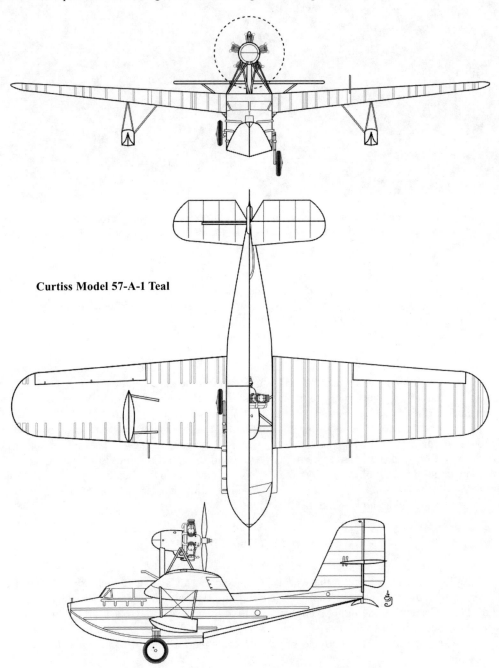

Curtiss Model 57-A-1 Teal

N969V pictured here is the A-1, the first of two Teals built. Although the Teal's design was fairly advanced for its day, the private aircraft market had all but disappeared by the time it flew.

The Curtiss A-1 Teal was first flown in 1930 as an effort to introduce a small flying boat of relatively modern design to the civilian airplane market. It came with innovative features such as an all-aluminum, single step hull and fully-cantilevered, wooden-skinned wings similar to those of the contemporaneous Lockheed Vega. The single pusher engine was mounted above the wing on struts and its manually-operated landing gear could be retracted to the sides of the hull. In 1930 the follow-on B-1 was introduced with a more powerful 225-hp J-6-7 engine and an extra seat. At the time the Teals were being completed at the Garden City plant, Curtiss was in the midst of a merger and reorganization, plus the nation was in the grip of a widespread economic depression that ruined the market for civilian aircraft, and as a result, none were sold.

Curtiss CW-3 Duck (1931)

TECHNICAL SPECIFICATIONS (CW-3L)

Type: 2-seat civil amphibian.
Total produced: 3
Powerplant: one 90-hp Lambert 7-cylinder air-cooled radial engine driving a two-bladed fixed metal propeller.
Performance: max. speed 80 mph (est.); ceiling (not reported); range (not reported).
Weights: empty (not reported), 1,200 lbs. gross (est.).
Dimensions: span 39 ft. 6 in., length 21 ft. 3 in., wing area (not reported).

The aircraft shown (N12325) is the CW-3L, powered by a 90-hp Lambert R-266 engine. Efforts to offer an amphibian version of the CW-1 Junior were not successful; only three were completed.

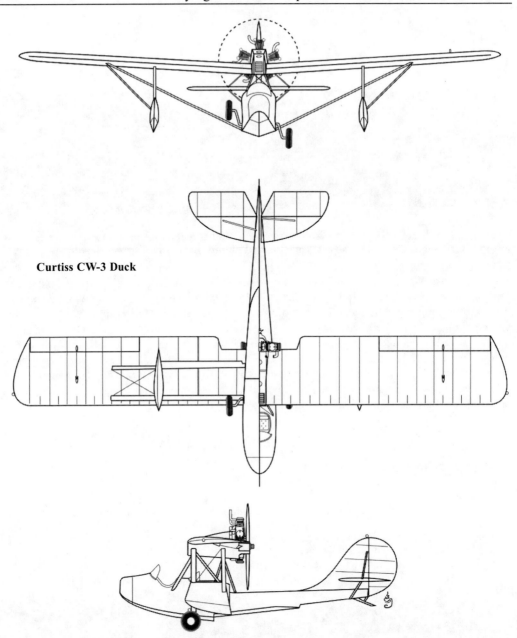

Curtiss CW-3 Duck

One of Curtiss' more successful civilian designs (reportedly the work of Walter Beech), the two-seat, parasol wing CW-1 Junior was introduced in 1931 with a 45-hp Szekely three-cylinder engine for a price of $1,490, and 270 were ultimately produced. The CW-3 Duck appeared the same year as a small flying boat version having twice the horsepower. The plywood hull was made up of a tubular steel CW-1 fuselage that had been modified with a V-chine bottom. For water operations, the landing gear was redesigned to rotate upwards and stabilizing floats were added below the lift struts. The first example was initially tested with a 60-hp Velie radial but soon retrofitted with the more powerful Lambert as the CW-3L, and the last of three built was equipped with a 90-hp Warner *Scarab Junior* as the CW-3W. Efforts to sell the CW-3 were unsuccessful, however, and the project was shelved. One CW-3 was the subject of a fatal air show crash that occurred at Miami in 1932 when, in the midst of a loop, both wings failed and the aircraft plunged to the ground.

Curtiss CA-1 Commuter (1935)

TECHNICAL SPECIFICATIONS

Type: 5-seat civil amphibian.
Total produced: 3
Powerplant: one 365-hp Wright R-975 9-cylinder air-cooled radial engine driving a two-bladed fixed metal
    propeller.
Performance: max. speed 151 mph, cruise 125 mph; ceiling 14,000 ft.; range 550 mi.
Weights: 2,980 lbs. empty, 4,650 lbs. loaded.
Dimensions: span 40 ft. 0 in., length 31 ft. 0 in., wing area (not reported).

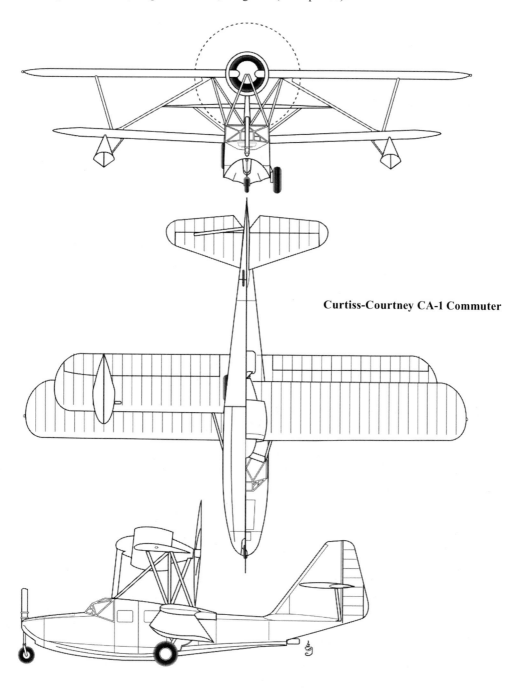

Curtiss-Courtney CA-1 Commuter

The first of three CA-1s built is shown here. Hull design by Edo Corporation was exceptionally modern. Curtiss' hierarchy decided against production despite above-average performance.

As a flying boat design of the mid–1930s, the Curtiss CA-1 Commuter represents a study in contrasts. It arose in 1933 after British aircraft designer and pilot Frank Courtney convinced Curtiss-Wright's board of directors to approve development and construction of a 5-seat amphibian for the civil market. But rather than give Courtney free rein on the design, the board imposed a remarkably obsolete requirement that the aircraft be completed in a biplane layout with a pusher engine. The modern aluminum hull of the first CA-1 was actually built by the Edo Corp. to Courtney's specifications, while the wings used old-fashioned wooden ribs and spars. The problem of tail-heaviness inherent to pushers was solved by moving the engine to the leading edge of the upper wing and connecting it to the propeller by means of an extension shaft. Another innovative feature was a tricycle landing gear system in which the nose gear retracted straight up into a vertical fairing and the main gear into recesses in sides of the hull.

Despite the biplane configuration, flight-testing of the CA-1 carried out in early 1935 revealed good overall performance for a civilian plane of that day. However, construction was thereafter limited to the three examples authorized and production was never undertaken. All three CA-1s, including their design data and rights, were later sold to Japan.

Douglas Aircraft Co.

One of the greatest names in aviation, the Douglas Aircraft Co. was established by Donald W. Douglas and David R. Davis at Santa Monica, California, in 1920. Its first design, the Liberty-powered Cloudster biplane of 1921, was the first American aircraft to lift its own weight in payload. Soon afterward, Douglas received its first military production contract for the Navy's DT land and floatplanes, then in 1923, was selected by the Army to build the Douglas World Cruisers for an around the world attempt. During the 1930s, Douglas enjoyed spectacular success with landplane designs and to a lesser extent, amphibians, but similar efforts to establish itself in the growing flying boat market were ultimately disappointing.

Douglas PD (1929)

TECHNICAL SPECIFICATIONS

Type: 5-place naval patrol boat.
Total produced: 25
Powerplant: two 525-hp Wright R-1750 *Cyclone* (later 575-hp R-1820) 9-cylinder air-cooled radial engines driving three-bladed, ground-adjustable metal propellers.
Armament: one flexible .30-calibre machine gun in bow, one flexible .30-calibre machine gun in rear cockpit, and up to 920 lbs. of bombs in underwing racks.
Performance: max. speed 114 mph, cruise 94 mph ; ceiling 10,900 feet; range 1,309 mi.
Weights: 8,319 lbs. empty, 14,988 lb. gross.
Dimensions: span 72 ft. 10 in., length 49 ft. 2 in., wing area 1,162 sq. ft.

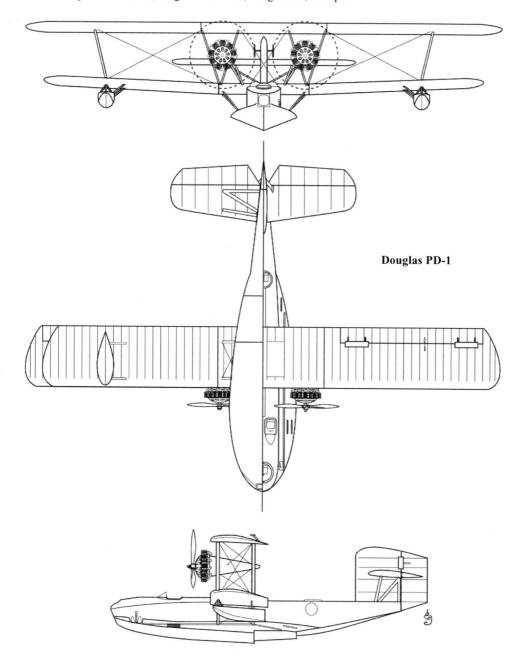

Douglas PD-1

Shown here from the rear quarter, the Douglas PD-1 appeared in 1929 as the first production derivative of the NAF PN-12 and was part of a broad Navy effort to replace older patrol boats like the H-16 and F-5L.

The first of four flying boat types to be manufactured to the specification of the Naval Aircraft Factory-designed PN-12, Douglas received a contract from BuAer on December 27, 1927 to build twenty-five aircraft under the designation PD-1. It was the first Navy flying boat to be manufactured in quantity since World War I and also the first flying boat of any type to be completed by Douglas Aircraft. Other than engine nacelles with flat top and bottom profiles, PD-1s were constructed according to the PN-12 specification without variation. The actual date of the first flight was not reported, but the first production PD-1s were listed as having been accepted and placed into service with San Diego-based VP-7 in June 1929. As deliveries proceeded, the type also equipped both VP-4 and VP-6 at Pearl Harbor, Hawaii. Like most of the Navy's second generation of biplane patrol boats, the career of the PD-1 was relatively brief, and all had been withdrawn from active service by the end of 1936.

Douglas Sinbad, Dolphin (RD, C-21, -26, and -29, OA-3 and -4) (1930)

TECHNICAL SPECIFICATIONS (RD-4)

Type: 8-place civil and naval utility amphibian.
Total produced: 59 (all versions)
Powerplant: two 450-hp Pratt & Whitney R-1340-96 *Wasp* 9-cylinder air-cooled radial engines driving a two-bladed, ground-adjustable metal propellers.
Armament: None.
Performance: max. speed 147 mph, cruise 110 mph ; ceiling 14,900 feet; range 660 mi.
Weights: 6,467 lbs. empty, 9,737 lbs. gross.
Dimensions: span 60 ft. 10 in., length 45 ft. 3 in., wing area 592 sq. ft.

Completed in July 1930 as the non-amphibious Sinbad under civil registration NX145Y, Douglas's first in-house flying boat design was initially conceived as a "flying yacht" to be offered on the civilian market. The Sinbad appeared as a monoplane having an all-metal hull of semi-monocoque construction and a two-spar cantilevered wing covered in plywood that featured slotted, Handley Page type ailerons. In original configuration, the 300-hp Wright J-5C *Whirlwind* engines were mounted directly above the wing and encased in nacelles that blended-in with its upper surface. After flight-testing revealed the need to raise the thrust line, the engines were moved above the wing

The Sinbad prototype after being modified and sold to the Coast Guard in 1931. In the Sinbad's original configuration as NX145Y, the engines were mounted directly above the wings in streamlined nacelles.

One of two RD-2s ordered by the Navy in 1932. This example entered service in 1933 with the Utility Unit based at Coco Solo in the Canal Zone.

on struts, along with an auxiliary airfoil mounted between the conical engine nacelles to add structural support and lift. When no civilian buyers surfaced, the Sinbad was sold to the Coast Guard in March 1931 for $31,500, where it was operated for a period of time as call-sign "24 G" without a military designation but later simply listed as the "RD" with no numeric suffix.

The improved Dolphin, equipped with amphibious landing gear and 400-hp Pratt & Whitney

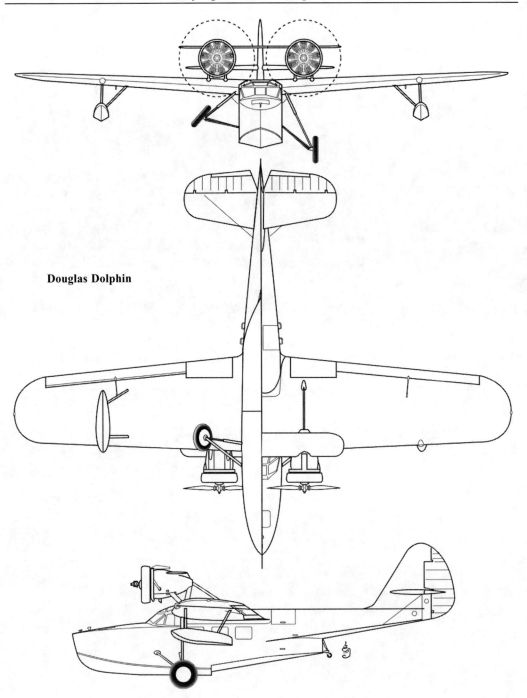

Douglas Dolphin

R-1340 engines, emerged in early 1931, and two, known as the Dolphin 1 Special, were sold in June the same year to the Wilmington-Catalina Airline where, over the next ten years, they completed close to 40,000 crossings without incident. Military orders followed for *Whirlwind*-powered (350-hp R-975-3s) examples, one for the U.S. Army Air Corps as the Y1C-21 (Y1 = service test) and another to the Navy as the XRD-1, both delivered in late 1931. Twenty-three more Dolphins variants were procured for the Navy and the Coast Guard between 1932 and 1934: three RD-2s in early 1933, two to the Navy and one to the Coast Guard, powered by 450-hp Pratt & Whitney R-1340-10

Sixteen Dolphins were delivered to civil purchasers between 1931 and 1934. NC14208, seen here, was one of two custom-built for the Vanderbilt family.

engines; six very similar RD-3s in mid–1933 to the Navy; and ten RD-4s in late 1934 to the Coast Guard, powered by 450-hp R-1340-96 engines. One of the Navy RD-2s was specially outfitted for President Franklin D. Roosevelt, but there is no record of it having been used for such purpose. Navy RDs were assigned to utility squadrons and used primarily as transports, whereas Coast Guard versions saw extensive service in the search and rescue role as flying lifeboats. Two RD-3s were subsequently assigned to the Marine Corps to be used as utility transports. One aircraft reportedly manufactured as an RD-2 was used as a government transport by the Secretary of the Treasury until 1937. After the U.S. entered World War II, RD-4s remaining in service with the Coast Guard were employed briefly for coastal patrol duties.

The authorities are in conflict as to the exact number of Dolphins accepted by the U.S. Army Air Corps, however, it appears that at least sixteen were delivered between 1932 and 1933, including the Y1C-21 mentioned above: two in 1932, powered by 300-hp Pratt & Whitney R-985-A engines, as the Y1C-26; eight also in 1932, powered by 350-hp R-985-5 engines, as the C-26A; four in 1932-1933, powered by 350-hp R-985-9 engines, as the C-26B; and two with enlarged cabins in 1933, powered by 575-hp R-1340-16 engines, as the C-29. Due to a change of the USAAC's designation system in the mid–1930s, the Y1C-21 became the OA-3, the Y1C-26 the OA-4, and the C-26A the OA-4B. In 1936 and 1937, four OA-4/-4As and one OA-4B were refitted with stainless steel wings, then another OA-4B became the OA-4C when modified with experimental tricycle landing gear.

Civilian Dolphins, of which sixteen (including the two Dolphin 1 Specials) are estimated to have been built between 1931 and 1934, came in many variations as dictated by the preferences of individual customers. One registered as NC14286 and later christened *Rover,* was completed as a personal transport for William E. Boeing. French industrialist Armand Esders purchased a Dolphin powered by 550-hp R-1340-S1 engines, Standard Oil Co. acquired two with 450-hp R-1340-96 engines to be used in overseas operations, and two more were built for the Vanderbilt family. In 1934 Pan American Airways bought two Dolphins that were operated by its China National Aviation Corp. subsidiary. Interestingly, after World War II began, two Dolphins (one Dolphin 1 Special and another from Standard Oil) ended up flying in Australia with the RAAF.

Douglas P3D, OA-5 (YO-44) (1935)

TECHNICAL SPECIFICATIONS (XP3D-2)

Type: 7-place naval patrol boat; 5-place amphibious military observation aircraft.

Total produced: 2

Powerplant: two 900-hp Pratt & Whitney R-1830-64 *Twin Wasp* 14-cylinder air-cooled radial engines driving three-bladed, variable-pitch metal propellers.

Armament: One .30-calibre machine gun in a bow turret, two flexible .30-calibre machine guns on each side of the dorsal position, and up to 4,000 lbs. (est.) of bombs, depth charges, and torpedoes carried on underwing racks.

Performance: max. speed 183 mph; ceiling 18,900 feet; range 2,050 mi.(normal loaded), 3,380 mi. (max.).

Weights: 15,120 lbs. empty, 22,909 lbs. normal gross, 27,946 lbs. max. takeoff.

Dimensions: span 95 ft. 0 in., length 69 ft. 7 in., wing area 1,295 sq. ft.

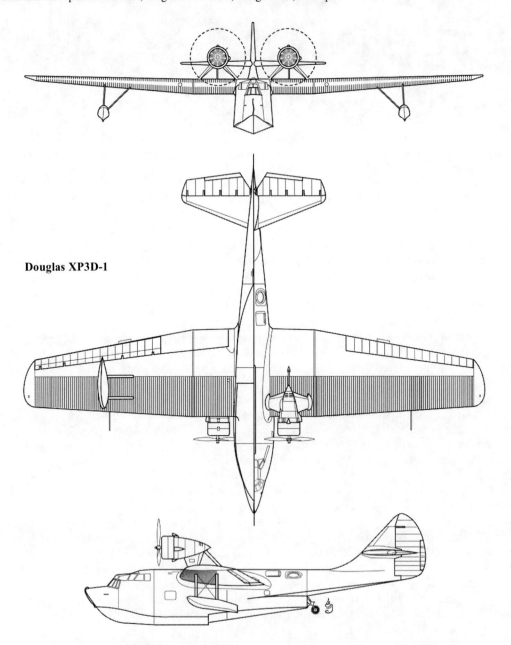

Douglas XP3D-1

The P3D and its amphibious Army counterpart represented a serious but ultimately unsuccessful attempt by Douglas to gain a share of the growing military flying boat market during the early and mid–1930s. The process actually began as far back as 1932 when the Navy and Army both expressed interest in a large, twin-engine flying boat that could be utilized for either patrol or bombing missions. In December 1932 the Army gave Douglas a contract to proceed with design work on

Chief contender against Consolidated's XP3Y-1 (later XPBY-1) in the Navy's 1935 patrol boat fly-off, the XP3D-1 reportedly lost the competition because of its higher unit cost.

The amphibious version, the YOA-5A shown here, was evaluated as part of an experimental Army project but never placed in production.

The modified XP3D-2 as seen during new patrol boat trials conducted in mid–1936. Despite the improvement in speed, the Navy elected instead to acquire 50 PBY-2s.

an amphibious flying boat under the designation XB-11, but after inspection of the mockup in April 1933, the designation was changed to YO-44. Only a month later, in an analogous project designated the XP3D-1, BuAer authorized Douglas to perform engineering studies with the option to order construction of a prototype. The Navy exercised its option in February 1934, and construction of the Army prototype was apparently approved around the same time, so that the two aircraft were built almost side-by-side. While the YO-44 was essentially an experimental Army project, the XP3D-1 would be competing directly with the Consolidated XP3Y-1 (see page 96) for a sizeable Navy production contract.

Apart from the engines specified and amphibious landing gear, the XP3D-1 and YO-44 were almost identical. As the shared design emerged, it featured a two-step metal hull and a fully-cantilevered, shoulder-mounted wing having the two engines mounted above on twin pylons. Stabilizing floats were fixed below the wings on struts. Positioned in front of the windscreen behind the mooring hatch, the bow turret was the first to appear on any type of military flying boat. The single fin empennage resembled a scale-up of the arrangement seen on the Dolphin. On February 6, 1935, the *Twin Wasp*-powered XP3D-1 was rolled-out for its first flight; the *Cyclone*-powered YO-44, under the new designation YOA-5 (observation-amphibian), followed just eighteen days later.

Competitive trials between the XP3D-1 and the XP3Y-1, conducted at Naval Air Station Anacostia, Maryland, during the spring of 1935, revealed acceptable performance and handling qualities from both aircraft. The selection of the XP3Y-1 for production over the XP3D-1 was apparently based on unit cost more than any other single factor. Soon afterward, the XP3D-1 returned to the factory to be readied for yet another round of patrol boat competition scheduled for the next year. When it reemerged in May 1936 as the XP3D-2, the engines had been upgraded to 900-hp R-1830-64s and moved down to nacelles on the wing, plus the floats now folded into the wings. These enhancements increased top speed by 22 mph and gave some improvement in range, but were not sufficient to gain the production contract, which BuAer subsequently awarded to Consolidated for 50 PBY-2s. While the YOA-5 underwent extensive evaluations with the U.S. Army Air Corps, no production was ever ordered.

Douglas DF (1936)

TECHNICAL SPECIFICATIONS

Type: 32-passenger transport.
Total produced: 4
Powerplant: two 1,000-hp Wright R-1820-53 *Cyclone* 9-cylinder air-cooled radial engines driving three-bladed, variable-pitch metal propellers.
Performance: max. speed 178 mph, cruise 160 mph; ceiling 20,000 ft. (est.); range 2,700 mi.
Weights: 15,000 lbs. empty (est.), 26,185 lbs. normal gross.
Dimensions: span 95 ft. 0 in., length 64 ft. 6 in., wing area 1,295 sq. ft.

One of two DFs, known as DF-195s, sold to the Soviet Union and used by Aeroflot as transports. Ironically, after being sold to Japan and dismantled, one of the DFs provided much useful data that went into the design of Kawanishi's H8K.

As prospects of producing the P3D and OA-5 for the military declined, Douglas turned to the civil market with the hope of interesting airline companies in a commercial variant. Making use of the wings and tail group derived from the XP3D-2, the DF (Douglas Flying-Boat) was created with an entirely new hull that accommodated thirty-two passengers in day seating or sixteen in sleeper berths. With this capacity and the performance projected, the DF was expected to not only out-perform existing twin-engine flying boats but four-engine types like the like the Sikorsky S-40 and S-42 as well. The aircraft's construction makeup was very advanced for the day: flush-riveting on the bottom of the hull, a multi-cellular aluminum wing structure held together with molybdenum steel fittings, beaded metal skins in areas subjected to high drag loads, hydraulically-retracted stabilizing floats, large trailing-edge flaps, and Frise (i.e., slotted) ailerons. The entire airframe was skinned in anodically-treated alclad except for a stainless steel bow post and fabric-covered flaps and control surfaces.

The DF made its first flight from Cover Field in California on September 24, 1936, and subsequent flight-testing revealed acceptable handling qualities combined with general performance well within design projections. The company had sufficient confidence in the aircraft's potential market to go ahead with construction of three more; but, surprisingly, no orders for the type were received from American air carriers despite the best efforts of the Douglas sales force. Pan American Airways, the number one prospect, had already begun purchasing twin-engine Sikorsky S-43s (see below). Faced with no domestic market, Douglas obtained export permits from the U.S. government and was authorized to sell two examples to Japan as the DF-151. Registered as J-ANES and J-ANET, the D-151s were ostensibly purchased to be used for commercial service with Greater Japan Air Line; however, one of them was in fact given to the Kawanishi aircraft company where it was dismantled and used to provide much of the design and structural data for what ultimately

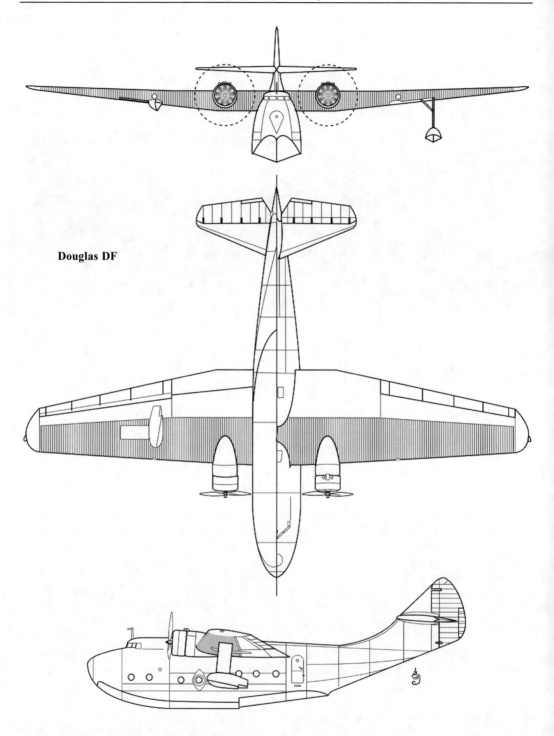

Douglas DF

became the four-engine Kawanishi H8K flying boat (later code-named "Emily"). The other D-151 was lost on a survey flight in October 1938. After being outfitted for cold weather operations, the two remaining aircraft were sold to the Soviet government as the DF-195. Though little is known about them, Aeroflot is reported to have used both DF-195s on its Leningrad (St. Petersburg)-Sevastopol route until 1940.

Fairchild Aircraft Corp.

Sherman M. Fairchild started the Fairchild Aerial Camera Corp. in 1920 and formed the Fairchild Aircraft Mfg. Co. in Farmingdale, New York, in 1925. After the company began designing and building airplanes in 1928, it underwent several corporate reorganizations, acquiring Kreider-Reisner Aircraft Co. in 1929, being acquired by Aviation Corp. (AVCO), also in 1929, then reappearing in 1934 as the Fairchild Aircraft Corp., with its principal production facility in Hagerstown, Maryland. Fairchild's first endeavor to produce a flying boat, the FB-3 of 1929 (see Appendix A, page 318), was limited to one prototype.

Fairchild F91 (1935)

TECHNICAL SPECIFICATIONS

Type: 8-passenger amphibious transport.
Total produced: 7
Powerplant: one 750-hp Pratt & Whitney R-1690-S2EG *Hornet* [or 760-hp Wright R-1820-52 *Cyclone*] 9-cylinder air-cooled radial engine driving a three-bladed, variable-pitch metal propeller.
Performance: max. speed 173 mph, cruise 155 mph; ceiling 18,000 ft.; range 730 mi.
Weights: 6,593 lbs. empty, 10,507 lbs. normal gross.
Dimensions: span 56 ft. 0 in., length 46 ft. 8 in., wing area 482 sq. ft.

Known variously as the "Baby Clipper" and the "Jungle Clipper," the F91 was designed by Fairchild engineer Alfred A. Gassner to a specification issued in 1934 by Pan American Airways for a single-engine amphibian to be operated on coastal and riverine routes. Gassner evolved a highly modern design presenting a two-step hull of all-metal semi-monocoque construction and a cantilevered wing on top of which the engine was mounted on a streamlined pylon. The landing gear consisted of a novel pivoting mechanism that retracted all the way upward into flush wheel wells in the wings. In its original configuration, the prototype was completed with retractable wing floats and an unusual Zap flap system (i.e., full-span flaps that interconnected with ailerons), but these innovations were not incorporated into the versions that followed it.

The F91 made its first flight on April 1, 1935, and testing soon revealed acceptable flight characteristics and good overall performance. The prototype was purchased by a covert intermediary

The second F91 completed, the *Cyclone*-powered F91B built to the order of Dr. Richard Archbold of the New York City Museum of Natural History and registered as NR777. It was later damaged beyond repair after arriving in New Guinea.

who intended ship it to the Spanish Republican forces, but while en route, the aircraft was intercepted by the Spanish Nationalists, who assembled it and used it for themselves. The second aircraft completed, an F91B powered by a *Cyclone* engine and identified as the Jungle Clipper, was built to the order of Dr. Richard Archbold, who was affiliated with the New York City Museum of Natural History and planned to use the aircraft for expeditionary purposes in the Southwest Pacific.

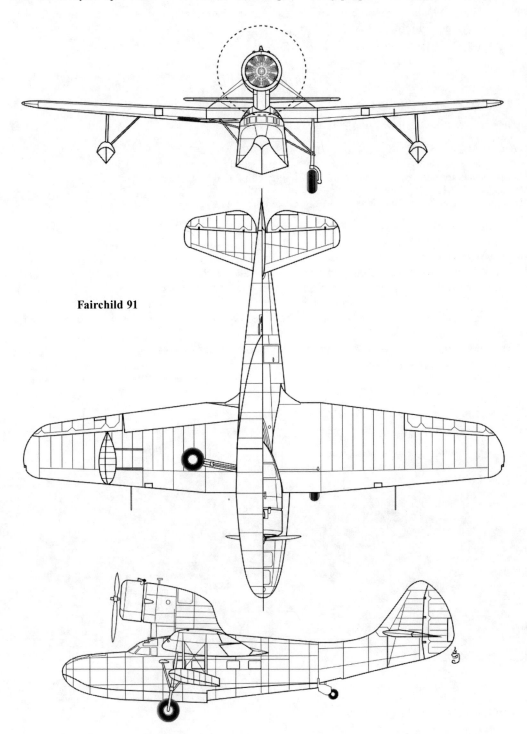

Fairchild 91

After being registered as NR777, the F91B was damaged beyond repair soon after arriving in New Guinea. Baby Clippers refer to six F91s originally ordered by Pan American but subsequently limited to the two aircraft accepted in 1935. The Baby Clippers replaced Sikorsky S-38s and were operated up and down the Amazon River by Pan American subsidiary Panair do Brasil until being removed from service in 1945. Two F91s acquired by the Japanese government were taken into military service as the LXF-1 Type F. The seventh and final F91, dubbed "Wings of Mercy," was bought by American millionaire Gar Wood and donated to the Royal Air Force during early World War II. The RAF later repainted the aircraft in a camouflage scheme and operated it in search and rescue missions out of Alexandria, Egypt until it was accidentally destroyed in 1943.

Fleetwings, Inc.

Fleetwings, Inc. was organized at Bristol, Pennsylvania, in 1930 by Frank and Cecil de Ganahl for the express purpose of fabricating airframes from stainless steel. The company continued to operate under the same name after being acquired by Hall Aluminum Aircraft Co. in 1934, then became Kaiser-Fleetwings in 1941 after its assets had been purchased by industrialist Henry J. Kaiser. The company's first airplane, the Model F-101, was built in 1931 to demonstrate the practicality of stainless steel spot-welding techniques rather than aerodynamic design. It reportedly did not fly very well.

Fleetwings F-4 and -5 Sea Bird (1936)

TECHNICAL SPECIFICATIONS (F-5)

Type: 4-place amphibian.
Total produced: 6
Powerplant: one 285-hp [or 300-hp] Jacobs R-755 L-5 [L-6] 7-cylinder air-cooled radial engine driving a two-bladed, variable-pitch metal propeller.
Performance: max. speed 150 mph, cruise 139 mph; ceiling (not reported); 430 mi.
Weights: 2,600 lbs. empty, 3,750 lbs. normal gross.
Dimensions: span 40 ft. 6 in., length 31 ft. 6 in., wing area (not reported).

NC16918, shown here, was one of five F-5s completed during 1936 and 1937. Pattern of "knurling" of stainless steel skin on sides of hull and float is evident.

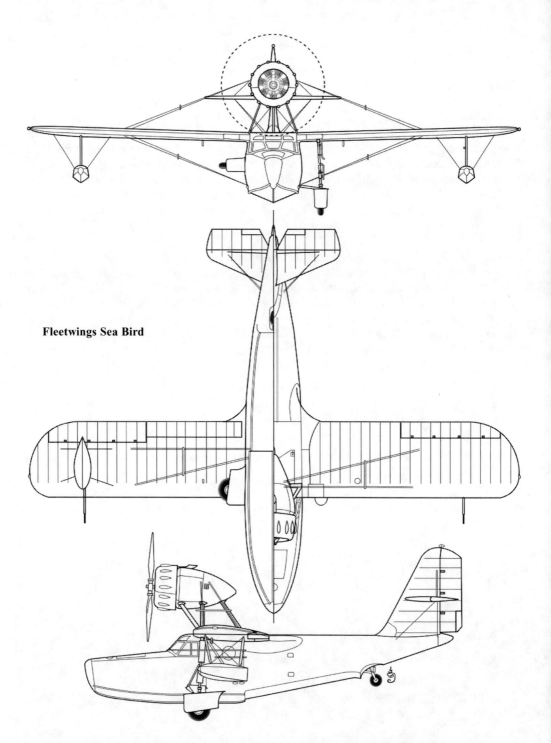

Fleetwings Sea Bird

Designed by Cecil de Ganahl and James Reddig, the Fleetwings Sea Bird was actually the second American flying boat (see American Marchetti BB-1, Part I, page 17) to possess a structure fabricated entirely from stainless steel. The two-step hull consisted of spot-welded stainless steel formers and stringers to which a very thin stainless skin was riveted; the wings and tail group, while fabric-covered, were likewise made up of a spot-welded stainless steel framework. Because of the corrosion problems inherent to water-borne operations, the company perceived stainless steel to be an ideal material for the construction of an amphibious flying boat. Aerodynamic design was straightforward, featuring a strut and wire braced constant-chord monoplane wing and a cruciform empennage having a single fin and rudder. The Jacobs radial engine, contained in a tight NACA-type cowling and nacelle, was strut-mounted in tractor fashion above the wing center-section and further braced by drag wires; stabilizing floats were fixed below the outer wing panels. The hand-operated landing gear utilized a wing-mounted retraction jack that folded it against the sides of the hull.

Powered by a 225-hp early version of the L-5, the F-4 was flown for the first time in 1936 under civil registration NX16793. After flight testing, it was sold to a Canadian mining company and subsequently re-registered as C-FBGZ. Returning to the U.S. in the 1940s as NC16793, this aircraft was evidently re-engined at some point with a more powerful J-5 or J-6 and is the only known flying example in existence today. The F-4 was followed in 1936 and 1937 by five essentially identical F-5s powered variously by 285-hp J-5 or 300-hp J-6 engines. The F-5 was originally offered to private owners for between $18,500 and $22,500, depending on engine and accessories (i.e., radios, etc.). According to the Seaplane Pilot's Association (SPA), one F-5 registered as NC19191 remained active until recently, when it was accidentally destroyed in a hangar fire.

Fokker Aircraft Corp. of America (General Aviation Mfg. Corp.)

Originally organized by Anthony Fokker as the Atlantic Aircraft Corp. in 1923, it was renamed Fokker Aircraft Corp. of America, Atlantic Aircraft Division, in 1927. The aircraft manufacturing plant was located in Hasbrouck Heights, New Jersey. Due to financial difficulties, Fokker became a subsidiary of General Motors in 1929, operating as General Aviation Corp. until 1931. In a stock swap, all assets were transferred to General Aviation Manufacturing Corp. in 1933 as a subsidiary of the newly organized North American Aviation, Inc., and the manufacturing facilities relocated to Dundalk, Maryland.

Fokker F-11 Flying Yacht (1929)

TECHNICAL SPECIFICATIONS (F-11A)

Type: 4 to 5-passenger transport.
Total produced: 7 (est.)
Powerplant: one 525-hp Wright R-1750D *Cyclone* 9-cylinder air-cooled radial engine driving a three-bladed, ground-adjustable metal propeller.
Performance: max. speed 112 mph, cruise 95 mph; ceiling (not reported); range 400 mi.
Weights: not reported; useful load listed as 2,430 lbs.
Dimensions: span 59 ft. 0 in., length 45 ft. 0 in., wing area (not reported).

F-11A operating with Western Air Express, probably in 1929 or 1930, on the Wilmington to Catalina Island route. This route (and its aircraft) were sold to the Wrigley family in 1933 after the reorganization of WAE into TWA.

The F-11 Flying Yacht combined the all-metal, cantilevered wing of a Fokker F-14 parasol land-plane transport (Army Y1C-14) with an entirely new metal boat hull designed by Alfred A. Gassner, who worked for Fokker (later General Aviation) from 1928 to 1931. Except for a fabric-covered tail group, the entire airframe was clad in aluminum. The design originally appeared with retractable side sponsons but these were later replaced by conventional strut-braced floats under the outer wing panels. F-11As reportedly underwent a variety of engine combinations after they were sold. The first example, under civil registration NX148H, flew sometime in 1929 with a single, pusher-mounted 525-hp *Cyclone*. Two or three more were built for private owners, and one was sold to the Army as the C-16. The last F-11A, also sold privately, was delivered with a 575-hp Pratt & Whitney R-1690B *Hornet* engine. NX148H was said to have been later modified for installation two pusher-mounted *Hornet* engines, and even later, to a single *Hornet* in a tractor configuration. At

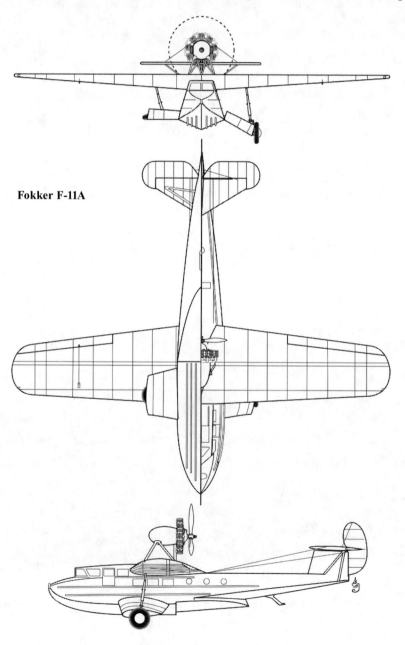

Fokker F-11A

least one, and possibly three, more aircraft were completed as the F-11AHB, powered by single 575-hp *Hornets*. One F-11AHB, used by Tony Fokker as a personal transport, was modified with two *Cyclones* mounted in a tandem configuration and had accommodations for up to ten passengers.

General Aviation PJ/FLB Flying Lifeboat (1932)

TECHNICAL SPECIFICATIONS (PJ-1)

Type: 7-place search and rescue boat.
Total produced: 5
Powerplant: two 420-hp Pratt & Whitney R-1340C-1 *Wasp* 9-cylinder air-cooled radial engines driving two-bladed, ground-adjustable metal propellers.
Performance: max. speed 120 mph; ceiling 15,000 ft. (est.); range 1,150 mi.
Weights: 7,000 lbs. empty, 11,200 lbs. gross.
Dimensions: span 74 ft. 2 in., length 55 ft. 0 in., wing area 754 sq. ft.

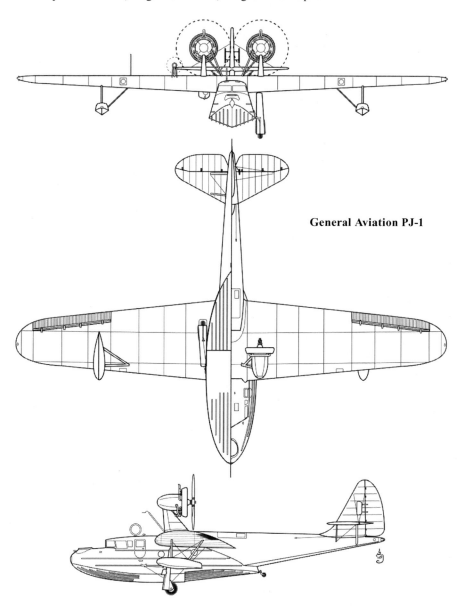

General Aviation PJ-1

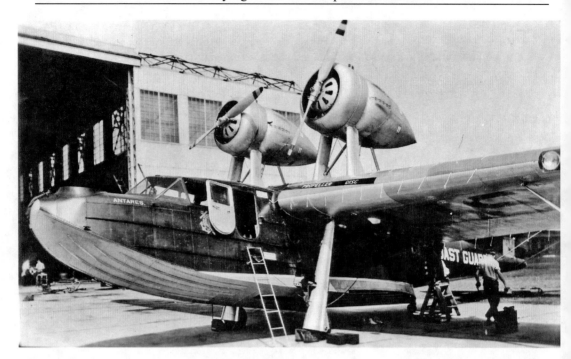

The first FLB delivered in early 1932 as FLB-8, it became the PJ-2, FLB-51 (V116) *Antares,* after being converted to tractor engines by the Naval Aircraft Factory in 1933. No other PJs received the modification.

Flying Life Boat 53, *Acrux,* shown later in its career when the Coast Guard had gone to an overall silver paint scheme. *Acrux* was one of the last PJs retired, in late 1940.

The General Aviation PJ, designed to a U.S. Coast Guard specification calling for a twin-engine aircraft to be used primarily in open-sea search and rescue operations, started life in 1930 as the company Model AF-15. After reviewing competitive proposals from several manufacturers, the Coast Guard selected General Aviation's design as the winning entry and initially identified the new aircraft as the flying life boat (FLB) without assigning a specific military designation. Though fifteen percent larger and better streamlined, the general layout of the FLB was very similar to the Fokker F-11A that preceded it. The date of the first flight is not a matter of record, however, the first aircraft was evidently completed sometime in late 1931 and accepted by the Coast Guard in January 1932 as FLB-8. Shortly after General Aviation was merged into North American, FLB-8, and the four production examples that followed it, received the designation PJ-1. As completed, the PJ-1 featured an all-metal hull reinforced with numerous external strakes on the sides and bottom so it could withstand the stresses of landing and taking off in heavy seas. The two *Wasp* pusher engines, encased in ring cowls behind conical nacelles, were mounted atop the wing on streamlined pylons. For beaching, small wheels enclosed in fairings could be folded-down from the wings.

As all five PJ-1s entered operational service during 1932, they were assigned the following USCG serial numbers and names: FLB-51 (formerly FLB-8) *Antares*, FLB-52 *Altair*, FLB-53 *Acrux*, FLB-54 *Acamar*, and FLB-55 *Arcturus*. Three of the PJs were based at the Coast Guard station at Cape May, New Jersey, and the other two, Miami, Florida. In 1933, FLB-51 was sent to the Naval Aircraft Factory in Philadelphia to be fitted with new 500-hp Pratt & Whitney R-1690 *Hornet* engines that would be remounted in a tractor configuration. When the aircraft reappeared as the PJ-2, its engines rested on struts rather than pylons and featured tight-fitting NACA-type cowlings that blended into the nacelles. Although the PJ-2 proved to be 15 mph faster and had slightly better range, the four PJ-1s were never modified. In their role as flying lifeboats, the five aircraft began accumulating a very impressive record, making many noteworthy rescues in the open ocean that would have otherwise been impossible. But as a consequence of the tremendous wear and tear on the airframes due to operations in heavy seas, the Coast Guard was forced to start retiring them after less than ten years of service: FLB-54 *Acamar* was withdrawn in mid–1937; FLB-52 *Altair* in early 1940; FLB-53 *Acrux* in late 1940; and finally, both FLB-51 *Antares* and FLB-55 *Arcturus* by the end of 1941.

Goodyear Aircraft Corp.

Known in aviation circles primarily for dirigibles and blimps, Goodyear Aircraft Corp. of Akron, Ohio began building military aircraft under license during World War II (i.e., Vought F4U as Goodyear FG) and also made plans to produce a small, two-place amphibian for the civilian market once the war ended.

Goodyear GA-1, -2 Duck (1944)

TECHNICAL SPECIFICATIONS (GA-2B)

Type: 2 to 3-place place civil amphibian.
Total produced: 21
Powerplant: one 165-hp Franklin 6A4-B3 6-cylinder air-cooled opposed engine driving a two-bladed, variable-pitch (Aeromatic) wooden propeller.
Performance: max. speed 125 mph, cruise 112 mph; ceiling 15,000 ft.; range 300 mi.
Weights: 1,600 lbs. empty, 2,300 lbs. gross.
Dimensions: span 36 ft. 0 in., length 26 ft. 0 in., wing area 178 sq. ft

Designed during the middle of World War II by a team consisting of David B. Thurston of Grumman and Karl Arnstein of Goodyear, the GA-1 featured an all-aluminum one-step hull and shoulder-mounted cantilevered wings of fabric-covered metal construction. For water operations, the landing gear folded up against the hull using a manual retraction jack. The 107-hp Franklin 4AC engine initially used on the prototype was mounted in a pusher configuration on a type of pylon that would later appear on Thurston's Colonial Skimmer (see Part III, page 222). Stabilizing floats were fixed to the outer wing panels on streamlined strut fairings. After completing its first flight in September 1944, the two-seat GA-1 Duck underwent tests and evaluations over the next year, during which time it was refitted with a 125-hp Franklin 6A4-A3 engine. The first production version, the GA-2, appeared in 1946 with a 145-hp Franklin engine and a third seat. A total of fourteen GA-2s were delivered to dealers over the next two years, but none were sold to private individuals. The final Ducks, six GA-2Bs built in 1948 and 1949, featured yet another upgrade to a 165-hp Franklin 6A4-3B engine. As before, there were no private sales, except that one GA-2B was reportedly delivered to a buyer in Sweden. Goodyear finally decided not to undertake further production because the cost of manufacturing the aircraft prevented it from being offered at price that most private pilots could afford. Goodyear scrapped the last remaining GA-2 in 1965.

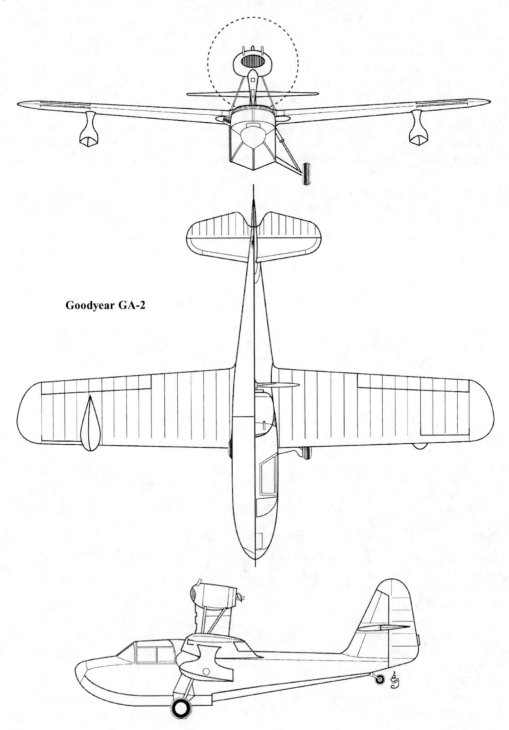

Goodyear GA-2

GA-2 production version first flown in 1946 with a 145-hp Franklin engine and a third seat. Although 14 GA-2s were delivered to dealers in 1946 and 1947, none were reportedly sold to private owners.

Great Lakes Aircraft Corp.

This short-lived manufacturer commenced operations in 1928 on the site of the former Martin plant in Cleveland, Ohio. Despite moderate success in securing Navy contracts (i.e., TG-1/-2 torpedo plane and BG-1/-2 dive-bomber) and selling civil sportplanes (i.e., 2T-1), the company was forced to cease operations in 1936. Production rights were sold to Bell Aircraft Corp., but no new Great Lakes aircraft were seen until 1973, when the company was reformed in Wichita, Kansas, to resume limited production of the modernized 2T-1A.

Great Lakes SG (1932)

TECHNICAL SPECIFICATIONS (XSG-1)

Type: 2-place scout amphibian.
Total produced: 1
Powerplant: one 400-hp Pratt & Whitney R-985-38 9-cylinder air-cooled radial engine driving a two-bladed, ground-adjustable metal propeller.
Armament (proposed): one flexible .30-calibre machine gun in the observer's position.
Performance: max. speed 124 mph; ceiling 8,400 ft.; range 695 mi.
Weights: 2,707 lbs. empty, 4,218 lbs. gross.
Dimensions: span 35 ft. 0 in., length 32 ft. 7 in., wing area 347 sq. ft.

Whether or not the Great Lakes SG was a flying boat or a floatplane is debatable, but it is included here because of its association with two other boat-hulled amphibians reported below (see Loening S2L and Sikorsky SS). It was part of an ultimately unsuccessful Navy experiment, conducted in 1932 and 1933, to find a small scout amphibian as a replacement for the conventional floatplanes then serving aboard cruisers. In 1932, three companies, Great Lakes, Loening, and Sikorsky, received contracts from BuAer under a specification calling for a single-engine amphibian stressed for catapult launches and, with wings folded, small enough to fit into the hangar space aboard Navy cruisers. The Great Lakes entry, designated the XSG-1, was delivered to Naval Air Station Anacostia for trials in November 1932. Its design presented a curious two-story layout: two-bays of biplane wings resting on a main pontoon, with the engine and pilot being situated in a separate nacelle between the upper and lower wings. The gunner/observer's position was located down in the pontoon aft of the wings. When, following brief trials, the XSG-1 failed to meet BuAer's performance expectations, further development was cancelled.

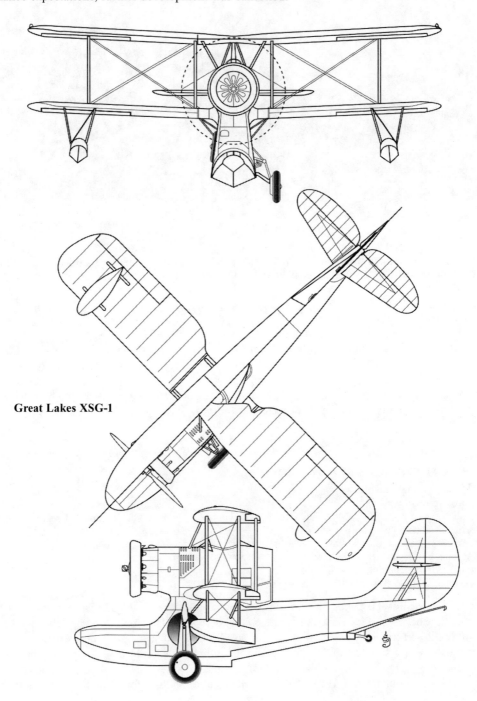

Great Lakes XSG-1

Sole prototype XSG-1, probably off the Maryland coast near NAS Anacostia in 1933. Its unusual configuration is evident in this side view. The Navy eventually abandoned the idea of an amphibious cruiser scout.

Grumman Aircraft Engineering Corp.

As a designer and builder of U.S. Navy and Marine Corps aircraft, Grumman is arguably the most famous name in the history of twentieth century aviation. The origins of the company can be traced to early 1930, when Leroy R. Grumman and Leon A. (Jake) Swirbul, both engineers employed by Loening, left to form the Grumman Aircraft Engineering Corp., initially located at the site of the old Cox-Klemin plant in Baldwin, New York. Grumman, an ex–naval aviator with engineering degrees from Cornell and MIT, obtained the company's first Navy contract by designing an innovative landing gear retraction system for seaplane floats. Using an arrangement of chain-driven pivots, the wheels retracted almost flush into the sides of the pontoon. The Navy was sufficiently impressed with this work to award Grumman a contract in early 1931 to build one of its earliest in-house airplane designs, the FF-1 two-seat fighter. As the company expanded, its operations moved to Farmingdale, New York, in 1932, and then to Bethpage, New York, in 1937.

Grumman JF/J2F (OA-12) Duck (1933)

TECHNICAL SPECIFICATIONS (JF-1 [J2F-5])

Type: 4 to 5-place utility amphibian.
Total produced: 626 (including Columbia Aircraft Corp.)
Powerplant: one 700-hp Pratt & Whitney R-1830-62 *Twin Wasp* 14-cylinder [850-hp Wright R-1920-50 9-cylinder] air-cooled radial engine driving a three-bladed, ground-adjustable [variable-pitch] metal propeller.
Armament: one (two on J2F-2A) flexible .30-calibre machine gun in the rear cockpit [and one fixed .30-calibre machine gun in the nose] and up to 200 lbs. [650 lbs. (400 lbs. on J2F-2A)] of bombs carried on underwing racks.
Performance: max. speed 168 mph [188 mph]; ceiling 18,000 ft. [27,000 ft.]; range 686 mi. [780 mi.].
Weights: 3,700 lbs. [4,300 lbs.] empty, 5,399 lbs. [6,711 lbs.] gross.
Dimensions: span 39 ft. 0 in., length 33 ft. 0 in. [34 ft. 0 in.], wing area 409 sq. ft.

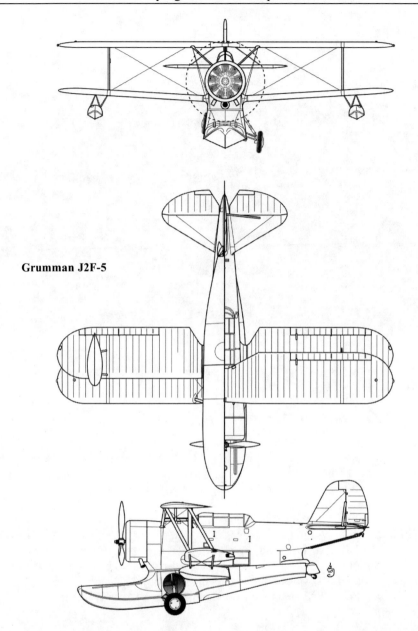

Grumman J2F-5

Like the Loening "Shoehorns" with which Grumman had been closely associated, the JF/J2F series of amphibians were flying boat-floatplane hybrids in which the fuselage structure formed an integral part of the main float. In 1931, BuAer asked Grumman to initiate a study for an amphibian designed to the Navy's new "utility" category, which specified that the aircraft also be capable of operating from an aircraft carrier. After reviewing Grumman's proposal for the model G-7, BuAer awarded the company a contract in late 1932 for construction of a prototype under the designation XJF-1. Not surprisingly, the design combined the shoehorn outline of Loening's OL series with the more modern aerodynamic and structural features of the FF-1. Along with Grumman's already proven gear retraction system, drag was minimized by utilizing all-metal, semi-monocoque construction methods to streamline the junctions between the fuselage and the main float. The single-bay biplane wings and all moveable control surfaces were conventional metal-framed structures with fabric covering.

The very first Duck, the XJF-1, shown on the ramp at NAS Anacostia as delivered in May 1933. Ducks would ultimately be produced in two major variants (JF and J2F) over a 12-year period (1933–1945).

One of 14 JF-2s accepted by the Coast Guard in 1934 and 1935. The aircraft shown (V148) was initially based at CGAS Port Angeles in Washington state.

The first flight of the XJF-1 took place on April 25, 1933, near the Grumman factory in Farmingdale, and it was delivered to Naval Air Station Anacostia in Maryland for military trials on May 4. As originally built, the tail group of the XJF-1 was similar in size and shape to that of the FF-1, but after early testing revealed stability problems, all vertical and horizontal tail surfaces were reshaped and enlarged. Following official acceptance, the Navy placed an order for twenty-seven

The J2F-1 depicted here was delivered to the Marine Corps at MCAS Quantico in June 1938 where it served with utility squadron VMJ-1. The Marines also operated several more JFs and J2Fs at other stations.

production models to be delivered as the JF-1. The only noticeable difference between the production JF-1 and the prototype was the rounded fin and rudder shape that became standard throughout the series. As JF-1s began entering service in late 1934, they replaced Loening OL-9s aboard the Navy's four carriers, and as deliveries proceeded, began replacing older observation and torpedo types in utility (VJ) squadrons; and between 1936 and 1939, four of these were transferred to the Marine Corps. The fourteen JF-2s ordered by the Coast Guard in early 1934 differed in having single-row 750-hp Wright R-1820-20 *Cyclone* engines that came with ring-type cowlings and a direction-finding loop antenna behind the canopy. Initial deliveries of JF-2s commenced later the same year, and on December 4, 1934, a USGC JF-2 established a new amphibian world speed record of 191 mph. One of the last JF-2s produced was reassigned to the Marines and entered service with VJ-6M at Quantico, Virginia, in late 1935. The last of the JF series, five *Cyclone*-powered JF-3s completed in late 1935, came without carrier arresting gear and were delivered directly to naval reserve units. An additional eight model G-20s (JF-2s without arresting gear) were sold to Argentina and delivered in 1937.

Grumman began design work on the improved model G-15 in 1935, and in March 1936, BuAer ordered twenty production aircraft as the J2F-1. Powered by the same R-1820-20 engine as the JF-2, changes included a lengthening of the main float with accommodation for an additional crewmember or a medical stretcher in the compartment below the cockpit, removal of the inter-aileron struts, and a strengthening of the airframe to allow catapult launches from ships. The first J2F-1 was flown on April 3, 1937, and all had been delivered to Navy and Marine units by the end of the year. To keep pace with the general expansion of the fleet, BuAer ordered four more batches of J2Fs from Grumman in 1937 and 1938, which all entered service during 1939: twenty-one J2F-2s equipped with 790-hp R-1820-30 engines and one fixed .30-calibre machine gun firing between cylinders; nine J2F-2As for the Marines featuring the addition of two bomb racks and twin machine gun mounts in the rear cockpit; twenty J2F-3s specially outfitted to serve as VIP transports; and thirty-two J2F-4s that differed from -2s only in minor details.

With war clouds on horizon, BuAer placed an order with Grumman in early 1940 for 144

One of 330 J2F-6s completed by Columbia Aircraft Corp. from 1942 to 1945. They were identical to Grumman-built J2F-5s except for uprated engines (R-1820–54) and constant-speed propellers.

J2F-5s, and deliveries started before the end of the year. J2F-5s were powered by 850-hp R-1820-50 engines, upping top speed by 10 mph, and could be distinguished by their full-chord cowlings. At some point during J2F-5 production the airplane acquired the name "Duck." Five J2F-5s were transferred to the Coast Guard and twenty to the Marines starting in early 1942. Because Grumman's assembly lines were urgently needed to manufacture fighters and torpedo-bombers after the U.S. entered World War II, license-production of the J2F was shifted to the Columbia Aircraft Corp. at Valley Stream, New York, and from mid–1942 to late 1945, a further 330 Ducks were completed there as the J2F-6 (initially designated JL-1). J2F-6s were identical to -5s except for a 1,050-hp R-1820-54 engines and constant-speed propellers. Besides Navy production, five J2F-6s were delivered to the Coast Guard and an unspecified number to the Marines. In wartime service, J2Fs were used for a variety of functions, flying reconnaissance, air-sea rescue, and armed patrol missions in addition to their normal ship-to-shore transportation duties. The Navy and Coast Guard began phasing-out J2Fs from service soon after the war ended, with the very last examples being retired in 1948. Interestingly, five ex–Navy J2F-5s and two J2F-6s were transferred to the U.S. Air Force in 1948, as the as the OA-12A and -12B, respectively, where they operated out of Elmendorf AFB with the 10th Air Rescue Squadron until the early 1950s. Surplus Ducks were also given to the air forces of Argentina, Columbia, and Mexico. In civilian hands, small numbers of Ducks were employed as air-taxis and fire-bombers, and some were used in movies. A few survivors may be seen today in aviation museums, and at least one flying example, Columbia J2F-6, civil registration number N1196N, is maintained by the Experimental Aircraft Association in Oshkosh, Wisconsin.

Grumman G-21 (J3F, JRF, OA-9 and -13) Goose (1937)

TECHNICAL SPECIFICATIONS (JRF-5)

Type: 8 to 9-place utility amphibian.
Total produced: 345 (military and civilian)
Powerplant: two 450-hp Pratt & Whitney R-985-AN-12 *Wasp Junior* 9-cylinder air-cooled radial engines driving two-bladed, variable-pitch metal propellers.
Armament (JRF-4, -5, and -6): 250 lbs. of bombs or depth charges.
Performance: max. speed 201 mph, cruise 150 mph; ceiling 21,300 ft.; range 800 mi.
Weights: 5,245 lbs. empty, 8,000 lbs. gross.
Dimensions: span 49 ft. 0 in., length 38 ft. 6 in., wing area 375 sq. ft.

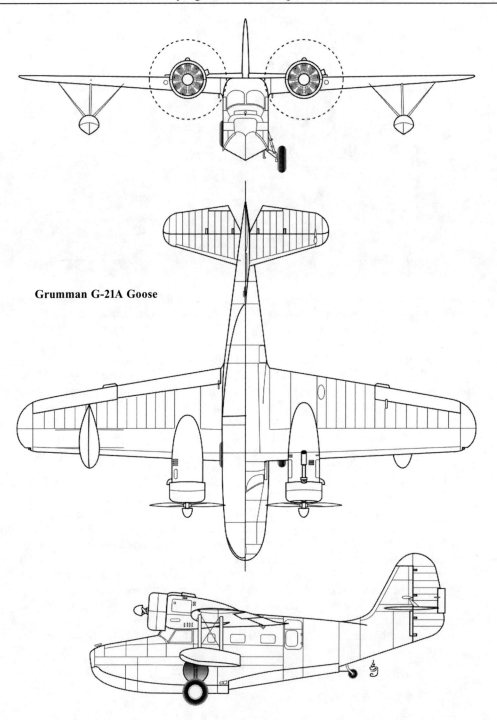

Grumman G-21A Goose

Certainly one of the longest-lived amphibians of all time, the Goose is also recognized as having been the very first monoplane to be designed by Grumman. The original impetus leading up to
its design reportedly came from a group of wealthy New York businessmen, who in 1936 approached
Leroy Grumman with the proposition of developing a modern twin-engine amphibian to be used
as a fast executive transport. Once Grumman agreed to build the aircraft, he assigned the project
to design engineer William Schwendler and hydrodynamicist Ralston Stalb as the company model

One of the early prewar civil G-21s, initially offered at a selling price of $68,000 in 1937. Small improvements to the hull, uprated engines, and a 500-lb. increase in useful load resulted in the G-21A.

Coast Guard JRF-5G in postwar paint livery. The last examples were retired from USCG service during mid–1954. One ex–Coast Guard JRF-5G was used to conduct hydrofoil experiments until 1962.

G-21. Working quickly, the team conceived a deep-bodied, two-step hull of exceptionally clean design, which joined to a cantilevered wing incorporating split-type flaps to keep takeoff and landing speeds within acceptable limits. Power was derived from two tightly cowled 450-hp *Wasp Junior* engines mounted in nacelles on the wings. Other than fabric-covered control surfaces, the entire airframe consisted of light-alloy aluminum construction. The only concessions to drag were fixed stabilizing floats and a strut-braced horizontal stabilizer. After making its first flight on May 29, 1937, the G-21 demonstrated superb handling qualities combined with performance that exceeded most twin-engine landplane designs.

Despite an expensive asking price ($68,000 compared to $37,500 for a new Beechcraft B18 landplane), Grumman promptly received orders for twelve G-21s. Early purchasers included such luminaries as Wilton Lloyd-Smith, Marshall Field, Henry H. Morgan, E. Roland Harriman, Robert R. "Colonel" McCormick, and Lord Beaverbrook. Two G-21s were also purchased in 1937 by Asiatic Petroleum. Refinements to the hull, upgraded SB2 engines, and a 500-lb. increase in takeoff weight resulted in the introduction of the G-21A as the standard civil production model. As interest in the new amphibian became more widespread, Grumman began receiving additional orders

G-21A of Catalina Air Lines seen on the run between Long Beach and Avalon, Catalina Island in the mid–1960s. This carrier had operated as Avalon Air Transport until 1963.

The first significant Goose upgrade, the G-21C, with four 340-hp Lycoming engines and retractable wing floats.

from airline, military, and overseas customers. The first actual military sale transpired in June 1938 when a G-21A was sold to the Royal Canadian Air Force. This was followed the same year by a sizeable U.S. Army Air Corps contract for twenty-six examples to be delivered as the OA-9. Later in 1938, the Navy obtained a G-21A for evaluation as a shore-based utility amphibian under the designation XJ3F-1, and in early 1939, following brief trials, gave Grumman an order for ten more as the JRF-1. Shortly after entering Navy service, one JRF-1 was transferred to the Marine Corps as a command aircraft and five others, including the original XJ3F-1, after receiving modifications for target-towing and photographic work, were returned to service as the JRF-1A. Military orders continued through the year: ten new aircraft accepted by the Coast Guard in 1940, seven as JRF-2s with seats interchangeable with stretchers as and three as JRF-3s with autopilots and de-icing equipment; and ten by the Navy in 1940 and 1941 as JRF-4s having wing racks that carried either two 250-lb. bombs or depth charges. Twelve G-21Bs, the only non-amphibious variants of the series to be produced, were delivered to the Portuguese Naval Service in 1940.

As the U.S. stepped-up its preparations for war, Grumman received a large-scale contract in 1940 to produce 185 examples as the JRF-5, with deliveries scheduled to begin in 1941. As the principal wartime production variant, the JRF-5 featured small detail refinements, uprated AN-12 engines, as well as camera equipment. Six more specially outfitted for rescue work entered service with the Coast Guard as the JRF-5G, and four were supplied to Great Britain under Lend Lease as the Goose I, which subsequently became the type's popular name. In 1942 an estimated seven or eight civilian examples joined the military inventory when they were impressed into service by the USAAF, G-21s as the OA-9 and G-21As as the OA-13. The final production variant, forty-seven JRF-6Bs completed between 1942 and 1945, appeared with improved electrical systems and specialized equipment for navigational training, forty-three of which were allocated to Great Britain as the Goose 1A and five to the USAAF as the OA-9GR. During the early days of World War II, Navy and Coast Guard JRFs armed with depth charges saw extensive use in antisubmarine patrols off the U.S. coast, but as the submarine threat diminished, Navy JRFs reverted to their utility transport role, while Coast Guard and USAAF types were employed mainly for search and rescue operations. Navy JRFs virtually disappeared from service as soon as World War II ended, while small numbers of Coast Guard JRF-5Gs remained active until the mid–1950s. Some ex–Navy JRFs continued in post-war military service with the armed forces of Argentina, Bolivia, Brazil, Cuba, France, Japan, Paraguay, Peru, and Sweden. Given the large numbers of war surplus G-21As available, Grumman never resumed civil production.

But if the cessation of hostilities in 1945 spelled the end of the type's usefulness as a military aircraft, it simply marked the beginning of what became a long and successful civil career in scheduled airline, air-taxi and charter, and freight hauling services. In fact, more than any other type of

G-21D "Turbo Goose" shown with Pratt & Whitney PT-6 turboprop engines. First introduced by McKinnon in 1963, at least 12 are believed to have been converted.

small transport, the Goose was uniquely suited for operations in coastal and inter-island environ-ments like the Caribbean, California, and Alaska. Some (but not all) of the airlines known to have operated G-21As in the post-war era were Reeve Aleutian Airways, Alaska Coast Airways, Chalk's Flying Service (Florida), Mackey Airlines (Florida), Antilles Air Boats (U.S. Virgin Islands), and Avalon Air Transport (California). Foreign air carriers and flying services also found the Goose to be ideal for operations in the coastal regions around Australia, Canada, the East Indies, Iceland, and Norway. But starting in the 1960s, as a consequence of irreparable damage, airframe fatigue, and a general lack of spare parts, the commercial fleet of G-21As began to dwindle, so that by the 1990s only a handful remained in operation. From 1958 to 1970, McKinnon Enterprises of Sandy, Oregon began marketing a series of G-21A conversions that were intended to extend the type's use-ful life. The first, listed as the G-21C, entailed a modification in which four 340-hp Lycoming GSO-480 engines were installed in place of the two R-985s and the wing floats made to retract into the wingtips. The G-21D (and E) or Turbo-Goose, introduced in 1966, came with two 600-hp Pratt & Whitney PT-6A turboprop engines, and the G-21G, in 1970, featured a modified and improved cabin area. An estimated twelve or more of these conversions are believed to have been completed.

Today, seventy years after the first flight, an internet website listed as Goose Central (see www.geocities.com/alaskangoose/) claims that more than fifty G-21 variants are still in existence, though the actual number in flyable condition is not reported. At least five are preserved in air muse-ums in the U.S. (including Alaska) and Canada, including a completely restored 1938-vintage G-21A maintained by the National Air and Space Museum's Udvar-Hazy Center at Dulles Airport in Washington, D.C. Most recently (late 2007), Antilles Seaplanes, LLC of Gibsonville, North Car-olina (see www.antillesseaplanes.com), who presently holds production rights to the G-21, announced that it will be offering *brand new* airplanes in two versions: a stock G-21A with R-985-AN12 engines or a "Super Goose" having PT-6A turboprops plus the cabin refinements of the McKinnon G-21G.

Grumman G-44 (J4F, OA-14, and Gosling I) Widgeon (1940)

TECHNICAL SPECIFICATIONS (J4F-1)
Type: 5-place patrol/utility amphibian.
Total produced: 266 or 291 (all versions)
Powerplant: two 200-hp Ranger L-440-5 6-cylinder air-cooled inline engines driving two-bladed, fixed-pitch wooden propellers.
Armament (J4F-1): one 200-lb. depth charge under right wing.
Performance: max. speed 153 mph, cruise 138 mph; ceiling 17,500 ft.; range 780 mi.
Weights: 3,240 lbs. empty, 4,525 lbs. gross.
Dimensions: span 40 ft. 0 in., length 31 ft. 1 in., wing area 245 sq. ft.

Originally conceived in 1940 for the civilian market, Grumman's Ranger-powered model G-44 found itself conscripted into military service by the time it reached production. While utilizing the proven two-step hull configuration, hand-operated landing gear, and all-metal construction of the model G-21, the smaller G-44 materialized with the squared-off wings and tail surfaces that typified newer Grumman designs (e.g., F4F-3, TBF-1). An all-new wing planform, presenting a con-stant-chord center-section on which the inline engines were mounted high up out of the spray, fea-tured a sharply tapered trailing edge from mid-chord to the tip and fully-articulated trailing-edge flaps. The first flight of the G-44 prototype took place on June 28, 1940 from Grumman's plant at Bethpage, and as flight trials proceeded, the only aerodynamic change consisted of adding mass balance horns to the elevators.

The first twenty-five production G-44s, assigned the BuAer designation J4F-1, were allocated to the Coast Guard, with deliveries commencing in mid–1941, and the next batch of twenty-six, including ten originally destined for Portugal and sixteen ordered by civilians, were impressed into U.S. Army Air Force service in early 1942 as the OA-14. From 1942 to 1945, Grumman completed another 131 G-44s under Navy contracts as the J4F-2, fifteen of which were subsequently Lend-Leased to Great Britain as the Gosling I (later Widgeon I, which developed into the type's official

Grumman resumed Widgeon production, an improved G-44A, in 1945. The final 40 of the 90 G-44As built were completed under license in France by SCAN from 1949 to 1952.

Known as "Super Widgeons," McKinnon Enterprises began converting G-44s to Lycoming inline engines in the mid–1950s, and 70 are thought to have been modified.

name), plus several more to the Portuguese Naval Air Service and the Brazilian Air Force. Coast Guard J4F-1s, after being retrofitted to carry a 200-lb. depth charge beneath the right wing between the fuselage and the engine nacelle, began flying antisubmarine missions off the American coast. On August 1, 1942, while operating out of the USCG base at Houma, Louisiana, a J4F-1 flown by Chief Aviation Pilot Henry White was credited with the sinking of *U-166*. (Ironically, following discovery of the wreck by an oil exploration team in 2001, it was determined that the submarine had not been sunk by an aircraft but by PC-556, a Navy coastal patrol ship.) In other military branches, J4F-2s, OA-14s, and Widgeon Is were most often employed as land-based utility transports, though the Navy also used some as instrument trainers.

Grumman resumed civil production of the Widgeon even before the war ended, introducing the improved model G-44A in early 1945. Refinements included a six-seat cabin and modified hull profile that improved water handling. When Grumman completed the last of fifty (seventy-five according to some authorities) G-44As in 1949, license-production of forty more between 1949 and 1952 was taken over by the firm of SCAN (Société des Constructions Aéro-Navales) located in France. Most of the French-built aircraft, known as the SCAN 30, were delivered to American customers. All G-44 military variants remaining in Navy, Coast Guard, and USAAF inventories were

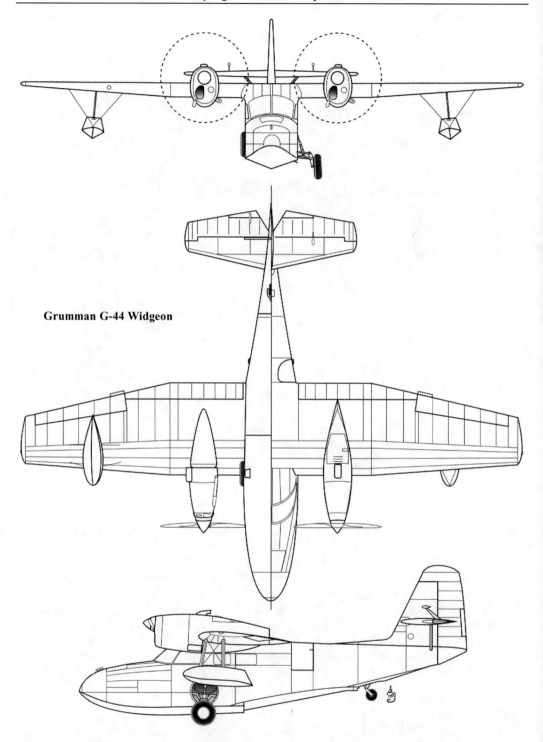

Grumman G-44 Widgeon

phased-out and sold surplus between 1946 and 1948. Five G-44As sold to the Royal Thai Air Force served from 1951 to 1956.

Due to the limited power available from the 200-hp Ranger engines, especially in single-engine operations, efforts to upgrade Widgeons with better powerplants were seen early on. During the mid–1950s, McKinnon Enterprises of Sandy, Oregon, began converting both G-44s and G-44As to

Recent photograph of this G-44 depicts the McKinnon Super Widgeon conversion.

260-hp (GO-435-C2B) or 270-hp (GO-480-B1D) Lycoming six-cylinder air-cooled engines that drove more efficient three-bladed Hartzell constant-speed propellers. Performance was significantly enhanced, top speed increasing to 190 mph and rate-of-climb doubling to 1,750 ft./min. Marketed as the "Super Widgeon," seventy or more examples are thought to have received the McKinnon conversion by 1970. Similar uprgrades have been performed on other Widgeons, such as the McDermott conversion to 260-hp Continental IO-470-D engines, recognizable by a comparitively flatter cowling profile. Virtually all of the privately owned G-44s and G-44As that remain active today have undergone engine upgrades and been subjected to extensive restorations. A classified advertisement appearing on the Seaplane Pilots Association website as recently as January 2008 listed a restored G-44 with the McDermott conversion for sale at $345,000.

Hall Aluminum Aircraft Corp.

Founded by Charles W. Hall in 1927, the Hall Aluminum Aircraft Corp. started manufacturing operations in Buffalo, New York, and moved in 1934 to Bristol, Pennsylvania, when it took over the site of Keystone Aircraft. Charles Hall designed a small metal flying boat in 1923 (see Appendix A, page 306), and after organizing his company, completed the XFH-1 experimental fighter prototype for the Navy in 1929. Although the XFH-1 was not selected for production, BuAer was sufficiently impressed to give Hall a shot at producing another aircraft. The company was ultimately acquired by Consolidated in 1940.

Hall PH (1929)

TECHNICAL SPECIFICATIONS (PH-3)

Type: 4 to 5-place patrol and rescue boat.
Total produced: 24 (all versions)
Powerplant: two 875-hp Wright R-1820-F51 *Cyclone* 9-cylinder air-cooled radial engines driving three-bladed, variable-pitch metal propellers.
Armament: four flexible .30-calibre machine guns in bow and waist positions (PH-1 and 2 only) and up to 1,000 lbs. of bombs or depth charges carried under the wings.
Performance: max. speed 159 mph, cruise 136 mph; ceiling 21,350 ft.; range 1,937 mi. normal, 2,300 mi. max.
Weights: 9,614 lbs. empty, 16,152 lbs. normal, gross, 17,679 lbs. max. takeoff.
Dimensions: span 72 ft. 10 in., length 51 ft. 0 in., wing area 1,170 sq. ft.

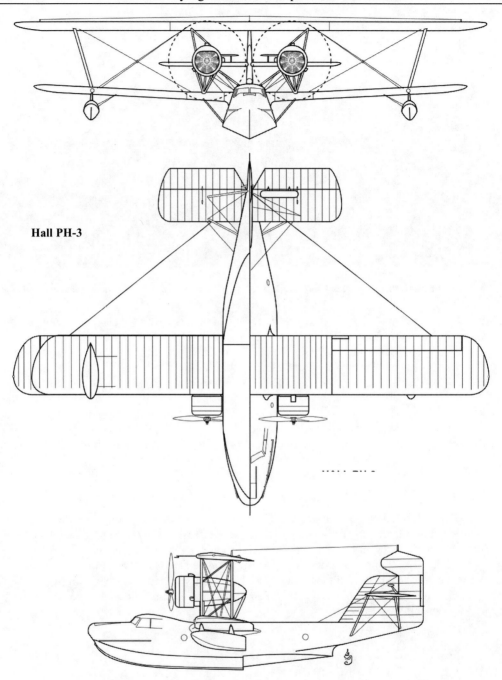

Hall PH-3

The longest-lived of the series derived from the design of the Naval Aircraft Factory PN-12, the Hall PH was the last type of biplane flying boat in American military service. Hall Aluminum became the second of four companies ultimately selected to manufacture the NAF design, receiving a contract in December 1927 to build a prototype under the designation XPH-1. While all of the patrol boats based on the PN-12 were very similar in general layout, they differed in details according to the manufacturer. The XPH-1, when delivered to Anacostia for trials late in 1929, appeared with a raked forward hull having a more blended sponson, a taller elephant-ear rudder, and full-chord cowlings that faired into the engine nacelles. In its test program, the XPH-1 demonstrated

The XPH-1, first of the Hall-built flying boats, as seen in late 1929. The nine production PH-1s, delivered through 1932, came with ring cowls and enclosed cockpits. All served with VP-8 out of Pearl Harbor.

One of 7 PH-3s ordered by the Coast Guard in 1939. This aircraft is shown in its wartime paint scheme on the ramp at CGAS San Francisco in 1942. The last PH-3s were removed from active service in 1944.

superior aerodynamic efficiency by posting better speed and range than the similarly equipped PN-12. BuAer awarded Hall a contract in June 1930 to produce nine examples as the PH-1, and deliveries started late in 1931. Production models differed in having enclosed cockpits, uprated R-1820-86 engines, and ring-type cowlings. All nine PH-1s were subsequently assigned to VP-8 operating out of Pearl Harbor, Hawaii and remained in service until replaced by PBYs during 1937.

As the Navy trended toward larger and more complex monoplane patrol boats in the mid–1930s, the Coast Guard still needed a smaller aircraft to operate in the search and rescue role. The biplane planform, allowing lower landing and takeoff speeds, was also better suited to the rough sea conditions likely to be encountered. Thus, nearly five years after last PH-1 had been completed, Hall received a new contract in June 1936 to manufacture seven aircraft for the Coast Guard as the PH-2. Built to a slightly revised specification, PH-2s featured special rescue equipment that included facilities for as many as twenty survivors plus air-to-ship and direction-finding radio systems. As the PH-2s entered service on both coasts during 1938, they effectively doubled (i.e., 750 miles) the Coast Guard's operational radius in search and rescue operations. To keep pace with Coast Guard expansion and attrition of the existing PH-2 fleet, Hall received an order in early 1939 for seven more aircraft to be completed as the PH-3, with deliveries scheduled to begin in the spring of 1940. The PH-3 differed in having a revised cockpit enclosure, no gun armament, NACA-type cowlings, and a 1,300-lb. increase in useful load. After the U.S. entered World War II, the PH-2s and -3s were repainted in non-spectacular intermediate blue over gray schemes, but continued to operate primarily in the search and rescue role. The last examples, replaced by newer types such as Consolidated PBYs and Martin PBMs, were retired from Coast Guard service during 1944.

Hall P2H (1932)

TECHNICAL SPECIFICATIONS (XP2H-1)

Type: 6-place naval patrol boat.
Total produced: 1
Powerplant: four 600-hp Curtiss V-1670-54 *Conqueror* 12-cylinder water-cooled inline engines driving three-bladed, ground-adjustable metal propellers.
Armament: five flexible .30-calibre machine guns in bow, waist, and tail positions and up to 2,000 lbs. of bombs or depth charges carried under the wings.
Performance: max. speed 139 mph, cruise 120 mph; ceiling 10,900 ft.; range 2,150 mi. normal, 3,350 mi. max.
Weights: 20,856 lbs. empty, 35,393 lbs. normal gross, 43,193 lbs. max. takeoff.
Dimensions: span 112 ft. 0 in., length 70 ft. 10 in., wing area 2,742 sq. ft.

Massing over twice the weight of the PH, the XP2H-1 was tested to evaluate long-range patrol missions. However, by the time trials were trials were completed in 1933, BuAer had decided to pursue monoplane designs instead.

The largest Navy flying boat to be built since the Curtiss NC-4, the Hall P2H represented an experimental effort to enlarge both the range and offensive capabilities of a naval patrol boat. Notably, it became the last type of biplane patrol boat completed to a Navy specification and the first to feature tail gun armament. When ordered in June 1930 as the XP2H-1, BuAer departed from standard practice by specifying water-cooled Curtiss engines rather than the customary air-cooled radials. Hall evolved a design in which the dimensions of the PH-1 were increased by a factor of approximately fifty percent, yielding over twice the wing area and interior hull volume. The four engines, tandem-mounted at the lower wing roots, sat on wide, raised pylons that also contained the radiators. The XP2H-1 was flown for the first time on November 15, 1932, and was accepted by the Navy soon afterward. By mid–1933, however, BuAer had reached the decision to concentrate

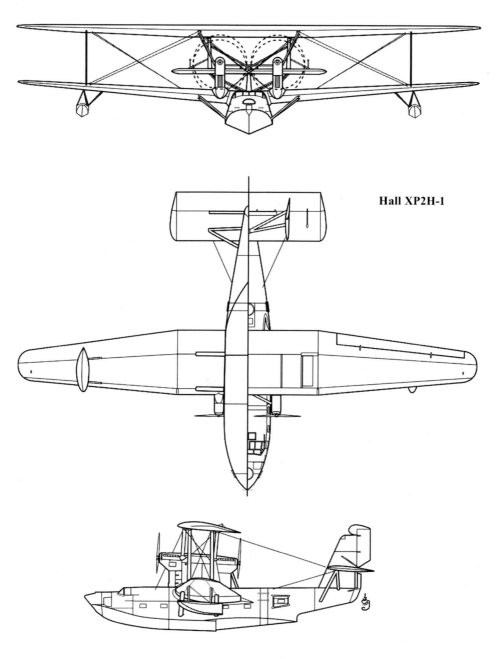

Hall XP2H-1

on more modern monoplane designs like the Consolidated XP3Y-1 and Douglas XP3D-1, and as a consequence, development of the XP2H-1 was discontinued.

Keystone Aircraft Corp.

Starting as Huff-Daland in 1920, this company was reorganized in 1927 as the Keystone Aircraft Corp., with manufacturing facilities located in Bristol, Pennsylvania. In 1928 Keystone acquired Loening Aeronautical as a wholly separate division with its own plant in New York. Keystone and Huff-Daland are probably best remembered for the series of large biplane bombers (i.e., LB/B-1, -3, -4, -5, and -6) it built for the Army between 1923 and 1932. Following a merger with Curtiss-Wright Corp. in 1931, the Bristol plant ceased manufacturing operations in 1932.

Keystone PK (1931)

TECHNICAL SPECIFICATIONS (PK-1)

Type: 5-place naval patrol boat.
Total produced: 18
Powerplant: two 575-hp Wright R-1820-64 *Cyclone* 9-cylinder air-cooled radial engines driving three-bladed, ground-adjustable metal propellers.
Armament: one flexible .30-calibre machine gun in bow, one flexible .30-calibre machine gun in the rear cockpit, and 920 lbs. of bombs carried under the wings.
Performance: max. speed 120 mph, cruise 100 mph; ceiling 9,700 ft.; range 1,250 mi. normal, 1,355 mi. max.
Weights: 9,387 lbs. empty, 16,534 lbs. normal gross, 17,074 lbs. max. takeoff.
Dimensions: span 72 ft. 0 in., length 48 ft. 11 in., wing area 1,226 sq. ft.

In November 1929, BuAer selected Keystone as the fourth and last airframe contractor to manufacture a derivative of the Naval Aircraft Factory PN-12. It was the only type of flying boat ever produced at the Bristol plant. Though not an established Navy contractor, Keystone had a proven record of building and delivering large aircraft to the Army. As built, the PK-1 (no experimental

PK-1 as seen from the rear. In late 1929 , Keystone became the last of four manufacturers selected to build derivatives of the NAF PN-12. All of the 18 built were assigned to patrol squadrons operating out of Pearl Harbor.

prototype) differed from other PN-12 types in having the twin-fin tail group seen on the PN-11 (see P4N, page XXX) and engines in NACA-type engine cowlings mounted in a slightly lower position. The only variation from the standard, sponson-type hull was a flattened bow having an access hatch. While the date of the first flight was not recorded, all of the eighteen PK-1s ordered are known to have been delivered to the Navy by September 1931. PK-1s were assigned to VP squadrons based at Pearl Harbor, Hawaii and remained active until being retired in July 1938. They were the last biplane patrol boats to serve in the Navy.

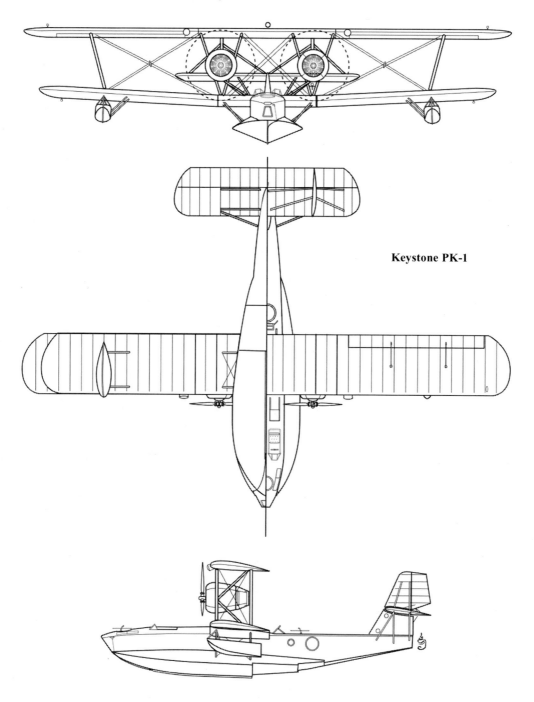

Keystone PK-1

Loening Aeronautical Division of Keystone Aircraft Corp.

As mentioned in Part I, above, Loening merged with Keystone Aircraft Corp. in 1928, but continued to independently design and manufacture aircraft from its East River location in New York City. Even though Grover Loening left the company in 1929 to form a separate engineering consulting firm, he apparently remained involved in the division's design work for some time afterward. The status of the Loening division following the acquisition of Keystone by Curtiss-Wright Corp. in 1931 is not clear, but, in any case, the East River plant had reportedly ceased all operations by 1938.

Loening (Keystone) C-4/K-85 Air Yacht (1928)

TECHNICAL SPECIFICATIONS (K-85)

Type: 10-place amphibious transport.
Total produced: 2.
Powerplant: one 525-hp Wright R-1750D *Cyclone* 9-cylinder air-cooled radial engine driving a three-bladed, ground-adjustable metal propeller.
Performance: max. speed 130 mph, cruise 107 mph; ceiling 10,900 ft.; range 575 mi.
Weights: not reported; useful load listed 2,091 lbs.
Dimensions: span 46 ft. 8 in., length 37 ft. 2 in., wing area (not reported).

The model C-4 originally appeared in 1928 as a fairly straightforward adaptation of the four-bay biplane wings and tailplane of the C-1, -2, and OL-9 (see Part I, above) to a much wider, pure boat fuselage in which the R-1340 *Wasp* engine had been relocated to the upper wing. In addition to a spacious cabin, the new hull provided far easier access through an entry hatch located in the bow. However, testing in 1928 and 1929 evidently indicated that the C-4 was underpowered for its weight, resulting in its being refitted with a more powerful *Cyclone* engine and re-introduced in

Using the 2-bay wings of the C-2, the boat-hulled C-4 initially appeared in 1928. Efforts to market the type as the *Cyclone*-powered C-4C and later as the Keystone K-85 were not successful and only two were completed.

1931 as the model K-85. The K-85's hull also had been lengthened two and a half feet to provide more space for passengers or cargo. Whether this amphibian was intended as a private transport or small airliner is not clear from available data, but in any event, efforts to market the K-85 were ultimately unsuccessful, and other than the original prototype, only one example, civil registration number NC10588, was completed.

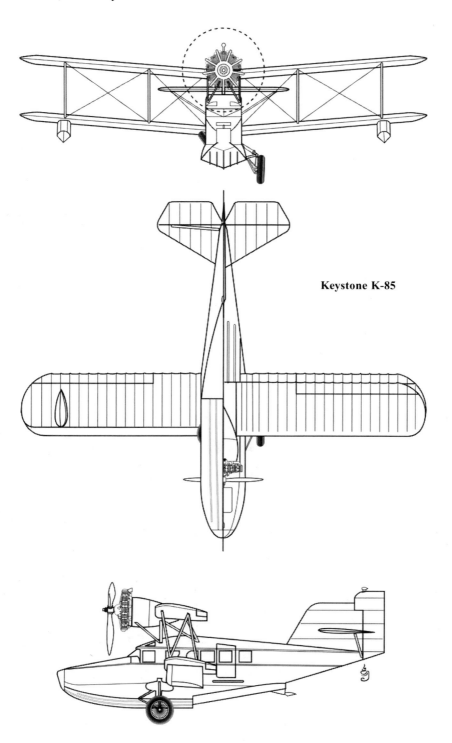

Keystone K-85

Loening (Keystone) C-6/K-84 Commuter (1929)

TECHNICAL SPECIFICATIONS

Type: 6-place amphibious transport.
Total produced: 31
Powerplant: one 300-hp Wright J-6 *Whirlwind* or 330- Pratt & Whitney R-985 *Wasp Junior* 9-cylinder air-cooled radial engine driving a two-bladed, ground-adjustable metal propeller.
Performance: max. speed 115 mph, cruise 90 mph; ceiling 12,000 ft.; range 506 mi.
Weights: not reported; useful load listed as 1,223 lbs.
Dimensions: span 36 ft. 0 in., length 32 ft. 5 in., wing area (not reported).

In 1929, by which time the airplane had gained wider acceptance as a private executive transport, Loening introduced the model K-84 Commuter (listed as the model C-6 prior to the Keystone merger) with the aim of marketing them to wealthy businessmen, in New York City especially, who regularly commuted between their offices in the city and homes in nearby suburban areas. And an amphibian would give them the added ability to fly directly from Manhattan Island to the coastal areas of Long Island or Connecticut where many of their residential estates were located. Like the C-4/K-85 which preceded it, the K-84 offered the more comfortable accommodations of a pure boat hull, but on a reduced scale.

Its general design incorporated most of the features see on earlier Loening amphibians: fabric-covered biplane wings, reduced to one bays of struts, but otherwise similar to those of the OL-9; a boxy metal boat hull that contained an enclosed cockpit and passenger cabin; and the cruciform tailplane characteristic of Loening designs. Unlike the C-5, the engine was mounted on struts between the upper and lower wings. The alternative *Wasp*-powered version was advertised as the K-84W. Offered at a base price of $16,800, thirty-one K-84s were sold to private owners between 1929 and 1931, making it one of the most popular private amphibians until the advent of the Grumman G-21 in 1937.

One of the most successful private amphibians of its day, a total of 31 C-4s/K-84s were delivered between 1929 and 1931.

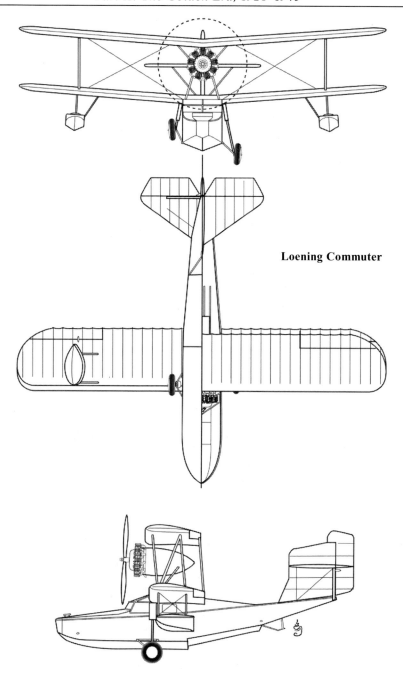

Loening Commuter

Loening (Keystone) O2L (1932)

TECHNICAL SPECIFICATIONS (XO2L-1)

Type: 3-place observation/utility amphibian.
Total produced: 1
Powerplant: one 450-hp Pratt &n Whitney R-1340-4 *Wasp* 9-cylinder air-cooled radial engine driving a
    three-bladed, ground-adjustable metal propeller.
Performance: max. speed 132 mph, cruise 110 mph; ceiling 16,200 ft.; range 350 mi.
Weights: 2,742 lbs. empty, 4,053 lbs. gross.
Dimensions: span 37 ft. 0 in., length 29 ft. 10 in., wing area 348 sq. ft.

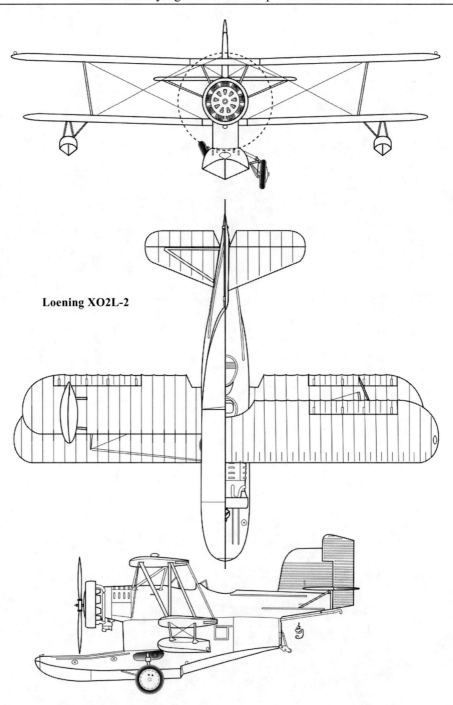

Loening XO2L-2

The O2L represented the ultimate evolution of the design series that had begun in 1923 with the Liberty-powered OL-1 (see Part I, above). In 1931, while deliveries of the OL-9 were still underway, Loening received a contract to design and built a substantially revised prototype under the designation XO2L-1. Though sharing many similarities with the OL-9, including the *Wasp* powerplant, the XO2L-1 made extensive use of semi-monocoque construction techniques that improved streamlining of the fuselage and main pontoon; and a thirty percent decrease in weight allowed smaller wings supported by a single bay of struts. Directional stability problems encountered soon

The sole prototype at NAS Anacostia in 1932, re-designated XO2L-2 after installation of a larger fin and rudder. Fleet tested aboard battleships with VO-1B but not placed in production.

after the prototype's first flight in early 1932 led to the addition of finlets on the horizontal stabilizers. But when performance and handling still fell below Navy expectations, the prototype was returned to the factory and subjected to modifications which included installation of a 550-hp R-1340D engine, lengthening the fuselage and pontoon three and a half feet, and enlarging the fin and rudder. Under the new designation XO2L-2, trials continued into late 1932, but Navy officials judged that the small performance improvement over the OL-9 did not merit production. BuAer then turned to Grumman for a new amphibian, ultimately resulting in the creation of JF/J2F Duck series.

Loening (Keystone) SL (1931)

TECHNICAL SPECIFICATIONS (XSL-1)

Type: 1-place scout.
Total produced: 1
Powerplant: one 110-hp Warner *Scarab* 7-cylinder air-cooled radial engine driving a two-bladed fixed-pitch metal propeller.
Performance: max. speed 101 mph, cruise 88 mph; ceiling 13,000 ft.; range (not reported).
Weights: 1,114 lbs. empty, 1,512 lbs. gross.
Dimensions: span 31 ft. 0 in., length 27 ft. 2 in., wing area 148 sq. ft.

The Loening SL was the last type of aircraft used in a series of Navy experiments, conducted intermittently from 1923 to 1933, to develop a small seaplane scout that could be deployed from a submarine. The aircraft had to be designed so that it could easily be dismantled and stowed in a watertight, eight-foot-diameter tube carried on the deck of the submarine. The earliest experiments had been carried out with diminutive float-equipped biplanes (Cox-Klemin XS-1 and -2, Martin MS-1) and actual submarine trials conducted in 1926, but these small aircraft were deemed unsatisfactory. Four years later, BuAer decided to reinstate the idea with a small monoplane flying boat, and in June 1930, awarded Loening a contract to construct a single prototype as the XSL-1. The

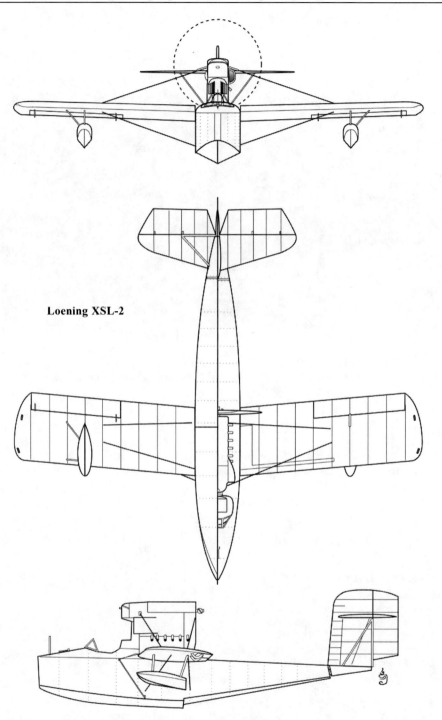

Loening XSL-2

design emerged with a semi-cantilevered monoplane wing which attached to the top of single-step metal boat hull. The Warner engine, mounted on struts in a pusher configuration, featured a ring cowl and a small bullet-shaped nacelle. Stowage in the deck tube was accomplished by simply removing the wings and stabilizing floats. The prototype, date of first flight unknown, was delivered to NAS Anacostia for trials February 1931. When testing revealed the XSL-1 to be underpowered with the Warner engine, it was returned to the factory for installation of a 160-hp Menasco

XSL-1, shown in original configuration in 1931, was underpowered with the Warner engine. The Navy abandoned the program in 1933 after the modified XSL-2 was damaged during exercises with a submarine.

B-6 and a more streamlined engine mount. The revised aircraft, re-designated XSL-2, resumed testing at Anacostia in early 1933, but these trials indicated only a nominal improvement in performance. Soon afterward, the Navy abandoned the entire program when the XSL-2 suffered serious damage during exercises with a submarine.

Loening (Keystone) S2L (1933)

TECHNICAL SPECIFICATIONS (XS2L-1)

Type: 2-place amphibian scout.
Total produced: 1
Powerplant: one 400-hp Pratt & Whitney R-985-28 *Wasp Junior* 9-cylinder air-cooled radial engine driving a two-bladed, ground-adjustable metal propeller.
Armament: One flexible .30-calibre machine gun in the observer's position.
Performance: max. speed 130 mph; ceiling 12,400 ft.; range 633 mi.
Weights: 2,833 lbs. empty, 4,053 lbs. normal gross, 4,317 lbs. max. takeoff.
Dimensions: span 34 ft. 6 in., length 30 ft. 7 in., wing area 355 sq. ft.

Like the Great Lakes SG reported above and the Sikorsky SS (see below), the Loening S2L was one of three amphibian designs to be considered as possible replacements for conventional floatplanes aboard Navy cruisers. The Navy had previously experimented with adding amphibious floats to existing observation types, but the resulting weight penalty had degraded performance unacceptably. A designed-for-purpose amphibian, however, was viewed as a potentially better solution to the current problem of periodically re-rigging floatplanes to wheeled undercarriage, then back to floats again. Loening received a contract in 1932 to construct a single amphibian prototype as the XS2L-1.

Its design followed a conventional biplane layout that seemed to derive features from both the OL-9 and the K-85 Air Yacht. A rather odd looking cabin resulted from glazed panels being placed

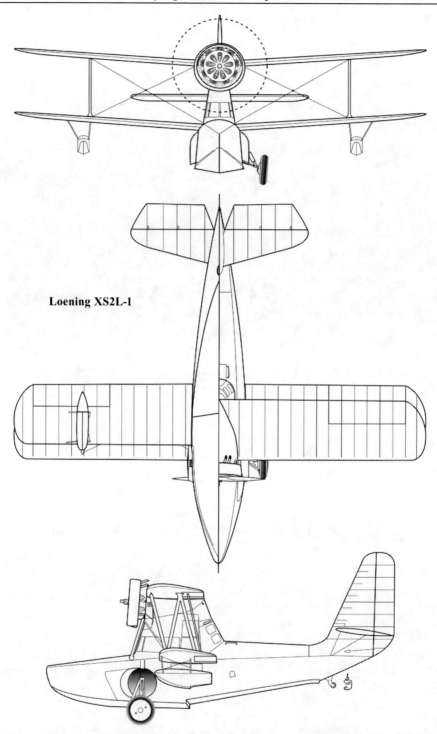

Loening XS2L-1

around the cabane struts below the engine and wing center-section. Landing gear was the improved type developed by Grumman. By the time the XS2L-1 arrived at Anacostia in February 1933, the Great Lakes entry had already been graded as unsatisfactory. Although the XS2L-1 exhibited marginally better performance in acceptance trials, it still fell below that of cruiser-based floatplanes like the Berliner-Joyce OJ-2, and no production resulted.

The XS2L-1 prototype, pictured here, was part of an unsuccessful experiment to replace floatplanes aboard Navy cruisers with boat-hulled amphibian. Development discontinued in 1933.

Glenn L. Martin Co.

One of the oldest American aircraft manufacturers, Glenn L. Martin originally founded his company at Santa Ana, California in 1909. Martin had operated under three different names at four different locations by the time his company started work on its first flying boat at the Baltimore (Middle River) plant in 1929. From that time onwards, Glenn Martin was said to have had an obsession with large flying boats, one that he seriously pursued until his death in 1955. Martin himself was not a design engineer but had a talent for recruiting gifted people, many of whom, like Donald W. Douglas, Lawrence D. Bell, and James S. McDonnell, went on to form their own aviation companies. But whether by accident or design, historical references (including internet sources) on Martin's aircraft do not reveal the identity of the engineers who designed his flying boats—a most curious oversight. While Martin rarely led the field in numbers of aircraft produced, his company, perhaps more than any other, set the pace in establishing new technology for flying boat designs.

Martin PM (1930)

TECHNICAL SPECIFICATIONS (PM-2)

Type: 5-place patrol boat.
Total produced: 55 (both versions)
Powerplant: two 575-hp Wright R-1820-64 *Cyclone* 9-cylinder air-cooled radial engines driving three-bladed, ground-adjustable metal propellers.
Armament: One flexible .30-calibre machine gun in the bow, one flexible .30-calibre machine gun in the rear cockpit, and 920 lbs. of bombs carried under the wings.
Performance: max. speed 119 mph, cruise 100 mph; ceiling 10,900 ft.; range 937 mi. (normal), 1,347 mi. (max.)
Weights: 9,919 lbs. empty, 17,284 lbs. normal gross, 19,062 lbs. max. takeoff.
Dimensions: span 72 ft. 0 in., length 49 ft. 0 in., wing area 1,236 sq. ft.

PM-1 serving with VP-9, based in Norfolk, Virginia, in the mid–1930s. PMs were the very first of a long line of flying boats that would be produced by Martin over a 30-year interval. Enclosed cockpit and cowl rings were added later.

Reshaped bow and twin-fin empennage distinguishes this factory-new PM-2. The 55 PM-1s and -2s, as the most numerous PN-12 derivatives, equipped five patrol units from 1930 to 1938.

Martin's first flying boat, the PM, also became the most numerous of the patrol boat types derived from the design of the Naval Aircraft Factory PN-12. In May 1929, when Martin received a contract to build twenty-five aircraft as the PM-1, the company already enjoyed a well-deserved reputation as one of the Navy's most reliable airframe contractors. The following October, after construction had started, BuAer added five more of the flying boats to the order. Listed as the company model 117, PM-1s were virtual duplicates of the PN-12, varying only slightly in finished weight. Deliveries of the new aircraft to fleet units started right on schedule in July 1930, but before the process could be completed, three of the PM-1s were diverted to the Brazilian government to assist it in putting down a rebellion; in an ironic turnabout, the rebels, who staged a successful coup while the planes were still en route, ultimately took delivery of them when they arrived. After entering Navy service, all PM-1s were later upgraded with ring cowlings and fully enclosed cockpits.

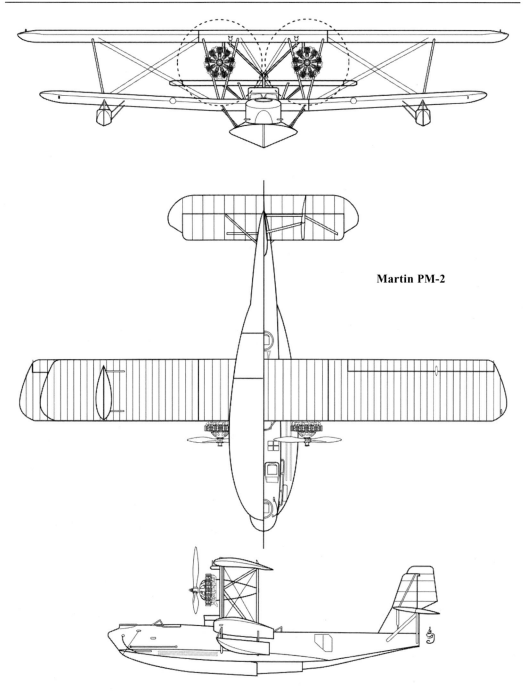

Martin PM-2

In June 1930, Martin received a third contract for twenty-five improved PM-2s (model 122), which differed from -1s in having a reshaped forward hull profile and the twin fin empennage of the PN-11. Deliveries of all PM-2s were completed between June and September of 1931, making Martin-built patrol boats the most numerous types in Navy service at the time. Replacing T4M-1 floatplanes, PM-1s and -2s were assigned to the Navy's two large seaplane tenders, VP-2 and -7 aboard the *Wright* based in the Canal Zone and VP-8, -9, and -10 aboard the *Argonne* in Pearl Harbor. The phase-out of PM-1s and -2s began in the late 1930s as they were replaced by P2Ys and PBYs, with the last examples being retired in early 1938.

Martin P2M and P3M (1931)

TECHNICAL SPECIFICATIONS (P3M-2)

Type: 5-place patrol boat.

Total produced: 10 (all versions)

Powerplant: two 525-hp Pratt & Whitney R-1690-32 *Hornet* 9-cylinder air-cooled radial engines driving three-bladed, ground-adjustable metal propellers.

Armament: One flexible .30-calibre machine gun in the bow and one flexible .30-calibre machine gun in the rear cockpit (no bomb load listed).

Performance: max. speed 115 mph, cruise 100 mph; ceiling 11,900 ft.; range 1,010 mi. (normal), 1,570 mi. (max.)

Weights: 10,032 lbs. empty, 15,688 lbs. normal gross, 17,977 lbs. max. takeoff.

Dimensions: span 100 ft. 0 in., length 61 ft. 9 in., wing area 1,119 sq. ft.

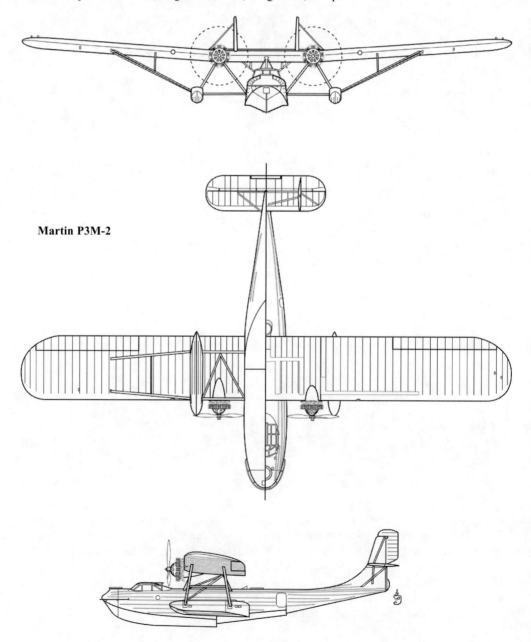

Martin P3M-2

As direct developments of the Consolidated XPY-1 of 1929 (see above), the P2M and P3M were both were byproducts of a naval aircraft procurement system which permitted one manufacturer's design to be produced by an altogether different company according to a competitive bidding process. In this case, Martin underbid Consolidated, receiving two contracts in June 1929 to build one development aircraft as the XP2M-1 plus nine others as the P3M-1. With the XP2M-1, Martin was given

One-of-a-kind XP2M-1 as seen at NAS Anacostia in mid–1931. Because of the additional weight and drag, the third engine (as with the XPY-1) was deemed impractical.

One of nine *Hornet*-powered P3M-2s. The first three P3M-1s were underpowered with two *Wasp* engines. The remaining six came with 525-hp *Hornets* as P3M-2s, and the three P3M-1s were subsequently modified to the same standard.

considerable leeway in making certain engineering changes, while the XP3M-1s were to be exact copies of the XPY-1, including its original two-engine layout. The first of three P3M-1s, powered by 450-hp R-1340 *Wasp* engines and having an open cockpit, was delivered in January 1931; however, when overall performance fell substantially below expectations, BuAer directed Martin to complete the six remaining aircraft to a revised specification under the designation P3M-2 and modify the three P3M-1s to the same standard. The upgrade included installation of 525-hp *Hornet* engines encased in ring cowlings, plus fully enclosed cockpits. But even after trials with the new engines, the P3M's performance was still substandard, causing them to be replaced in frontline service within a year and reassigned to NAS Pensacola as trainers. The last two P3M-2s were stricken from the naval inventory in 1941.

The one-of-a-kind XP2M-1 was rolled-out for its first flight in June 1931. It differed from the P3Ms in having three 575-hp Cyclone engines, two mounted directly to the wings in nacelles and a third on top. The wing itself was positioned lower in relation to the fuselage. Shortly after the XP2M-1 commenced flight trials, Navy officials determined that the extra weight and drag of the third engine effectively offset any advantage in speed and climb, and ordered it removed. However, by the time the aircraft resumed testing later in the year as the XP2M-2, the Navy had decided to award Consolidated a construction contract for the very similar P2Y-1. The wing-mounted nacelle arrangement was later adopted on the P2Y-3.

Martin M130 (1934)

TECHNICAL SPECIFICATIONS

Type: 41-passenger long-range civil transport.
Total produced: 3
Powerplants: four 830-hp Pratt & Whitney R-1830-S2 *Twin Wasp* 14-cylinder air-cooled radial engines driving three-bladed, variable-pitch metal propellers [later upgraded to 950-hp R-1830-S3 engines with constant-speed propellers].
Performance: max. speed 180 mph, cruise 163 mph; ceiling 17,000 ft.; range 3,200 mi. (normal), 1,570 mi. (max.)
Weights: 25,363 lbs. empty, 51,000 lbs. [52,252 after upgrade] gross.
Dimensions: span 130 ft. 0 in., length 90 ft. 10½ in., wing area 2,315 sq. ft. (including sponsons).

Probably the most celebrated of all Martin flying boat designs, the M130 was the first passenger-carrying aircraft in the world to truly possess trans-oceanic range. The original idea actually dated back to 1931, when Pan American Airways approached Sikorsky and Martin to both submit proposals for a passenger-carrying flying boat capable of traversing routes across the North and South Atlantic. Then in 1933, after the British government refused to grant landing concessions in Newfoundland and Bermuda, Pan American completely revised the requirements so that Sikorsky's route encompassed Latin America and Martin's, the Pacific area. As surveyed and mapped by Charles A. Lindbergh, the Pacific route entailed an 8,200-mile flight from San Francisco, California to Manila in the Philippines (Hong Kong added later), with intermediate stops in Hawaii, Midway, Wake, and Guam. At minimum, the specification dictated an aircraft that could safely carry the requisite payload of fuel, passengers, and mail over the 2400-mile segment between California and Hawaii. Taking these requirements as their baseline, Martin's engineering staff concluded such an aircraft would need four of the most powerful engines available and operate at entirely new levels of aerodynamic efficiency.

As the design of the new M130 came together, Martin evolved a very streamlined, two-step hull that supported the massive wing and tail structures without the usual profusion of struts and braces seen on most multi-engine flying boats. Airfoil-shaped sponsons, attached to the hull below the wings, eliminated the need for strut-braced wing floats and provided additional lift. To strengthen the long hull against the large hydro- and aerodynamic forces that would be encountered, the upper section was skinned in a corrugated Alclad. Wing efficiency was maximized by encasing the *Twin Wasp* engines in tight cowlings that blended into nacelles in an unbroken line. The two lobe design

China Clipper **(NC14716), the first and most famous of the three M130s built. After proving flights in the Atlantic during the fall, this aircraft inaugurated the world's first transpacific service in late November 1935.**

The last M130 completed, *Philippine Clipper* **(NC14714) in 1936. This aircraft, impressed into Navy service in 1942, was destroyed in January 1943 when it struck a mountain coming into San Francisco.**

of the hull created an upper space for the flight deck and the seven-man crew, leaving a spacious lower deck that provided accommodations for up to forty-six passengers in a day configuration or eighteen in sleeper berths. (Despite the number of seats, the fuel load required between San Francisco and Honolulu effectively limited the complement to only nine or ten passengers.)

The first of three M130s ordered by Pan American made its maiden flight on December 30, 1934. Its four engines and advanced aerodynamic concept allowed the new flying boat to lift more than twice its empty weight, exceeding the payload ratios of contemporary landplanes like the Boe-

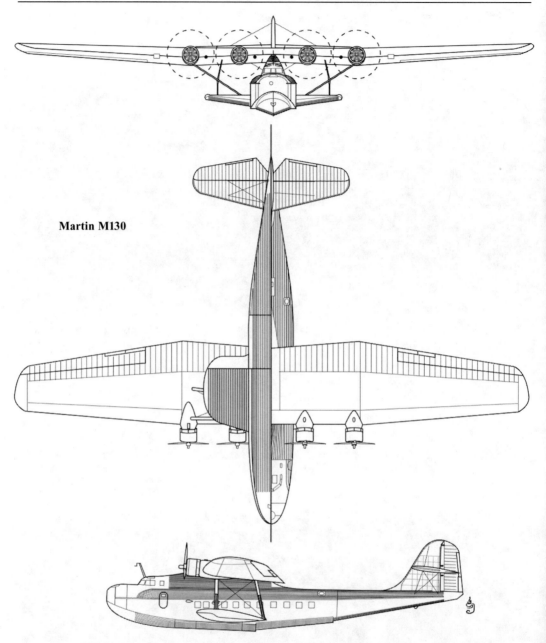

Martin M130

ing 247 and Douglas DC-2 by a factor of 50 percent. Two of them, christened *China Clipper* (NC14716) and *Hawaiian Clipper* (NC14715, later shortened to *Hawaii Clipper*), were delivered to the airline during 1935, and the third, *Philippine Clipper* (NC14714), in early 1936. After completing proving flights over the Atlantic in the fall of 1935, the *China Clipper*, captained by Edward Musick, was ferried to Pan American's West Coast base at Alameda and, carrying mail only, departed San Francisco on November 22, 1935, and arrived in Manila five days later after a total flying time of 59 hours and 48 minutes. With all three M130s in service, Pan American commenced cargo operations in March 1936; and the world's first passenger-carrying transpacific flight took place on October 21, 1936. *China Clipper* opened the new route to Hong Kong in April 1937. Thereafter, Pan American established a weekly (13–14 days roundtrip) service between San Francisco, Manila, and Hong Kong. Tragedy forced a reduction in Pacific service in July 1938 when the *Hawaii Clipper* simply disappeared on a scheduled flight between Guam and Manila. Although the M130s were a stunning commercial success, Martin lost money on the deal: offered at a contact price of $417,000 each (huge compared to $242,000 for a Sikorsky S-42 or $78,000 for a Douglas DC-2 landplane), the sale of only three aircraft was not sufficient to allow the company to recover its development and infrastructure costs.

Taking all of the Pan American staff with it, *Philippine Clipper* departed Wake Island on December 8, 1941, one day after the Japanese attacked Pearl Harbor. Shortly afterward, both *China Clipper* and *Philippine Clipper* were impressed into wartime service with the Navy as the M130. In January 1943, while inbound from Honolulu, *Philippine Clipper* struck a mountain coming into San Francisco. *China Clipper* survived until January 1945, when it was damaged beyond repair during a landing at Port of Spain, Trinidad.

Martin M156 (1938)

TECHNICAL SPECIFICATIONS

Type: 53-passenger long-range civil transport.
Total produced: 1
Powerplants: four 850-hp Wright R-1820-G2 *Cyclone* 9-cylinder air-cooled radial engines driving three-bladed, variable-pitch metal propellers.
Performance: max. speed 190 mph, cruise 156 mph; ceiling 15,000 ft.; range 2,410 mi. (normal), 3,290 mi. (max.)
Weights: 29,691 lbs. empty, 62,000 lbs. gross.
Dimensions: span 157 ft. 0 in., length 90 ft. 7 in., wing area 2,460 sq. ft. (including sponsons).

The sole Martin M156 shown flying over Baltimore in January 1938. With no airline orders, the aircraft was sold to the Soviet Union. Rather than fly it, Soviet officials crated it up and shipped it to Russia.

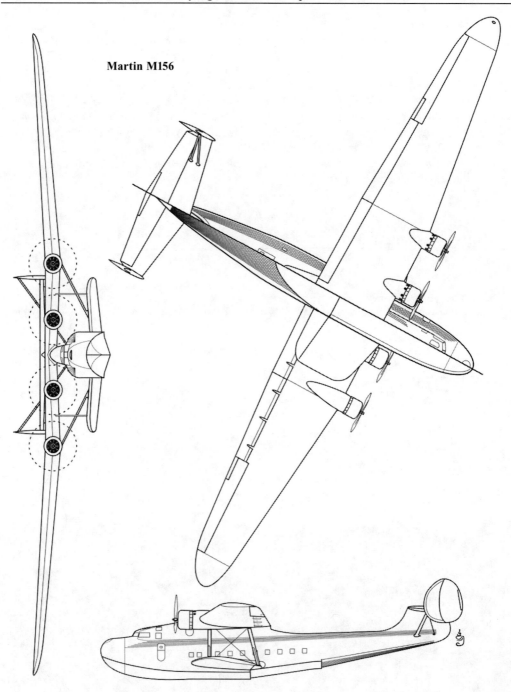

Martin M156

The Martin model 156 was briefly—until the Boeing 314 appeared four months later—the largest flying boat in the world. The modest sales of the M130 never discouraged Glenn L. Martin. He was firmly convinced large flying boats were the wave of the future and envisaged new types having takeoff weights upwards of 250,000 lbs. (i.e., fives time that of the M130) that would possess the range to comfortably span the world's oceans. In 1936, out of an effort to expand exports, Martin entered negotiations with the Soviet Union for the sale of an enlarged version of the M130, and once the contract price was fixed at $1,050,000, the company's engineers began laying down the blueprint of the company model 156. With only a slight boost (+80 hp) in available engine power, total wing area had to be enlarged 20 percent to lift the projected 11,000-lb. increase in take-off weight; and a larger, twin-fin empennage was needed to offset the directional problems that would be generated by the twenty-seven-foot increase in wingspan. Construction of the M156 continued through 1937, and it was rolled-out for it first flight in January 1938. Martin invited many airline executives to the event with the hope of interesting them with his proposed model 163 (similar in size to the model 170 XPB2M, reported below), but Pan American was already committed to the Boeing 314 and none of the other airlines apparently took notice of the project.

Rather than fly it home, Soviet officials crated-up the M156 and shipped it to Russia. Like most aircraft sold to the Soviets during that time, very little was known about the M156's operational career until recently. Registered as SSSR L2940, the aircraft entered service in 1940 with Aeroflot in the Far East area. On shorter routes, the M156 was said to have been routinely overloaded to a capacity of seventy passengers. Although it received the official designation SP-30, the aircraft was popularly referred to as the "Glenn Martin." Aeroflot was forced to retire the plane sometime in 1944 for lack of spare parts.

Martin M162A Tadpole Clipper (1937)

TECHNICAL SPECIFICATIONS

Type: 2-place flying testbed.
Total produced: 1
Powerplant: one 120-hp Martin-Chevrolet 4-cylinder water-cooled inline engine driving two belt-driven two-bladed, fixed-pitch metal propellers.
Performance: max. speed 120 mph; ceiling and range not available.
Weights: 2,600 lbs. empty, gross (not reported).
Dimensions: span 43 ft. 5½ in., length 28 ft. 6 in., wing area 525 sq. ft.

Martin M162A "Tadpole Clipper" parked under port wing of the XPBM-1. This three-eighths (37.5 percent) scale flying testbed was intended to prove the design concept upon which the full-size aircraft would be based.

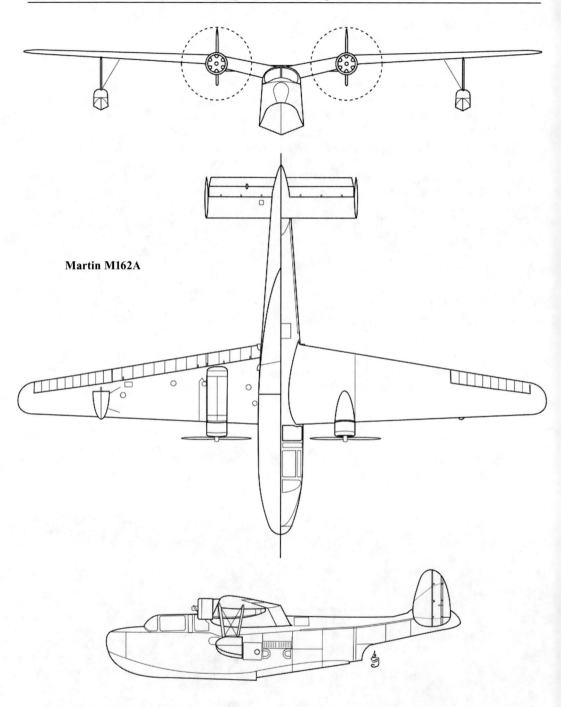

Martin M162A

Sometimes referred to as the "Tadpole Clipper," the Martin model 162A may have been the earliest flyable proof-of-concept demonstrator to be built by an American aircraft manufacturer. Aviation companies of that era frequently used small-scale models for wind tunnel testing but flying demonstrators, other than full-size prototypes, were unheard of. The motivation behind Martin's decision to build the M162A is more fully explained in text accompanying the model 162 PBM Mariner, which is reported next. As a three-eighths scale (37.5%) replica of the PBM, the M162A was intended to test, evaluate, and ultimately prove the design concept upon which the full-size aircraft would be based. From the very start, the project's primary aim was not so much to test general flight characteristics as to assess and improve upon the hydrodynamic qualities of the hull, which was something that could not be duplicated in a wind tunnel.

Construction of the wood-framed, metal and fabric-skinned model commenced in mid–1937. The configuration of the engine nacelles on the gull-wing planform was replicated by driving the propellers through a network of V-belts, connected to a four-cylinder automotive engine (one previously developed by Martin for a lightplane project) buried in the hull. Just weeks after the M162A's first flight on December 3, 1937, continuation of the project actually became unnecessary when Martin received approval to proceed with construction of twenty-one PBM-1s; nevertheless, with the M162A at such an advanced stage, the company chose to move forward with the test program in order to identify and implement any time-consuming and costly hull problems that might arise on the full-size plane. A wise move as it turned out, because, as designed, the hull revealed a tendency to develop pitch oscillations (i.e., "porpoising") while planing on the step. After Martin's engineering team solved the problem by lengthening the keel and reinforcing the hull in areas of maximum stress, similar improvements were incorporated into the design of the XPBM-1. Further testing also resulted in changes to the contour of the bow which eliminated sea-spray in the propeller arc. Because of frequent failures in the belt-drive mechanism, actual air testing of the M162A was kept to a minimum.

In early 1938, when the small flying boat was displayed to the public for the first time in a hangar next to the massive M156, the press jokingly referred to it as the "Tadpole Clipper." After the test program ended, the M162A was placed in storage in one of Martin's factory buildings and remained there until being received by the Smithsonian Institution in 1973. After the aircraft underwent a total restoration in 1987, the Smithsonian loaned it to the Museum of Industry in Baltimore, Maryland, where it may be seen today.

Martin PBM Mariner (1939)

TECHNICAL SPECIFICATIONS (PBM-1 [PBM-5])

Type: 7 to 10-place naval patrol boat.
Total produced: 1,366 (all versions)
Powerplants: two 1,600-hp Wright R-2600-6 *Twin Cyclone* 14-cylinder air-cooled radial engines driving three-bladed, electric controllable-pitch metal propellers [2,100-hp Pratt & Whitney R-2800-22 *Double Wasp* 18-cylinder air-cooled radial engines driving four-bladed, electric controllable-pitch propellers].
Armament: One [two] .50-calibre machine gun[s] in powered nose, dorsal, and tail turrets, one .50-calibre machine gun in each waist position, one .30-caliber machine gun firing downward in aft tunnel position (PBM-1 only), and up to 4,000 lbs. [8,000 lbs.] of bombs, torpedoes, or depth charges carried in nacelle bays.
Performance: max. speed 200 mph [215 mph], cruise 147 mph; ceiling 20,200 ft. [21,000 ft.]; range 2,590 mi. [2,480 mi.] (normal), 3,424 mi. [2,700 mi.] (max.)
Weights: 24,143 lbs. [32,803 lbs.] empty, 41,139 lbs. [56,000 lbs.] normal gross, 56,000 lbs. [60,000 lbs.] max takeoff.
Dimensions: span 118 ft. 0 in., length 77 ft. 2 in. [79 ft. 10 in.], wing area 1,400 sq. ft.

The Martin PBM, in terms of general design and structure, was arguably the most advanced twin-engine flying boat of its day. But the real impetus behind the design had been economic: faced with financial losses on the M130 and dismal prospects for commercial sales, Martin had little choice but return to the highly competitive arena of military patrol boat contracts. Since Consolidated commanded such a strong position in the twin-engine market with its PBY, Martin sought to interest the Navy in a proposal for a larger, four-engine patrol boat listed as the model 160. Coincidentally, BuAer had already contracted for two other four-engine flying boat prototypes (see Consolidated XPB2Y-1 and the Sikorsky XPBS-1), and Martin hoped to insert itself into the eventual competition for a production contract. As an unsolicited private venture, however, Martin would be obliged to fund development of a prototype, which it was in no position to do; instead the company

PBM-3, first major production variant, featured a hull stretch, lengthened engine nacelles, enlarged weapons bays, and fixed stabilizing floats. It was produced in four major sub-variants until it was superseded by the PBM-5 in 1944.

Martin XPBM-1 in original configuration, as seen in 1939 with straight horizontal stabilizer. Testing revealed a tail flutter problem that was remedied by adding dihedral to the horizontal stabilizers, thus producing the "pinwheel" tail.

planned to build a one-fourth (25%) scale flying demonstrator that would validate the main characteristics of the design. When BuAer declined to consider another four-engine project, Martin went back to the drawing boards and returned in early 1937 with an all-new proposal for the twin-engine model 162, which the company promised would deliver substantially better speed, range, and payload than the twin-engine PBY. Consolidated's president, Reuben Fleet, disputed Martin's performance claims and threatened the Navy with political repercussions if his company lost a production contract. As a compromise, BuAer awarded Martin a development contract the following June for a single XPBM-1 prototype with the understanding that future production plans would hinge on test results.

Timing was critical: construction of the XPBM-1 prototype would take eighteen months or longer, and Martin feared this interval might give Consolidated the opportunity to introduce an

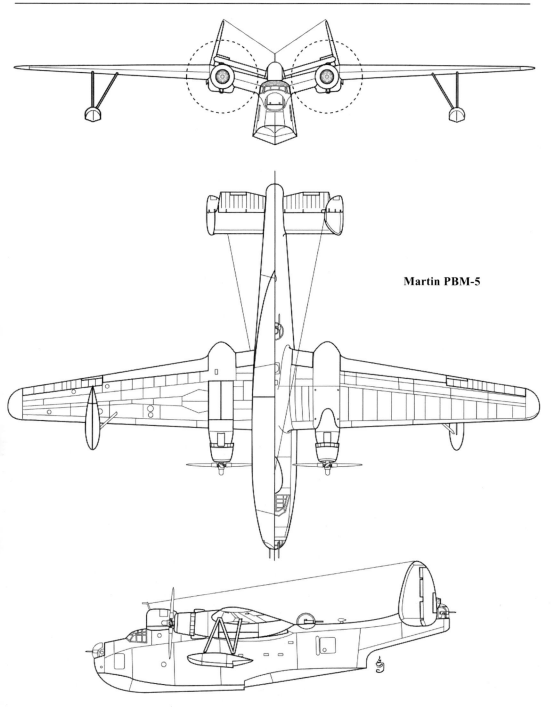

Martin PBM-5

altogether new twin-engine prototype (i.e., Consolidated Model 3l/P4Y). To speed progress, Martin's engineering staff reworked the plan for the M160 demonstrator into a three-eighths scale
(37.5%) replica of the XPBM-1, and as the M162A, had it flying before the end of the year. Despite
receiving a production contract for twenty-one PBM-1s in late December 1937, which had achieved
the main purpose of a demonstrator, Martin continued the M162A test program and in doing so,
obtained much valuable data subsequently incorporated into the final arrangement of the XPBM-1
hull.

The amphibious PBM-5A, as seen here, was initially tested in the late wartime period, but all production models were produced in 1948 and 1949. A few PBM-5As were active in the Dutch Navy until 1960.

When rolled-out for its first flight on February 18, 1939, the XPBM-1 represented a state-of-the-art flying boat concept. The design attained new levels of aerodynamic efficiency by mounting the fully-cantilevered wings to the upper hull in a gull configuration which raised the engines well above the sea-spray without need for drag-inducing struts or pylons. Aft of the rear step, the hull curved upward to support a high-mounted twin-fin empennage designed to provide adequate directional stability and single-engine control when needed. To keep the airframe clean, droppable munitions were housed in enclosed nacelle bays and the stabilizing floats folded into the wings so that only one side remained exposed to the slipstream. A tail flutter problem revealed in early testing was cured by adding an amount of dihedral to the horizontal stabilizers that matched the gull angle of the inner wings, thereby giving the type its distinctive "pinwheel" tail. Performance trials indicated a 17-mph increase in top speed over the PBY-4, but the real difference was that the PBM-1 would go thirty percent further carrying twice the load of bombs or depth charges. And defensive armament was the most formidable yet seen on any twin-engine patrol boat: powered nose and dorsal turrets each armed with a .50-calibre machine gun, flexible .50-calibre guns in two waist positions and in the tail, plus a .30-calibre tunnel gun firing downward in the aft fuselage.

Even as deliveries of the first PBM-1s began during the fall of 1940, the Navy was making plans for unheard of levels of aircraft production. Between November 1940 and August 1941, as part of the buildup, Martin received a series of contracts for 379 aircraft to be delivered as the PBM-3. The sole XPBM-2, a long-range version with increased fuel tankage and stressed for catapult launches (similar in concept to the Boeing XPBB-1 reported on page 88), was tested but never placed in production. The first major version, the PBM-3, featured 1,700-hp R-2600-12 engines, a two-foot eight-inch hull stretch, lengthened nacelles with larger weapons bays, enlarged strut-braced stabilizing floats for improved water handling, and an 11,000-lb. increase in takeoff weight. Soon after the U.S. entered World War II, total PBM-3s on order rose to 677 aircraft. Initial deliveries commenced in the spring of 1942, and over the next two years, PBM-3s were produced in four principal variants. A single example, fitted with a large radome that housed an APS-15 search radar, was tested as the XPBM-3E. Thirty-one of the first PBM-3s accepted were subsequently modified

Postwar PBM-5 shown in overall glossy sea blue paint scheme. The -5s formed a major part of the Navy's Patrol forces until the mid–1950s and also served with the Coast Guard until 1958.

by the Navy as PBM-3R over-ocean transports after being stripped of armament and armor and given strengthened floors, and a further eighteen were completed as transports at the factory. The 274 PBM-3Cs delivered from mid–1942 to mid–1943 came standard with four-bladed propellers, radomes (empty initially; radar sets installed as they became available), and an additional .50-calibre gun added to the bow, dorsal, and tail turrets. Thirty-two PBM-3Cs allocated to Great Britain began entering service in mid–1943 as the *Mariner* G.R.1, thus giving the type its official name; twenty were later returned to the Navy and twelve transferred to the Royal Australian Air Force. From July to October 1943, production shifted to ninety-four PBM-3S antisubmarine variants, which were completed without armor or powered gun turrets in order to achieve a twenty-five percent increase in patrol range. An upgrade to 1,900-hp R-2600-22 engines and self-sealing fuel tanks, plus restoration of armor and powered turrets, resulted in the introduction of the PBM-3D in October 1943, and 259 examples had been accepted by June 1944. Starting in late 1943, twenty-seven PBM-3s, mostly the lighter -3S version, were assigned to the Coast Guard, where they were used primarily for search and rescue operations.

Despite the uprated engines of the -3D, the PBM was still considered underpowered at high takeoff weights under certain conditions. The need for more power had been recognized back in mid–1941, when the Navy ordered 180 R-3350-powered versions as the PBM-4; however, this plan had to be abandoned once it became clear all R-3350 engines would be allocated to B-29 production. As an alternative, two PBM-3 airframes were refitted with 2,100-hp Pratt & Whitney R-2800-34 engines in early 1944 and tested as the XPBM-5. Flight trials indicated improved takeoff and climb performance, as well as a 12-mph increase in top speed, though range was slightly reduced. All production shifted to the PBM-5 in mid–1944, with 592 having been completed by the time the war ended, and a further 137 being delivered by June 1947. From late 1944 through 1945, forty-one examples lacking armament were delivered to the Coast Guard as the PBM-5G. Thirty-four postwar amphibious variants, the PBM-5A, were manufactured from April 1948 to March 1949, ending all PBM production.

PBM-1s initially became operational during the fall of 1940 with VP-55 and VP-56, based at Norfolk, Virginia, then after combining as VP-74 in mid–1941, moved to a new base in Bermuda. Using newly installed British radar, a PBM-1 of VP-74 attacked and sank a German U-Boat on June 30, 1942. Due in part to the U-Boat threat, converted PBM-3Rs were rushed into Navy service in 1942 to transport essential military personnel and supplies over routes in the mid and south Atlantic, and later saw extensive service in the southwest Pacific area while operating from bases in Australia. As deliveries continued throughout 1942 and 1943, PBM-3Cs and -3Ss went on to equip seventeen Navy patrol squadrons in the Atlantic and were credited with sinking ten U-boats by the end of 1943. More importantly, patrolling PBMs effectively protected thousands of tons of merchant shipping by simply keeping the marauding submarine packs submerged, away from the convoy lanes. In the Pacific Theater, where the submarine threat was less serious, armed PBMs flew long-range reconnaissance, often attacking targets of opportunity along the enemy-held coasts. In the anti-ship role, primarily in night operations dubbed "nightmares," PBMs laden with bombs or torpedoes flew air strikes against Japanese shipping targets. As PBM-5s became available during the latter half of 1944, most were sent to reequip Navy combat units in the Pacific Theater. Like their PBY counterparts, PBMs assigned to patrol units in various combat zones were often called upon to perform other duties such as air-sea rescue, medical evacuation, and transportation.

Remaining PBM-3s were withdrawn almost as soon as the war ended, while PBM-5s continued to form an important component of the Navy's maritime patrol strength well into the post-war era. Some PBM-5s received modifications that enabled them to perform new roles: a few aircraft fitted with ECM equipment for electronic surveillance were re-designated PBM-5E; a number of lightened versions, configured especially for antisubmarine patrol, became the PBM-5S (the PBM-5S2 also included a 50-million candlepower searchlight); and one equipped with special instruments for night/all-weather operations was tested as the PBM-5N. Post-war improvements given to most active PBM-5s included APS-15 radar sets characterized by smaller, teardrop radomes, plus the installation of RATO, a system of four rockets attached to sides of the aft hull which dramatically improved takeoff performance. Once the Korean War started in June 1950, five squadrons of PBM-5s, which included three called-up reserve units, were deployed to fly convoy patrol missions along the Korean coastline and in the Sea of Japan. Virtually all PBM-5s were phased-out of Navy service during the mid–1950s, succeeded in many instances by newer Martin P5Ms (see Part III, above). The Coast Guard operated its PBM-5Gs a while longer, not retiring the final example until 1958.

Small numbers of ex–Navy PBMs were supplied to foreign navies during the 1950s. Seventeen PBM-5As were transferred to the Dutch Navy, where they were operated in the East Indies around New Guinea from 1955 to 1960. Eight PBM-5s went to Argentina and three to Uruguay, a few of which are thought to have remained active until the mid–1960s. Only small numbers of PBMs made it into civilian hands. A company named Flying Lobster Transport used a PBM-5 to fly live lobsters from Maine to New York during the late 1940s. Five or six surplus PBM-5s were acquired to haul cargo by a Columbian firm in the late 1940s but reportedly ceased operations after a year. Today, only one complete example remains, an unrestored PBM-5A owned by the Smithsonian Institution, which is currently being held in storage at the Pima County Airport in Tucson, Arizona. The nose section of one PBM-5 is preserved at the Air Force Association Museum in Western Australia.

Martin PB2M Mars (1942)

TECHNICAL SPECIFICATIONS (XPB2M-1)

Type: 11-place long-range naval patrol boat; 40 to 133-passenger military transport.
Total produced: 1
Powerplants: four 2,200-hp Wright R-3350-8 *Double Cyclone* 18-cylinder air-cooled radial engines driving three-bladed, electric controllable-pitch laminated wooden propellers (XPB2M-1R refitted with metal propellers).
Armament: one .30-calibre machine gun each in nose, dorsal, waist, and tail turrets and up to 10,000 lbs. of bombs, torpedoes, or depth charges carried in two upper hull bays.
Performance: max. speed 221 mph, cruise 149 mph; ceiling 14,600 ft.; range 4,375 mi. max.
Weights: 75,573 lbs. empty, 144,000 lbs. gross.
Dimensions: span 200 ft. 0 in., length 117 ft. 3 in., wing area 3,683 sq. ft

The Martin XPB2M-1 in 1942, soon after its first flight, July 1942. At the time it flew it was the largest flying boat in the world. By then, however, the Navy had abandoned the "Sky Dreadnought" concept in favor of more carriers.

The third of four "Sky Dreadnoughts" to be considered by the Navy (see also Consolidated PB2Y [Consolidated PB3Y, Appendix B, page 341] and Sikorsky PBS), preliminary design work on the Martin model 170 began in 1937 while the XPBM-1 was under construction. When presenting the proposal to BuAer in early 1938, Glenn L. Martin characterized the ambitious project as a veritable flying battleship, able to defend itself while delivering a 10,000-lb. bomb load to attack targets well beyond America's frontiers. On August 23, 1938, naval officials were sufficiently interested to award the company a contract to build a single prototype as the XPB2M-1. Though considerably larger, the structural, aerodynamic, and hull design of the XPB2M-1 was similar in most respects to that of the XPBM-1, and its final configuration owed much to the data accumulated from the XPBM-1 test program. Rather than nacelle bays, munitions were stored in two hull compartments located just below the wings from which weapons would be deployed on sliding racks. Due to an unprecedented production schedule (i.e., B-26 bombers for the Army; *Maryland* and *Baltimore* bombers on foreign contracts), Martin was unable to begin construction of the prototype until mid–1940. The giant aircraft was christened "Mars" in line with Martin's practice of choosing names starting with the letter M.

The completed XPB2M-1 was rolled-out out of the Martin factory and launched in the Middle River for taxi tests during the first week of November 1941, but within days, the program suffered a critical setback when the number three engine threw a propeller blade and caught fire. The starboard wing and number three nacelle sustained serious damage from the fire, and the hull was damaged where the propeller blade penetrated. It took Martin over six months to complete repairs, and the first flight of the XPB2M-1 did not occur until July 2, 1942. It was the largest flying boat

The Mars prototype in 1943 following conversion to a long-range transport as the XPB2M-1R. Production plans remained on hold until mid–1944, when the Navy ordered 20 JRM-1s.

to have flown and the second largest aircraft in the world (the Douglas XB-19 of 1941 being fractionally larger). But in the interval, the Navy had discarded the notion of the Sky Dreadnought in favor of acquiring huge numbers of twin-engine flying boats (i.e., PBYs and PBMs) to accomplish the patrol function, effectively leaving the big *Mars* without a combat role. At the same time, the enormous danger posed to Allied shipping by German U-Boats dictated the need for very large, transoceanic air transports; thus, in early 1943, it was no surprise when BuAer directed Martin to remove all armament and associated bombing equipment from the *Mars* prototype and modify it as a transport under the new designation XPB2M-1R. Industrialist Henry J. Kaiser reportedly offered to license-build the *Mars* by the hundreds; however, Glenn L. Martin was reluctant to share production rights, causing Kaiser to ultimately join forces with Howard Hughes.

Martin completed factory testing of the XPB2M-1R in mid–1943 and delivered it to the Navy for operational trials and crew training. Meanwhile, the U-Boat threat had diminished to the extent that the Navy was fast abandoning the idea of moving large amounts of war material by air rather than by sea. Any plans to place the *Mars* in production were again on hold; the single XPB2M-1R was turned over to VR-2, a regular Naval Air Transportation Service (NATS) unit operating out of NAS Alameda, California, where it began making regular cargo runs between the West Coast and Hawaii.

During the first half of 1944, however, naval officials came to the conclusion that limited numbers of long-range, over-ocean air transports would be needed to support the invasion of Japan, and in June the same year, Martin received a contract to manufacture twenty new transport versions of the *Mars* under the designation JRM-1 (reported in Part III, page 254.) The XPB2M-1R, now affectionately known as the "Old Lady," continued to accrue an impressive record with VR-2, routinely hauling over ten tons of freight (i.e., over twice the average payload of a PB2Y or Douglas C-54) over the California-Hawaii run. Toward the close of its flying career, the XPB2M-1 was used to train the VR-2 aircrews that would be transitioning to the new JRM-1s. The aircraft finally ended its days at NATC Patuxent in Maryland, where it was used for maintenance training until 1949.

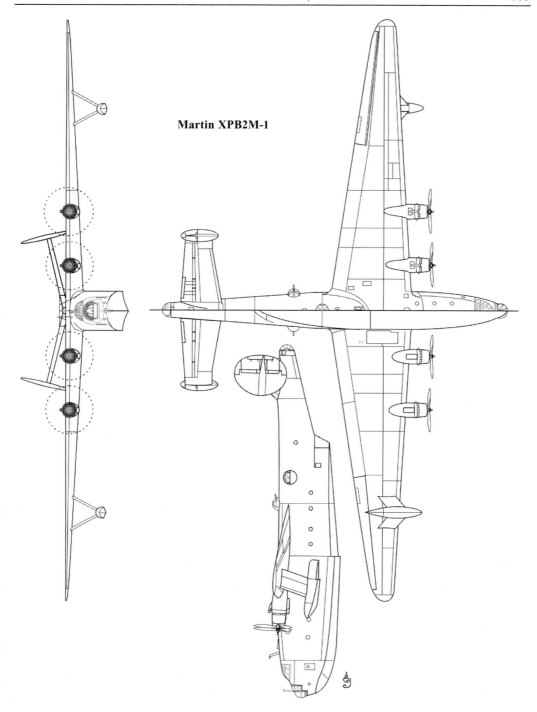

Martin XPB2M-1

Naval Aircraft Factory

The Naval Aircraft Factory's role in flying boat development diminished rapidly during the decade of the 1930s, with most of the emphasis being shifted to large manufacturers like Consolidated, Martin, and Sikorsky. As Naval Aviation began its massive expansion in the years just prior to World War II, NAF returned to its original role of supplementing the production of private contractors by license-building aircraft like the PBN-1 (see Consolidated PBY, page 96).

Naval Aircraft Factory P4N (PN-11) (1928)

TECHNICAL SPECIFICATIONS (XP4N-1)

Type: 5-place naval patrol boat.

Total produced: 5

Powerplants: two 575-hp Wright R-1820-64 *Cyclone* 9-cylinder air-cooled radial engines driving three-bladed, ground adjustable metal propellers.

Armament: one flexible .30-calibre machine gun in bow, one flexible .30-calibre machine gun in rear cockpit, and up to 920 lbs. of bombs in underwing racks.

Performance: max. speed 115 mph; ceiling 9,000 ft.; range 1,510 mi. normal, 1,930 mi. max.

Weights: 9,770 lbs. empty, 17,900 lbs. normal gross, 20,340 lbs. max. takeoff.

Dimensions: span 72 ft. 10 in., length 54 ft. 0 in., wing area 1,154 sq. ft.

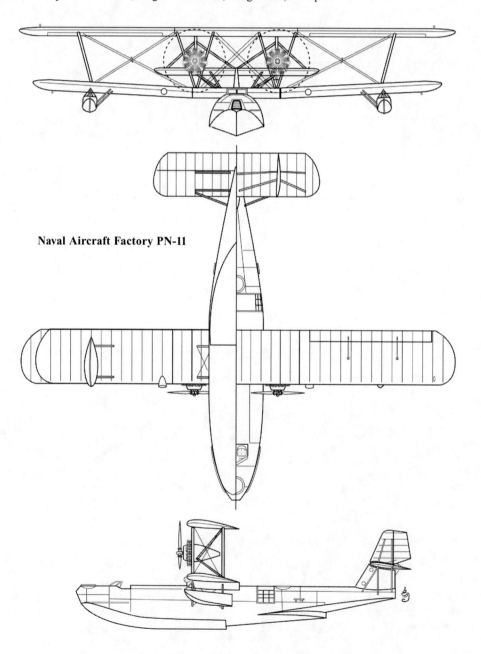

Naval Aircraft Factory PN-11

The PN-11/XP4N-1 was a hybrid design, incorporating a narrower hull and twin-fin empennage with the biplane wings of the PN-12. The new hull shape became a key element in the designs of the PY/P2Y and P2M/P3M.

The PN-11 and P4N represented an effort to achieve better performance by combining a more streamlined hull with the biplane wings and powerplants of the PN-12. (Note that the PN-12 actually preceded the PN-11 by a year.) Since its introduction on the Curtiss H series in 1915, nearly every large Navy flying boat had been designed with some variation of the Porte sponson-type hull. Comparatively, the new hull was longer, deeper in profile, and approximately thirty percent narrower in beam. The chief advance expected was not speed but improved hydrodynamic efficiency allowing higher takeoff weights, which corresponded to more fuel and range. The new hull also introduced a new empennage arrangement featuring twin fins and rudders on top of a high-mounted horizontal stabilizer. In 1927 BuAer ordered two aircraft with the new hull as the PN-11, and the first, powered by 525-hp Pratt & Whitney R-1690 *Hornet* engines, was flown in October 1928, and the second, with 525-hp Wright *Cyclones*, in June 1929. Trials indicated that the PN-11, with the same takeoff power as the PN-12, had picked up a 2,500-lb. increase in useful load that could be translated to a 600-mile improvement in range.

BuAer placed an order in mid–1929 for three similar aircraft as the XP2N, but changed the designation to XP4N-1 before the first example was accepted in December 1930. The XP4N-1 was virtually identical to the PN-11, while the other two, both completed in March 1932 as the XP4N-2s, carried an extra 150 gallons of fuel that raised takeoff weight by 1,250 lbs. Although the PN-11s and P4Ns never served operationally, the new hull became a key element of new monoplane patrol boats like the XPY/P2Y and P2M/P3M.

Sikorsky Aviation Division of United Aircraft Corp.

Igor Sikorsky's company reached its peak as a designer and manufacturer of flying boats in the 1930s. In many ways the flying boats were simply a means that enabled Sikorsky to pursue his life long dream of developing a truly practical helicopter. In 1939 the operation was renamed Vought-Sikorsky Division, and the model numbers of Sikorsky designed aircraft were thereafter preceded by VS. Today, as one of the world's largest manufacturers of helicopters, the company exists as Sikorsky Aircraft Corp., a wholly owned subsidiary of United Technologies Corp. Founder Igor I. Sikorsky died in 1972.

Sikorsky S-39 (1930)

TECHNICAL SPECIFICATIONS (S-39-A/B)

Type: 5-passenger civil amphibian.

Total produced: 21 (all versions)

Powerplant: one 300-hp Pratt & Whitney R-985 *Wasp Junior* 9-cylinder air-cooled radial engines driving a two-bladed, ground adjustable metal propeller.

Performance: max. speed 115 mph, cruise 97 mph; ceiling 18,000 ft.; range 375 mi.

Weights: 2,678 lbs. empty, 4,000 lbs. gross.

Dimensions: span 52 ft. 0 in., length 31 ft. 11 in., wing area 320 sq. ft.

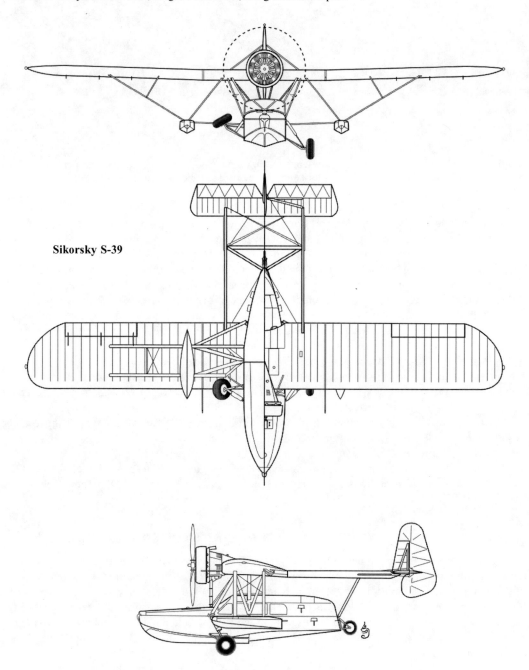

Sikorsky S-39

N887W, shown here, was one of 13 aircraft completed by Sikorsky during 1929 and 1930 as the S-39-A, powered by a 300-hp version of the *Wasp*. Most were later modified with larger rudders and upgraded engines.

Following the success of the S-38 (see Part I, page 73), Sikorsky down-scaled the basic elements of its design to create the smaller S-39. It was apparently intended for the emerging executive transport market as well as air-taxi operators in coastal regions. The original S-39 prototype, completed with two 115-hp tractor-mounted Cirrus *Hermes* inline engines, was test flown in mid–1929 but crashed later in the year during an attempt to recover from the loss of one engine. Sikorsky enjoyed better success with the S-39-A, flown in early 1930 with a single R-985 *Wasp Junior* engine mounted directly to the wing. (Interestingly, the S-39-A was the first U.S. aircraft to be certificated with the R-985, which became one of the most widely used radial engines in the world.) Despite the onset of the Depression, twelve S-39-As, marketed at an average price of $17,500, were sold to civil owners by the end of 1930. The S-39-B, introduced in 1931 with a larger fin and rudder, resulted in six more private sales plus one example to the U.S. Army Air Corps as the Y1C-28. Two S-39-Bs refitted with 400-hp R-1340 *Wasp* engines were subsequently re-certified as S-39-Cs. The final example produced, an S-39-CS Special named the "Spirit of Africa," was built in 1932 to the order of Martin and Osa Johnson, well-known explorers and photographers. Appearing in a distinctive giraffe paint scheme, the Spirit of Africa logged more than 60,000 miles of exploratory flights across Africa and the East Indies. Several civilian S-39s were operated by the Civil Air Patrol during World War II on search and rescue missions, and one of these, restored to its wartime CAP markings, is presently on display at the New England Air Museum at Windsor Locks, Connecticut. The only known flyable example, an S-39-B registered as NC50V, was repainted in the colors of the Spirit of Africa while undergoing a complete restoration and is presently listed for sale at www.spiritofigor.com.

Sikorsky S-40 (1931)

TECHNICAL SPECIFICATIONS (S-40-A)

Type: 32-passenger civil amphibian.
Total produced: 3
Powerplants: four 660-hp Pratt & Whitney R-1690-44 *Hornet* 9-cylinder air-cooled radial engines driving two-bladed, ground adjustable metal propellers.
Performance: max. speed 140 mph, cruise 120 mph; ceiling 13,000 ft.; range 900 mi.
Weights: 21,000 lbs. empty, 34,000 lbs. gross.
Dimensions: span 114 ft. 0 in., length 76 ft. 8 in., wing area 1,740 sq. ft.

The first S-40, the *American Clipper*, probably in late 1931. This aircraft departed Miami for the Canal Zone on November 19, 1931, with Charles A. Lindbergh at the controls.

Head-on view of S-40 in displacement taxi. All S-40s were fully amphibious, but the wheels could be removed, optionally, to reduce weight and drag.

The ultimate development of the aerodynamic and structural concept that began with the S-34 in 1926, the S-40, at the time it flew, was not only the largest amphibian in the world but the largest civil aircraft of any type in the United States. Since Pan American Airways had used the S-36 to perform its Caribbean surveys and S-38s to establish Caribbean service, it is not surprising that the airline turned to Sikorsky for the design of a flying boat large enough to span the planned routes extending to South America. Minimally, the aircraft would need to have the range to carry passen-

The *American Clipper* outbound in early 1930s. When it flew, the S-40 was the largest amphibian in the world and the largest type of civil aircraft in the Unites States.

gers and mail over the 600-mile over-water segment between Jamaica and the Panama Canal Zone. On December 20, 1929, Pan American awarded a contract to build three aircraft as the S-40, with deliveries starting in mid–1931. To lift the S-40's projected sixteen tons of mass, Sikorsky determined that a four engine layout would be necessary, a feature not seen on an American flying boat since the Curtiss NC-4. Its two-step all-metal hull, divided into seven watertight compartments and almost sixty feet in length, was wider than a Pullman railway car, providing spacious accommodations for up to thirty-two passengers. The engine mounts, tail booms, and empennage of the S-40 followed a configuration analogous to the S-38, but Sikorsky selected a pure monoplane layout for the wing with stabilizing floats mounted to outrigger booms in the same fashion as the Consolidated Commodore.

Flight testing of the first S-40 began in early 1931, and it was delivered to Pan American the following October, as soon as its ATC certificate was granted, where it was christened *American Clipper*, the very first. With the famous Charles A. Lindbergh at the controls, *American Clipper* inaugurated service when it departed Miami for the Canal Zone on November 19, 1931. It was joined by the second S-40, *Caribbean Clipper*, later the same year, then by the third, *Southern Clipper*, in early 1932. The three S-40s thereafter established regular airline service between the U.S. east coast and South American destinations such as Rio de Janeiro and Buenos Aires, taking the place of Consolidated Commodores on longer routes. S-40s, when the need arose, could be operated without their amphibious gear to achieve an improvement in range. During 1935, after all three of the aircraft were upgraded to supercharged *Hornet* engines, their designation was changed to S-40-A. By the end of 1939, the S-40-As had been withdrawn from service by Pan American, however, *Caribbean Clipper* later served with the Navy as a navigational trainer and is said to have amassed a total of 13,000 flying hours before being scrapped in 1944.

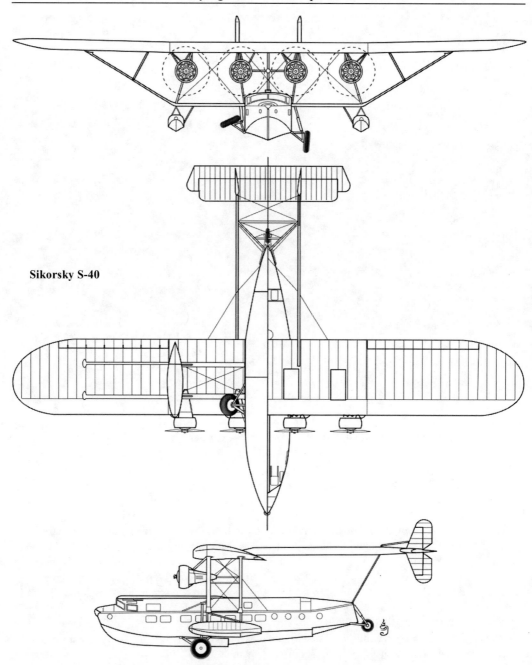

Sikorsky S-40

Sikorsky S-41 (RS) (1931)

TECHNICAL SPECIFICATIONS (S-41)

Type: 15-passenger civil amphibian.
Total produced: 6
Powerplants: two 575-hp Pratt & Whitney R-1690-34 *Hornet* 9-cylinder air-cooled radial engines driving two-bladed, ground adjustable metal propellers.
Performance: max. speed 133 mph, cruise 115 mph; ceiling 13,500 ft.; range 575 mi.
Weights: 8,100 lbs. empty, 13,800 lbs. gross.
Dimensions: span 78 ft. 9 in., length 45 ft. 2 in., wing area 790 sq. ft.

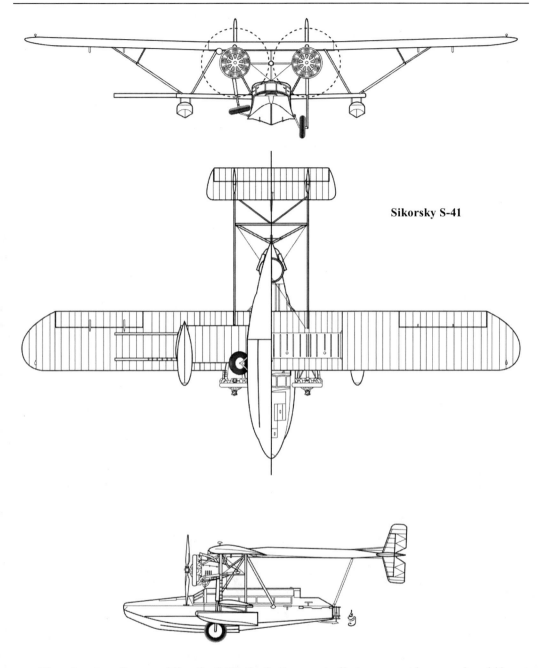

Sikorsky S-41

Though outwardly resembling the S-38, the S-41 was actually ten percent larger and could boast almost half again the useful load. Besides a five-foot lengthening of the hull plus bigger, fully-cowled *Hornet* engines, the S-41 discarded the lower sesquiplane layout of the S-38 for a single upper wing having ten percent more area. The first three S-41s were delivered to Pan American Airways in late 1931, where they were used in operations along the northeast U.S. coast and also between Miami and Cuba. Three more were delivered to the Navy during 1933 as RS-1 utility amphibians, with one being assigned to Marine Corps squadron VO-9M in Haiti. The chronology of the military designations can be misleading, in that the S-38s acquired by the Navy in the late 1920s as the PS-2 and -3 became the RS-2 and -3, while the four later impressed from Pan American became the RS-4 and -5.

The S-41 was 10 percent larger than the S-38 and could lift half again the useful load. This photograph depicts one of three RS-1s delivered to the Navy in 1933, one of which was subsequently assigned to the Marine Corps.

Sikorsky P2S (1932)

TECHNICAL SPECIFICATIONS (XP2S-1)

Type: 3-place naval patrol boat.
Total produced: 1
Powerplants: two 450-hp Pratt & Whitney R-1340-88 *Wasp* 9-cylinder air-cooled radial engines driving two-bladed, ground-adjustable metal propellers.
Armament: one flexible .30-calibre machine gun the bow, one flexible .30-calibre machine gun the rear cockpit, and up to 1,000 lbs. of bombs carried under the wings.
Performance: max. speed 124 mph; ceiling 13,900 ft.; range (not reported).
Weights: 6,040 lbs. empty, 9,745 lbs. gross.
Dimensions: span 56 ft. 0 in., length 44 ft. 2 in., wing area 762 sq. ft.

Sole prototype XP2S-1, delivered to NAS Anacostia in June 1932. After a year of trials, the Navy decided not to pursue the small patrol boat concept and cancelled development.

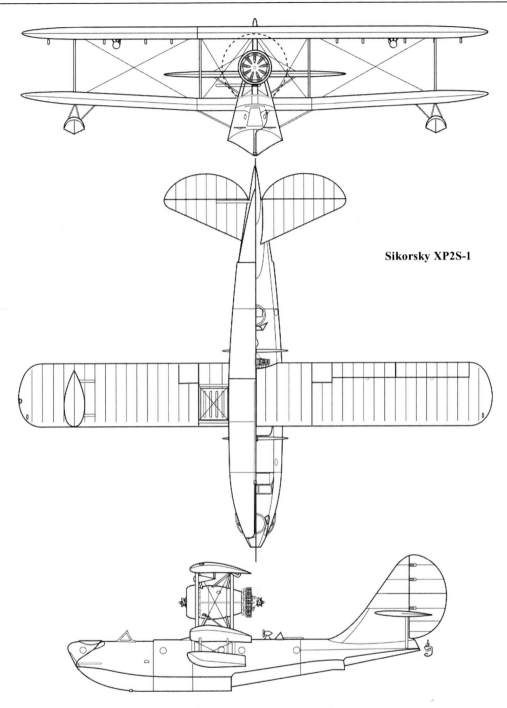

Sikorsky XP2S-1

After selling one S-36 and four S-38s to the Navy between 1927 and 1929 (see Part I, pages 71–73), Sikorsky endeavored to interest BuAer in a dedicated patrol bomber having a more conventional biplane layout and a full-length hull supporting the tail group. Sikorsky received a development contract in mid–1930 to build one prototype as the XP2S-1, but did not deliver a completed aircraft to NAS Anacostia, Maryland, for testing until June of 1932, nearly two years later. Using an all-metal hull similar in shape to that of the Hall PH-1, the XP2S-1 appeared to as a two-bay, equal-span biplane with its two *Wasp* engines mounted in a tandem configuration. Overall performance was on a par with the larger biplane patrol boats of that era, though its range was not revealed. After approximately one year of official trials, the Navy cancelled the project.

Sikorsky SS (1933)

TECHNICAL SPECIFICATIONS (XSS-2)

Type: 2-place naval patrol boat.
Total produced: 1
Powerplants: one 550-hp Pratt & Whitney R-1340-12 *Wasp* 9-cylinder air-cooled radial engines driving a
    two-bladed, ground-adjustable metal propeller.
Armament: one flexible .30-calibre machine gun in the observer's position.
Performance: max. speed 159 mph; ceiling 22,600 ft.; range 618 mi.
Weights: 3,274 lbs. empty, 4,526 lbs. normal gross, 4,790 lbs. max. takeoff.
Dimensions: span 42 ft. 0 in., length 33 ft. ½ in., wing area 285 sq. ft.

The Sikorsky SS appeared as the last of three amphibian designs (see Great Lakes SG and Loening S2L, above) to be considered as possible replacements for conventional floatplanes aboard Navy cruisers. In addition to adequate scouting range, the requirement specified that the aircraft be stressed for catapult launches and small enough, with wings folded, to fit within the confines of existing cruiser hangars (i.e., a width of 14 feet 6 inches). Compared to his rivals, Sikorsky emerged with a remarkably modern aeronautical concept: a very streamlined two-step hull of all-metal semi-monocoque construction with monoplane wings that were raised above the spray in a gull configuration. The single *Wasp* engine, contained in a clean cowling-nacelle combination, was strut-mounted between the V of the wings. In stowed position, the wings folded back from the gull break to rest against the tail fin. The aircraft employed a Grumman-type amphibious landing gear and per

The XSS-2 was the last of the three amphibious cruiser scouts (see Great Lakes SG and Loening S2L) evaluated by the Navy in 1932 and 1933 and the only monoplane. All were ultimately deemed unsatisfactory.

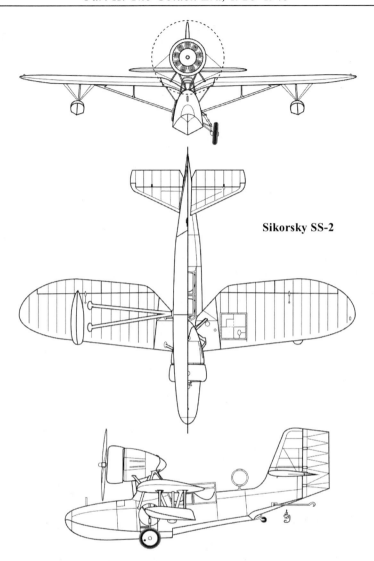

Sikorsky SS-2

specification, came with a tailhook to permit arrested landings aboard carriers. Sikorsky delivered the XSS-1 prototype to Anacostia sometime in 1933, and following modifications, it was subsequently evaluated as the XSS-2. Though its range was similar to the XSG-1 and XS2L-1, the XSS-2 demonstrated itself to be 50 mph faster with a much better rate-of-climb. In the interval, however, the Navy had decided to abandon the amphibian idea in favor of new types of cruiser-based floatplanes, and thus no production of the XSS-2 was ordered.

Sikorsky S-42 (1934)

TECHNICAL SPECIFICATIONS (S-42-A)

Type: 32-passenger civil flying boat transport.
Total produced: 10
Powerplants: four 750-hp Pratt & Whitney R-1690-52 *Hornet* 9-cylinder air-cooled radial engines driving three-bladed, variable-pitch metal propellers.
Performance: max. speed 188 mph, cruise 165 mph; ceiling 16,500 ft.; range 1,200 mi.
Weights: 24,000 lbs. empty, 38,000 lbs. gross.
Dimensions: span 114 ft. 2 in., length 68 ft. 0 in., wing area 1,340 sq. ft.

The first S-42, NC822M *Brazilian Clipper*, which entered service in August 1934. Compared the S-40, the S-42 cruised 40 mph faster while carrying the same number of passengers.

Design work on the S-42 actually began in 1931 in response to a Pan American Airways requirement, issued to Martin and Sikorsky, respectively, calling for a flying boat design that possessed transatlantic range. Then in 1933, for purely diplomatic reasons, Sikorsky's requirement was changed to encompass routes to South America. In order to achieve the performance required of the new S-42, Sikorsky made a bold departure from his previous designs to come up with an entirely new two-step hull and a semi-cantilevered wing supported by a streamlined pylon and lift struts only on the sides. More drag was eliminated by mounting the engines directly on the wings in tight cowlings that blended into streamlined nacelles, and the flying boat's full-length hull permitted a far cleaner twin-fin empennage arrangement on a pylon raising it out of the spray. Structure of the airframe was all aluminum except for fabric covering on the ailerons, tail surfaces, and the wing area aft of the main spars. In 1933, after the design was settled, Pan American ordered three S-42s, to be powered by the current 700-hp versions of the *Hornet* engine. The maiden flight of the first S-42 took place on March 29, 1934, and after being christened *Brazilian Clipper* the following August, the aircraft entered service on the Miami–Rio de Janeiro route. It was soon followed by *West Indies Clipper* the same year, but the third S-42 (NC824M) was destroyed in 1935 at Port of Spain, Trinidad, before being named.

Once in service, the two S-42s proved to have far better performance than any other flying boat operated by Pan American at the time. They were not only 40 mph faster than S-40s in cruise configuration, but fully loaded, could still post a range of 750 miles. Pan American liked the design well enough to place an order in 1934 for four improved S-42-As. With 750-hp supercharged *Hornet* engines, cruise speed rose 15 mph, and the addition of a trailing-edge flap kept takeoff and landing speeds within limits. All four S-42-As entered operational service on South American routes during 1935 and 1936 as *Jamaica Clipper, Antilles Clipper, Colombian Clipper,* and *Dominican Clipper.* In the spring of 1935, *Brazilian Clipper* was temporarily removed from regular service and refitted with long-range tanks to perform survey flights for the Pacific routes that would be undertaken by the Martin M130 later in the year. As Pan American's operations expanded in 1935

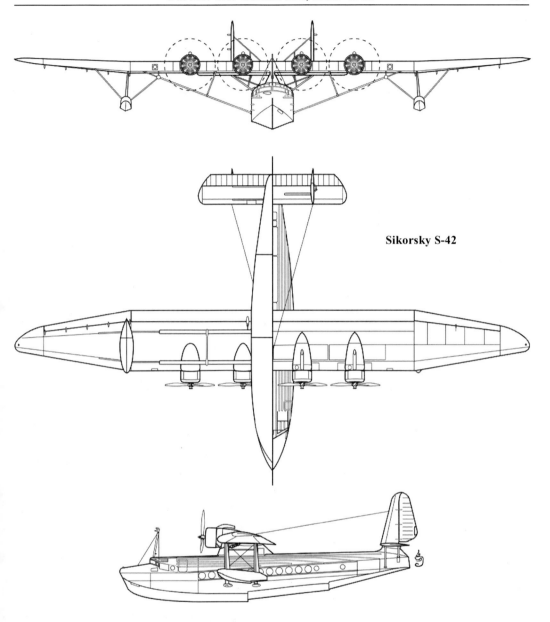

Sikorsky S-42

and 1936, Sikorsky received orders for three extended range (1,900 mi.) S-42-Bs featuring four additional feet of wingspan, greater fuel capacity, and small refinements to the hull. The first, as *Pan American Clipper II* (later renamed *Samoan Clipper*), after making a survey flight to New Zealand in early 1937, entered service on the Manila–Hong Kong extension. *Bermuda Clipper* (later renamed *Alaska Clipper,* then *Hong Kong Clipper II*), the second S-42-B, opened Pan American's New York-Bermuda service in June 1937; the last S-42-B, as *Pan American Clipper III*, commenced South American operations in mid–1937, then as the second *Bermuda Clipper*, took over the New York-Bermuda route in 1940.

Two S-42-As, *Samoan Clipper* in 1938 and *Dominican Clipper* in 1941, were accidentally destroyed prior to the U.S. entering World War II; S-42-B *Hong Kong Clipper II* was lost during the Japanese invasion of Hong Kong in December 1941; S-42-B, the second *Bermuda Clipper*, crashed at Manaus Brazil in 1943; and S-42 *West Indies Clipper* sank at Antilla, Cuba, in 1944. During the war, the American government never impressed Pan American's S-42s into military serv-

**The Last S-42-B, the *Pan American Clipper III*, delivered in mid–1937. The -Bs featured more pow-
erful engines, extended wingspan, and greater fuel capacity. The last examples were retired by Pan
American in 1946.**

ice, and the four surviving examples continued in airline operations until early 1946 and were
scrapped soon afterward.

Sikorsky S-43 (JRS, OA-8 and -11) (1935)

TECHNICAL SPECIFICATIONS (S-42)

Type: 15 to 19-passenger civil/military amphibious transport.
Total produced: 53
Powerplants: two 750-hp Pratt & Whitney R-1690-52 *Hornet* 9-cylinder air-cooled radial engines driving
    three-bladed, variable-pitch metal propellers.
Performance: max. speed 194 mph, cruise 167 mph; ceiling 20,700 ft.; range 775 mi.
Weights: 12,750 lbs. empty, 19,096 lbs. gross.
Dimensions: span 86 ft. 0 in., length 51 ft. 2 in., wing area 781 sq. ft.

Incorporating all the aerodynamic refinements seen on the S-42, plus a Grumman-type gear
retraction system, the S-43 was originally conceived to fulfill a Pan American Airways requirement
for a twin-engine amphibian that would replace Consolidated Commodores on secondary Latin
American routes. Due to its smaller size, the S-43 employed a single-step hull and a single-fin tail
group. The wing rested on a small center pylon, supported on either side by N-struts. Wing flaps
occupying forty-eight percent of the span reduced stall speed to a comfortable 65 mph, permitting
takeoffs and landings in tighter areas. After the type made its first flight in June 1935, the first of
fourteen S-43s delivered to Pan American entered Latin American service in April 1936, though
most were subsequently turned over to Panair do Brasil and other subsidiary operations. While
often referred to as the "Baby Clippers," none were assigned official names. In 1938 Pan American
used one of its S-43s to perform survey flights for planned route extensions into Alaska. Addition-
ally, four were sold to Inter-Island Airways in the Hawaiian Islands, four to Aéromaritime in West
Africa, and one to DNL-Norwegian Airlines. Twenty-two amphibians were delivered as S-43s, plus
one S-43-A and three S-43-Bs with minor detail changes. Two S-43s were custom built in 1937 as
personal transports, one to Howard Hughes and another to Harold Vanderbilt. Three delivered in
1937-1938 to Iliolo-Negros for inter-island operations in the Philippines were registered as S-43-
Ws with a one-foot fuselage extension and *Cyclone* engines, plus one as the S-43-WB without
amphibious landing gear.

Between 1937 and 1939, the Navy acquired seventeen S-43s that entered service as utility amphibians under the designation JRS-1, with two being assigned to the Marine Corps. During the same period, five were also delivered to the U.S. Army Air Corps as the Y1OA-8, and later, in 1942, a commercial S-43, after being reequipped with 875-hp R-1690-S2C engines, was impressed into USAAF service as the OA-11. Navy, Marine, and USAAF variants of the S-43 are reported to have

One of 14 S-43s delivered to Pan American in 1935 and 1936. Most were assigned to Latin American service, either with Panair do Brasil or other subsidiaries. Four others were sold to Inter-Island Airways in Hawaii.

Navy JRS-1, probably in 1937, shown before application of unit markings. The 15 Navy and two Marine Corps JRS-1s reportedly remained in service up through the end of World War II.

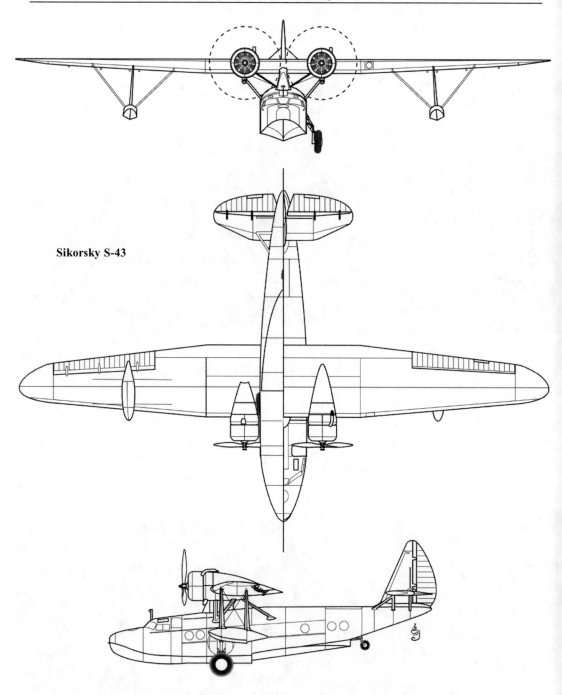

Sikorsky S-43

remained in service throughout most of World War II. One S-43 was sold to the Soviet Union and several ex–Pan American examples were used in Brazil to transport rubber along riverine routes. Reeve Aleutian Airways acquired an S-43, possibly ex–Pan American, which it operated in Alaska as late as the 1950s; another served with Avalon Air Transport, flying between Southern California and Catalina Island, until the early 1960s. At least two compete S-43s are known to exist today: one JRS-1 preserved in Marine Corps colors at the Pima Air Museum in Tucson, Arizona; and the S-43 once owned by billionaire Howard Hughes, which is reportedly still maintained in flying condition.

Sikorsky VS-44 (PBS, JR2S) (1937)

TECHNICAL SPECIFICATIONS (VS-44A)

Type: 24 to 47-passenger civil flying boat; naval patrol bomber.

Total produced: 4

Powerplants: four 1,200-hp Pratt & Whitney R-1830-S1C Twin Wasp 14-cylinder air-cooled radial engines driving three-bladed, constant-speed metal propellers.

Armament (XPBS-1 only): one 50-calibre machine in a bow turret, one flexible . 30-calibre machine gun in each waist position, and one 50-calibre machine in a tail turret (presumed to carry bomb load similar to PB2Y but no information available).

Performance: max. speed 210 mph, cruise 175 mph; ceiling 18,996 ft.; range 3,598 mi.

Weights: 26,407 lbs. empty, 48,540 lbs. normal gross, 57,500 max. takeoff.

Dimensions: span 124 ft. 0 in., length 79 ft. 3 in., wing area 1,670 sq. ft.

The first of the "Sky Dreadnoughts," the XPBS-1 as delivered in August 1937. In June 1942, after being assigned to transport duties, this aircraft was lost when it struck a log in San Francisco Bay and sank.

One of three VS-44As delivered to American Overseas Airways between January and June 1942. Soon afterward, they were impressed into Navy service as JR2S-1s.

The last of a long line of flying boats built by Igor Sikorsky, the S-44 (later VS-44) came into being as one of four "Flying Dreadnoughts" (see also Consolidated PB2Y and Martin PB2M, and Consolidated PB3Y, Appendix B, page 341) to be considered by the Navy between 1937 and 1942. When BuAer requested proposals for its ambitious four-engine project in early 1935, the competition was limited to Consolidated and Sikorsky initially; Martin came in three years later. From the start, because of the enormous expense involved (i.e., $300,000+ per aircraft, not including devel-

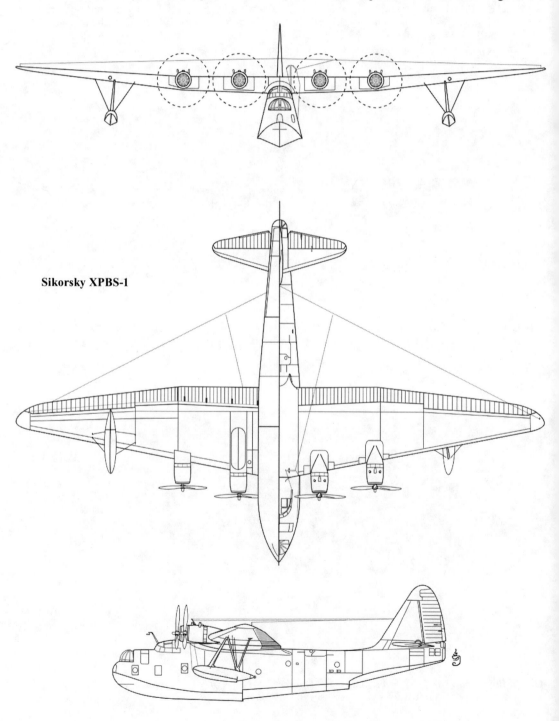

Sikorsky XPBS-1

opment cost), the Navy viewed the Flying Dreadnoughts as an experimental program, limited to single prototypes. Production, if undertaken, would be based upon extensive testing and operational evaluation. The S-44 was selected first, Sikorsky receiving a development contract in June 1935 to construct one prototype as the XPBS-1. As design work progressed, Sikorsky and his staff evolved an advanced flying boat concept that was both elegant and functional. While sharing some similarities with the earlier S-42, the XPBS-1 eliminated the need for supporting pylons or struts by employing a very deep, two-step hull which curved upward from the second step to raise the tail

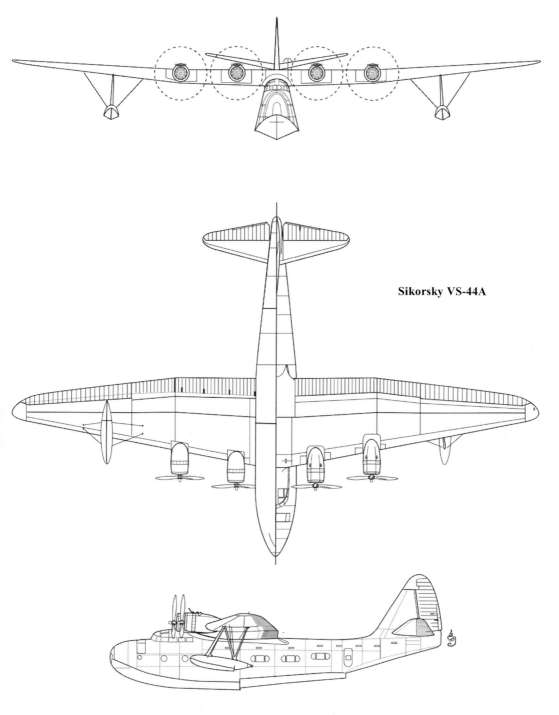

Sikorsky VS-44A

group clear of the sea-spray. Equally as innovative, the tapering, fully-cantilevered wing smoothly blended into the top of the hull and incorporated fully-articulated trailing flaps occupying fifty-five percent of the span.

After a two-year construction period, the XPBS-1 prototype completed its maiden flight on August 13, 1937. Initial testing (with the original 1,050-hp R-1830-68 engines) revealed a top speed of 227 mph and a loaded range well within design specifications (i.e., 3,000 miles+). Stability problems traced to the turbulence generated by the wings resulted in the addition of dihedral to the horizontal stabilizers. After being delivered to the Navy in October 1937, the XPBS-1 was joined by the Consolidated XPB2Y-1 in mid–1938, and extensive trials between the competing prototypes followed throughout the balance of the year. Even though the Navy officially accepted the XPBS-1 in January 1939, BuAer announced that Consolidated's entry had narrowly won the competition on a point basis and would be selected for limited production as the PB2Y-2. The XPBS-1 was thereafter assigned to Patrol Wing Five at NAS Norfolk, Virginia, where it was used to evaluate long-range patrol-bomber operations until shortly after the U.S. entered World War II. In the spring of 1942, the aircraft was reassigned to VR-2 out of NAS Alameda, California for transport duties between the West Coast and the Hawaiian Islands. On June 30, 1942, while returning from Pearl Harbor, the XPBS-1 struck a log in San Francisco Bay and sank. Included among the passengers and crew, all of whom safely escaped, was Admiral Chester W. Nimitz, Commander of the Pacific Fleet.

Given the very limited market for large, four-engine flying boats, efforts to continue development of the S-44 might have ended with loss of the Navy contract but for the intervention of American Export Airlines (AEA), a newly formed venture that was attempting to break Pan American's effective monopoly on Atlantic mail, cargo, and passenger routes. In December 1939, as a component of its plan, AEA approached Sikorsky (by then operating as the Vought-Sikorsky Division) with the proposition of creating a commercial variant of the S-44, with the option of acquiring three aircraft as the VS-44A. Six months later, after obtaining government approval to commence transatlantic operations, AEA exercised its option to purchase the three flying boats at a total cost of $2,100,000. Redesigned as a transport, the VS-44A could accommodate 32-passengers in day seating or 16 in sleeper berths, with the same amenities of a Pan American Clipper; but more important, it possessed a 3,100-mile range, fully-loaded, that would allow it to fly transatlantic routes nonstop.

The first VS-44A, christened *Excalibur*, made its first flight on January 17, 1942. The same month, due to the intervention of World War II, AEA contracted with the Naval Air Transportation Service (NATS) to provide wartime transatlantic service, and starting in May, *Excalibur* began making regular flights between New York City and Foynes, Ireland, with an intermediate stop in Botswood, Newfoundland. The second VS-44A, named *Excambian*, was delivered in May 1942, and the third, *Exeter*, in June. Shortly after all three VS-44As become operational, they were formally impressed into naval service under the designation JR2S-1. Tragedy struck in early October 1943 when *Excalibur* was destroyed during a takeoff from Botswood, killing eleven of twenty-six people aboard in an accident attributed to pilot error. At the end of 1944, the remaining two VS-44As were returned to AEA, and after being repainted in an all-white civilian scheme, continued to make transatlantic runs on military contracts. In the interval, the assets of AEA were acquired by American Airlines, Inc., which planned to discontinue all flying boat operations when hostilities ended. Soon after the last AEA transatlantic flight was completed in late October 1945, both aircraft were offered for sale.

In the period right after the war, the two VS-44As went through a series of new owners, who attempted, most of them unsuccessfully, to employ the big flying boats in charter and cargo operations. In mid–1946, while operating with the very short-lived Tampico Airlines, *Excambian* made a record nonstop flight from Lima, Peru, to New York City. Ostensibly on a charter operation for Skyways International and loaded with guns and ammunition intended for Paraguayan rebels, *Exeter* was destroyed in mid–1947 during a night landing on the Rio de la Plata River in Uruguay. Then just a few years later, *Excambian* was impounded by the City of Baltimore for nonpayment of stor-

Excambian **as seen in the 1960s while flying the Long Beach–Catalina run for Avalon Air Transport. The aircraft made a total of 8,172 flights before being retired in 1967.**

age fees and thereafter sold for $500! In the hands of new entrepreneurs during the early 1950s, the aircraft was completely refurbished with the goal of turning it into a flying trading post that would operate up and down the Brazil's Amazon River. The venture eventually failed, however, and *Excambian* found itself derelict again, this time in Ancou, Peru. Finally, in 1957, the aircraft was purchased by Dick Probert, one of the owners of Avalon Air Transport, and ferried to Long Beach, California. Following extensive repairs and modifications that included accommodations for up to forty-seven passengers, *Excambian* was placed in service with Avalon Air Transport on the Long Beach-Catalina Island run. When withdrawn from service in 1967, the big flying boat had made a total of 8,172 flights carrying 211,246 passengers.

After being sold to Antilles Air Boats in late 1967, the VS-44A flew to St. Croix, U.S. Virgin Islands, where it commenced flying commercial operations in the Caribbean. Sadly, the flying career of *Excambian* came to an abrupt end on January 10, 1969, when it struck on object after an aborted takeoff and sank in four feet of water. Although the aircraft was drained and towed ashore, the owners reached the conclusion that the repairs needed to bring to it back into airworthy condition were simply too costly. As a consequence, the aircraft sat out in the open, deteriorating, for six years until 1976, when it was donated to the Naval Aviation Museum and moved to Pensacola, Florida. But this was not much of an improvement, as the VS-44A was still forced to remain in outside storage. Rescue came in 1983: for eventual restoration and display, NAM agreed to a long-term loan of the aircraft to the New England Air Museum; after a move to Bridgeport, Connecticut, volunteers, many from Sikorsky's Stratford plant, subjected *Excambian* to a 300,000+ hour restoration that ultimately entailed replacing thirty-seven percent of the structure and ninety-seven percent of the skin. Resplendent in its original AEA markings, the VS-44A may be seen today at the Museum, which is located at Windsor Locks, Connecticut, near Bradley International Airport.

Spencer Aircraft Co.

In 1937, Percival H. Spencer joined forces with Sikorsky engineer Vincent A. Larsen to form Larsen Aircraft Co. in Farmingdale, New York. Their sole product, the SL-12C amphibian, is reported in Appendix A, below. Spencer left Larsen to start his own company in 1940, but there was no corporation on record. In December 1941, he left this business to become a test pilot for Republic, and then resumed company operations sometime in 1943.

Spencer S-12 Air Car (1941)

TECHNICAL SPECIFICATIONS

Type: 2-place civil amphibian.
Total produced: 1
Powerplant: one 110-hp Franklin 4A 4-cylinder air-cooled opposed engine driving a two-bladed, fixed-pitch wooden propeller.
Performance: max. speed 95 mph, cruise 86 mph; ceiling (not reported.; range (not reported).
Weights: 1,000 lbs. empty (est.), 1,600 lbs. gross (est.).
Dimensions: span 33 ft. 7 in., length 23 ft. 3 in., wing area 160 sq. ft. (est.)

Spencer's S-12 Air Car as seen in its original 1941 configuration. Fuselage pod was later revised to a more rounded shape. After Spencer sold the design rights to Republic, it evolved into the Seabee.

The modified S-12 Air Car, with a more rounded cabin configuration, seen taxiing up to dock in 1943. Its similarity to Seabee is evident.

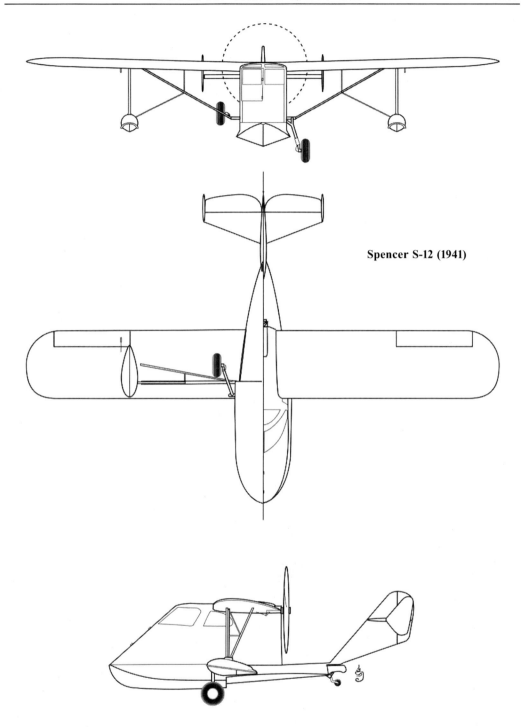

Spencer S-12 (1941)

Although a one-of-a-kind homebuilt design, the Spencer S-12 Air Car deserves recognition as the progenitor of the Republic Seabee (see Part III, below) and other amphibian designs, some of which are still being built today.

Spencer's amphibian concept was similar in many respects to Grover Loening's S-1 Flying Yacht of 1922 (see Part I, page 54): a pod arrangement containing a cockpit and pusher engine, which rested on a long pontoon extending aft to support a high-mounted tail group. Spencer started construction of the project in March 1941, using a metal framework skinned in a wooden veneer for the hull and fabric-covered wooden structures for the wings and tail surfaces. Stabilizing floats were fixed below the wings and braced to the lift struts. The rear aspect of the plane was dominated by a very tall fin and rudder incorporating a cruciform horizontal stabilizer. An innovative feature seen on later developments was a split windscreen that also formed a front entry door during water operations. The amphibious landing gear was a simple arrangement that could be rotated upward ninety

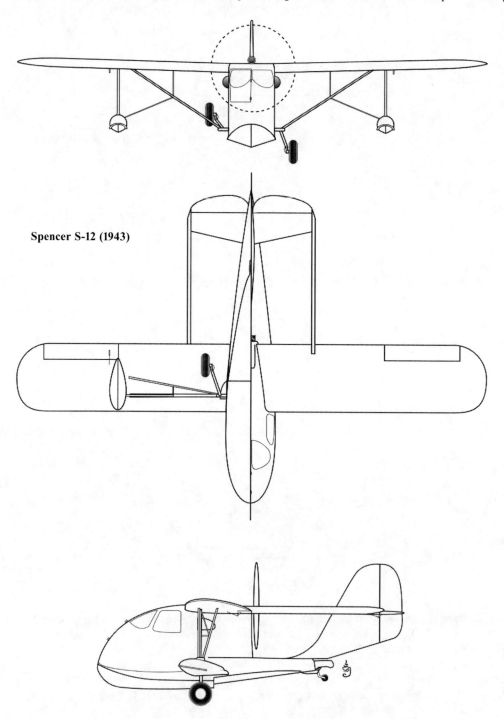

Spencer S-12 (1943)

degrees. With Spencer at the controls, the S-12 made it first flight on August 8, 1941, under civil registration NX29098. But because of his wartime duties, Spencer placed the project on hold for the next two years, then in mid–1943, using wood forming equipment, constructed an all-new, streamlined forward hull. In December 1943, after demonstrating the S-12 before his former employers at Republic Aircraft, he sold his design rights to the company, and it would reappear two years later as the all-metal RC-1 Seabee.

Viking Flying Boat Co.

Viking was apparently formed in 1930 at New Haven, Connecticut, as a spin-off of the earlier Bourdon Aircraft Corp., then in 1931, was acquired by Stearman-Varney, Inc., a company started by Lloyd Stearman and Walter Varney, presumably to build mailplanes and transports. Production of aircraft at the New Haven plant continued until 1936.

Viking OO (V-2) (1930)

TECHNICAL SPECIFICATIONS (OO-1)

Type: 4-place civil and military observation flying boat.
Total produced: 6
Powerplant: one 250-hp Wright R-760 Whirlwind 9-cylinder air-cooled radial engine driving a two-bladed, fixed-pitch wooden propeller.
Performance: max. speed 104 mph, cruise 88 mph; ceiling 15,300 ft.; range 390 mi..
Weights: 4,200 lbs. empty, 5,900 lbs. gross.
Dimensions: span 42 ft. 4 in., length 29 ft. 4 in., wing area 250 sq. ft.

After importing three 17HT-4 flying boats manufactured in France by Schreck Hydroavions FBA, the first license-built version to be completed by Viking, the Wright J-6-powered V-2, was tested and certified in the United States in 1930. No more V-2s were manufactured, but one of

The second OO-1 (V152), but the first to be completed by Viking, as delivered to the Coast Guard in 1936. The identical French-built Schreck 17HT-4 (V107) had been destroyed in 1934. The type remained in active service until 1941.

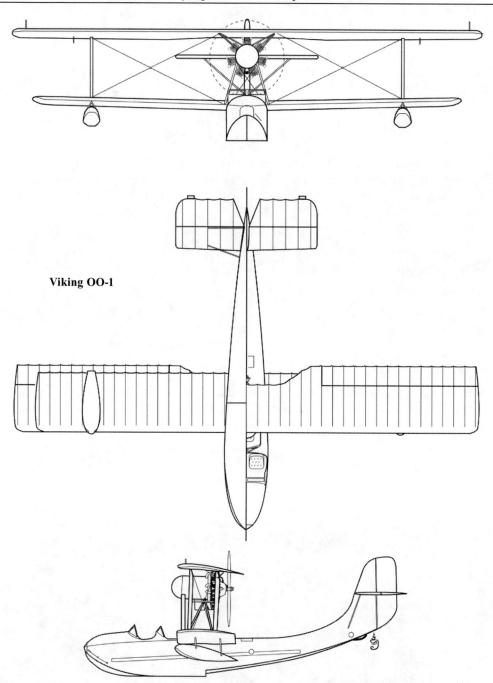

Viking OO-1

the Schreck 17HT-4s was sold to the Coast Guard in 1931. Although a comparatively outdated biplane design, the small wooden-hulled and framed aircraft nevertheless exhibited good open-sea handling qualities. After its 17HT-4 was accidentally destroyed in a fire in 1934, the Coast Guard awarded Viking a contract to build five license-copies under the designation OO-1, and all were delivered between October and December 1936. Once in service, the OO-1s operated from stations at Biloxi, Mississippi, Cape May, New Jersey, Charleston, South Carolina, and Miami and St. Petersburg, Florida. Their active career was relatively brief, however, the last example being retired in April 1941.

PART III

The Post-War Era, 1945–Present

HISTORICAL OVERVIEW

*"I put the sweat of my life into this project, and if it's a failure,
I'll leave the country and never come back."—Howard R. Hughes,
testimony in reference to H-4 before U.S. Senate in 1947.*

Aeronautical Progress

As the post-war era dawned in America, big flying boats had been displaced in the role of overseas transports by new four-engine landplanes but still held great promise in the military sphere. The military services not only released the design freeze that characterized wartime aircraft development but began issuing highly ambitious specifications calling for new aircraft that would achieve unprecedented levels of flight performance. Probably the greatest single influence was the introduction of jet propulsion, both turbojet and turboprop engines. Another important breakthrough had come from a wealth of captured German experimental research data relative to high-speed aerodynamics. The power available from jet engines combined with the possibilities to be derived from advanced aerodynamic concepts such as swept or delta wings confronted flying boat designers with a whole new set of problems. Efforts to move flying boat design into the Jet Age would in the end produce many interesting, if not always practical, ideas.

Despite increased power-to-weight ratios and the higher wing-loading it allowed, a flying boat still demanded a careful blend of hydro- and aerodynamic features that would permit reasonably safe operations on the water. Designers from companies like Convair and Martin conducted extensive tests using the water drag tanks and wind tunnels at NACA's Langley facility. They discovered that by increasing length-to-beam ratios, hull drag was considerably lessened (e.g., 10:1 for the Convair P5Y and Martin P5M; 15:1 for the Martin P6M), and at the same time, the weight of the aircraft in displacement could be supported by extending the afterbody. Spray characteristics of the narrower hulls were little altered, and the longer afterbody dampened the tendency of the hull to porpoise and skip at higher speeds. Less success was achieved in attempts to completely lift the hull from the water during high-speed takeoffs and landings (e.g., 145 mph) with devices like hydro-skis and hydrofoils (see Convair F2Y). Other sophisticated concepts such as blending the wing into the hull to form part of the buoyant surface (see Convair Skate in Appendix B, page 348) were studied but never materialized into a full-size aircraft. Wing design benefited from new low-drag, laminar-flow airfoil sections, and takeoff and landing speeds were kept within acceptable limits (e.g., 100 mph) by using large-span, Fowler-type flap systems. During the late 1950s, Convair and Martin developed boundary layer control systems (i.e., air generated by one or more jet engines, ducted to blow over the flaps and ailerons) that were designed to reduce takeoff and landing speeds to

213

levels low enough (e.g., 35 to 40 mph) to permit open-ocean operations; however, both programs (see Convair P6Y and Martin P7M, in Appendix A) were cancelled before any prototypes were built.

Amphibian development during the same time period was more conservative. In fact, only one manufacturer—Grumman—made a serious effort to produce large, multi-engine amphibians for the military and commercial markets (see G-44 Widgeon in Part II, and G-73 Mallard and SA-16 Albatross in Part III). From the mid–1950s onwards, efforts to extend the service life of older Grumman amphibians like the Goose and Widgeon resulted in a number of modification programs that included airframe rebuilds, engine upgrades, or both; and from the mid–1960s, availability of small, lightweight turboprop engines such as the 600-hp Pratt & Whitney PT6A led to extensive conversion programs known as the Turbo-Goose (G-21D/E) and Turbo-Mallard (G-73T). A similar effort to convert the Albatross to Rolls-Royce *Dart* turboprops (Conroy Turbo-Albatross) was not ultimately successful. While Supplemental Type Certificates (STC) were issued with respect to modification and testing of preexisting designs (e.g., Grumman G-21D/E, G-73T, and G-111 [Albatross]), no factory-built multi-engine amphibians have been produced in the United States since 1961. During the mid–1990s, efforts to raise sufficient capital to place the G-73T Mallard into production (in the Czech Republic) failed; however, as of November 2007, according to a website maintained by Antilles Seaplanes, LLC (see http://www.gooseseaplanes.com), plans to manufacture an all-new G-21 Super Goose, available in either piston-engine or turboprop versions, still appear to be moving forward.

In an interesting contrast to previous eras, the most energetic category of new amphibian design was (and still is to some extent) directed at the emerging single-engine, lightplane market. This was aided by small engine manufacturers like Continental, Franklin, and Lycoming, who began introducing a wide variety of four- and six-cylinder air-cooled, horizontally opposed engines that were inexpensive, reliable, and relatively powerful for their weight (e.g., the four-cylinder Lycoming O-320 of 1953 produced 150 hp for a weight of 272 lbs. [1:1.8]). These new engines also generated their rated power at higher RPMs, thus requiring smaller diameter propellers, and due the low frontal area of their flat geometry, could be better streamlined. Performance, especially in terms of takeoff and climb, was further enhanced by the availability of variable-pitch and constant-speed propellers for use on the opposed engines.

Another phenomenon unique to the post-war era has been the increasing popularity of amateur-built aircraft, which includes its fair share of amphibian designs. Unlike the mostly self-designed homebuilt types of the earlier eras, this new category of homebuilts is characterized by fully-tested designs that commonly feature comprehensive plan sets, patterns, and highly detailed building instructions. The growth of the homebuilt aircraft movement has been encouraged and sustained by the nearly simultaneous rise of the Experimental Aircraft Association (see http://www.eaa.org), and even further by builder's networks on particular aircraft types (e.g., http://www.coot-builders.com and http://volmeraircraft.com). Since the 1980s in particular, kit-built aircraft have become an important force in the overall growth of the homebuilt trend. A major innovation underlying the success of kits has been the development of complete airframe components (e.g., fuselage, wings, and tail group) that are molded from lightweight composite materials like fiberglass and Kelvar-epoxy, and many regularly include hard-to-make items such as engine mounts, landing gear, and canopies. Kits not only reduce and simplify the building process but offer, at a fraction of the cost, a completed aircraft that rivals the quality and performance of one manufactured under a standard type certificate.

Changes in Federal Aviation Regulations (FARs) over the years have also provided a stimulus to amphibian development. FAR Part 103, in force since 1982, allows "ultralight air vehicles" to fly virtually unlicensed as long as they meet certain criteria: single-place, empty weight no more than 254 lbs, fuel capacity of 5 gallons or less, and maximum speed not exceeding 55 mph; and for water operations, an extra weight allowance of ten percent or 25.4 lbs. In the interval, besides conventional ultralights adapted to floats, several different types of amphibious mono-hull designs have appeared in kit form (see Advanced Aeromarine Buccaneer and Diehls XTC, in Appendix A, pages

325 amd 329) and new types are reported to be in the offing (see Moyes Connie in Appendix A, page 332). Another important regulatory development occurred as recently as 2004 with the introduction of new "Light Sport" Aircraft and Airman categories (see generally http://www.aopa.org/ whatsnew/regulatory/regsport.html). As applied to amphibians, an aircraft may be certificated as Light Sport (manufactured) or Experimental Light Sport (homebuilt or kit-built) as long as it falls within the following guidelines: two-place, single-engine, gross weight no more than 1,430 lbs., and maximum speed not exceeding 120 knots (138 mph). This rule not only opens the door for easier licensing of kit-built amphibians like the Aventura HP and II (see Appendix A, below) and Progressive Aerodyne SeaRey (see page 333) but also manufactured aircraft like the Icon A5 (see page 247). As important, a Light Sport Aircraft under these rules may be flown by a person holding a Sport Pilot Airman's Certificate. Although a Sport Pilot cannot fly for hire and is confined to operations within certain types of airspace, the new category offers an very economical alternative to Private Pilot training, and perhaps most significant, requires only a valid state driver's license as evidence of medical fitness.

Military Procurement

Even while World War Two was in progress, the Navy had begun the process of replacing its flying boats with land-based patrol aircraft (e.g., Consolidated PB4Y) and had newer types under development (e.g., Lockheed P2V and Martin P4M). In the massive demobilization that followed V-J Day, nearly all flying boats other than amphibious PBY variants and PBM-5s were rapidly phased-out of service. Similarly, most of the Navy's single- (Grumman J2F) and twin-engine (Grumman JRF, J4F and Sikorsky JRS) utility amphibians were removed from the inventory and offered surplus. Yet, in the midst of this, the Navy still envisaged important roles for flying boats and amphibians in its future operations. In 1945 and 1946, BuAer continued production of the PBM-5 and JRM-1/-2 Mars (reduced to six of 20 originally ordered) and likewise authorized development of the Convair (formerly Consolidated-Vultee) XP5Y-1 and Martin XP5M-1 as new maritime patrol types. At almost the same time, with Navy and Air Force endorsements, Grumman began construction of the XJR2F-1, a large amphibian that would fulfill the utility, reconnaissance, and air-sea rescue roles.

But the Navy's most audacious plans for new flying boats contemplated far-reaching new missions: lack of funding for new carriers combined with the difficulties of adapting jet aircraft to existing carriers impelled naval planners to consider the feasibility of developing advanced jet aircraft capable of operating from the sea. The "Sea Fighter" program was started in 1948 with the aim of creating a jet-propelled interceptor that could takeoff and land on water. A contract awarded to Convair in 1951 resulted in the first flight of the twin-engine, delta-wing XF2Y-1 Sea Dart in early 1953, and a little over a year later, it became to first seaplane of any type to exceed the speed of sound. But after four years of nonstop development, which included testing of two YF2Y-1s with revised hydro-ski configurations (note that two more YF2Y-1s were delivered but never flown), the Sea Fighter program was cancelled in the fall of 1957 due to persistent control problems related to hydro-ski operations.

In 1949, while the Sea Fighter was still on the drawing board, the Navy embarked on the even more ambitious Seaplane Striking Force (SSF) project. SSF envisaged large flying boats that could carry out long-range nuclear strike, conventional bombing, mine-laying, or reconnaissance missions. After a lengthy period of evaluating various design concepts, BuAer, in October 1953, issued Martin a contract to build two XP6M-1 SeaMaster prototypes, the first of which was test flown in July 1955. Despite the loss of both prototypes during the first two years of testing, the program continued with six service test YP6M-1s, and Martin was allowed to initiate production of the definitive P6M-2. Then in mid–1959, only months after delivery of the first of eight P6M-2s, the Navy reversed its position and cancelled the entire SeaMaster program. In the final analysis, the SSF concept was rendered obsolete by two late-arriving naval developments: (1) super carriers capable of launching long-range nuclear strike aircraft and (2) nuclear submarines carrying intercontinental ballistic missiles.

The Naval Air Transport Service operated the four remaining Martin JRMs (one was destroyed in 1945 and another in 1950) until 1956. Convair's turboprop XP5Y ultimately evolved into the R3Y Tradewind long-range transport; however, due to chronic problems with the complex engines, the type was removed from service in 1957 after delivery of only nine production aircraft. The piston-engine Martin P5M became the Navy's mainstay patrol boat during the 1950s and 1960s, and was the very last type of flying boat to serve, the final examples being withdrawn in late 1967. Grumman's JR2F Albatross, after a designation change to UF-1 (USN and Coast Guard) and SA-16 (USAF), then again to HU-16 (all services), enjoyed a long-lasting career, serving in the USAF until 1974 and with the Navy until 1976, and ended the 72-year era of American military seaplanes when the final example left Coast Guard service in early 1983.

Civil Developments

Post-war attempts to use large flying boats like Boeing 314s and Sikorsky VS-44As in unscheduled overseas operations proved to be fruitless. One VS-44A (*Excambian*) did enjoy a 10-year career with Avalon Air Transport, making short-haul trips between Long Beach and Catalina Island, but came to grief in 1969 while operating in the U.S. Virgin Islands. In a complete contrast, the availability of surplus military utility amphibians, in particular the Grumman Goose and Widgeon, provided a huge stimulus to smaller commercial carriers all over the world. From the late 1940s well into the 1970s, this fleet of about 500 Grumman amphibians was the backbone of passenger and cargo-carrying services of many island, coastal, and bush operations; but attrition, as a consequence of irreparable damage, airframe fatigue, and lack of spares, left only a handful of these irreplaceable aircraft in commercial service by the 1990s. In smaller numbers, ex-military Grumman Albatrosses and Turbo-Mallards were placed in scheduled airline operations during the 1970s; however, all Albatrosses had been withdrawn by 1987, and scheduled passenger services ended altogether in late 2005, when the FAA grounded the remaining Turbo-Mallards operated by Chalk's Ocean Airways. The traditional role of twin-engine amphibians in both scheduled and charter operations has largely been supplanted by large, float-equipped aircraft like the Viking (formerly de Havilland) Turbo-Beaver and Twin Otter and the Cessna Caravan. Today, most of the large amphibians remaining in airworthy condition are privately owned and many others are non-flying static displays in various aviation museums.

It is probably safe to say that the thirty-five years following the end of World War II (1945–1980) became the "golden age" of privately-owned, single-engine amphibians. According to wartime statistics, approximately 260,000 military pilots were trained between 1939 and 1945, which was among the factors leading many big aircraft companies (e.g., Boeing, Goodyear, Grumman, Lockheed, Republic, etc.) to foresee an enormous boom in the post-war civil lightplane market. Despite the fact the boom never actually materialized, approximately 2,000 single-engine amphibians (see Colonial, Lake, Thurston, and Republic, below) were nonetheless manufactured under standard type certificates during this period and still comprise the majority of today's private amphibian fleet. Since 1980, as a result of the general downturn in the lightplane market and rising production costs (e.g., compare $53,000 for a Lake LA-200 in 1980 to $700,000+ for a new LA-250 today), less than 150 standard category amphibians have been completed. It remains to be seen whether or not new types such as the Leader Industries Privateer, Seawind 300C, Thurston TA-16, or Trident TR-1 (Canada) will ever achieve type certification and production. In terms of organization and support, the Light Sport Icon A5 appears to be a good candidate for future production and has the potential to become a trendsetter.

Interestingly, in the U.S. since 1980, the greatest numbers (an estimated 1,000 or more) of new single-engine amphibians entering the ranks of privately owned aircraft have been generated by homebuilders and kit-builders. And as the used fleet of standard category amphibians diminishes through the natural process of attrition, the amateur-built trend, kitplanes especially, is likely to continue in the foreseeable future.

THE POST-WAR ERA • 1945–PRESENT

Aircraft Manufacturer	Model	First Flight
Aerocar International, Inc.:	Coot	1969
Anderson Aircraft:	Kingfisher	1969
Colonial Aircraft Corp.:	C-1, C-2 Skimmer	1948
Columbia Aircraft Corp.:	JL	1946
Convair Aircraft Corp.:	P5Y (R3Y) Tradewind	1950
	F2Y Sea Dart	1953
Grumman Aircraft Engr. Corp.:	G-73 Mallard	1946
	SA-15 (JR2F, UF) Albatross	1947
Hughes Aircraft Corp.:	HK-1 (H-4) Hercules	1947
Icon Aircraft:	A5	2008
Lake Aircraft Corp.:	LA-4, LA4-200	1960
	LA-250, -270, -270T	1984
Glenn L. Martin Co.:	JRM Mars	1945
	P5M Marlin	1948
	P6M Seamaster	1955
Pereira Aircraft Co.:	Osprey I	1970
	Osprey II	1974
Republic Aviation Corp.:	RC-1, RC-3 Seabee	1944
Seawind/SNA, Inc. (Seawind, LLC):	Seawind	1982
Spencer-Anderson:	S-12C/E Air Car	1970
Thurston Aircraft Corp.:	TSC-1 Teal	1968
	TA-16 Seafire	1981
Volmer Aircraft Co.:	VJ-22 Sportsman	1958

Aerocar International, Inc.

Moulton B. (Molt) Taylor, best known for the Aerocar design that appeared in 1950, formed Aerocar International, Inc. at Longview, Washington, in 1961, then after moving to Saginaw, Texas, in 1970, reorganized under the name Mini-IMP Aircraft Co. Taylor died in 1995.

Taylor Coot (1969)

TECHNICAL SPECIFICATIONS (COOT-A)

Type: 2-place homebuilt civil amphibian.
Total produced: 70 (est.)
Powerplant (prototype): one 180-hp Franklin 6A4-B 6-cylinder air-cooled opposed engine driving a two-bladed, constant-speed metal propeller.
Performance (prototype): max. speed 120 mph, cruise 100 mph; ceiling (not reported); range 438 mi.
Weights: 1,450 lbs. empty, 1,950 lbs. gross.
Dimensions: span 36 ft. 0 in., length 22 ft. 0 in., wing area 180 sq. ft.

One of the most popular and best-supported homebuilt amphibian designs ever introduced, an estimated seventy Coot-As have been completed since Molt Taylor flew the first example in 1969 and more are under construction. Two Coot prototypes originally appeared: the single tail A and the twin boom B, with the A becoming the definitive model. Departing from orthodox amphibian design, the Coot's wings are located in the middle of the hull where, in place of drag-producing tip floats, the wing roots act as lateral stabilizing sponsons. Landing gear is tricycle type, with the main

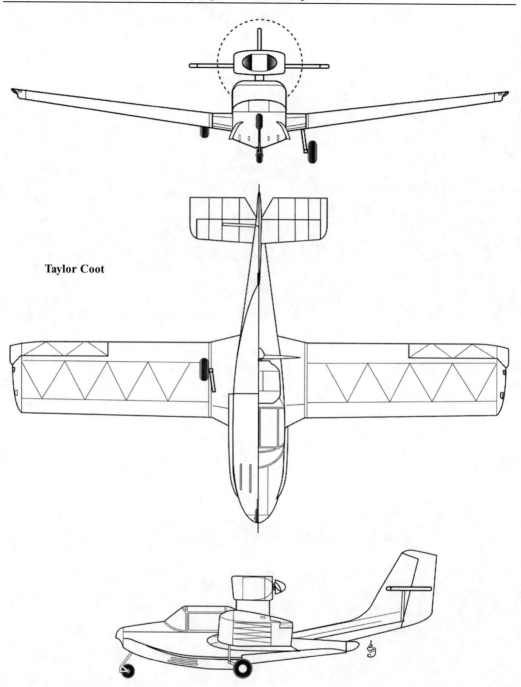

Taylor Coot

wheels folding rearward into the wing and the nose wheel retracting forward into a bow recess. Another innovative feature is folding wings and horizontal stabilizers that permit the aircraft to be placed on a trailer and towed. The hull, consisting of a pod and tail boom arrangement, is made up of molded fiberglass sections, internally stiffened by wooden formers and stringers that are fiberglass-bonded; wings are fabric-covered wooden structures with fiberglass leading edges.

Coot builders have installed various Franklin, Continental, and Lycoming powerplants, ranging from 100 hp to 220 hp, but engines having 180 hp or more, equipped with constant-speed propellers, have been recommended in order to achieve acceptable performance under average load

Since the first Coot-A flew in 1969, an estimated 70 have been completed and flown by homebuilders. The wings were intentionally mounted at mid-hull so that the roots would function as sponsons.

conditions. Two Coots are reported to have flown with modified Mazda automotive engines of undisclosed horsepower. Auxiliary sponsons, located below and forward of the wings, have been added to some recently built Coots to enhance buoyancy and keep water-spray away from the propeller. The molded structures and other airframe components, originally offered by Taylor, are currently available (see www.coot-builders.com) from Ken Welter of Camas, Washington.

Anderson

Earl Anderson, at the time a captain for Pan American Airlines and a resident of Delray Beach, Florida, designed, built, and tested a two-place amphibian in 1969, and thereafter offered construction plans to homebuilders.

Anderson EA-1 Kingfisher (1969)

TECHNICAL SPECIFICATIONS
Type: 2-place homebuilt civil amphibian.
Total produced: Unknown
Powerplant (prototype): one 100-hp Continental O-200 4-cylinder air-cooled opposed engine driving a two-bladed, fixed-pitch metal propeller.
Performance (prototype): max. speed 96 mph, cruise 85 mph; ceiling 10,000 ft.; range 322 mi.
Weights: 1,032 lbs. empty, 1,540 lbs. gross.
Dimensions: span 36 ft. 2 in., length 23 ft. 6 in., wing area 178.5 sq. ft.

To the amateur aircraft builder, the Anderson Kingfisher offers a simple amphibian design which can utilize the wings of a Piper J-3 Cub or similar Piper aircraft. The one-step hull consists of plywood construction with internal longerons and formers and, though not denoted, the tail group appears to be a welded steel tube framework with fabric covering. Whether derived from Piper components or scratch-built, the wings are of the fabric-covered, two-spar type, supported by metal V-struts. The engine, tractor-mounted on struts incorporated into the wing center-section, overhangs the cockpit area. Material and construction of the engine nacelle are not mentioned, but the nose bowl looks like an off-the-shelf item. Some Kingfishers are reported to have been fitted with other engines, most commonly the 115-hp Lycoming O-235. Earl Anderson flew the Kingfisher prototype for the first time on April 24, 1969. While the actual number of Kingfishers completed and

Designed by airline pilot Earl Anderson, the original EA-1 utilized the wings and other miscellaneous components of a Piper J-3 Cub. The hull is of built-up plywood construction.

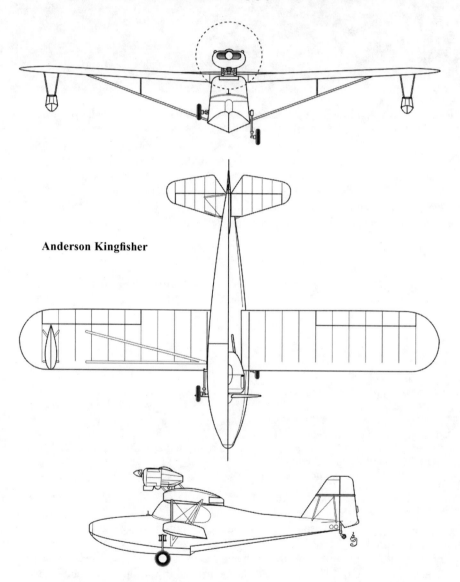

Anderson Kingfisher

flying is not published, over 200 sets plans had been sold by 1978 and 100 were thought to be at some stage of construction. At one time, Kingfisher kit components were being offered to builders, but the website (see members.eaa.org/home/homebuilders/selecting/kits/Kingfisher.html) apparently is no longer active. Plans may still be obtained through the Experimental Aircraft Association.

Colonial Aircraft Corp.

Founded as a side venture in 1946 by David B. Thurston, an aeronautical engineer working for Grumman, and Herbert P. Lindbad, who was employed by Republic, the Colonial Aircraft Corp. built and tested its first amphibian prototype at Long Island, New York, during 1947 and 1948, and upon receiving the aircraft's Type Certificate of Airworthiness in 1955, the company moved to a new manufacturing facility in Sanford, Maine. After Colonial was acquired by Lake Aircraft Corp. in 1959, with John F. Strayer as the new president, Thurston left the company to pursue other interests while Lindbad stayed on.

Colonial C-1 and -2 (IV) Skimmer (1948)

TECHNICAL SPECIFICATIONS (C-2)

Type: 2 to 4-place civil amphibian.
Total produced: 43 (all versions)
Powerplant: one 180-hp Lycoming O-360-A1A 4-cylinder air-cooled opposed engine driving a two-bladed, constant-speed metal propeller.
Performance: max. speed 135 mph, cruise 130 mph; ceiling (not reported); range 625 mi.
Weights: 1,525 lbs. empty, 2,350 lbs. gross.
Dimensions: span 34 ft. 0 in., length 23 ft. 6 in., wing area 170 sq. ft.

Using some of the ideas taken from his previous association with the Goodyear GA-1 Duck (see Part II, above) and Grumman G-65 Tadpole (see Appendix A, below), David Thurston evolved an all-new amphibian design featuring a shallower hull and a raised turtledeck, together with a pusher engine mounted high up on a pylon between the wings. The hull consisted of all-metal, semi-monocoque construction, and the fully-cantilevered wings joined the fuselage in a high-middle position behind the cockpit enclosure. Characteristics taken almost directly from the G-65 included a tricycle gear retraction system in which the main wheels folded into the wings and one-piece, streamlined stabilizing floats. The nose wheel, when retracted, left half of the tire exposed to act as a bumper. Construction of the prototype, dubbed the C-1 "Skimmer," began during 1947 and continued into the next year. Originally, power was derived from a 115-hp Lycoming O-235-C1 driving an Aeromatic propeller (i.e., automatic low to high-pitch change via counterweight mechanisms).

The C-1 prototype, registered as N6595K, made its first flight on July 17, 1948, and development proceeded over the next six years. In the interval, a 125-hp Lycoming O-290-D replaced the

The original C-1 prototype (N6595K) in its final form just prior to Type Certification in September 1955. It became the forerunner of over 1,000 production amphibians (i.e., Colonial and Lake combined).

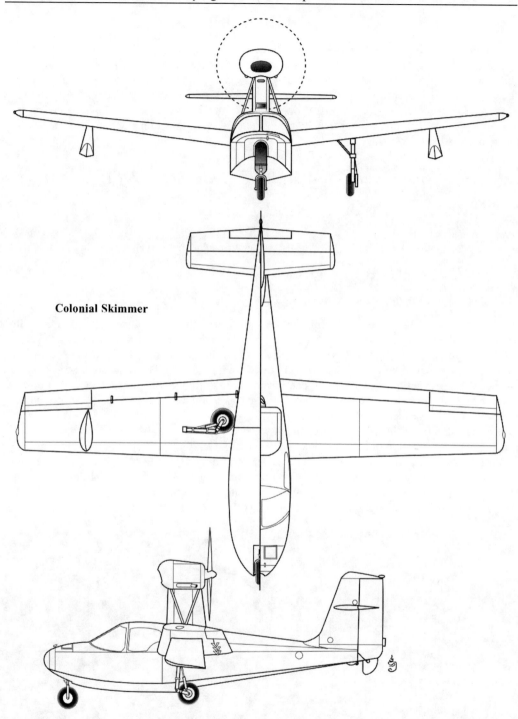

Colonial Skimmer

original engine and the pylon was modified. Other refinements included a strengthened rear tur-tledeck and a retractable water rudder instead of an extended air rudder. As the C-1 reached its final production standard during 1954 and 1955, the powerplant was changed again to a 150-hp Lycoming O-320-A2B engine, the pylon modified, a taller fin and rudder added, and the floats lengthened. The cabin was arranged with two side-by-side seats in front, with a third optional seat mounted sideways in the rear. In early 1955, Colonial moved its operations to Sanford, Maine, in anticipa-

N246B shown here was the fifth C-1 off the assembly line. In the mid–1960s the aircraft went to Canada and was re-registered as CF-LML.

tion of production plans, and issuance of the aircraft's official Type Certificate followed in September 1955. From that point until late 1957, Colonial manufactured and delivered a total of twenty-three aircraft as the C-1 Skimmer.

During 1957 Colonial developed the improved C-2 Skimmer IV, which featured a 180-hp Lycoming O-360-A1A engine, a cabin redesigned to accommodate four seats, enlarged horizontal tail surfaces, modified wing floats, plus structural strengthening of the wings and pylon for the increased gross weight. Type Certificate approval came in December 1957, and twenty C-2s had been completed at the time Colonial sold its assets to Lake Aircraft Corp. in late 1959. According to a website devoted to Colonial Aircraft (see http://home.c2i.net/otter32/colonial/colonial_history. htm), seven C-1s, including the original prototype, and eight C-2s remain in flying condition today under U.S. and Canadian registrations, and at least five more are known to be in various stages of restoration. The sixty-year legacy of the Colonial Skimmer continues, manifested today as the Lake LA-250 and -270T.

Columbia Aircraft Corp.

Located in Long Island, New York, near Grumman's Bethpage plant, the pre-war origins of this company are not clear. In 1942 Grumman assigned production of the J2F Duck to Columbia, and 330 aircraft were subsequently completed as the J2F-6. The assets of Columbia were sold to Commonwealth Aircraft Corp. in 1946.

Columbia JL (1946)

TECHNICAL SPECIFICATIONS (XJL-1)

Type: 6-place military utility amphibian.
Total produced: 3
Powerplant: one 1,200-hp Wright R-1820-56 *Cyclone* 9-cylinder air-cooled radial engine driving a three-bladed, constant-speed metal propeller.
Performance: max. speed 174 mph, cruise 119 mph; ceiling (not reported); range 2,070 mi.
Weights: empty (not reported), 13,000 lbs. gross (est.).
Dimensions: span 50 ft. 0 in., length 45 ft. 11 in., wing area (not reported).

Grumman began laying down the design of the Model G-42 in mid–1939, a monoplane intended as a successor to the J2F Duck series; however, as a consequence of wartime priorities placed on

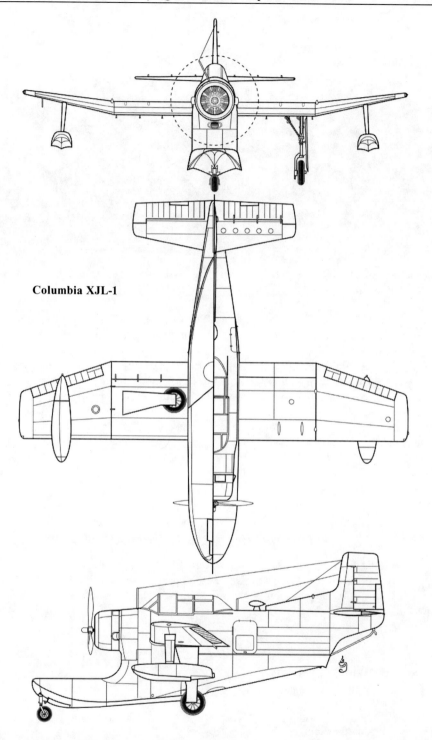

Columbia XJL-1

the company to mass produce other aircraft (e.g., F4F, TBF, F6F), the project remained on hold until being transferred to Columbia Aircraft sometime in 1943. The overall design of the G-42 was characterized by the shoehorn fuselage/pontoon configuration of the J2F with squared-off, tapered wings similar in shape to those of the G-44 Widgeon. Other new features included a tricycle type landing gear in which the main wheels fully retracted into the wing. BuAer awarded Columbia a

One of two Columbia XJL-1 prototypes as delivered to NATC for testing in 1947. The design had actually been initiated by Grumman in 1939 as the G-42, intended as a successor to the Duck, but was assigned to Columbia in 1943.

contract to build two flying prototypes and one static test example under the designation XJL-1, but the war ended before construction of the aircraft was completed. The maiden flight of the first XL-1 prototype took place on October 15, 1946, and both prototypes were delivered to NATC in 1947 for evaluation. After testing in 1947 and 1948 revealed structural weakness in the airframe, the Navy elected to abandon any further development. Both aircraft were afterward placed in storage at NAS Norfolk, Virginia and remained there until being sold surplus in 1959.

One of the XJL-1s, civil registry N48RW, was restored to flying condition during the late 1980s but crashed at Camp Pendleton, California, in 1997. It is now reportedly undergoing restoration. The other XL-1, civil registry N54205, is currently preserved at the Pima Air Museum in Tucson, Arizona.

Convair Aircraft Corp.

In 1943, two years after merging with Vultee Aircraft, Consolidated shortened its name to Convair Aircraft. Following another reorganization in 1953, the company became the Convair Division of General Dynamics Corp. Along with Grumman and Martin, Convair became one of the few large military contractors to continue development of flying boats after World War II. None of the projects, however, were ultimately successful and all (including the unbuilt XP6Y-1 reported in Appendix B) had been cancelled by 1959.

Convair P5Y/R3Y Tradewind (1950)

TECHNICAL SPECIFICATIONS (R3Y-1)

Type: 8-place patrol boat; 103-passenger military transport.
Total produced: 11
Powerplants: four 5,500-shp Allison T40A-10 paired turboprop engines driving six-bladed contra-rotating, fully-reversible metal propellers.
Armament (XP5Y-1 only): Remote-controlled turrets in nose, forward and aft waist positions on each side, and tail, each containing two 20-mm cannons, and up to 8,000 lbs. of bombs, torpedoes, or depth charges carried in internal bays.
Performance: max. speed 388 mph, cruise 300 mph; ceiling 39,700 ft.; range 2,785 mi. (normal), 3,450-mi. (max.)
Weights: 71,824 lbs. empty, 145,500 lbs. normal gross, 165,000 max. takeoff.
Dimensions: span 145 ft. 9 in., length 139 ft. 8 in., wing area 2,102 sq. ft.

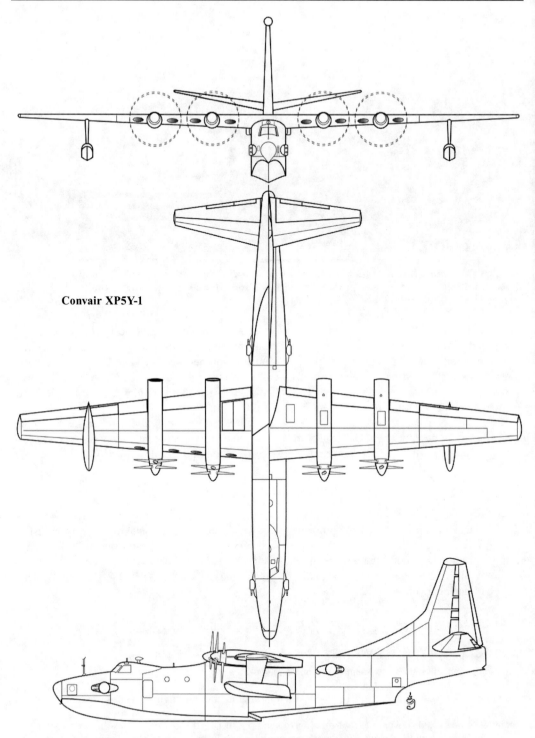

Convair XP5Y-1

The only type of turboprop flying boat to enter service with the Navy, the design and development of the Convair Tradewind originated from a requirement issued by BuAer in 1945 calling for a long-range flying boat that would utilize turboprop propulsion and take advantage of recent advances in aerodynamic design. Antisubmarine warfare (ASW) was envisaged as the new aircraft's primary role, with a secondary emphasis on transportation of troops and supplies. In May 1946,

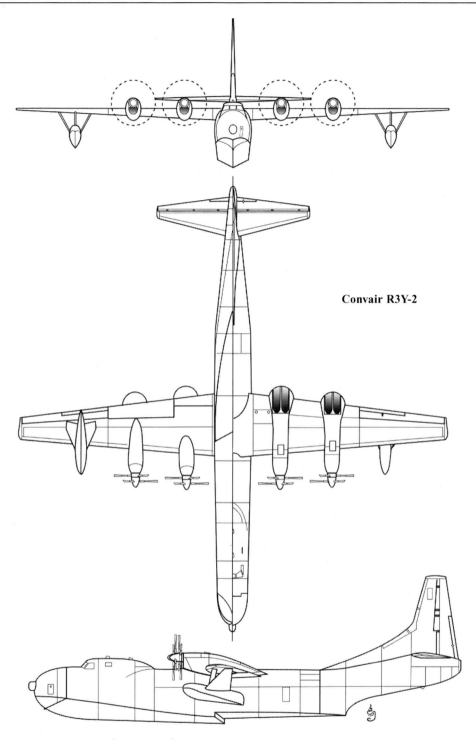

Convair R3Y-2

after reviewing competing designs, the Navy awarded Convair a contract to build two prototypes of its proposed model 117 under the designation XP5Y-1. At virtually the same time, Allison commenced a parallel program to develop the T40 powerplant, which, in order to reach the levels of power needed (i.e., 5,000 shp+), would entail mounting two T38 turboprop engines side-by-side and driving a propeller shaft through a common gearbox. The aerodynamic concept created for the

The first XP5Y-1 prototype. This aircraft was destroyed in a crash in July 1953 and the second proto-type never flew. The Navy decided instead to proceed with the more conservative Martin P5M.

One of six R3Y-2s configured as an amphibious assault transport. The nine R3Ys were the only type of turboprop-powered flying boats to ever reach operational service with the Navy.

XP5Y-1 was strikingly innovative: a exceptionally low-drag hull possessing a length/beam ratio of only 10:1 in combination with a high-aspect ratio wing employing a laminar-flow airfoil of very thin section. Fowler-type flaps occupying sixty percent of the wingspan would lower landing and take-off speeds to the 100-mph range, depending on weight. Due to the thinness of the wings, stabilizing floats were placed outboard on streamlined fairings. The tail group consisted of a very tall fin and rudder and a horizontal stabilizer with slight dihedral.

Problems with the engine gearboxes delayed the first flight of the XP5Y-1 until April 18, 1950, by which time the Navy had already ordered the more conventional Martin P5M-1 (see below) into production to fulfill the patrol boat function. The following August, however, shortly after the XP5Y-1

R3Y-2, dubbed "Caribbean Sea Tradewind," seen on beaching gear while serving with VR-2 at NAS Alameda. Chronic problems with the engine gearboxes resulted in the grounding of all R3Ys in April 1958.

had established a turboprop endurance record of eight hours six minutes, BuAer directed Convair to commence development of an unarmed transport version as the R3Y-1. Despite the loss of one of the XP5Y-1 prototypes in July 1953 in a non-fatal accident attributed to engine failure, work on the R3Y-1 continued without interruption. In addition to deletion of armament, major design changes involved modifying the nacelles for T40A-10 engines, raising the aft hull to elevate the entire tailplane and removing dihedral from the horizontal stabilizer, plus adding two twelve-foot cargo hatches on the port side. Other changes included pressurized accommodations for up to 103 fully equipped troops or 73 stretcher cases in an ambulance configuration. Full cargo payload was 48,000 lbs. The first R3Y-1 completed its maiden flight on February 24, 1954, and five of the six ordered had been delivered before the end of year. During operational testing, one of the R3Y-1s set a new transcontinental seaplane record by flying coast-to-coast at an average speed of 403 mph, a record which still stands today. The last R3Y-1 became the R3Y-2 assault transport when completed in December 1954 with a shorter, more bulbous nose that hinged upward to allow loading of troops, supplies, and vehicles from a beach, and five more R3Y-2s were delivered to the Navy during 1955.

In early 1956, once operational trials had been concluded, the five R3Y-1s and six R3Y-2s entered service with VR-2 at NAS Alameda, replacing the unit's Martin JRM Mars. Two of the R3Y-2s were afterward fitted with probe and drogue in-flight refueling systems, and in September 1956, one of them set a record when it simultaneously refueled four Grumman F9F-8 aircraft. Operations, however, were plagued by serious problems with the propeller gearboxes, resulting in the loss of one aircraft in May 1957 and another in January 1958. All remaining R3Y-1s and R3Y-2s were grounded in April 1958, and after being stricken in early 1959, sold for scrap.

Convair F2Y Sea Dart (1953)

TECHNICAL SPECIFICATIONS (YF2Y-1)

Type: single-seat fighter.
Total produced: 5
Powerplants: two Westinghouse J46-WE-12 turbojets, each rated at 4,500 lbs./s.t. dry, 6,000 lbs. in afterburning.
Armament (planned but never installed): four fixed 20-mm cannons in the nose and an unspecified number of 2.75-in. folding-fin aircraft rockets in a canister.
Performance: max. level speed 724 mph (0.95 Mach) at s.l., ceiling 54,800 ft.; range 513 mi.
Weights: 12,625 lbs. empty, 16,500 lbs. normal gross, 21,500 max. takeoff.
Dimensions: span 33 ft. 8 in., length 52 ft. 7 in., wing area 568 sq. ft.

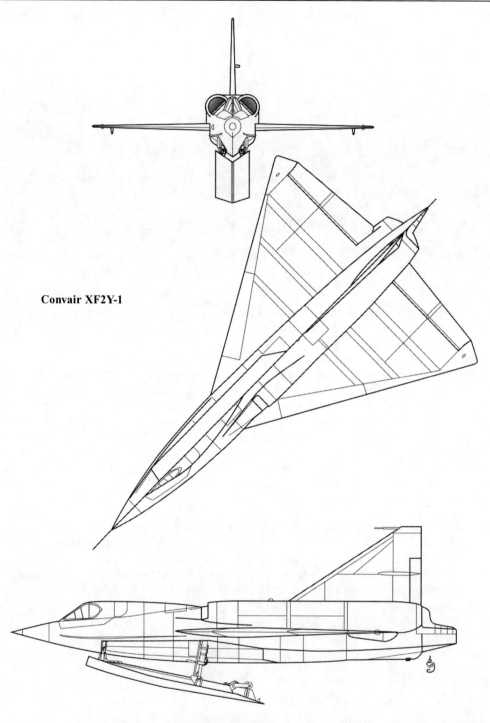

Convair XF2Y-1

The Convair F2Y Sea Dart was (and still is today) the only type of seaplane in the world to have achieved supersonic flight. Its origins can be traced to a highly ambitious Navy competition initiated in 1948 to generate designs for a jet-propelled supersonic fighter capable of operating from the sea. Convair's sea fighter proposal called for a twin-engine, pure delta-wing (tailless) planform on a blended hull which would rise up on two retractable hydro-skis for takeoffs and landings. Before settling on a two-ski arrangement for the project, Convair was said to have tested a number

The XF2Y-1 seen during takeoff at full ski extension. The Navy's interest in the "Sea Fighter" program was motivated in part by the difficulties of operating high-performance jets from carriers.

of different variations on conventional seaplanes (type unknown). Convair's proposal was deemed to hold the most promise, and in January 1951, the company received a contract to build two prototypes under the designation XF2Y-1. In mid–1952, even before a prototype had flown, BuAer was sufficiently enthusiastic about the program to order twelve production models as the F2Y-1, then, before the end of the year, increased the contract to a total of twenty-two aircraft. The Navy's motivation was largely influenced by the difficulties it was facing in adapting high-performance jet aircraft to carrier operations. The contract was later changed to provide that the first four production examples be completed as unarmed YF2Y-1 service test aircraft.

Much of the technology utilized in the sea fighter concept was derived from Convair's previous experience with the XF-92A, the world's first pure delta-wing jet aircraft, as well as other technical data from associated Convair projects on the YF-102 supersonic fighter and XB-58 supersonic bomber, both under development for the U.S. Air Force. As with the XF-92A, pitch and roll control of the XF2Y-1 would be effected by "elevons" on the trailing edges of the wings, interconnected to simultaneously function as elevators and ailerons. The J46 powerplants specified, essentially fifty percent scale-ups of the J34, were still under development by Westinghouse. Convair minimized the problem of engine ingestion of water-spray by locating the intakes high up on the upper hull behind the leading edges of the wings. The lower hull, in addition to a characteristic V-chine bottom, included speed brakes which also doubled as water brakes for differential water steering. Floating at rest, the XF2Y-1 sat slightly tail low, with the leading edges of the wings elevated about eighteen inches above the waterline and the trailing edges actually touching the water. The one-piece canopy, consisting of two tear-shaped windscreens, hinged backward for ingress and egress.

As the first XF2Y-1 airframe neared completion in mid–1952, the J46 engines were not ready for installation, causing Convair to substitute two non-afterburning J34-WE-32s of 3,400 lbs./s.t. each. Thus completed, with test pilot E. D. (Sam) Shannon at the controls, the XF2Y-1 commenced taxiing tests in San Diego Bay in December 1952. In a normal takeoff sequence, the skis remained fully retracted until reaching a speed of 10 to 11 mph, then extended to an intermediate position up to about 55 mph, and then extended fully while the aircraft accelerated to a takeoff speed of

One of the two YF2Y-1s shown on ramp with redesigned skis and oleos. The first YF2Y-1, in August 1954, became the world's only seaplane to exceed the speed of sound. The other two YF2Y-1s were never flown.

145 mph. On January 14, 1953, during a high-speed taxi test, the aircraft inadvertently lifted off the water and flew about 1,000 feet before touching down; its first "official" flight did not occur until April 9, 1953. Further testing revealed that the XF2Y-1 was not only seriously underpowered for its weight, but also nearly impossible to control due to severe buffeting and vibration generated by the hydro-skis during takeoffs and landings. Convair sought to remedy the problem by redesigning the hydro-skis and supporting oleo struts, but these efforts only provided a partial solution. Around the same time, the program received another setback linked to discovery of the "area-rule" principle by NACA engineer Richard T. Whitcomb (i.e., due to the straight-bodied shape of its fuselage, the induced drag at the wing junction would prevent the XF2Y-1 [like the YF-102] from reaching super-

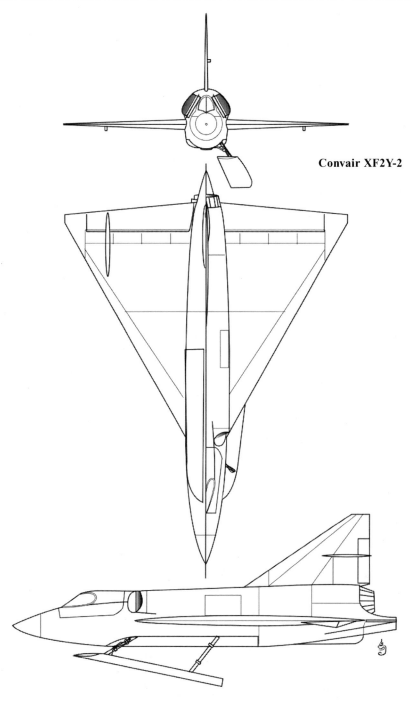

Convair XF2Y-2

sonic speed in level flight). Meanwhile, afterburning J46 engines were installed in the prototype, but performance trials held afterward soon demonstrated that the new powerplants would not produce the anticipated levels of thrust. Navy officials were sufficiently disillusioned at this point to cancel the second prototype and reduce the contract to four service test and eight production aircraft. Even so, Convair was authorized to proceed with the extensively redesigned F2Y-2, which would feature an area-ruled fuselage section and a single Pratt & Whitney J75-P-9 engine developing 15,000 lbs./s.t. in afterburner.

The XF2Y-2 after being converted to a single-ski configuration in 1954. The ski would not retract fully into the hull, thereby restricting the aircraft to low-speed operations. The entire program was terminated in 1957.

The first service test YF2Y-1, powered by J46s, joined the Sea Dart program in early 1954. It differed from the prototype in having somewhat elongated engine nacelles and exhaust nozzles but lacked built-in beaching gear. On August 3, 1954, Convair test pilot Charles E. Richbourg placed the YF2Y-1 in a shallow dive and exceeded the speed of sound, the first seaplane to ever do so. Problems encountered with airflow over the wings resulted in span-wise fences being installed on the upper surfaces near the tip. Although a number of modifications were made to the skis in the course of tests, the aircraft remained dangerously unstable during takeoffs and landings. Misfortune struck the following November when, during a demonstration before Navy officials and the press over San Diego Bay, the YF2Y-1 disintegrated in mid-air, killing test pilot Richbourg. An investigation revealed that the aircraft had exceeded its stress limits due to pilot induced oscillations. Given the results thus far, combined with the fact that much progress had been made in the interim on the carrier jet problem, the Navy cancelled the remaining eight production F2Y-1s and terminated further development of the F2Y-2. What remained of the program—the single XF2Y-1 and three YF2F-1s under construction—was reduced to experimental status only.

Through the balance of 1954, the XF2Y-1 underwent a series of modifications in which the twin skis were replaced by a single, wider hydro-ski. Since the single ski could not fully retract into the belly recesses, the aircraft was restricted to low-speed flight operations. When takeoff and landing trials with the new configuration began in late December 1954, the XF2Y-1 experienced nearly uncontrollable hydrodynamic oscillations; however, changes subsequently made to the rate of elevon deflection and revision of the oleo damping systems solved the problem to the extent that the aircraft could safely make crosswind takeoffs and landings and be operated in seas with six to ten-foot waves, which exceeded even the original requirements. After completing the single-ski test program in early 1956, the XF2Y-1 was placed in storage. The second YF2Y-1 flew for the first time on March 3, 1956. It was powered by the same J46 engines and came in a twin-ski configuration, but featured the final revisions made to the ski after-bodies seen on the first YF2Y-1, plus foldable beaching wheels similar to the XF2Y-1. During the open sea takeoff and landing trials that followed, Navy officials rated the control problems associated with the buffeting and vibrations of the twin skis to be completely unsatisfactory. Further trials were halted on April 28 and the aircraft never flew again. The other two service test YF2Y-1s were completed and delivered but never flown. But the program did not entirely end: after the XF2Y-1 was modified yet again to receive a small, rigidly-mounted hydrofoil in place of the single ski, the Navy resumed non-flying, water-testing in March 1957. Because a takeoff angle of attack (i.e., 20-degrees nose up) could not be achieved with the hydrofoil, no actual flights were planned. Early testing revealed pitch oscillations of such magnitude that runs had to be aborted between 60 and 70 mph. Subsequent efforts to revise the hydrofoil were not successful, and the entire program was finally terminated in the fall of 1957.

Four Sea Darts survive today. The XF2Y-1, reported to be in very poor condition, is in storage at the Smithsonian's Paul Garber facility awaiting restoration. Of the three YF2Y-1s, the second example now resides in the San Diego Aerospace Museum at Balboa Park, the third in the Wings of Freedom Air and Space Museum at NAS Willow Grove, Pennsylvania, and the last at the Florida Air Museum (Sun n' Fun) in Lakeland.

Grumman Aircraft Engineering Corp.

Even before World War II ended, Grumman was actively engaged in plans to design and develop large amphibians for both the military and commercial aviation markets. Indeed, during the post-war era, the company became the largest manufacturer of multi-engine amphibians, producing more boat-hulled aircraft (575, including 50 G-44As) than Convair and Martin combined. In 1969, as prime contractor for the Lunar Excursion Module (LEM) in the Apollo program, the company changed its name to Grumman Aerospace Corp., then in 1994, after being acquired by Northrop Corp., emerged as Northrop-Grumman Corp. Founder Leroy Grumman died in 1982 at age 87.

Grumman G-73 Mallard (1946)

TECHNICAL SPECIFICATIONS

Type: 12-passenger commercial/civil amphibian.
Total produced: 59

Grumman's original G-73 prototype in late 1946, after Type Certification and re-registration as NC41824. This aircraft was ultimately sold to a Canadian mining company.

Powerplants: two 600-hp Pratt & Whitney R-1340-S3H1 *Wasp* 9-cylinder radial engines driving three-bladed, constant-speed metal propellers.

Performance: max. speed 215 mph, cruise 180 mph, ceiling 23,000 ft.; range 863 mi. (normal), 1,400 mi. (max.).

Weights: 9,350 lbs. empty, 12,750 lbs. gross.

Dimensions: span 66 ft. 8 in., length 48 ft. 4 in., wing area 444 sq. ft.

In December 1944, with the aim of offering a post-war successor to the G-21 Goose, an engineering team led by Gordon Israel began laying down the blueprint for the new G-73 Mallard. Leroy Grumman and his staff were convinced that once the war ended there would be an explosion of public air transportation which, in turn, would create a ready market among feeder airlines for a ten to fifteen-passenger twin-engine amphibian. In fact, a post-war market analysis performed by the company went as far as to suggest that as many as 250 of these aircraft might be sold. Though sharing characteristics with the Goose in terms of layout, the design of the G-73 emerged with a larger and cleaner airframe having a more modern tricycle landing gear arrangement. The single-strut wing floats also doubled as auxiliary fuel tanks. Israel believed the new amphibian would perform best with engines producing 700 to 800 hp; however, since none were available in that power range, he was forced to compromise with supercharged R-1340s delivering 600 hp up to 3,000 feet and 550 hp up to 5,000 feet, which left the G-73 slightly underpowered for its weight. Normal accommodation was two crewmembers and ten passengers, with access through a door on the port side of the hull; a lavatory and baggage compartment was located aft. For short-range operations, five additional seats could be located in the lavatory and baggage area. According to a customer's wishes, the cabin could be special ordered with sofas, tables, and overstuffed chairs.

The first G-73 rolled out for its maiden flight on April 30, 1946, and like the Goose and Widgeon, testing revealed the aircraft to have superb handling qualities both on the water and in the

A recent photograph of the G-73T Turbo-Mallard serving with Chalk's Ocean Airways. All G-73Ts were suspended from commercial operations following a fatal crash in December 2005.

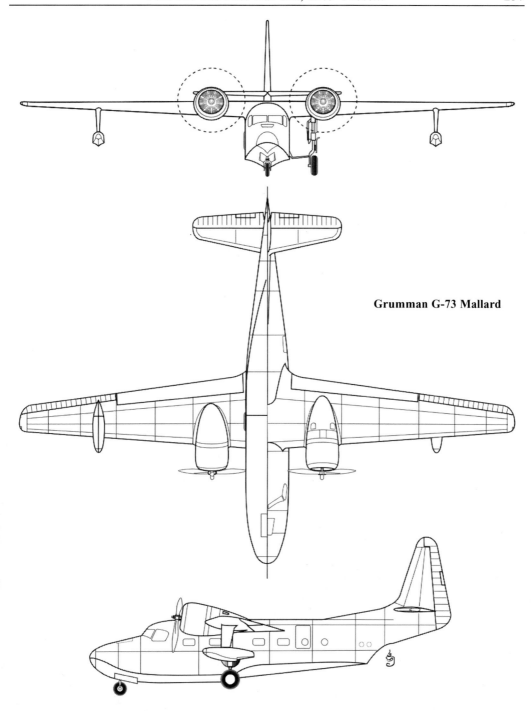

Grumman G-73 Mallard

air. After receiving its Type Certificate in September 1946, this aircraft was delivered to the first Mallard customer, a Canadian mining company. But sales to feeder airlines were not forthcoming as expected, with only one G-73 purchased by Air Commuting in 1947, a New York City–based carrier that ceased operations before actually starting any scheduled services. The only military operator was the Egyptian Air Force, which received two Mallards in 1949. These aircraft were in fact outfitted with luxury accommodations for then Egyptian ruler, King Farouk, and following Farouk's overthrow in 1952, used as personal transports by the new government established under

Gamal Abdel Nasser. Limited production continued until March 1951, at which point Grumman had delivered a total of fifty-nine G-73s, primarily to corporate customers in the United States and Canada. The last Mallard built was initially retained by Grumman as a company transport but later sold to a Canadian firm. Later resale of corporate aircraft saw many G-73s registered in coastal and inter-island regions like Australia, New Zealand, and the East Indies, mainly as executive transports. Starting in the mid–1950s, a number of ex-corporate Mallards saw service as airliners with small regional carriers in the U.S., Canada, Caribbean, Australia, Japan, and French Polynesia (Tahiti).

As with the Goose and Widgeon, efforts to upgrade the Mallard with more power started in the mid–1960s. A Mallard owned by Northern Consolidated Airlines (Alaska) was tested for fifty hours in 1964 and 1965 with two 578-shp Pratt & Whitney PT6A-6 turboprop but later returned to standard configuration. The same aircraft was modified again in 1969, this time with 652-shp PT6A-27s, resulting in the award of a supplemental Type Certificate in 1970 as the G-73T Turbo Mallard, rated for seventeen passengers. Thereafter, Frakes Aviation performed a number of G-73T PT6A conversions (652 shp to 715 shp), and similar modifications on several other Mallards were undertaken by an Australian company listed as Aero Engineers. During the early 1990s, in a venture coordinated by Duncan Aviation in the U.S., efforts were made to raise sufficient investment capital to place the Mallard (presumably the G-73T) back into limited production using the manufacturing facilities of Aero and Levov in the Czech Republic; however, the plan apparently never came to fruition. Most recently, Turbo Mallards flying regular passenger services between Florida and the Bahamas with Chalk's Ocean Airways were all grounded in December 2005 after one of them experienced a complete separation of its right wing following takeoff, killing the two crewmembers and all eighteen passengers. An investigation of the crash (see NTSB/AAR-07/04) attributed the wing failure to a combination of corrosion in the main spar and fatigue cracks in the strap added to the spar, and Chalk's other G-73Ts were subsequently found to have the same problem. Once the investigation was concluded, the Federal Aviation Administration issued an airworthiness directive that effectively removed G-73Ts from further air carrier operations. Today, over thirty *Wasp*-powered Mallards are believed to remain on the U.S. Aircraft Registry, though the actual number in airworthy condition is not known.

Grumman SA/HU-16 (G-64 and -111, JR2F and UF) Albatross (1947)

TECHNICAL SPECIFICATIONS (SA-16A [HU-16B])

Type: 18-passenger military amphibian; 30-passenger commercial amphibian (G-111).
Total produced: 466
Powerplants: two 1,225-hp Wright R-1820-76 Cyclone 9-cylinder radial engines driving three-bladed, constant-speed metal propellers.
Performance: max. speed 236 mph, cruise 150 mph, ceiling 21,500 ft.; range 1,581 mi. [1,811 mi.] (normal), 2,415 mi. [2,645 mi.] (max.).
Weights: 20,800 lbs. [22,884 lbs.] empty, 29,500 lbs. [32,000 lbs.] max takeoff (water), 33,500 lbs. (water).
Dimensions: span 80 ft. 0 in. [96 ft. 8 in.], length 60 ft. 7 in. [62 ft. 2 in.] , wing area 883 [1,035] sq. ft.

The last type of large, multi-engine flying boat to be mass-produced by a manufacturer in the United States, the design of Grumman's G-64 originated from a 1944 Navy requirement calling for a twin-engine utility amphibian with a capacity for four crewmembers and ten passengers or 5,000 lbs. of cargo. Since extended range (2,000 mi.+) and multi-mission capability (i.e., maritime reconnaissance and antisubmarine patrol) were essential factors, the specification included provision to carry extra fuel in tip floats and for wing pylons that could be rigged to carry drop tanks, bombs, depth charges, or torpedoes. In late 1944, BuAer authorized Grumman to built two prototypes as the XJR2F-1, however, by the time construction was actually underway (delayed apparently by Grumman's other wartime production priorities), the war had ended, and the new amphibian's potential roles had been expanded to encompass search and rescue missions with the recently-established

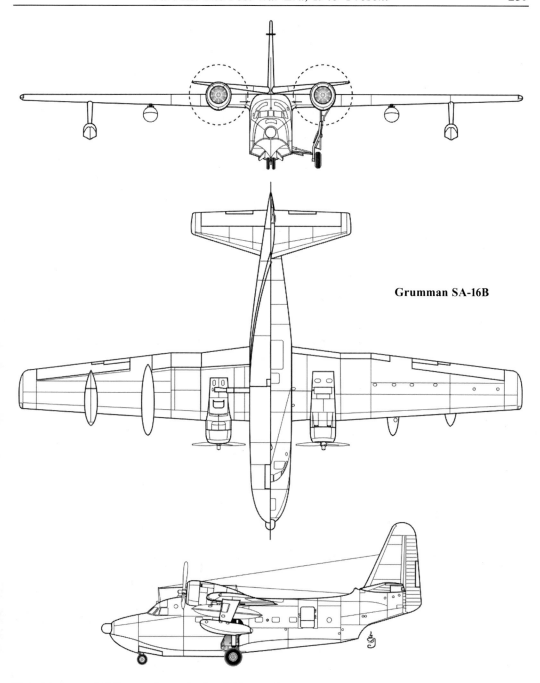

Grumman SA-16B

U.S. Air Force. While aerodynamically similar to the G-73 Mallard, the much larger G-64 emerged with over twice the mass and horsepower. The design of the two-step hull incorporated a deep V-section that would enable the aircraft to operate in very rough seas. As also seen on the G-73, the G-64 utilized a new, much stronger, tricycle gear arrangement consisting of dual nose wheels and main gear struts that pivoted out from the wings and the hull.

The maiden flight of the first XJR2F-1 took place on October 24, 1947, and the aircraft was thereafter delivered to the Navy for official evaluations, followed shortly by the second prototype. Grumman originally selected the name "Pelican" for the XJR2F-1 but later changed it to "Albatross." Very favorable performance trials conducted during 1947 and 1948 led to a series of produc-

Grumman XJR2F-1 prototype as seen in late 1947. Although the aircraft was ordered in 1944, other wartime priorities delayed completion of the project.

tion contracts from both the Navy and the USAF. In the interim, the Navy had discarded the JR designation, and G-64s were initially ordered as PF-1As, but before any aircraft could actually be delivered, the designation had changed again to UF-1 under a new utility category. From 1948 to 1954, 138 of the amphibians were manufactured under Naval Bureau Numbers, though not all entered service with the Navy. Eleven specially equipped variants, designated UF-1G, were delivered to the Coast Guard; eight (PB-517 through -524) to Indonesian Air Force under a government-sponsored Military Assistance Program (MAP); and five more accepted by the Navy in 1953 as UF-1T dual-control trainers. Contracts under USAF serial numbers accounted for production of 305 G-64s between 1949 and 1953. The USAF originally ordered the Albatross under the designation OA-16A but changed it to SA-16A by the time deliveries started. Like the Navy contract, not all of the aircraft were accepted by the USAF, with fifty-three being allocated to the Coast Guard as UF-1Gs, plus, under MAP, three to the Portuguese Air Force and two to the Spanish Air Force. During 1953, 154 USAF SA-16As, sometimes referred to as "triphibians," received skis kits for operations on snow and ice. Two other USAF SA-16As, after undergoing factory conversions for cold weather operations in Antarctica, were reassigned to the Navy as UF-1Ls.

In 1955 Grumman introduced an extensive upgrade to the type (commonly referred as the "B" conversion) in which wingspan was increased sixteen feet six inches with new outer wing panels incorporating enlarged ailerons and fixed leading edge camber in place of the original slots. Other improvements included a taller fin and rudder and an aerodynamic cleanup of aerials and antennas. Over a period extending to 1961, Grumman converted 242 of the amphibians to the B standard: ninety-four for the USAF as the SA-16B; thirty-six antisubmarine versions for export as the SA-16B/ASW; seventy-one for the Coast Guard as the UF-2G; and thirty-three for the Navy as the UF-2. During the same timeframe, Grumman built twenty-seven new aircraft to the B standard: ten for the Royal Canadian Air Force as the CSR-110; six to the Japanese Multi-Service Defense Forces as the UF-2S; five to the West German *Deutsche Marine* as the SA-16B; plus six more retained by the factory for resale. Other than those mentioned above, foreign air arms receiving SA-16Bs and SA-16B/ASWs included Argentina, Brazil, Chile, Republic of China (Taiwan), Greece, Iceland, Italy, Malaysia, Mexico, Norway, Pakistan, Peru, Philippines, Thailand, and Venezuela. In 1962, following adoption of the tri-service system, all Albatross designations were changed as follows: SA-16A

Opposite: **UF-2G (HU-14E after 1962) serving with the Coast Guard. The last operational HU-16E flight was made in March 1983. The type is reported to have operated with foreign air forces until the mid–1990s.**

A total of 305 SA-16As were accepted by the USAF between 1949 and 1953 for search and rescue duties. Ninety-four of these later underwent the conversion to SA-16B (HU-16B after 1962).

to HU-16A; SA-16B to HU-16B; SA-16B/ASW to SHU-16B; UF-1 to HU-16C; UF-1L to LU-16C; UF-1T to TU-16C; UF-2 to HU-16D; and UF-2G to HU-16E. One UF-1 converted in 1962 to a four-engine configuration (two R-1340s added) by Shin Meiwa Industries in Japan became the UF-XS. This aircraft also featured a T-tail and a General Electric T58 turboshaft engine mounted in the fuselage to provide bleed air over the flaps for boundary layer control.

Navy UF-1s and USAF SA-16As began entering operational service in 1949, and the first UF-1Gs were delivered to the Coast Guard in 1951. Navy versions were used for a variety of duties, including transportation of personnel and cargo, maritime reconnaissance, air ambulance, and air-sea rescue. All USAF and Coast Guard variants were specifically dedicated to the search and rescue role, with most USAF SA-16s being assigned to the Air Rescue Service (ARS) branch of the Military Air Transport Service (MATS). During the Korean War, ARS SA-16s began flying rescue missions in the Yellow Sea in the summer of 1950 and served throughout the conflict. Often, SA-16s would accompany Sikorsky H-19 helicopters to the area of the downed aircraft where the helicopter would make the actual pickup. In operational service, most SA-16s were adapted to use JATO bottles for improved takeoff performance and also retrofitted with an AN/APS-31A search radar, carried under the wing initially but later housed in a nose radome. One of the type's serious deficiencies was the inability to maintain altitude on one engine when loaded. The wing extension of the B conversion, in reducing stall speed by almost 10 mph, rendered single-engine operations much safer.

At the time the U.S. entered hostilities in Southeast Asia in mid–1964, HU-16Bs serving as a component of the USAF's Aerospace Rescue and Recovery Service commenced operations in the Gulf of Tonkin, and by the end of 1965, had been credited with saving 60 downed airmen. In addition to rescue duties, HU-16Bs orbiting off the coast of Vietnam were used as command and control platforms to coordinate multi-aircraft missions. As more Sikorsky HH-3 (i.e. "Jolly Green Giant") helicopters entered USAF service during the mid–1960s, HU-16s were withdrawn from SAR duties. In later service, they were employed for surveillance of ice flow and oil slicks, as well as transportation of troops and supplies in support of Army Special Forces operations. The USAF

The sole Conroy Turbo Albatross as seen at Lakeland, Florida, in 1992. Even though the *Dart* engines more than doubled available horsepower, efforts to market the type were unsuccessful. *Credit:* Derek Heley.

phased-out its last HU-16 in 1974, and the Navy retired its last active examples in 1976. Starting in 1955, ex–USAF SA-16/HU-16s were transferred to four different Air National Guard squadrons (California, Maryland, Rhode Island, and West Virginia), where they served until being withdrawn between 1971 and 1975. The last operational Coast Guard HU-16E made its final flight on March 10, 1983. Albatrosses are reported to have continued in service with some foreign air forces as late as the mid–1990s.

As they were released from military service, significant numbers of UH-16s found their way into civilian hands. In 1970, Conroy Aircraft Corp. (an affiliate of Aero Spacelines, creator of the "Super Guppy"), converted an HU-16 to 2,280-shp Rolls-Royce *Dart* turboprop engines and attempted to market it as the Conroy Turbo Albatross, but no sales resulted and only a single prototype (civil registration N16CA) was ever completed. In the late 1970s, through a collaborative effort with Resorts International, Grumman Aerospace acquired 57 HU-16s with the intention of converting them to airline use. The conversion amounted to a complete remanufacture of the airframe in which all military equipment was removed, structural components stripped down and repaired or replaced as needed, and the engines rebuilt to zero-time. Additions included a twenty-eight passenger interior, a galley and provision for a flight attendant, plus all new instruments, avionics, and mechanical systems. The first factory-converted Albatross flew in February 1979 and in April 1980, the aircraft received a new Type Certificate as the G-111. In the interval, only thirteen G-111s were actually completed, twelve for Resorts International and one for Conoco Oil Corp., to be used in its Malaysian operations. Other programs to upgrade Albatrosses to turbine power (four engines) have been proposed—one to 1,100-hp Garrett TPE-331 turboprops and another, by Frakes, to 1,000-hp Pratt & Whitney PT-6As—but never pursued. In 1981, Chalk's International Airways (a subsidiary of Resorts International) commenced scheduled airline operations with its G-111s between south Florida and the Bahamas, but in 1987, after Resorts International was acquired by entrepreneur Donald Trump, the aircraft were flown to Arizona and placed in storage. As of 2006, according to one source (see http://www.warbirdalley.com/hu16.htm), a total of ninety-two G-64s and G-111s remain on the U.S. Aircraft Registry, of which approximately thirty are said to be in airworthy condition.

Hughes Aircraft Division, Hughes Tool Co.

After making a start in Culver City, California, as Hughes Development Co. in 1934, the company reorganized in 1936 as the Hughes Aircraft Division of Hughes Tool Co. During its formative years, it functioned as an alter-ego of its immensely wealthy and sometimes eccentric owner, Howard R. Hughes, Jr. Hughes had a passion for breaking records, and his first in-house aircraft design, the H-1, set new records for closed course speed (352 mph in 1935) and average transcontinental speed (332 mph in 1937). In 1938, with his modified Lockheed 14, he established a new around-the-world record of three days, nine hours. World War II provided the pretext for yet another record: the largest aircraft in the world.

Hughes H-4 (HK-1) Hercules (1947)

TECHNICAL SPECIFICATIONS

Type: long-range military transport.
Total produced: 1
Powerplants: eight 3,000-hp Pratt & Whitney R-4360-4 *Wasp Major* 28-cylinder air-cooled radial engines driving four-bladed, constant-speed metal propellers.
Performance (est.): max. speed 225 mph, cruise 199 mph, ceiling 20,900 ft.; range 2,983 mi. (max.).
Weights: empty (not reported), 400,000 lbs. gross.
Dimensions: span 319 ft. 11 in., length 218 ft. 8 in., wing area 11,430 sq. ft.

The concept for what ultimately became the Hughes H-4 originated with industrialist Henry J. Kaiser. As America entered World War II, losses of Allied ships to German U-boats were reach-

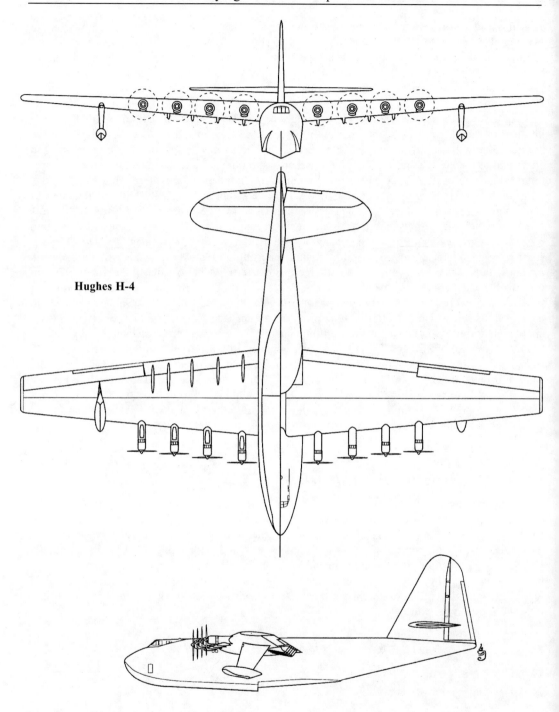

Hughes H-4

ing catastrophic levels (i.e., 1,160 ships sunk in 1942 alone). Kaiser believed the risk of submarine attack could be avoided by building hundreds of mammoth (150–200 ton), cargo or troop-carrying flying boats—"Sky Freighters"—in much the same manner that his shipyards turned-out Liberty ships. After unsuccessful efforts to interest Donald W. Douglas and Glenn L. Martin in the venture, Kaiser persuaded Howard R. Hughes to join him. A War Department development contract issued to Hughes and Kaiser in late 1942 called for three prototypes, designated HK-1 (Hughes-Kaiser-One), to be completed within a two-year deadline. To fund development, the project was

The massive H-4 during the final stages of construction in Long Beach, California. The aircraft was completed in 1947, three years behind schedule.

H-4 seen on November 2, 1947, just prior to its one and only flight. Hughes made the flight during a recess in the U.S. Senate hearings held to investigate the project.

scheduled to receive $18 million over time from the government-sponsored Reconstruction Finance Company.

Hughes, though retaining supervisory capacity, assigned the actual design work on the aircraft to an engineering team led by Glenn E. Odekirk. Many different configurations (e.g., twin-hull; four, six, or engines, etc.) were studied before the HK-1's single-hull, eight-engine layout was adopted. In its final form, the giant aircraft emerged with a projected weight of 400,000 lbs., fully loaded, and the capacity to carry 700 fully-equipped troops. Due to the wartime restrictions placed on strategic materials such as aluminum, most of the airframe would be fabricated according to the "duramold" process, a method developed by Hughes in which laminations of plywood bonded with resin were molded under pressure to form very large components.

The H-4 in 1980, being readied for public display at Long Beach after acquisition by the California Aero Club. In 1995, the aircraft was moved again, this time to the Evergreen Aviation Museum in McMinnville, Oregon.

After more than a year had passed, with the project still lingering in the design stages, Kaiser, who originally believed that the first aircraft could be designed, built, and flown in less than twelve months, became frustrated and withdrew. Hughes continued under his own name, initially as the HFB-1 (Hughes-Flying-Boat-One), but later changed the aircraft's designation to H-4, signifying the fourth aircraft to be designed by his company. Actual construction of the prototype did not begin until mid–1944, sixteen months after the contract award, and work proceeded at such a slow pace that the H-4 remained unfinished at the time the war ended in September 1945. Many reasons have been cited for the delays, most notably Hughes' own preoccupation with perfection and his alleged mental breakdown during development. After the war, Hughes continued construction of the H-4, government cancellation of production plans notwithstanding. Although Hughes had given the name Hercules to the huge airplane, the popular press tagged it the "Spruce Goose," a misnomer, since it was made mostly of birch.

In fall of 1947, around the time the H-4 was completed, the Senate War Investigating Committee subpoenaed Hughes to explain and justify the usage of government funds on the project. While giving his testimony, Hughes remained unruffled in the face of the Committee's evident hostility and skepticism. During a break in the Senate hearings, he returned to California for the ostensible purpose of running taxi tests on the H-4. On November 2, during the last of three taxi runs near Long Beach, with twenty-seven people aboard (including three members of the press), Hughes lifted the H-4 off the water, maintaining an altitude of seventy feet at an airspeed of 135 mph for just under a mile before setting it back down. Critics of the project claimed that the aircraft had remained in the ground effect and lacked sufficient power to climb any higher. In any case, the aircraft never flew again and was maintained in flying condition in Hughes' hangar until his death in 1976.

In 1980, the H-4 was acquired by the California Aero Club and thereafter placed on display under a large dome adjacent to the *Queen Mary* ocean liner exhibit in Long Beach. Disney purchased both attractions in 1988, but after disappointing revenues, sold the H-4 to Evergreen Aviation Museum in 1995, located in McMinnville, Oregon (southwest of Portland), where it may be seen today.

Icon Aircraft

This Los Angeles, California–based company was founded by Kirk Hawkins in 2005, a year after the Federal Aviation Administration enacted new rules creating the Light Sport Aircraft category and the Light Sport Pilot Certificate. Hawkins, himself an engineer, former USAF pilot, and Stanford Business School graduate, thereafter assembled a design team that included individuals who had previously worked for Burt Rutan at Scaled Composites, Inc. For more information, see http://www.iconaircraft.com/about-icon.html.

Icon A5 (2008)

TECHNICAL SPECIFICATIONS

Type: 2-place light sport civil amphibian.
Total produced: 1
Powerplant: one 100-hp Rotax 912 ULS 4-cylinder air and liquid-cooled opposed engine driving a three-bladed, fixed-pitch composite propeller.
Performance: max. speed 120 mph; ceiling (not reported).; range 345 mi.
Weights: 900 lbs. empty, 1,430 lbs. gross.
Dimensions: span 34 ft. 0 in., length 22 ft. 0 in., wing area (not reported).

The best word for the Icon A5 is audacious. Although there are still other candidates in offing (i.e., Seawind 300C and Thurston TA-16, both reported below), no Standard Airworthiness Certificate has been issued by the FAA for a new amphibian design since the appearance of the Thurston Teal in 1969. In addition to being Light Sport qualified, everything about the A5 is innovative: molded, carbon-fiber airframe, high-performance wing/airfoil design, new lightweight engine, sports car type interior appointments, trailerable with folding wings, and optional LCD (glass) instrument display.

Icon A5 prototype as seen during flight-testing in July 2008. Icon Aircraft has announced plans to proceed with Type Certification and possibly have the aircraft in production sometime in 2010.

Instead of tip floats, the A5 employs seawings (sponsons) that not only add lift, but also function as entry platforms on the water. The A5 will apparently be available as either an amphibian with retractable tricycle landing gear or a flying boat without any gear. According to the manufacturer's estimates, at gross weight, the A5 will take off within 750 feet on a standard day.

The A5 prototype made its first flight on July 9, 2008, and has since been undergoing trials to access general flying characteristics such as takeoffs and landings on land and water, low-speed maneuvering, and water handling. Icon expects the experimental phase of the flight test program to be completed in 2009. Once the design is finalized, the company plans to build a production prototype that will verify all FAR Part 23 airworthiness standards. Production is scheduled to begin

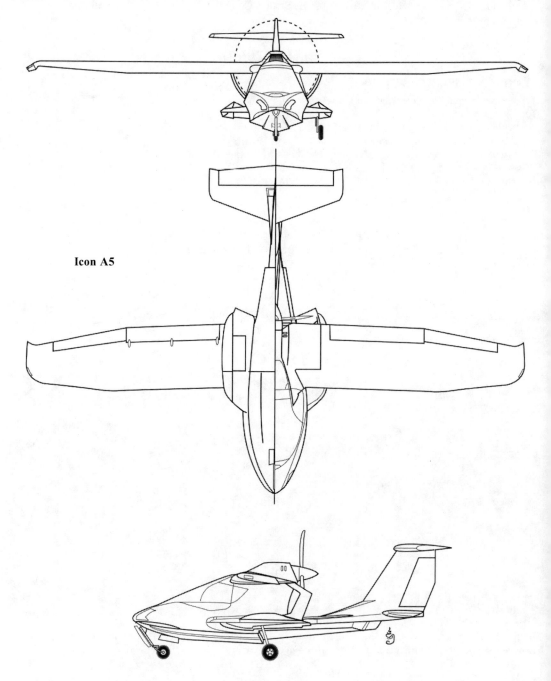

Icon A5

sometime in late 2010. According to Icon's website (see http://www.iconaircraft.com/buy-your-model.html), the target price for an A5 standard model will be $139,000.

Lake Aircraft Corp.

After acquiring the assets of Colonial Aircraft Corp. in 1959 (see page 221), Lake Aircraft Corp. was formed on Colonial's site in Sanford, Maine with Jack F. Strayer, a former Colonial distributor, as its president. Since that time, over a forty-plus year interval, the company has undergone a series of reorganizations in which the original Aircraft Type Certificate changed hands at least four times. In late 2002, under the name Sun Lake aircraft (a subsidiary of LanShe Aerospace, LLC), all production rights were acquired by Wadi Rahim, a native of Bangladesh, and all manufacturing operations relocated from Maine to Fort Pierce, Florida. Most recently, as reported on the Lake Amphibian Flyers Club website (see www.lakeflyers.com/lake_history.htm), Armand Rivard (i.e., Revo, Inc.), who had sold Lake's assets and ATC to Rahim, regained control in 2005 following a default in payments.

Lake LA-4, LA4-200, and LA4-200EP Buccaneer (1960)

TECHNICAL SPECIFICATIONS (LA4-200)

Type: 4-place civil amphibian.
Total produced: 873 (both versions, est.)
Powerplant: one 200-hp Lycoming IO-360-A1B 4-cylinder air-cooled opposed engine driving a two-bladed, constant-speed metal propeller.
Performance: max. speed 140 mph, cruise 121 mph; ceiling (not reported).; range 600 mi.
Weights: 1,559 lbs. empty, 2,600 lbs. gross.
Dimensions: span 38 ft. 0 in., length 24 ft. 11 in., wing area 189 sq. ft.

Soon after the takeover by Lake, in order to offset the increased gross weight of the proposed four-seat LA-4 Buccaneer prototype, the twenty-first Colonial C-2 built (serial number 121) was modified by extending wingspan four feet, plus one foot added to each aileron. Other changes included lengthening the nose seventeen inches to allow for complete enclosure of the nose gear when retracted and revising the cockpit arrangement. The modified aircraft, designated the LA-4P, retained the 180-hp Lycoming O-360-A1A powerplant of the C-2 and was tested during 1960. Listed as LA-4As, the next two production aircraft retained the shorter nose of the C-2, while all of the other estimated 182 LA-4s completed between 1961 and 1969 came with long noses. It is an interesting point of fact, that from 1963 to 1985, Lake Aircraft, under several different variations of ownership, subcontracted actual construction of the aircraft to Aerofab, Inc., a separate company formed for that purpose by Herbert P. Lindbad, who had co-founded Colonial with David B. Thurston back in 1946.

In 1969, Lake Aircraft introduced the 200-hp LA4-200 with the aim of increasing certificated gross weight. The 200-lb. increase in takeoff weight rendered four-seat operations far more practical. Other refinements made during production of the LA4-200 included moving the battery to the baggage compartment and the pitot tube under the wing, replacing the cabin roof and upper nose with fiberglass panels, and adding fourteen gallons of fuel capacity to the tip floats. A single LA-4, registration number N7637L, built as a flying boat without amphibious landing gear, was completed as a special order in 1969. The LA4-200 Buccaneer became most numerous of the entire Colonial/Lake series, with approximately 645 examples having been delivered by the end of 1981. From 1981 to 1986, LA4-200 production was superceded by the LA4-200EP or Buccaneer EP (extended performance), which featured a balanced IO-360-A1B6 engine, a larger propeller, a prop shaft extension, and new rear cowling. According to reported serial numbers used, forty-three LA4-200EPs are believed to have been built, bringing total LA-4 production to an estimated 873 aircraft. Since being manufactured, many LA-4s have been retrofitted with after-market Rayjay turbo-superchargers to improve performance at altitude.

Lake LA-4, the first production model of the series, powered by a 180-hp Lycoming O-360-A1A. An estimated 182 were sold between 1960 and 1969, when production shifted to the LA4–200.

Recent photograph of the LA4–200, the most numerous of the series, with 641 having been delivered by the end of 1981. The fairing and scoop ahead of the pylon houses a retrofitted heating system.

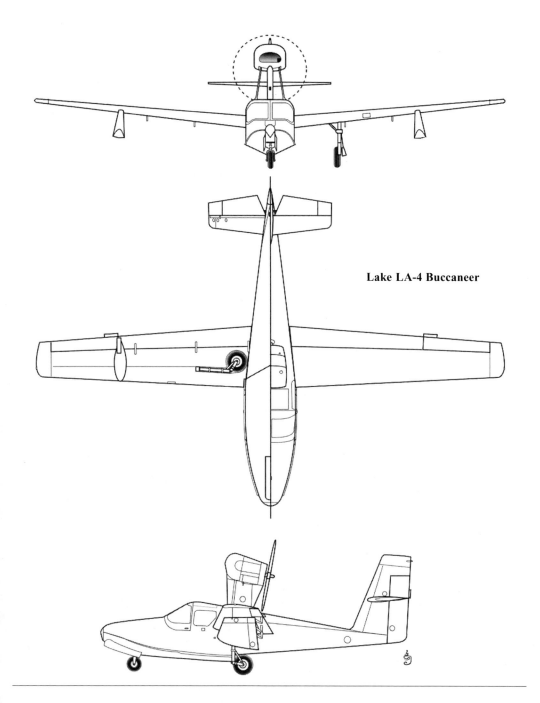

Lake LA-4 Buccaneer

Lake LA4-250 and -270T Renegade, Seafury, and Seawolf (1982)

TECHNICAL SPECIFICATIONS (LA4-250)

Type: 4 to 6-place civil amphibian.

Total produced: 137 (all versions, est.)

Powerplant: one 250-hp Lycoming IO-540-C4B5 6-cylinder air-cooled opposed engine driving a three-bladed, constant-speed metal propeller.

Performance: max. speed 168 mph (est.), cruise 150 mph; ceiling 14,700 ft.; range 1,050 mi.

Weights: 2,070 lbs. empty, 3,050 lbs. gross.

Dimensions: span 38 ft. 0 in., length 28 ft. 4 in., wing area 189 sq. ft.

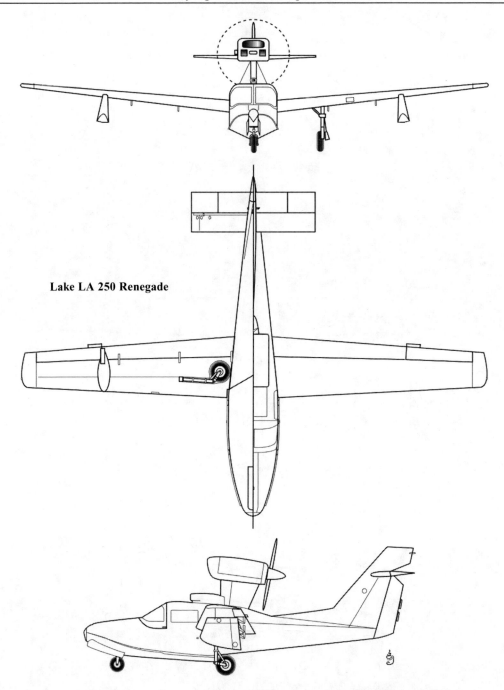

Lake LA 250 Renegade

Major changes in the Lake production standard seemed to have occurred whenever the company changed hands. Evidence of this trend was seen when Armand Rivard (as a subsidiary of Revo, Inc.) acquired the Lake Type Certificate in 1979, followed in two years by the introduction the LA4-200EP. But even as new standard was put into operation, plans were afoot to offer a far more extensive upgrade in the form of the larger LA4-250. The prototype LA4-250 (N250L), completed and test flown during 1982, was derived from an existing LA4-200 airframe in which the hull was lengthened three feet six inches in the cabin area to accommodate two additional seats and more baggage space, and the pylon and nacelle were modified to accept the larger IO-540 engine.

Lake LA4–270T Renegade N84142 shown in 2008. The Renegade series uses a standard LA4 wing with a 3-foot 5-inch fuselage stretch and enlarged fin and rudder area to offset the increase in power. *Credit*: **Julian Mönch.**

The hull extension also produced a deeper V-section, enabling operations in rougher waters than previous versions. To compensate for the added power (and modernize appearance), the fin and rudder were enlarged and given sweepback, and the horizontal surfaces raised to a higher position in the thrust line. First deliveries of LA-250s, marketed under the new name Renegade, commenced in late 1983. Interestingly, Rivard purchased Aerofab, Inc., from Herbert Lindbad in 1985, thus combining Type Certificate ownership of Lakes with their manufacturing operations for first time in over twenty years.

More power became available in 1987 with the introduction of the LA4-270T, equipped with a 270-hp turbo-supercharged TIO-540-AA1AD. According to the manufacturer's claim, the 270T boasted a 26-mph increase in cruise speed and an almost forty percent improvement in ceiling (i.e., 23,800 ft.), though useful load diminished by 100 lbs. The LA4-250 and 270T were offered in two versions: the standard civil Renegade and the commercial Sea Fury, which featured beefed-up construction and increased salt water protection. A military variant, appearing sometime later as the Seawolf, reportedly featured major structural enhancements, wing hardpoints for stores and munitions, plus an engine boost to 290 hp. Available data does not reveal how many, if any at all, Seawolfs have been manufactured besides the prototype. Sales of LA4-250s from 1983 to 1995 are believed to have numbered over 100 aircraft; sales of LA-270Ts from 1987 to 2002, numbered about thirty. LanShe Aerospace, which acquired Lake as Sun Lake in 2002, resumed production in 2003 and 2004, but the number of aircraft completed before Rivard regained control is uncertain. Today, Team Lake, LLC (see www.teamlake.com), Rivard's current operation, indicates that a new Seafury, in either 250-hp or and 270-hp (T) versions, can be built to order in the $700,000-$800,000 price range. There are also plans, according to the site, to resume production of the military Seawolf.

Glenn L. Martin Co.

Glenn L. Martin's fascination with large flying boats continued unabated into the post-war years. Even after his death in 1955, his company redoubled its efforts to push the flying boat paradigm up to new levels of technology. But the trend of history, specifically, changing military requirements, went against it, and Martin's flying boat era abruptly ended when the last P5M-2 rolled off the Middle River assembly line in 1960. It also marked the end of Martin's fifty-one-year history as an airframe designer and manufacturer. In 1961, the company changed its name to Martin-Marietta Aerospace, specializing in missile systems, and following a merger with Lockheed in 1994, reappeared as Lockheed-Martin.

Martin JRM Mars (1945)

TECHNICAL SPECIFICATIONS (JRM-2, -3)

Type: long-range military transport.
Total produced: 6 (all versions)
Powerplants: four 3,000-hp Pratt & Whitney R-4360-4 *Wasp Major* 28-cylinder air-cooled radial engines driving four-bladed, constant-speed (fully-reversible on inboard engines) metal propellers.
Performance: max. speed 238 mph, cruise 215 mph; ceiling 14,600 ft.; range 6,750 mi.
Weights: 75,573 lbs. empty, 148,500 lbs. normal gross, 165,000 max. takeoff.
Dimensions: span 200 ft. 0 in., length 120 ft. 3 in., wing area 3,683 sq. ft.

During the latter stages of World War II, although the "Sky Freighter" concept had been completely abandoned, Navy planners nonetheless perceived the need for limited numbers of large flying boats to augment Naval Air Transportation Service (NATS) operations in the Pacific. In June 1944, in consideration of the XPB2M-1R's (see Part II, page 182) established performance record in service, BuAer awarded Martin a contract for twenty new aircraft under the designation JRM-1. Though retaining the original wing planform and R-3350 engines of the XPB2M-1R, the JRM-1 (company model 170A) was essentially a new airframe. The hull was lengthened six feet forward of the wings while the aft fuselage was shortened three feet and reshaped to support a large single

Caroline Mars, **the sixth production aircraft and the only JRM-2, as seen in 1946 prior to application of Navy markings. This aircraft, after being converted into a civilian fire-bomber, was destroyed by a typhoon in 1962.**

fin and rudder. Internally, cargo handling was optimized by installing an overhead hoist and deleting many of the bulkheads between compartments. In tooling up for the Navy order, Martin also began work on the model 170-24A, an R-4360-powered civil version of the Mars it hoped to offer on the post-war airliner market.

The first JRM-1, christened *Hawaii Mars*, was delivered to the Navy for evaluations in late

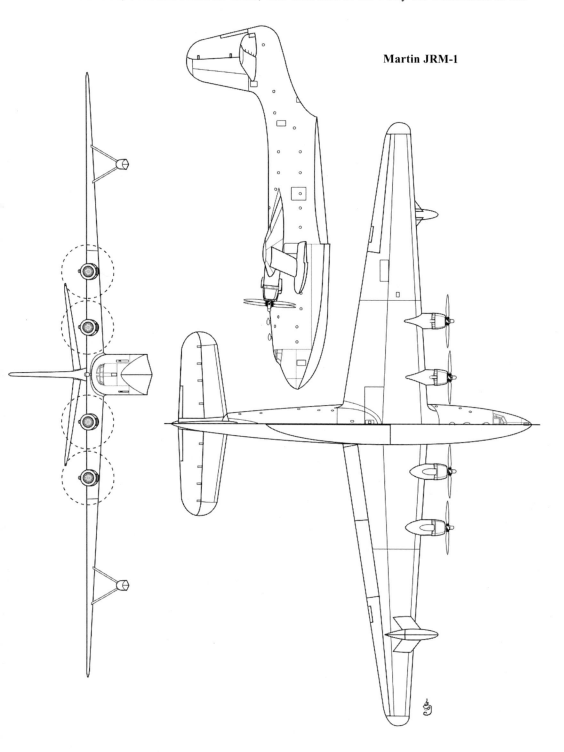

Martin JRM-1

Photograph of *Hawaii Mars* (C-FLYL) made in 2006 at Sproat Lake, B.C., while owned by Forest Industries Flying Tankers. This aircraft and *Philippine Mars* were sold to Coulson Flying Tankers in 2007.

July 1945, but was accidentally destroyed two weeks later in a landing accident on Chesapeake Bay. Martin delivered four more JRM-1s by the end of the year; however, as a result of the V-J Day cutbacks, the original order was reduced to only six aircraft. Added to that, airline operators, though expecting a post-war air travel boom, expressed no interest in the model 170-24A or any other large flying boat for that matter. After entering Navy service, all four JRM-1s received names in Bureau Number order, i.e., *Philippine Mars, Marianas Mars, Marshall Mars*, and *Hawaii Mars* (No. 2). The sixth and final Mars, delivered in 1946 as the JRM-2 and subsequently named *Caroline Mars*, was completed with the 3,000-hp R-4360-4 engines originally intended for the 170-24A and distinguishable by longer-chord cowlings. It also featured fully-reversible propellers on the two inner engines, which improved water handling to the extent that the aircraft could now back up. The increase in power upped takeoff weight by 16,000 lbs. and added over 10,000 lbs. to useful load. Over time, in order to bring them up the JRM-2 payload standard, all four JRM-1s were refitted with R-4360 engines and returned to service as JRM-3s.

As they became fully operational, the five Mars were assigned to VR-2, based in San Francisco Bay at Naval Air Station Alameda. Though used primarily to haul cargo and personnel between the West Coast and Hawaii, the big flying boats did occasionally depart from routine duties to perform some impressive feats: in 1949, the *Caroline Mars* carried a payload of 68,282 lbs. (double the normal load) from Baltimore to Cleveland (Lake Erie); in 1950, the *Caroline Mars*, again, transported 144 Marines from San Diego to Honolulu; and in 1949, the *Marshall Mars* carried a record 301 servicemen plus a crew of seven from San Diego to Alameda. In May 1950, while operating off Diamond Head in Hawaii, the *Marshall Mars* was forced to make an open sea landing after one of its engines caught fire. All of the crew escaped to safety, but the aircraft was entirely consumed by the fire. Other than this incident, the JRMs enjoyed a virtually unblemished safety record during their tenure with VR-2. In 1956 the Navy began the process of reequipping VR-2 with Convair R3Ys

The second JRM-1, *Philippine Mars,* **making a JATO-assisted takeoff from San Francisco Bay in its 1950s heyday with VR-2. It survives today as a fire-bomber under Canadian registration C-FLYK.**

(see page 225), and the final Mars flight took place in August of that year. Thereafter, the four Mars were hauled out of the water on beaching gear and consigned to the boneyard at Alameda; three years later, all four aircraft were sold to a scrap dealer for a combined price of $23,650.

Fortunately, the Mars' career did not end there: in 1959, due to the persistent efforts of an experienced Canadian pilot named Dan McIvor, who envisaged the huge flying boats as ideal platforms with which to fight forest fires, the four JRMs were re-sold to a consortium of British Columbia-based lumber corporations and registered in the name of Forest Industries Flying Tankers (FIFT). In addition to the planes, McIvor acquired most of the Navy's remaining inventory of JRM parts, plus thirty-five spare R-3350-24WA engines. The switch to the less powerful (2,500 hp) but less complex R-3350s, even with the consequent reduction in payload (-10,000 lbs.), was seen as a more practical long-term maintenance scenario. As they were returned to flyable condition, each Mars, one at a time, was flown to Fairey Aviation of Canada in Victoria, British Columbia, where they underwent extensive conversions to aerial fire-bombing tankers. Besides the engine change and a general refurbishment, the conversion involved removal of all military equipment and installation of 6,000-gal. (50,100-lb.) water tanks in the bottom hull where fuel tanks had been. The hull planing surfaces were equipped with retractable scoops designed to enable the aircraft to recharge its water tanks while skimming across a lake, thereby allowing a rapid turnaround between water drops. The first JRM converted, the *Marianas Mars* (Canadian registration CF-LYJ), flew in early 1960, but was destroyed the following June when the pilot (not McIvor, who was ill at the time) cartwheeled the aircraft into the forest, killing himself and three crewmembers. The second, *Caroline Mars* (CF-LYM), commenced fire-fighting operations in early 1962, this time with McIvor at the controls; the following October, however, while ashore for maintenance, the aircraft was wrecked beyond repair by typhoon *Freda*. Despite these misfortunes, *Philippine Mars* (CF-LYK) and *Hawaii Mars* (CF-LYL) entered service as tankers during 1963 and 1964, respectively.

It is an amazing testament, that in the forty-three years that followed, these two huge flying boats flew hundreds of firebombing sorties over western Canada virtually without mishap. In 2006, FIFT disclosed plans to discontinue operations and offer the *Philippine Mars* and *Hawaii Mars* for sale to the highest bidder. Soon afterward, the Glenn L. Martin Aviation Museum in Baltimore launched a fund-raising campaign to acquire at least one of these historic aircraft. But in April 2007, FIFT announced that both of the big flying boats were being sold to Coulson Arcane, Ltd., another British Columbia-based company, for an undisclosed price. According to a website maintained by Coulson Flying Tankers, a subsidiary of Coulson Arcane (see http://martinmars.com/), both aircraft are back in service and available for fire-fighting calls.

Martin P5M (SP-5) Marlin (1948)

TECHNICAL SPECIFICATIONS (P5M-2)

Type: 8 to 12-place maritime and antisubmarine patrol boat.
Total produced: 267 (all versions)
Powerplants: two 3,450-hp Wright R-3350-32WA *Double Cyclone* 18-cylinder air-cooled radial engines driving four-bladed, fully-reversible metal propellers.
Armament: two 20-mm cannons in a powered tail turret and 8,000 lbs. of torpedoes (4), bombs, depth charges, or mines carried in two wing nacelle bays.
Performance: max. speed 251 mph, cruise 159 mph; ceiling 24,000 ft.; range 2,471 mi. (normal), 3,060 mi. (max.).
Weights: 50,485 lbs. empty, 76,595 lbs. normal gross, 78,000 lbs. max. takeoff.
Dimensions: span 118 ft. 2 in., length 100 ft. 7 in., wing area 1,406 sq. ft.

XP5M-1 seen in its original configuration. This aircraft flew with a standard PBM-5 wing mated to the new hull. Some historians believe the hull design was influenced by the Japanese Kawanishi H8K "Emily" of World War II.

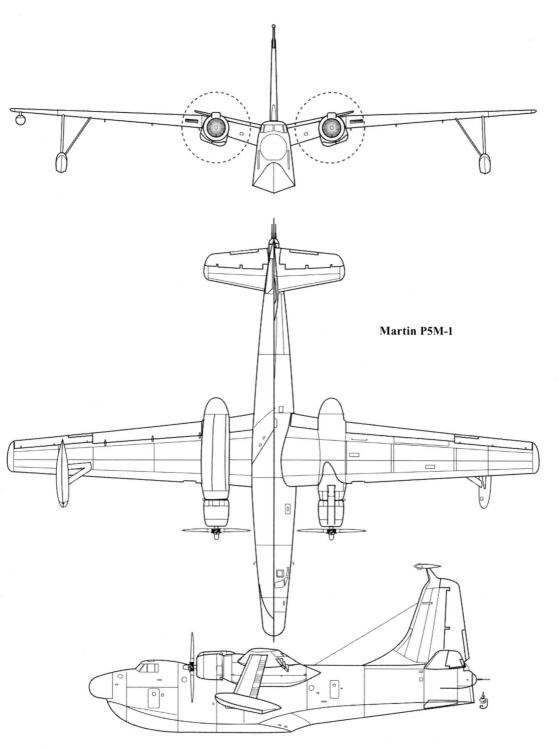

Martin P5M-1

The Martin P5M, though more conservative than its rival Convair P5Y, nevertheless represented a landmark advance in large flying boat design when it appeared in 1948. During the early 1940s, in the midst of wartime production, Martin was quick to acknowledge that the R-3350-powered Consolidated XP4Y-1 and Boeing XPBB-1 (see Part II, above) both demonstrated superior speed and range over the PBM-3. Martin was sufficiently impressed, in fact, to consider the possibility of license-building PBBs at the Middle River plant; however, the wartime priorities on R-3350 engines rendered such a plan impractical. Instead, the company commenced work on a wholly new

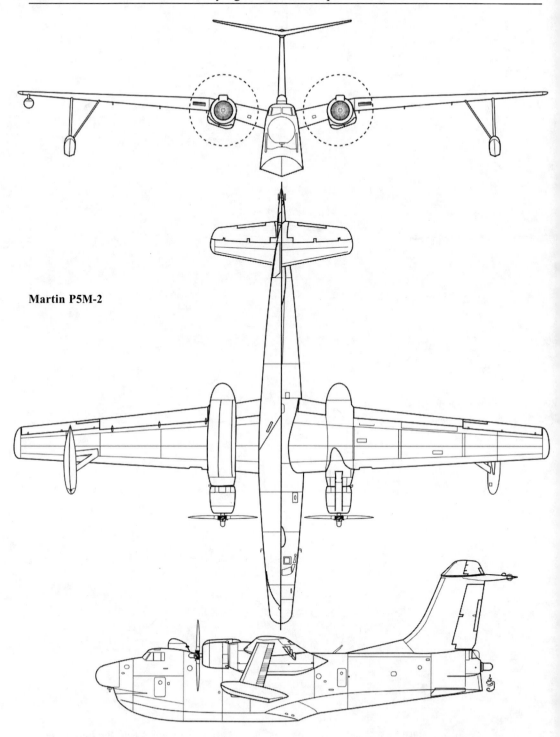

Martin P5M-2

R-3350-powered design, the model 237, which was seen as a future candidate to replace current production PBM-5s. While sharing some characteristics with the PBM, such as the gull wing planform, the model 237 emerged with a noticeably larger single fin and rudder and a hull afterbody (allegedly inspired by the Japanese Kawanishi H8K) extending all the way to the tail. The new single-step hull pattern not only created a more streamlined length-to-beam ratio (9.45 to 1 on the proto-

Three P5M-1s of VP-56, based at NAS Jacksonville, off the Florida coast, in the mid–1950s. Production P5Ms dispensed with the nose and dorsal armament of the prototype.

type; 10 to 1 on later versions), but also created more interior space and improved seaworthiness in rough water. Bottom-mounted "hydroflaps," another hull design innovation, permitted more precise maneuvering on the surface. While having almost the same wing area as the PBM, load factor increased by twenty percent, and fowler-type flaps occupying seventy-five percent of the span were used to keep landing speeds in the 100-mph range.

Despite the shift toward reliance on land-based aircraft to accomplish the maritime and anti-submarine patrol functions, post-war Navy officials still planned to maintain a sizeable fleet of flying boats which could be operated from mobile bases served by seaplane tenders. Thus, in June 1946, with PBM-5 production scheduled to end the next year (see Part II, page 177), BuAer authorized Martin to build one prototype of its proposed model 237, and after initially considering it as the XPBM-6, assigned the designation XP5M-1. Around the same time, the factory name "Marlin" was applied to the new aircraft. Planned defensive armament originally consisted of dual 20-mm power turrets in the nose and tail, plus a dorsal turret with two .50-calibre machine guns. The APS-15 search radar, similar to late production PBM-5s, was housed in a teardrop radome over the cockpit. As construction proceeded, the new hull and empennage of the XP5M-1 were mated to a PBM-5 wing modified to accept the larger R-3350 engines but otherwise unchanged. The prototype made its first flight on May 30, 1948 from Chesapeake Bay and was afterward delivered to the Naval Air Test Center for official trials.

In December 1949, Martin received an order for four P5M-1 production models, which differed substantially from the prototype in having uprated (3,250-hp) turbo-compound engines, increased wing dihedral, squared-off wingtips, greater flap area, revised engine nacelles with larger weapons

One of four P5M-2Gs delivered to the Coast Guard in 1956. The finish is an aluminized "varnish." All USCG P5Ms were transferred to the Navy in 1961 and used afterward as trainers.

bays, four-bladed propellers, larger tip floats on faired struts that had been moved further outboard, and a raised flight deck. Equipment changes included a bulbous nose radome housing an APS-44A radar in place of the nose turret, with defensive armament being reduced to only a twin 20-mm turret in the tail. Due to the naval buildup incident to the Korean War, Martin received contracts during 1950 to manufacture a further 156 P5M-1s for the Navy, plus seven more as the P5M-1G for the Coast Guard. Eary production P5M-1s began entering service in late 1951 and all, including the Coast Guard P5M-1Gs, had been delivered by April 1954. After acceptance, eighty P5M-1s dedicated to the ASW role were subsequently re-designated P5M-1S after being fitted with a magnetic anomaly detector (MAD) atop the tailfin, a "Jezebel" droppable sonarbuoy system, a high-intensity searchlight pod-mounted under the starboard wing, and an automatic integrated display system (AIDS) to track submarine targets. Coast Guard P5M-1Gs, lacking armament and most military equipment, were specially equipped for SAR missions.

As a result of a redesign effort begun in 1951, the improved P5M-2 was rolled out for its first flight in August 1953. The most noticeable changes included a new T-tail configuration with the MAD gear housed in a streamlined tail cone along with a more rounded bow and lowered chine that produced less sea spray. Crew accommodations were improved, and installation of -32WA engines added a 400-hp boost to takeoff power. Deliveries of P5M-2 production models commenced in the spring of 1954, and by mid–December 1960, when production terminated, Martin had delivered 117 examples, including four to the Coast Guard as the P5M-2G. P5M-2s subsequently receiving the ASW refit mentioned above were re-designated P5M-2S.

The XP5M-1 prototype continued to serve many years as a flying testbed for NATC, evaluating new hull and nacelle configurations plus experimental features like radar-directed armament and fixed leading edge slats, ending up, finally, with the 15 to 1 aspect hull for the proposed XP6M-1 (see below). Early production P5M-1s first became operational during December 1951 with VP-44, attached to the seaplane tender *Currituck* (AV-7) out of Norfolk, Virginia, and as deliveries proceeded (including P5M-2s from mid–1954 onwards), Marlins went on to equip a total of thirteen active duty Navy squadrons based at various locations on both coasts, i.e., VP-30, VP-31, VP-40, VP-42, VP-44, VP-45, VP-46, VP-47, VP-48, VP-49, VP-50, and VP-56 (for detailed unit information see, http://www.vpnavy.org/). Coast Guard P5M-1Gs, intended for use in long-range (i.e.,

The XP5M-1 prototype seen later in life as the model 270 after having been modified to test the 15:1 hull configuration of the P6M SeaMaster.

A Navy SP-5B (formerly P5M-2S) in the post–1958 paint scheme of insignia white over seaplane gray. SP-5s were the navy's last operational flying boats, the final examples being retired from VP-40 in late 1967.

up to 3,000 mi.) search and rescue operations, began entering service in early 1954, followed in 1956 by P5M-2Gs. In 1959, under a military assistance program (MAP), the French *Aéronavale* received twelve P5M-2s from the Navy order, where they were used for maritime patrol out of Dakar West Africa until 1964, after which time they were returned to the Navy. Citing unacceptably high operational costs, the Coast Guard turned over all of its P5Ms to the Navy in 1961, and since they lacked most military equipment, were placed into service as crew trainers under the designations P5M-1T and P5M-2T, respectively.

When all American military forces adopted the tri-service designation scheme in September 1962, the P5M-1 became the P-5A, the P5M-1S the SP-5A, the P5M-1T the TP-5A, the P5M-2 the P-5B, the P5M-2S and the P5M-2T the TP-2B. In 1964, in attempt to boost takeoff power, one SP-5B was tested with a tail-mounted 3,000-lbs./s.t. Pratt & Whitney J60 turbojet engine, but the feature was never incorporated as a program retrofit. Although the Navy had begun the process of replacing Marlins with land-based Lockheed P-2s and P-3s during the early and mid–1960s, three squadrons of SP-5Bs, operating in rotation out of NAS Sangley Point in the Philippines, engaged in combat operations from 1964 to 1966 when they deployed to Cam Ranh Bay in South Vietnam. In addition to coastal reconnaissance, SP-5Bs armed with rockets and machine guns were occasionally used to attack surface vessels supplying enemy forces. No Marlins went to the reserves, and as they were retired from active service, they were placed in storage until being sold for scrap. The Navy ended fifty-five years of flying boat operations when an SP-5B of VP-40 made its last operational flight on November 6, 1967. Today, the only known surviving example is an SP-5B maintained as an outdoor exhibit by the Naval Aviation Museum in Pensacola, Florida.

Martin P6M SeaMaster (1955)

TECHNICAL SPECIFICATIONS (YP6M-1)

Type: 4-place nuclear attack/minelayer/reconnaissance boat.
Total produced: 16 (all versions)
Powerplants: four Allison J71A-6 turbojet engines, each rated at 9,500 lbs./s.t. dry, 13,000 lbs. in afterburning.
Armament: two radar-directed 20-mm cannons in a powered tail turret and 30,000 lbs. of bombs, depth charges, mines, or nuclear weapons carried in a watertight rotary bomb bay.
Performance: max. speed 646 mph, cruise 540 mph; ceiling 40,000 ft.; range 1,595 mi. (armed), 2,745 mi. (max.).
Weights: 86,239 lbs. empty, 167,011 lbs. normal gross, 171,000 lbs. max. takeoff.
Dimensions: span 102 ft. 7 in., length 133 ft. ½ in., wing area 1,900 sq. ft.

XP6M-1 seen on the ramp at Martin's Baltimore plant during load verification tests sometime prior to its first flight in July 1955. Martin became prime contractor for the Navy's Seaplane Striking Force project in October 1953.

The Martin SeaMaster, by all accounts the most sophisticated American flying boat to ever achieve production, presents a prime example of what happens when a military aircraft's function is eclipsed by emerging technology. The SeaMaster's mission, termed the "Seaplane Striking Force" (SSF), originated during 1949, soon after the Department of Defense cancelled the Navy's "Super Carrier" program in favor of U.S. Air Force plans to build up its strategic bomber force (i.e., the

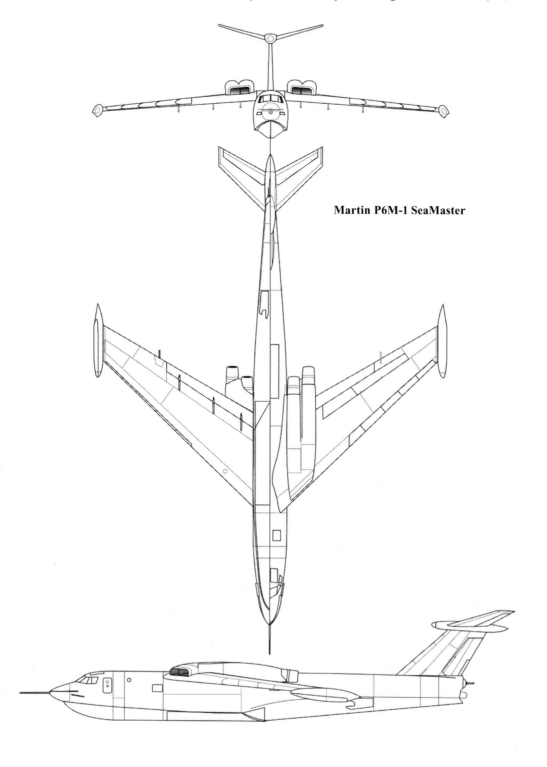

Martin P6M-1 SeaMaster

Convair B-36 and Boeing B-47). SSF foresaw a fleet of large, jet-propelled flying boats not only capable of long-range nuclear strike, but conventional bombing, mine-laying, and reconnaissance as well. Because the Soviet fleet would need to pass through several "chokepoints" when leaving port, mine-laying ability was seen as an effective means of blocking enemy access to open sea. And perhaps most important, the flying boats of the SSF, unlike landplane bombers, would be able to operate from hidden ocean bases, supported only by seagoing tenders or submarines.

In March 1951, once naval officials decided to move forward with the SSF program, BuAer circulated a formal requirement calling for a seaplane that could carry a 30,000-lb. weapons load over a 1,500-mile combat radius and also be capable of a low-altitude dash speed of Mach 0.9 (i.e., 685 mph at sea level). Given the highly ambitious and specialized nature of these specifications, Convair and Martin were the only airframe contractors having the in-house expertise to tender SSF proposals. Responsibility for Martin's design, known internally as the model 275, was assigned to George Trimble as project engineer, assisted by J. D. Pierson as hydrodynamicist and J. L. Decker as aerodynamicist. To minimize frontal area and at the same time offer good handling in open seas, Trimble's team evolved a deep-V, low-chine hull design that possessed an exceptionally slender 15:1 length-to-beam ratio. In mid–1952, after undergoing extensive modifications, the XP5M-1 was used as a flying testbed to validate the overall efficiency of their new hull concept. Martin's efforts ultimately paid off in October 1953 when BuAer declared it winner of the SSF competition and awarded a contract to construct two prototypes and a static test example under the designation XP6M-1.

During the early stages of the project, Martin considered powering the model 275 with experimental turbo-ramjet compound powerplants under development by Curtiss-Wright, but after a series of engine failures, abandoned the idea in favor of more conventional afterburning Allison J71 turbojets, a fairly straightforward adaptation of the axial-flow J35. To achieve transonic dash speeds (i.e., Mach 0.8+) on the power available (i.e., 52,000 lbs./s.t. in afterburning), the XP6M-1 emerged with very thin-section wings, swept to 40-degrees at the leading edge. By shoulder-mount-

One of the six service-test YP5M-1s, the first of which commenced flight-testing in January 1958. It is painted in the special SSF scheme of seaplane gray over insignia white.

ing the wings at a slight anhedral angle, the stabilizing floats could be placed outboard the wingtips rather than on drag-producing struts. Since the aircraft's mission called for high speeds at low altitudes, the wing structure was designed to be very rigid, utilizing machined aluminum skins having a thickness of one inch at the root. The wing featured a combination of retractable leading-edge slats and articulated trailing-edge flaps that would keep landing speeds below the 150-mph mark. Many of the innovations initially seen on Martin's XB-51 were adapted to the design of the P6M, such as the T-tail empennage, wing spoilers for roll control, and a rotary bomb bay which, for sea operations, included a pneumatic sealing system. Large, board-type "hydroflaps" on the aft hull bottom could be used for either water maneuvering or aerodynamic braking. The four J71 engines, in paired nacelles near the roots, were located over the wings to raise the intakes above the sea spray. A four-man flight crew, consisting of a pilot, copilot, navigator-radio operator, and flight engineer, would be housed in a fully-pressurized bow compartment. As prototype construction advanced, Martin adopted the name SeaMaster for the new aircraft, and Navy officials had sufficient confidence in the future of SSF to add six YP6M-1 pre-production models to the contract, with a future provision for up to twenty-four P6M-2 production versions.

Final assembly of the first XP6M-1 prototype was completed in late December 1954, but load-verification and other ground testing delayed the first flight until July 14, 1955. Early air testing, carried out by Martin chief test pilot George Rodney, demonstrated satisfactory flying characteris-

Canted engine nacelles are evident in this group photograph of the six YP6M-1s. All but one show the unique beaching cradles allowing them to make a quick transition from the water onto the ramp.

One of the eight P6M-2 production aircraft. The advent of *Forrestal* class carriers and missile-carrying nuclear submarines hastened the demise of the SSF program.

tics; however, high-speed flights had to be limited after prolonged afterburner operations were shown to cause serious scorch and sonic damage to the aft fuselage. Testing also revealed a recurring problem with airframe vibrations or "buzzing" during flight maneuvers. Even so, the Navy optimistically forged ahead with plans to officially unveil the SeaMaster program when it invited the press to the rollout ceremony of the second XP6M-1 in early November 1955. The second SeaMaster would be completed with the navigational and bombing equipment needed to evaluate the aircraft's military mission. A few weeks later, on December 7 (three days after Glenn Martin's death), the program suffered its first major setback: during a routine check flight with the first Navy pilot at the controls, the first XP6M-1 inexplicably crashed into Chesapeake Bay, killing all four of the crew. Since no flight data recorders were carried aboard the aircraft, the cause of the crash was not immediately apparent. The flight program did not resume until May 1956, by which time the second prototype had been fitted with ejection seats along with instrumentation to provide important flight telemetry data. As testing of the second XP6M-1 proceeded into the fall of 1956, the reasons for the earlier crash remained uncertain and the airframe vibrations continued. In an effort to solve the vibration problem, the horizontal stabilizer was changed to an all-flying surface rather than one with separate, moveable elevators. On November 9, while attempting a pull-out from a high-speed dive, the pilot of the XP6M-1 lost all pitch control and the aircraft went into an un-commanded outside loop. Fortunately, the entire flight crew was able to safely eject just before the airframe broke up. In the investigation that followed, data recovered from the flight recorders clearly showed that the aircraft had entered the maneuver because the hydraulic control actuators were unable to counteract the high-speed aerodynamic loads placed on the horizontal stabilizer.

Despite the loss of both prototypes, BuAer still believed the SSF program was viable and moved ahead with extensive preparations in anticipation of future operations. Navy plans included conversion of two seaplane tenders and one submarine as support vessels, development of beaching cradles to allow the P6Ms to taxi in and out of the water under their own power, plus establishment of a new air station at Harvey Point, North Carolina, as the SeaMaster's home base. At the same time, Martin's engineering staff worked to implement changes to the service-test YP6M-1s that would rectify the design flaws of the prototypes. The engine nacelles were moved rearward to reduce water ingestion and given a toe-out geometry of five degrees to direct engine exhaust away from the rear fuselage. Other changes included a completely redesigned horizontal stabilizer control system in which elevator movement was restored plus an upgrade to A-6 engines. The first of six YP6M-1s rolled out of the Middle River plant in November 1957 and commenced flight-testing in January 1958. Initial trials indicated that the earlier problems had been resolved, and as the other five YP6M-1s joined the program during 1958, SSF operational testing truly began in earnest. The aircraft and their weapons systems were evaluated over a broad range of missions that included high-speed mine-laying, bomb runs with both conventional and nuclear "shapes," and day and night operations using specialized reconnaissance cradles. An efficient beaching system, consisting of a float-stabilized dolly, enabled SeaMasters to easily move in and out of the water without outside assistance.

As the YP6M-1 test program proceeded apace, Martin turned its attention to construction of the definitive SeaMaster production model, the P6M-2. The -2 came with an upgrade to Pratt & Whitney J-75-P-2 engines, each delivering 15,800 lbs./s.t. in afterburner, which boosted available power by a factor of eighteen percent. Noticeable differences from earlier variants included a larger all-around vision cockpit enclosure, re-shaped nacelles to house new engines, and the removal of most wing anhedral due to the deeper draft produced by increased weight (i.e., 91,284 lbs. empty; 195,000 lbs. max. takeoff). Production models also featured an all-new, transistorized Sperry navigation and bombing system which would improve multi-mission capability. The SeaMaster acquired yet another role with the development of a probe and drogue refueling package, contained within the rotary bomb bay, that would enable it to refuel other aircraft. Soon after the first P6M-2 flew on March 3, 1959, it posted a top speed of Mach 0.95 (686 mph) at sea level, giving it higher low-level penetration speeds than any comparable land-based bomber (e.g., the Boeing B-52 was limited to 420 mph at sea level). However, despite the long-awaited success, a combination of protracted development and rising costs led to a cut back in the production contract to eighteen P6M-2s, and later still, to only eight. As two more P6M-2s joined the program during the summer of 1959, it looked as if SSF might still turn onto an operational reality, then on August 21, 1959, citing "unforeseen technical difficulties," the Navy abruptly cancelled the entire program; the other five P6M-2s were completed during the fall of 1959 but never flown. The thirteen aircraft—five YP6M-1s and eight P6M-2s—sat idle on a ramp at the Middle River plant for over a year until being dismantled and scrapped. All that remains today, two tail assemblies, one fuselage section, and a set of tip floats, currently reside at the Glenn L. Martin Aviation Museum in Baltimore.

Two developments ultimately spelled the demise of the SeaMaster: first, starting in late 1955, the introduction of *Forrestal* class aircraft carriers, and with them, the ability to deploy long-range nuclear strike, mine-laying, and reconnaissance aircraft such as the Douglas A3D (A-3) Skywarrior; and second, the emergence of nuclear submarines that could carry sixteen *Polaris* nuclear-tipped ballistic missiles, the first of which was launched in mid–1959 (i.e., the U.S.S. *George Washington*, SSBN-598). Afterward, Martin reportedly tried to promote an eight-engine, transport version of the P6M, unofficially dubbed the "SeaMistress," but the project never went beyond the idea stage.

Pereira (Osprey) Aircraft Company

This company evolved from several homebuilt designs developed by George Pereira and has been in business for nearly 40 years. According to its recently updated website (see http://www.ospreyaircraft.com), building plans are currently available from Osprey Aircraft, 3741 El Ricon Way, Sacramento, California 95864.

Pereira Osprey I (X-28A) (1970)

TECHNICAL SPECIFICATIONS

Type: 1-place civil/military flying boat.
Total produced: unknown
Powerplant: one 90-hp Continental C90-12 4-cylinder air-cooled opposed engine driving a two-bladed metal propeller.
Performance: max. speed 135 mph; ceiling 18,000 feet; range (not reported).
Weights: empty (not reported), 900 lbs. gross.
Dimensions: span 23 ft. 0 in., length 17 ft. 3 in., wing area 90 sq. ft. (est.).

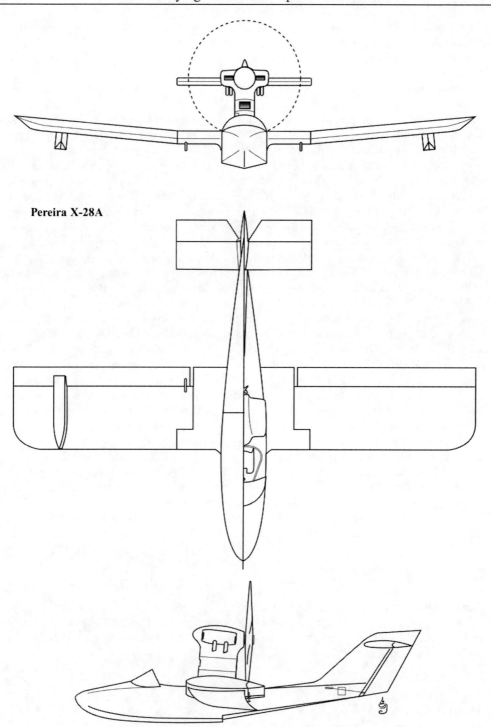

Pereira X-28A

Pereira's first design arose in connection with a Navy requirement for a lightweight, single-engine flying boat, to be operated in the river deltas of Southeast Asia for ostensible police-type duties. Except for the absence of landing gear, the hydro- and aerodynamic configuration was very similar to the Colonial/Lake amphibians reported above. Construction was all-wood, featuring a single-step, semi-monocoque hull reinforced with resin-bonded fiberglass and fabric-covered wings

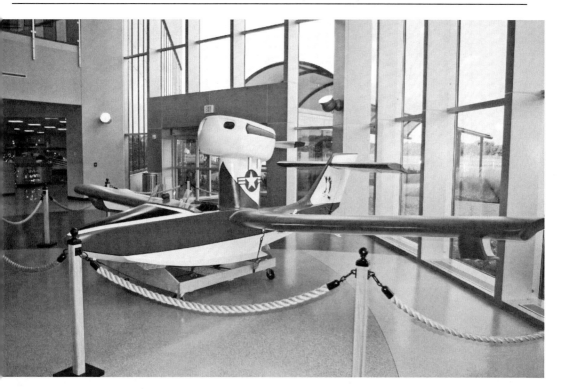

Photograph of X-28A as it appeared in 2007 on exhibit at the Kalamazoo/Battle Creek International Airport. *Credit*: **Glenn Chatfield.**

and control surfaces. Fully-cantilevered wings attached to the upper hull, and the empennage was characterized by a swept fin and rudder having a high-mounted horizontal stabilizer. The pilot sat in an open cockpit just forward of the pylon-mounted pusher engine. After being test flown sometime in 1970 as the Osprey I under civil registration N3337, the prototype was turned over to the Navy and thereafter evaluated as the X-28A (USN serial number 158786). No other X-28As were ordered or produced, due apparently to the U.S. withdrawal from Vietnam and Cambodia, and the sole example was donated to the U.S. Marine Corps Museum in Quantico, Virginia, in 1972. Other data suggests that one or more Osprey Is may have been built privately, but there is no evidence that any were flown or registered.

Pereira Osprey II (1974)

TECHNICAL SPECIFICATIONS

Type: 2-place civil homebuilt amphibian.
Total built or started: 500 (est.)
Powerplant: one 160-hp Lycoming O-320 4-cylinder air-cooled opposed engine driving a two or three-bladed metal or wooden propeller.
Performance: max. speed 145 mph; cruise, 130 mph, ceiling (not reported); range 350 mi.
Weights: 970 lbs. empty, 1,570 lbs. gross.
Dimensions: span 26 ft. 0 in., length 21 ft. 0 in., wing area 105 sq. ft. (est.).

The Osprey II represented an effort by George Pereira to offer amateur builders a fully-amphibious, two-place design that could be built in a workshop without molds. Soon after being introduced in 1974, the plans and construction methods were featured in *Mechanics Illustrated* magazine. Though sharing the general arrangement of the X-28A, the Osprey II featured a widened hull, an enlarged cruciform empennage, and a mechanically operated landing gear that folded into the wings.

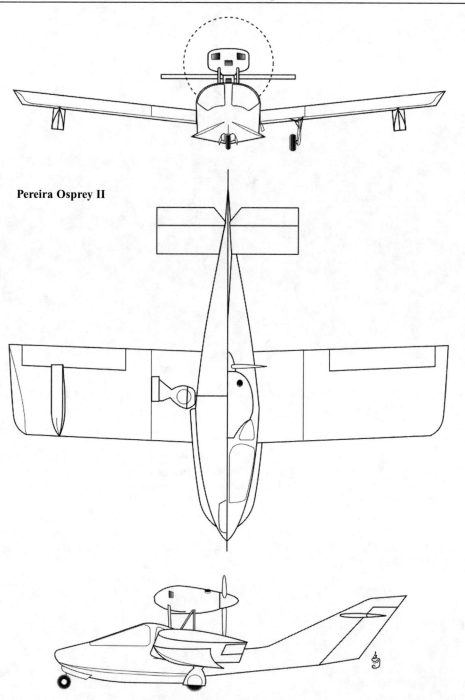

Pereira Osprey II

To simplify construction, the engine was mounted on struts behind a streamlined Plexiglas canopy that fully enclosed the cockpit area. Hull construction utilized a sandwich technique whereby the built-up wooden structure was sprayed with polyurethane form, then after cutting and sanding, covered in glass cloth impregnated with polyester resin, and three layers of cloth were applied to the hull bottom to withstand impact loads. The wings were of conventional two-spar wooden construction with fabric covering aft of the main spar, and the outer panels could be removed for storage.

When the Osprey II prototype was flown sometime in 1974 it was powered by a 150-hp Franklin

Osprey II N52JF seen during the Experimental Aircraft Association's annual fly-in at Oshkosh, Wisconsin. An estimated 500 have been built since the design appeared over 35 years ago.

4R engine but subsequently modified to accept installation of a Lycoming O-320 after production of the 4R was discontinued. Flight-testing revealed generally good flying and water handling characteristics and required only small changes to trim. Materials marketed by Osprey consist of a 46-page plan accompanied by an illustrated, step-by-step construction manual. While not originally intended to be kit-built, partial Osprey II kits (i.e., molded canopies and wood parts) are now available from Aircraft Spruce & Specialty Company of Corona, California. According to the Osprey website, 500 of these aircraft have been completed and thought to be flying at the time of this writing.

Republic Aviation Corporation

Having been started by Alexander de Seversky in 1931 as Seversky Aircraft Corp. in Farmingdale, New York, the company became Republic Aviation Corp. in 1939 following a financial restructure and change of ownership. Known throughout the industry as a military contractor, Republic began making plans in 1943 to capitalize on the anticipated post-war lightplane boom when it purchased the design and production rights to Percival H. Spencer's S-12 Air Car (see Part II, above). Spencer was employed by Republic as a test pilot at the time.

Republic RC-1 and -3 Seabee (1944)

TECHNICAL SPECIFICATIONS (RC-3)

Type: 4-place civil amphibian.
Total produced: 1,060
Powerplant: one 215-hp Franklin 6A8-215-B8F or B9F 6-cylinder air-cooled opposed engine driving a two-bladed, fixed-pitch wooden or metal propeller.
Performance: max. speed 120 mph, cruise 103 mph; ceiling 12,000 ft.; range 360 mi.
Weights: 2,190 lbs. empty, 2,810 lbs. gross.
Dimensions: span 37 ft. 8 in., length 27 ft. 10½ in., wing area 196 sq. ft

To date, the Republic Seabee holds the distinction of having been produced in greater numbers than any type of single-engine civil amphibian in the U.S. Although actually flown and tested during World War II, the Seabee is included in this era because it is most commonly identified with lightplanes introduced after 1945. Using the general design concept behind the wood and fabric S-

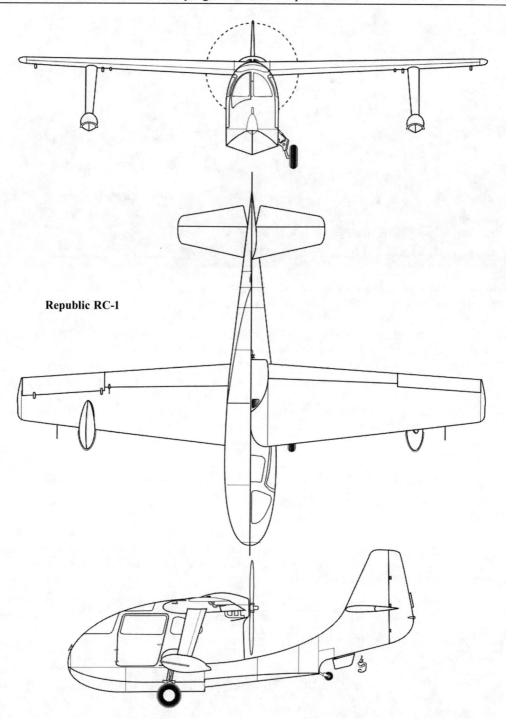

Republic RC-1

12 Air Car, construction of the prototype RC-1 (Republic Commercial One) "Thunderbolt Amphib-ian" commenced during 1944. Obvious design changes included all-metal construction methods, producing a stronger and more streamlined airframe, plus a fully-cantilevered, tapered wing with single-strut stabilizing floats. The conventional landing gear arrangement of the S-12 was retained, but with the main wheels neatly retracting flush into hull recesses. An upswept hull afterbody that smoothly blended up into the cruciform tail group gave the RC-1 the characteristic look of all

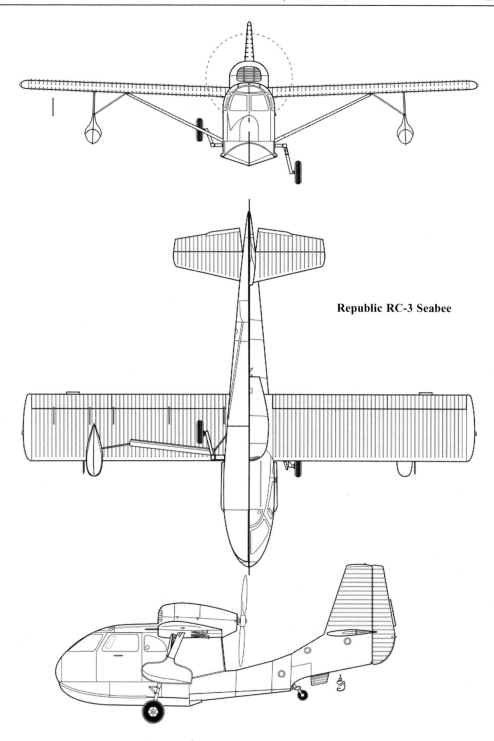

Republic RC-3 Seabee

Seabees. Further attention was given to drag reduction by burying the 175-hp Franklin 6A-6 pusher engine in the middle of the wing center-section and fairing it into the aft cabin pod.

The RC-1 prototype, civil registration NX41816, rolled out of the Farmingdale plant in late November 1944, and with Percy Spencer himself at the controls, made its first flight on November 30. Only weeks later, the prototype received much acclaim at an aviation industry convention in

RC-1 prototype as seen in 1944 and 1945. A cantilevered, tapered wing, recessed main landing gear, and lower-mounted engine distinguish it from the RC-3 production model.

St. Louis, Missouri, where Republic received deposits for 1,972 new amphibians to be sold at a price of $3,500 each. Soon after that, NX41816 was taken to the Washington National Airport and demonstrated before officials representing the U.S. military services. Then in early 1945, Republic obtained formal approval from the Navy for the commercial use of the name "Seabee." While still making plans to tool-up for post-war Seabee production, Republic received a sizeable order from the USAAF in April 1945 for amphibians to be delivered as the OA-15. The military version, intended mainly for rescue work, specified a more powerful, geared engine plus a cabin arrangement for two hospital litters. However, before any military examples could be completed, the contract was cancelled in late 1945 as part of the V-J Day cutbacks. Work on the RC-3, the definitive production model (note that the RC-2 had been assigned to a proposed commercial version of Republic's XF-12 Rainbow) continued through the rest of the year. To simplify mass production, the RC-3 differed from the prototype in a number of important respects. Instead of fully-cantilevered units, production models featured constant chord wings braced by single lift struts and stabilizing floats braced by jury struts. The recessed wheel wells were deleted and the geometry of the main landing gear changed to simply swivel up against the sides of the hull. The new engine, more powerful by 40 hp, was moved to the top of the wing in a larger nacelle.

The first RC-3, registered NX87451, emerged from the factory for its first flight on December 1, 1945, with Percy Spencer again serving as test pilot. Later the same month, Republic had sufficient confidence in the future of the Seabee and the lightplane market in general to acquire Aircooled Motors, Inc., manufacturer of Franklin engines. In March 1946, the Civil Aeronautics Authority granted Republic official type certification, and deliveries of production RC-3s commenced in late July, the first example (actually the thirteenth RC-3 built) being accepted by J. G. (Tex) Rankin of Rankin Aviation Industries of Tulare, California. But after such a hopeful start, the expected explosion in post-war lightplane sales never materialized, and added to that, rising production costs and inflation had driven the Seabee price to $6,000 by late 1946. In June 1947, the production line was suspended to await further sales, and finally, in October, Republic announced that all Seabee production was being terminated. The last of 1,060 Seabees built was sold and delivered in early 1948.

But despite a comparatively brief production life, the Seabee has enjoyed a long and fruitful career as a general aviation aircraft in both private and commercial hands. It was particularly well suited to coastal regions and wilderness areas served by lakes, and many were sold to foreign users in the Caribbean, Central and South America, the East Indies, South Africa, and Northern Europe. Seabees became well known as air taxis along major waterways and for hauling passengers and supplies in the isolated bush areas of Canada and Alaska, where they could make a swift transition

Production RC-3 during the type's heyday in the late 1940s. A total of 1,060 RC-3s had been built when production terminated in 1947. According to recent estimates, 250 or more are still flying.

UC-1 Twin Bee conversion by United Consultant Corp. The twin-engine configuration improved performance about 25 percent across the board. Twenty-three are said to have been converted between 1966 and 1987.

The last iteration of the Seabee, the Trident Trigull, as seen recently in Canadian registration. Efforts to place the type into production during the 1970s ran into a series of financial difficulties.

from land to water operations. As of 2006, some 250 Seabees (over 23 percent of the original fleet) are said to still be registered and flying in the U.S. and elsewhere. Through the course of their long service, surviving Seabees have typically undergone numerous rebuilds that have included upgrades to more powerful engines with controllable propellers. Starting in 1960, out of an effort to extend and improve the RC-3's usefulness, United Consultant Corp. of Norwood, Massachusetts, introduced the UC-1 Twin Bee, a conversion that involved removing the pusher engine and replacing it with two tractor-mounted Lycoming 180-hp O-360-A1A or 200-hp IO-360-B1D engines on the wings. The extra weight was offset by three-foot wing extensions, and the hull afterbody was lengthened three feet four inches to compensate for the change in center of gravity. Performance improved across the board—147-mph top speed, 131-mph cruise, 900-mile range, plus a 300-lb. increase in useful load—and extra cabin space was created where the engine had been located. At least twenty-three Twin Bee conversions were completed between 1966 and 1987.

The story of the Seabee does not end here and may not be over yet: In the mid–1960s, Percival Spencer and son-in-law Charles Herbst, an engineer, commenced an effort to design and produce a more modern amphibian based upon the RC-3. But before an aircraft was built, the project was taken over by David Hazelwood and C. S. Newton, who reorganized it in 1970 as the Trident Aircraft Ltd. of Vancouver, Canada. The first flight of the prototype, billed as the TR-1 Trigull under Canadian registry CF-TRI-X, took place on August 5, 1973. Though sharing the basic Seabee configuration, the TR-1 was in fact an all-new, four-seat airframe that featured tricycle landing gear, retractable tip floats, a swept fin and rudder, plus a 300-hp Continental IO-520 engine driving a three-bladed, constant-speed propeller. The nose wheel retracted into a hull recess with the partially exposed tire acting as a bumper, and the mains folded upward into the wings. Except for the cabin pod forward of the engine, which was formed from fiberglass, structure was all-metal. The second prototype, registered C-GATE-F, flew for the first time in July 1976. A third airframe was built for static tests and never flown. During the testing of the prototypes, the company made plans to develop a six-seat production version that would be powered by a Lycoming IO-540 engine, either normally aspirated or tubo-charged. A decision to go-ahead with production—based on firm orders for forty-three aircraft—was made in mid–1978; however, due to mounting financial difficulties, Trident was forced to cancel production plans and cease business in early 1980. Both Trigulls prototypes are currently owned by Viking Air Ltd. of Victoria, B.C., and CF-TRI-X (now C-FTRI) is maintained in airworthy status. As of April 2003, a magazine report appearing in *Air International* announced that a Canadian firm planned to revive efforts to produce a turbine-powered variant of the Trigull, however, the current status of the project is unknown. For more information, see http://www.seabee.info/trigull.htm.

Seawind/SNA, Inc. (Seawind, LLC)

The U.S. company was originally formed in the 1990s by Richard Silva of Kimberton, Pennsylvania, to market and distribute Seawind amphibian kits being fabricated in Canada. More recently, after being reorganized as Seawind, LLC, the company, together with its Canadian counterparts, has been involved in an effort to obtain official type certification for the Seawind in both the U.S. and Canada, with the ultimate aim of placing the aircraft in production. Presumably, Seawind, LLC will function as U.S. distributor for aircraft manufactured in Canada by Air Composites, Inc. of Saint Jean, Quebec.

Seawind (1982)

TECHNICAL SPECIFICATIONS (300C)
Type: 2 to 4-place civil amphibian.
Total produced: 120 (all versions, est.)
Powerplant: one 310-hp Continental IO-550-N 6-cylinder air-cooled opposed engine driving a three-bladed, constant-speed metal propeller.

The Seawind 300C (N46SW), the first 300-hp version to be built by Richard Silva. Efforts to certificate the aircraft and place it production are still ongoing.

Performance: max. speed 200 mph, cruise 180 mph; ceiling 18,000 ft.; range 1,040 mi.
Weights: 2,350 lbs. empty, 3,400 lbs. gross.
Dimensions: span 35 ft. 0 in., length 27 ft. 2 in., wing area 163 sq. ft.

Advertised as the fastest and longest-ranged amphibian on today's market, the Seawind 300C represents an interesting departure from the more orthodox single-engine amphibian layouts seen in the post-war era. Its most outstanding characteristic is a tightly cowled tractor engine which extends to the center of gravity from a horizontal pylon mounted on top of the large fin and rudder. The aft end of the pylon is used to support a vertical finlet and an all-moving horizontal stabilator. Molded fiberglass components, strengthened by cellfoam, merge together to form an airframe of exceptional aerodynamic cleanness. The 300C's cantilevered wings end in sponsons which are shaped to also function as drooped tips that improve takeoff and landing performance. The cabin, situated well forward of the wing, features a wrap-around windscreen offering nearly panoramic visibility.

The origins of the Seawind can be traced back to the 1970s when Roger, Len, and Kirk Creelman, all of Haliburton, Ontario, Canada, began laying down their concept for a composite-built amphibian having a tail-mounted engine. The original prototype, powered by a 200-hp Lycoming IO-360 engine, is thought to have made its first flight in 1982 under Canadian registration C-GNEW and was displayed in the U.S. for the first time at the Oshkosh EAA Fly-In in 1983. As originally designed, the main landing gear retracted into the hull behind the step. A second 200-hp example, featuring changes to the hull and sponsons, was flown under Canadian registration C-GFNL. The first U.S. registered Seawind (N540SW) appeared during the early 1990s, powered by a 300-hp Lycoming IO-540 engine driving a three-bladed propeller. Other changes included redesigned main landing gear legs that retracted upward into the wings. Since their introduction over fifteen years ago, approximately 115 Seawind kits have been sold to homebuilders and over 80 of them are reported to be flying. Some examples have been completed with turbo-charged Lycoming TSIO-540 engines and at least three are known to be powered by Allison 250-B17B turboprop engines delivering 400 shp.

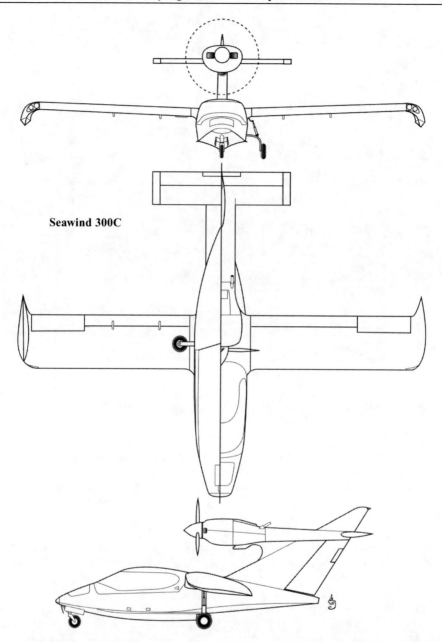

Seawind 300C

The process of bringing the Seawind design to full U.S. and Canadian type certification, preparatory to production, has been protracted, however. The test program got off to a good start in 2004 with the first factory-built, Continental-powered 300C prototype, and in the interval, the company received ninety-three deposits for production 300Cs. But in April 2007, at about 70 percent completion, the Seawind certification program suffered a severe setback when the prototype was lost in a fatal crash. A newsletter issued soon afterward (see http://www.seawind.biz/Seawind%20Flyer%20Fall%202007.pdf) indicated that further testing and production plans would be held in abeyance until additional funding was obtained for the project. Despite these problems, the company is still optimistic. A recent report (see http://www.seawind.biz/Seawind%20News.html) states that the second 300C prototype is about two-thirds complete and so far, the company has received half of the funding needed to resume testing. The current price listed for a VFR-equipped new 300C, should it come to pass, is $349,900 (about half of the suggested price for a new Lake LA-250, -270).

Spencer and Anderson

In the late 1960s, Percival H. Spencer (see Spencer S-12 Air Car in Part II, page 208, and Republic RC-1/-3 Seabee, Part III, page 273), at virtually the same time that he was working on a production aircraft intended to succeed the Seabee (i.e., Trident TR-1), teamed up with Dale L. Anderson in Chino, California, to develop more simplified amphibian designs for the homebuilt market. Spencer and Anderson remained involved in promoting their designs until 1991. Percival Spencer was an active pilot until 1987; he passed away in 1995.

Spencer-Anderson S-12C/E Air Car (1970)

TECHNICAL SPECIFICATIONS (S-12E)

Type: 4 -place homebuilt civil amphibian.
Total produced: unknown
Powerplant: one 285-hp Continental IO-520-B 6-cylinder air-cooled opposed engine driving a three-bladed, constant-speed metal propeller.
Performance: max. speed 155 mph, cruise 135 mph; ceiling 15,000 feet; range 800 mi.
Weights: 2,150 lbs. empty, 3,200 lbs. gross.
Dimensions: span 37 ft. 4 in., length 26 ft. 3 in., wing area 184 sq. ft.

In 1968 Spencer and Anderson commenced work on the S-12C, a modernized and slightly enlarged version of the old 1941 S-12 Air Car design that was to be powered with a 180-hp Lycoming O-360 engine driving a two-bladed, constant-speed propeller. To facilitate construction by home-builders, all major airframe components were fabricated from spruce and plywood or, in the case of the upper hull, engine cowling, and tip floats, from fiberglass molded over forms. The tricycle landing gear used spring-type main legs that rotated up against the hull and a pivoting nose wheel arrangement similar to the TR-1. Spencer made the first flight of the S-12C prototype from Chino on May 25, 1970, and began conducting water trials on Lake Havasu in early July. After flying the aircraft all over the U.S., Spencer and Anderson, in an effort to improve useful load and high

Percival H. Spencer, at left, standing in front of his last project, the S-14, with Dale Anderson in the early 1980s. Spencer died in 1995 at age 90.

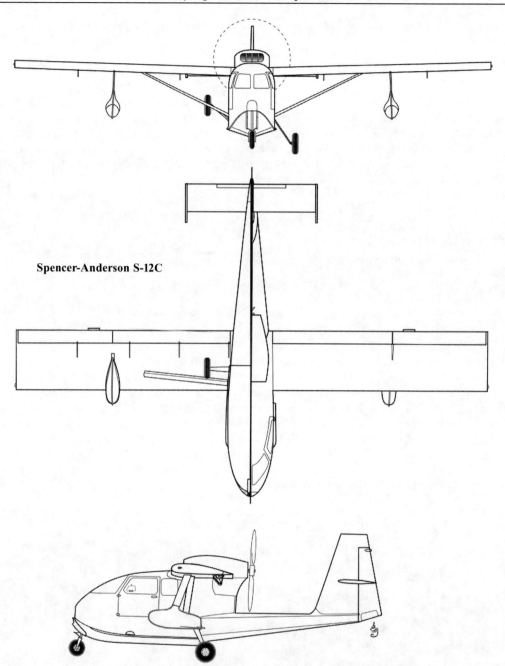

Spencer-Anderson S-12C

altitude performance, thereafter modified it for installation of a 260-hp Lycoming O-540-E4B engine and renamed it the S-12D. The definitive version, the S-12E, was designed to be powered by a 285-hp Continental IO-520-B.

Spencer and Anderson are thought to have sold over 300 sets of S-12C/E plans before selling the design rights to Robert Kerans in 1991. A number of S-12Es have been completed and flown by homebuilders, though the exact figure has never been published. Plans and building information may be obtained today from Spencer Amphibian Air Car, Inc., P. O. Box 327, Kansas, Illinois 61933, or by calling (847) 882-5678. Spencer's last amphibian design, the S-14 Air Car Junior, represented an effort to offer a scaled-down (two-seat) version with folding wings for road transport. Construc-

A Spencer S-12C Air Car as seen at the annual Experimental Aircraft Association fly-in in Oshkosh, Wisconsin. Spencer began selling construction plans to homebuilders in 1970, and they are still available today.

Another visitor to the Oshkosh fly-in, this Air Car (N14NX) was completed with a twin boom tail group and conventional landing gear.

tion of the S-14 started in 1980, and the aircraft was test flown, by Spencer himself at age 86, on November 4, 1983. No details are available, but after 37.5 hours of flight-testing, Spencer decided to terminate the S-14 project. The S-14 prototype was purchased by William Randolph Hearst, Jr., in 1984 and thereafter donated to the Experimental Aircraft Association Museum in Oshkosh, Wisconsin.

Thurston Aircraft (Aeromarine) Corporation

David B. Thurston is one of the most respected names in modern amphibian design. While working as a design engineer for Grumman, he co-founded Colonial Aircraft Corp. (see page 221), then in 1966, founded Thurston Aircraft Corp, in Sanford, Maine. In 1972 Thurston assigned production rights of his Teal amphibian design to Schweizer Aircraft of Elmira, New York, where he was also employed as a managing engineer. In yet another move, Schweizer sold the Teal production rights in 1976 to Teal Aircraft Corp. of St. Augustine, Florida, which listed David Thurston as vice-president. Later still, in the 1970s and 1980s, Thurston formed an engineering consulting firm, known as Thruston Aeromarine Corp., along with a development company, named Aeromarine International Corp., to pursue certification and production of his TA-16 Seafire design, which will be discussed in more detail below.

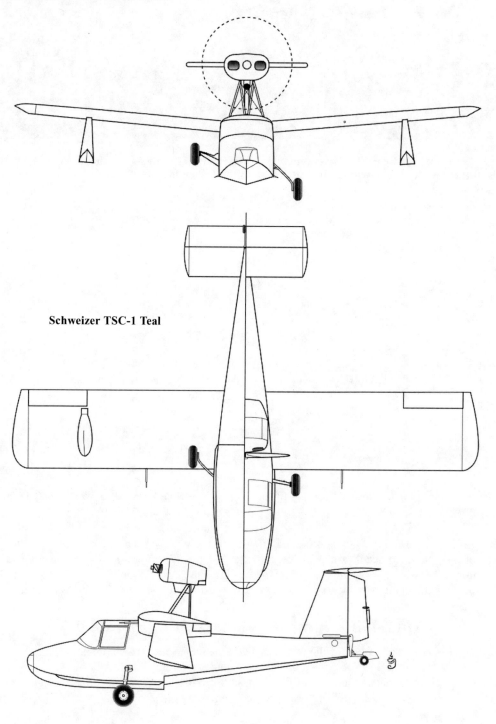

Schweizer TSC-1 Teal

Thurston TSC-1A, -1A1, and -1A2 Teal I and II (Marlin 150) (1968)

TECHNICAL SPECIFICATIONS (TSC-1A2 TEAL II)

Type: 2 -place civil amphibian.
Total produced: 38 (all versions)
Powerplant: one 150-hp Lycoming O-320-A3B 4-cylinder air-cooled opposed engine driving a two-bladed, constant-speed metal propeller.
Performance: max. speed 125 mph, cruise 115 mph; ceiling (not reported); range 400 mi.
Weights: 1,600 lbs. empty, 2,200 lbs. gross.
Dimensions: span 31 ft. 1 in., length 23 ft. 7 in., wing area 157 sq. ft.

David Thurston conceived the Teal with the idea of producing an all-metal, two-place amphibian that could be marketed at about half the cost of comparable three or four-place types like the Lake Buccaneer. Though sharing some characteristics with Thurston's earlier Skimmer design, the Teal was somewhat simpler, having constant-chord wings without flaps and a manually-operated, tailwheel-type landing gear. Other noticeable differences included a T-tail arrangement and a tractor engine mounted on struts above the wing. (Thurston later explained that tractors were generally more efficient, and the Skimmer had only been designed as a pusher because CAA regulations applicable at the time [i.e., 1946] required the propeller arc to be a certain distance away from the passenger cabin.)

Originally, Thurston had planned to develop both flying boat (TSC-1) and amphibious (TSC-1A) versions of the Teal but abandoned the flying boat idea before any construction started. The TSC-1A amphibian prototype, civil registry N1968T, was flown for the first time in June 1968, and following successful flight trials, received FAA type certification in August 1969. By mid–1971, when fifteen TSC-1As had been manufactured, Thurston introduced the improved TSC-1A1, which featured two 23-gallon wing tanks in place of the 24.5-gallon fuselage tank and a gross weight increase to 2,200 lbs. Four TSC-1A1s had been delivered at the time production was taken over by Schweizer in 1972. In mid–1973, after delivery of three more TSC-1A1s, production shifted to the improved TSC-1A2 Teal II, which incorporated slotted flaps, a change in horizontal stabilizer incidence, and increased elevator trim tab travel, and Schweizer went on to produce a total of nine -1A2s before production rights were assumed by Teal Aircraft in 1976. Over the next two years, Teal Aircraft completed seven TSC-1A2s, marketed under the new name Marlin 150, and was making plans to

Thurston TSC-1A seen at the Experimental Aircraft Association's annual fly-in Oshkosh, Wisconsin. Thirty-eight Teals had been completed by three different manufacturers when production terminated in 1978.

Schweizter-built TSC-1A1 in Monaco (LN) registration. Efforts to place the Teal back into production during the 1980s never materialized.

introduce two upgrades, the TSC-1A2/EP with a 160-hp Lycoming O-320-1A2 and the TSC-1A3 (Marlin 180) with a 180-hp Lycoming O-360, at the time it ceased all manufacturing operations. Although one TSC-1A2 was fitted with the 180-hp engine for test purposes, neither of the proposed upgrades ever achieved production status. During the early 1980s, under a proposed venture known as Advanced Aircraft, plans were made to offer a modification package for existing Teal IIs that would have comprised conversion to tricycle gear, upgrade to a 180-hp engine, plus refinements to other systems, but the effort failed before any aircraft were modified.

Of the thirty-eight Teals built, twenty-six are thought to still exist in some form, and at least twenty-one of these are either in flying condition or undergoing restoration. A website with current information and images on surviving Teals may be viewed at http://www.seabee.info/teal.htm.

Thurston TA-16 Seafire/Trojan (1982)

TECHNICAL SPECIFICATIONS

Type: 4-place civil amphibian.
Total built: 3 (est.)
Powerplant: one 250-hp Lycoming O-540-A4D5 6-cylinder air-cooled opposed engine driving a two-bladed, constant-speed metal propeller.
Performance: max. speed 175 mph, cruise 150 mph; ceiling 18,000 ft.; range 1,000 mi.
Weights: 1,950 lbs. empty, 3,200 lbs. gross.
Dimensions: span 37 ft. 0 in., length 27 ft. 2 in., wing area 183 sq. ft.

The TA-16 Seafire, when it flew in 1982, represented the sum of David Thurston's accumulated experience in amphibian design over a period spanning nearly forty years. It embodied Thurston's tried and tested all-metal structural methods with an updated airframe that promised above-average flight performance and excellent water handling. Though aerodynamically similar to the Teal II, the twenty percent larger TA-16 was designed to lift twice the useful load while producing significant increases in cruise speed (+40 mph) and range (+600 miles). Its tricycle landing gear system was reminiscent of the Skimmer, the trailing-arm type main wheels retracting flush into the

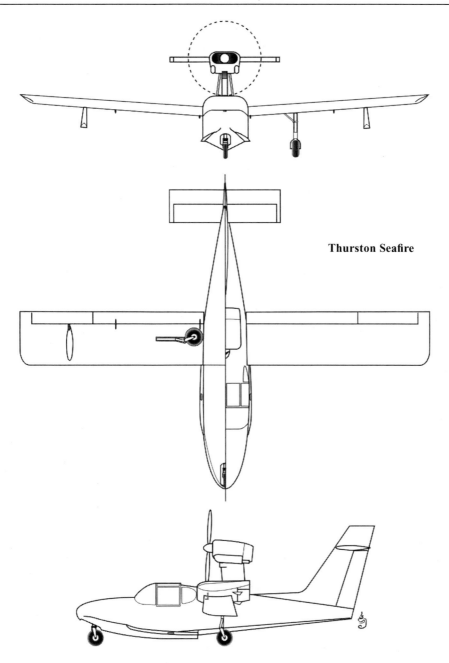

Thurston Seafire

wings, while half the nosewheel tire was left exposed to form a docking bumper. Other noticeable features included a single pylon engine mount and a one-piece, blown canopy which slid all the way back to permit easy access to the rear seats. A new cruciform empennage, given slight sweep-back, placed the horizontal surfaces directly behind the engine thrust line for maximum pitch authority. Special attention was given to hull design, a deep V-section with side strakes that would allow high-speed water turns and improve rough water handling. Less visible enhancements consisted of a steerable nosewheel for easier beaching and engine/propeller controls located on a central pedestal rather than overhead.

The genealogy of the TA-16 is somewhat unusual. From the first, Thurston envisaged both pro-duction versions (i.e., Seafire) and homebuilt versions (i.e., Trojan) of the same aircraft. The Seafire

The original amateur-built TA16 Trojan N1378J as seen at Camden, New Jersey, in 2003. Start and stop efforts to obtain FAA Type Certification for a manufactured Seafire version have been ongoing since 1983. *Credit:* **Derek Linder.**

would possess certain detail differences in systems that would enable it to meet type certification standards under FAR Part 23. Sets of plans for the homebuilt Trojan were first issued in 1975 while Thruston simultaneously waged a campaign to obtain investor support for a Seafire construction and certification program. During the late 1970s and early 1980s, while a number of Trojan home-built projects were at various stages of construction, Thurston himself commenced construction of the production model prototype. The first flight of the of the TA-16 Seafire prototype, registration number N16TA, took place on December 10, 1982; the first homebuilt TA-16 Trojan, registration number N1378J, made its first flight a little less than six months later, on May 20, 1983. Efforts to obtain type certification of the Seafire continued until 1987, at which point the program stalled at about 85 percent completion, and production plans were placed on hold. It should be noted that the Seafire certification program coincided with a time period in which the market for new production single-engine civil aircraft in the U.S. had all but disappeared.

In late 1990s, after a long hiatus, Thurston revived support for the Seafire certification and production program under the sponsorship a new company known as Aquastar, Inc. Following certification, Aquastar planned to offer production models at a unit price in the range of $325,000. The Seafire prototype, re-registered to Aquastar in 2000, was moved to Seagull Aviation Parts, Inc. of Clintonville, Wisconsin, where it underwent a complete airframe refurbishment that included installation of new avionics and test equipment. Test flying resumed sometime in 2002, and the pro-totype was displayed at the EAA's annual Oshkosh, Wisconsin fly-in the same year. The sequence of events after 2002 is not clear, but the certification project apparently stalled again. More recently, the project resurfaced at a website listed as the "Seafire Home Page" (see http://www.nelsonillus-tration.com/SeafireCoInfo.htm) under the aegis of Aeromarine Aircraft, Inc., headquartered in Ozark, Alabama. Although the site reported that the company hoped to achieve certification by the end of 2004, the current status of the project was not revealed. As to homebuilt Trojan variants, forty-five construction projects were reported to have been started in the U.S. and Canada during the 1970s and 1980s; however, according to an article that appeared in the February 2000 issue of *General Aviation News,* only two examples were actually completed and flown.

Volmer Aircraft Company

Volmer S. Jensen began designing and building sailplanes in the 1930s, and soon after World War II, acquired the assets of Jarvis Aircraft Co. in Burbank, California, to patent and build the VJ-21 Jaybird, a motor-glider type aircraft featuring a pod nacelle with a pusher engine and monowheel landing gear with outriggers. Outside of aviation circles, Jenson is probably best remembered for having created the model of the "Enterprise" seen in the original *Star Trek* television series. He passed away in 1997.

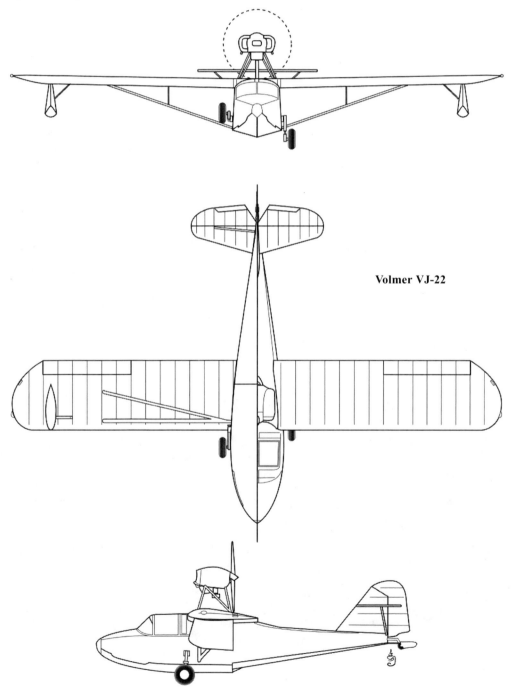

Volmer VJ-22

Volmer VJ-22 Sportsman (1958)

TECHNICAL SPECIFICATIONS

Type: 2-place homebuilt civil amphibian.
Total built: 100 (est.)
Powerplant: one 85-hp Continental C-85 4-cylinder air-cooled opposed engine driving a two-bladed, fixed-pitch wooden or metal propeller.
Performance: max. speed 105 mph, cruise 85 mph; ceiling 13,000 ft.; range 300 mi.
Weights: 1,000 lbs. empty, 1,500 lbs. gross.
Dimensions: span 36 ft. 6 in., length 24 ft. 0 in., wing area 170 sq. ft.

Almost fifty years after it first appeared, the VJ-22 stands as one of the most enduring amphibian designs in the history of the homebuilt aircraft movement and examples are still being built today. Volmer Jensen started construction of the first VJ-22 in the fall of 1957 and made the first flight in December 1958. All of the basic airframe components were of built-up wooden construction. The single-step hull, scaled-down from an old Savoia-Marchetti design, was framed with a keel, longerons, and formers of spruce, covered in a veneer of aircraft grade 1/16-inch and 3/32-inch mahogany, reinforced to 1/4-inch at the step location, then overlaid with fiberglass cloth for added strength.

Construction was speeded-up by utilizing the fabric-covered, wooden wings of an Aeronca 7AC Champion. Though not specifically mentioned, it appears Jenson also made use of the steel tube horizontal tail surfaces, metal lift struts, and other ready-made hardware from the Champ. By the time the VJ-22 was ready to fly, Jensen had dubbed it "Chubasco," a Spanish term for violent thunderstorms seen off the Pacific coast. Flight trials subsequently revealed docile flight characteristics and very good water handling.

In the intervening years, Jensen sold many sets of plans, marketed as the "Sportsman," and over 100 examples are estimated to have been built and flown. As is common with most homebuilts, VJ-22 builders have introduced a number of variations to the basic design. In recent years, for example, different powerplants have been installed, most commonly the 100-hp Continental O-200 and the 108-hp Lycoming O-235, and some have switched to a tractor type mount. Today, prospective builders have the option of buying a complete VJ-22 hull kit from Aircraft Spruce & Specialty Co., which retails for $4,526.00 (see http://www.aircraftspruce.com/), plus Aeronca wing parts and associated hardware are still obtainable from Univair Aircraft Corp. (see http://www.univairparts.com/).

Plans and building information are currently sold by the Volmer Club of America (see http://www.volmeraircraft.com/). Chubasco, the original VJ-22, following a recent refurbishment and recovering, is still registered and flying.

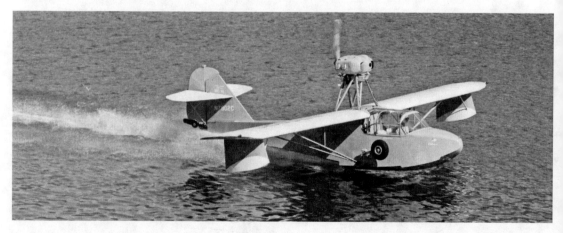

The first VJ-22, N7802C "Chubasco." Simple construction combined with docile handling qualities have made the Sportsman a popular choice with homebuilders. Complete hull kits are now available.

Appendix A: Lesser Known Flying Boats and Amphibians

THE EARLY ERA • 1912–1928

Aeromarine Model 80 (1920)

In addition to the NAF F-5Ls converted to Model 75s, Aeromarine also modified a number of ex–Navy Curtiss HS-2Ls in 1921 into six-passenger flying boats and offered them as the Model 80. At least one was placed into service with its Aeromarine Airways subsidiary and another is known to have operated out of Baltimore during 1921 and 1922 with the short-lived Easter Airways.

Aeromarine 80, an ex-Curtiss HS-2L, in Aeromarine Airways service with a highly modified bow for passenger accommodations.

Aeromarine EO (1924)

Resembling a down-sized version of its AMC (see Part I, page 13), the EO represented a final effort on Aeromarine's part to introduce a three-place sport plane to the civil market. Powered by

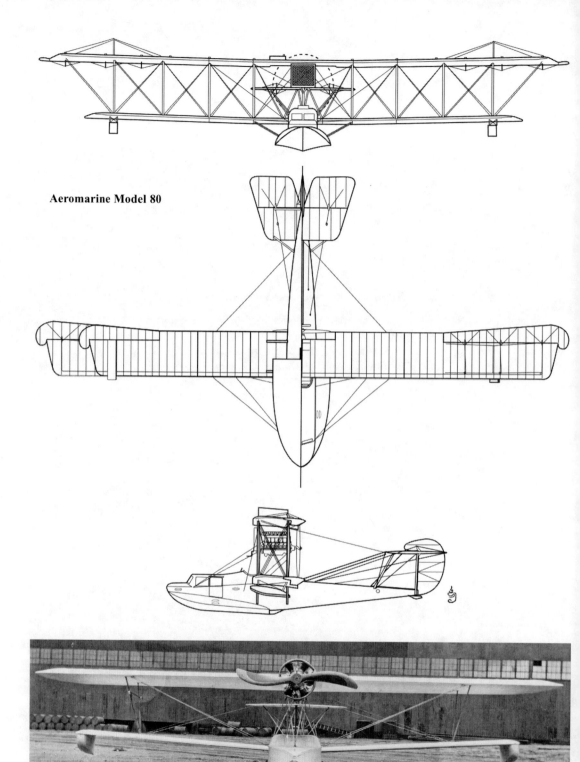

Aeromarine Model 80

Front view of Aeromarine EO with 5-cylinder Anzani engine. The rivet detail on the bottom of the metal hull is visible.

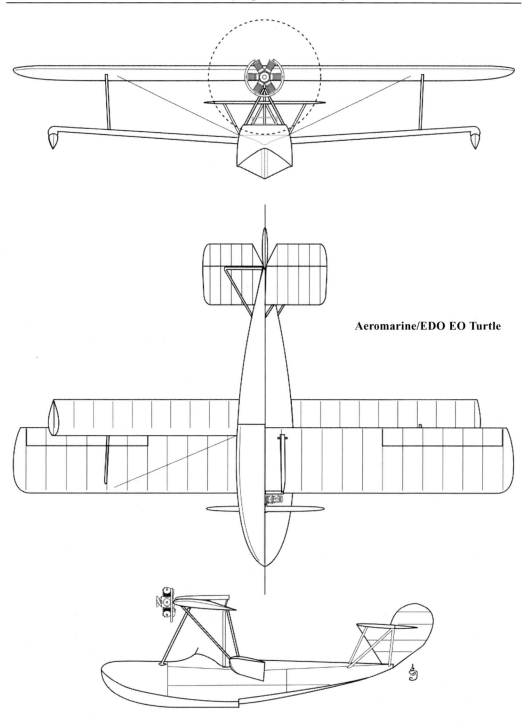

Aeromarine/EDO EO Turtle

a tractor-mounted 80-hp Anzani 5-cylinder radial engine, the EO featured an all-aluminum, deep-V hull of exceptionally modern design having a sesquiplane wing layout that was braced by V-struts. No performance data is available. One EO is known to have been competed in 1924, though whether its was subsequently registered to Aeromarine-Klemm or Edo Corp. seems to be a point of debate. In any case, after being reequipped with a 90-hp Kinner K-5 engine in 1929, the EO was destroyed in a crash in 1931.

Batson Air Yacht seen sometime in 1913. Powered by three 175-hp engines, the ungainly craft reportedly never achieved flight.

Batson Air Yacht (1913)

Probably the largest flying boat in the world at the time, Matthew A. Batson built this aircraft during 1912 and 1913 with the intention of flying it on a transatlantic flight from Savannah, Georgia, to Liverpool, England. The airframe consisted of six forty-foot wings and a gondola-type cabin, affixed with a plethora of struts and braces to a seventy-four-foot-long pontoon. The ungainly craft was powered by three 120-hp Emerson six-cylinder engines. Though successfully launched in the Herb River, it reportedly never achieved sustained flight.

Boland Flying Boat (1913)

Between 1910 and 1913, Frank and Joseph Boland of Rahway, New Jersey, built and tested several aircraft that featured unusual canard layouts. The 1913 flying boat appeared with a raised mono-

The Boland canard flying boat as it appeared in 1913. Its single vertical tail surface was mounted under the port wing.

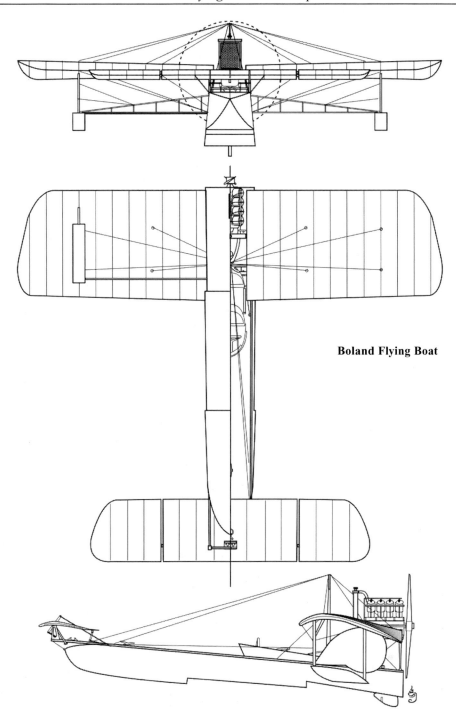

Boland Flying Boat

plane wing which tied into spanwise braces that also served as outriggers for the stabilizing floats. A single fin and rudder was mounted between the wing and the float on the port side. The forward canard, rigged as an all-flying stabilizer, was large enough to function as a tandem wing. Photographs indicate a water-cooled V-8 engine in a pusher configuration. The flat-bottomed hull possessed two transverse steps that would have been between the approximate center of gravity. No flight data was reported.

Burgess K (D-1, AB-6) (1913)

Built by the Burgess Co. of Marblehead, Massachusetts (acquired by Curtiss in 1916), the model K was flown in April 1913 with a 70-hp Renault pusher engine. Its two-bay biplane wings utilized inverted V-struts with a single tubular metal spar, and the wooden hull was similar in configuration to the Curtiss F Boat. The single example built, purchased by the Navy and taken into service as the D-1 (later AB-6), was destroyed in a crash in early 1914.

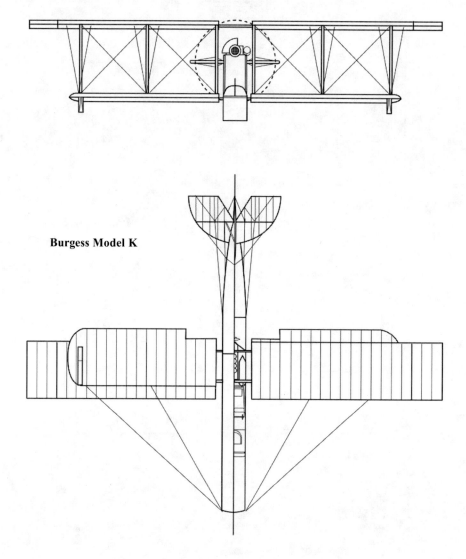

Burgess Model K

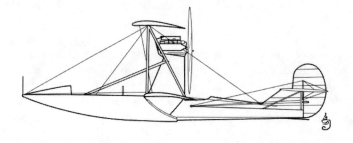

Burgess-Dunne B-D-F (1916)

The Burgess-Dunne series of aircraft were British tailless designs built in the U.S. under license. The B-D-F of 1916 was a boat-hulled version of the B-D land and hydroplane, powered by a 100-hp Curtiss OXX-2 engine. When the Army and the Navy expressed no interest in the type, Burgess tried unsuccessfully to sell them on the civilian market. Only one B-D-F was built.

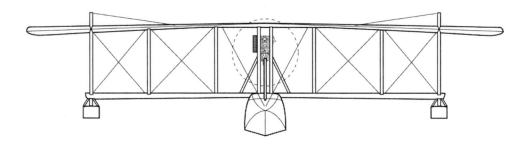

Burgess BDF

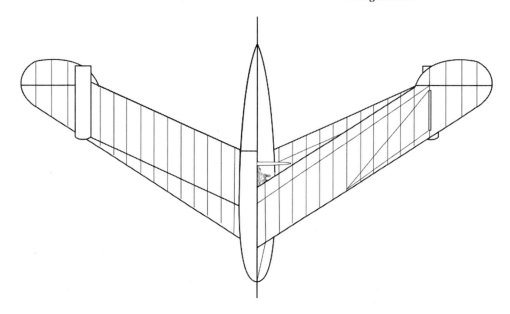

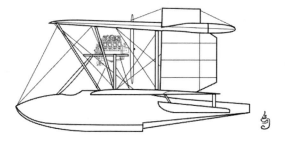

Christofferson Hydro (1913)

Constructed by Christofferson Aviation Co. in San Francisco, California, the Hydro flying boat, which flew sometime in 1913, was in all likelihood designed by Alan Loughead (later Lockheed) who worked for Christofferson at the time. The aircraft was powered by a 120-hp Hall-Scott V-8 engine and featured a two-bay biplane layout very similar to that of the Curtiss F Boat. Of the three or four examples known to have been completed in 1914, two were sold to explorer Roald Amundsen for a proposed Arctic flight, but never used in that capacity, and one was employed by Silas Christofferson's San Francisco–Oakland Aerial Ferry in 1914, thus becoming the second scheduled airline to operate in the U.S. Another Hydro is listed as having been sold to Japan.

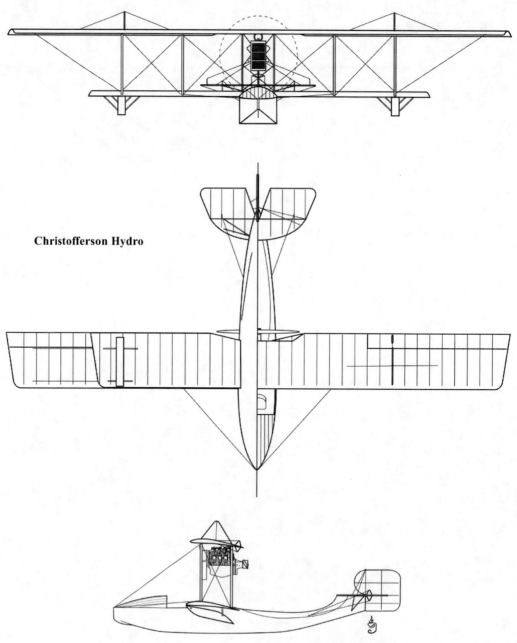

Christofferson Hydro

Cooke Tractor Flying Boat (1913)

Weldon B. Cooke, an early pioneer who taught himself to fly in a Curtiss pusher, apparently started construction of a flying boat project in California, and then sometime in 1913, shipped the parts by rail to Sandusky, Ohio, where the aircraft was completed and presumably flown from Lake Erie. The craft's biplane wings rested on a full-length boat hull that ended in a tail group supported by a profusion of struts. Its single tractor propeller, mounted forward of the wing, was driven by a belt running from a 75-hp Roberts engine. No performance data exists on this aircraft. After he left Sandusky to assist Benoist with the St. Petersburg-Tampa Air Boat Line, Cooke was killed during an exhibition flight in 1914.

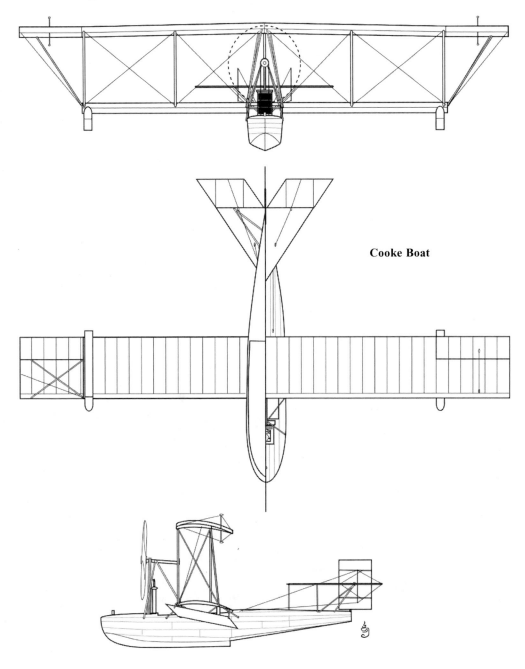

Cooke Boat

Weldon Cooke's flying boat seen on Lake Erie in Sandusky, Ohio, in 1913. Cooke was killed a year later while working with Benoist.

Curtiss OWL (A-2, E-1, and AX-1) (1912)

Ordered by the Navy in May 1911 as a standard model E pusher landplane and taken into service as the A-2, it became the amphibious OWL I (Over Water and Land) after being subjected to a series of experimental modifications during 1913 that entailed installation of a wide, stepped pontoon with built-in tricycle-type wheels, plus a fabric-covered enclosure over the two-man cockpit. This aircraft was re-designated E-1 after it flew in mid–1913, then as AX-1 in early 1914. Work was begun by Curtiss in late 1913 on the OWL II, which, while utilizing the same model E components, featured a more pointed V-bottom hull and improved housings for the tricycle wheels. The OWL II was reportedly completed sometime in 1914, but its final disposition is unknown.

The OWL I, depicted here, was really an "E Hydro" with a cabin built up onto the pontoon. It was probably the first amphibian.

Curtiss Tadpole (1913)

Curtiss built the Tadpole to test the aerodynamic relationship between the planing hull and the rigging of the wings. The first variation used a 100-hp Curtiss OX engine and came with the unequal span wings of the early F Boat, but with inset ailerons and several degrees of sweep. One of the devices tested on this aircraft was a set of moveable struts on the upper and lower wing center sections that enabled incidence to be adjusted. According to this notion, if the wing were adjusted to negative incidence while the plane was moored, it would not tend to become airborne during high winds. Continuing experiments were carried with the Tadpole in winter of 1914 when it was fitted with outrigger skis and flown from a frozen lake.

The one-of-a-kind Tadpole was built to test various wing configurations. In 1914, it was fitted with skis and flown off a frozen lake.

Curtiss M (Monoplane) (1914)

When it made its first flight in January 1914, the Curtiss model M became the world's first monoplane flying boat. Built to order for Raymond V. Morris, a Curtiss employee, the single-seat model

The Curtiss M Boat, the first monoplane flying boat, as it appeared in 1914. After unsatisfactory tests, it was converted to a biplane layout.

M was powered by a 90-hp OX engine and possessed a stepped, full-length hull similar in shape but narrower in beam to that of the F Boat. The single thirty-four foot wing, braced by two bays of V-struts attached to a bottom outrigger spar that also held the stabilizing floats, featured large tip ailerons, several degrees of sweep, and a thicker airfoil section derived from the Bleriot Type IXb. After Morris tested the M in San Diego during 1914, performance with the monoplane wing was found to be unsatisfactory, and a smaller lower wing was later added to this aircraft.

Curtiss H-7 Super America (1915)

The H-7 Super America, also referred to as the "Transatlantic," was a transitional flying boat design having features that would be incorporated on later types. While its wings and hull were similar to those of the H-4, the H-7 differed in having tractor-mounted 160-hp Curtiss VX experimental engines and a redesigned tail group that was reinforced by booms extending from the engine mounts to the horizontal tail surfaces. The cockpit, unlike the H-4, was left open. During the H-7's first flight in mid–October 1915, it demonstrated extreme tail-heaviness that nearly resulted in its destruction. Flight-testing was not resumed until May 1916 following a repositioning of the engines, re-rigging of the wings, and modifications to the hull. Despite successful trials, no Navy or RNAS orders were forthcoming. Two H-7s ordered by Russia subsequently became victims of the same shipping fiasco that involved the Curtiss K Boats. Nevertheless, the H-7's tractor engine arrangement would be seen again on the H-10 and became standardized on the H-12/-16 series. A scaled down version of the H-7's tail design appeared later on the the H-14.

H-7 TB, probably in 1916 following modifications. It was ordered by Russia, but not by the U.S. Navy or R.N.A.S.

Curtiss T Triplane (1916)

Designed to British Admiralty requirements and completed in 1916, the Curtiss T was the first type of American-built aircraft to possess four engines. It massed 22,000 lbs. loaded and boasted an upper wingspan of 134 feet. When the planned Curtiss V-4 powerplants failed to materialize, the aircraft was dismantled and shipped to Great Britain, where it was reassembled and fitted with four 240-hp Renault engines. One reference indicates that the big flying boat was damaged beyond repair on its maiden flight. In any case, the contract was cancelled before any of the other 19 examples on order could be completed.

Massive Curtiss T Triplane flying boat as seen after being shipped to Great Britain and readied for flight.

Curtiss FL (Model 7) (1917)

Tested during 1917 as an experimental project, the model FL combined the high-aspect ratio triplane wings of the model F landplane with the hull of a late F Boat. The type's 100-hp Curtiss OX engine was mounted in a pusher configuration in the center-section of the middle wing. After experimental trials, Curtiss reportedly sold the single FL to the American Trans-Oceanic Corp., but its final disposition in unknown.

One-of-a-kind FL Boat, also carried as the model 7, which tested a triplane configuration. It was reportedly sold to a corporate owner afterward.

Curtiss-Judson Triplane (1917)

Completed for an individual named Judson (no first name given) in early 1917, no specifications for this aircraft were ever listed, but it appears to have used a lengthened and improved F Boat hull, which was mated to an extra set of F Boat upper wings. Its single 150-hp Curtiss VX engine was pusher-mounted between the panels of the middle wing. This triplane is reported to have been refitted sometime later with a 400-hp Curtiss K-12 engine and used for exploratory work in South America.

It is not certain whether this aircraft was actually built by Curtiss or built using Curtiss components. One was completed in 1917.

Curtiss BT (1917)

The triplane BT or Baby T flying lifeboat was built to investigate an interesting theory that did not work well in practice. The idea arose from discussions between Curtiss and the U.S. Coast Guard regarding the feasibility of an aircraft which, after landing in the water near a stricken

The BT Boat, completed for the Coast Guard in 1917, represented an interesting idea that did not work in practice.

vessel, could discard its wings and tail group and thereafter function as a motorized lifeboat. In its initial configuration, the BT was powered by a single 200-hp Curtiss VX-3 engine buried in the hull, which drove two tractor propellers mounted on the middle wing through a transmission and shaft drive. When preliminary testing was carried out in mid–1917, the BT's transmission system proved to be so problematic that it had to be discarded. A modified BT having a tractor-mounted, direct-drive engine on the middle wing was flown in late 1917, however, the wings and tail group were no longer capable of being jettisoned. Though the Coast Guard apparently lost interest in the project, the Navy purchased the BT in December 1917 and tested it briefly. No further examples were ordered, and the aircraft was scrapped in mid–1919.

Curtiss Janin Patent Boat (1918)

Never intended to fly, the Janin Patent Boat was built for the express purpose of invalidating a patent filed by Albert Janin in 1913, which became the subject of an infringement lawsuit brought against Curtiss in 1914. After the aircraft, completed in 1918, failed to achieve flight as expected, Janin's lawsuit was dismissed.

Built by Curtiss in 1918 to disprove allegations of patent infringement, the aircraft was never flown.

Ecker Flying Boat (1912)

Neither the time of construction nor the first flight of this aircraft can be accurately verified. According to the records of the Smithsonian National Air and Space Museum (NASM), Herman A. Ecker of Syracuse, New York, built the Ecker Flying Boat in late 1912 or early 1913. The aircraft was powered by a converted 60-hp 6-cylinder Roberts marine engine that was pusher-mounted on

Though dated 1912, the time of Ecker's first flight was not documented. The Ecker Flying Boat used a Roberts engine but otherwise very similar to the Curtiss E Boat. *Credit*: **National Air and Space Museum.**

struts beneath the upper wing. The stepped wooden hull and three-bay wing design bear a conspicuous resemblance to the Curtiss E Boat of the same time period. Ecker was reported to have flown the flying boat successfully for several years before placing it into storage. The aircraft was acquired by NASM in 1961 and completely restored in 1982.

Hall Air Yacht (1923)

The 2-seat Air Yacht was Charles Hall's (see Hall Aluminum Aircraft Co. in Part II, page 149) first effort to produce an airplane. The small flying boat, powered by a 60-hp 3-cyliner radial, featured a sesquiplane and boom layout having an upper span of 25 ft. and a hull length of 25 ft. 1 in. No flight details are available.

Junkin-Bruckner Baby Flying Boat (1919)

Built in 1919 by Elwood J. Junkin and Clayton J. Bruckner of Lorain, Ohio, this aircraft is identified by some historians as having been the first product of what ultimately became the Weaver Aircraft Co. (WACO) formed by Junkin, Bruckner, and George E. Weaver a year later. The diminutive flying boat sported a single bay of 18-foot biplane wings, a boom-mounted empennage, and a 15-hp Hendee engine connected to a belt and pulley driving the propeller. Flight trials on Lake Erie quickly revealed that the craft was far too underpowered to achieve flight, plus the vibration produced by the engine almost shook the airframe apart. Afterward, Junkin and Bruckner reportedly stored the Baby Flying Boat in loft above a dance hall in Lorain.

Kirkham Air Yacht (1925)

The five-place Air Yacht was built by the Kirkham Aeroplane & Motor Co. of Long Island, New York, to the special order of millionaire Harold S. Vanderbilt. Featuring a fully-cantilevered

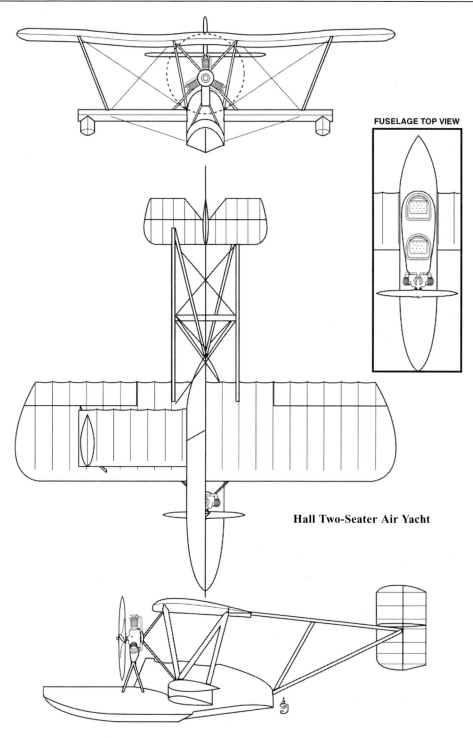

FUSELAGE TOP VIEW

Hall Two-Seater Air Yacht

gull wing and a 540-hp Napier Lion V-12 pusher engine, it was one of the most modern flying boats in the world when it flew for the first time in late 1925. The exceptionally clean aerodynamic contours of the Air Yacht were thoroughly tested in a wind tunnel before the design was finalized. After delivery, Vanderbilt is said to have used this aircraft to commute between New York City and his home in Newport, Rhode Island.

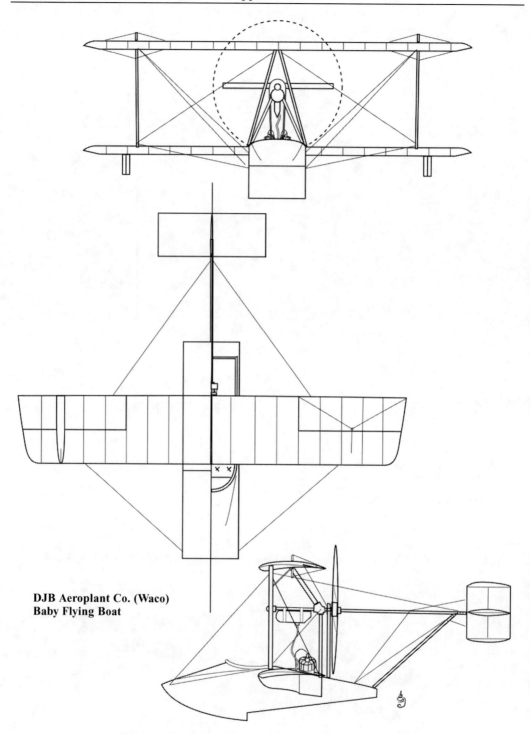

**DJB Aeroplant Co. (Waco)
Baby Flying Boat**

Lawrence-Lewis A and B Flying Boat (1915)

Under the business name Lewis Aeroplane Co., in Chicago, Illinois, George R. Lawrence and his business partner, Harry Lewis, are known to have built several types of small flying boats, starting in 1914 and 1915. All of them were biplanes featuring a long, enclosed cabin built onto a flat-

Exceptionally modern for its day, Kirkham's Air Yacht was built for the private use of millionaire Harold S. Vanderbilt.

Lawrence-Lewis type A flying boat taking off, probably in 1915. Unusual fuselage configuration shows to good effect.

bottomed pontoon. The first A type, thought to have flown sometime in 1915, was powered by a tractor-mounted 50-hp Kirkham C-4 engine and reportedly used a wing-warping system for lateral control. One source indicated that the A type completed many successful flights (see http://www.aerofiles.com/_la.html). The dimensionally larger B type, though sharing a similar cabin layout, was powered by a Hall-Scott engine of undisclosed horsepower and incorporated interplane-type ailerons.

Loening Duckling (1918)

In 1918, a year after starting his own company, Grover Loening designed and built a small flying boat which he named the Duckling. It emerged as a single-bay biplane powered by a tractor-mounted 60-hp Lawrence 3-cylinder radial engine. The hull resembled an enlarged seaplane pontoon, and the twin fin with its high-horizontal stabilizer was an arrangement seen later on Loening's record-breaking monoplane Flying Yacht of 1922. Although this small aircraft is known to have been completed, the limited information available does not confirm whether or not it was actually flown, and no specifications or performance data were ever published.

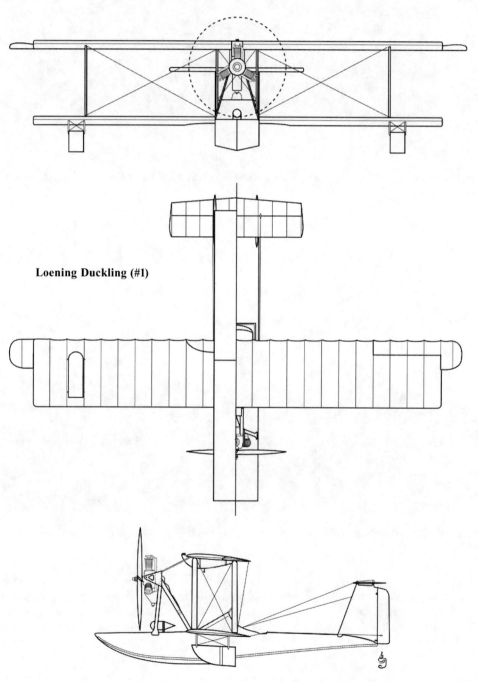

Loening Duckling (#1)

Loughead F-1 (1918)

One of Alan and Malcolm Loughead's (later changed to "Lockheed") earliest endeavors to obtain a military contract, the F-1 was a twin-engine flying boat of wooden construction having a three-bay biplane layout similar to the Curtiss HS-1, its chief competitor at trials conducted in 1918 at the Navy's North Island base in San Diego. The design was characterized by a triple fin empen-

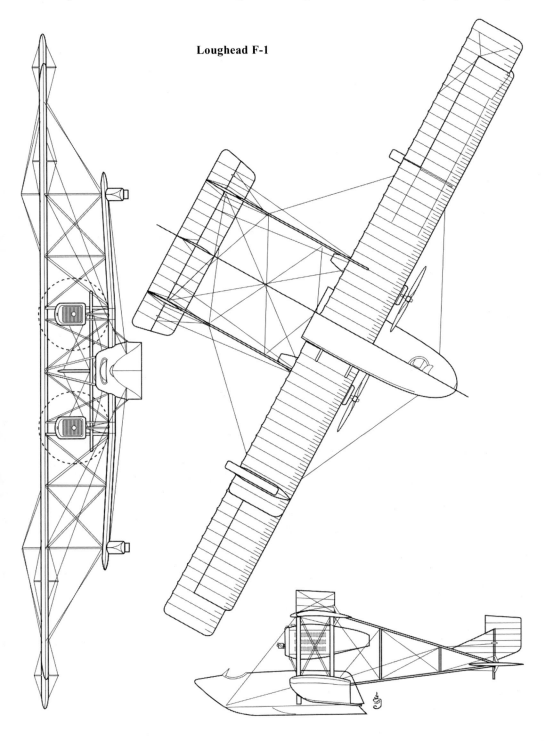

Loughead F-1

Loughead F-1, with outer wing panels removed, being moved to Long Beach in 1918 for its first flight.

nage supported by booms extending back from the hull and wings. Two tractor-mounted 160-hp Hall-Scott A-5 engines were positioned between the upper and lower wing on struts. Although Loughead's entry lost to Curtiss, the Navy Department was sufficiently impressed to give the brothers a contract to license-produce two HS-1Ls. Following the competition, the F-1 was reportedly used for sightseeing and charter flights around Santa Barbara, California. The aircraft eventually fell victim to vandals and was abandoned on the beach.

Queen Aeroboat (1912)

Designed by Grover C. Loening for the short-lived Queen Aeroplane Co. of Bronx Park, New York, some historians have speculated that this aircraft may have flown sometime in early 1912, before the Curtiss Flying Boat No. 2 (see Part I, page 31), which would make it the world's first flying boat. But unlike Curtiss's effort, which is well-documented, there appears to be no verifiable record of exactly when the Aeroboat made its first flight. According to the information posted on Aerofiles (see http://www.aerofiles.com/_pl.html#_Q), the initial version utilized a discarded speedboat hull and wings from a Blériot monoplane and was originally powered by a 35-hp Gnôme rotary engine driving a pusher-mounted propeller via a chain and sprocket. A 1913 version, equipped with a 50-hp Gnôme and improved wings, is thought to have flown sometime the same year; however, it was destroyed in a storm before it could be fully flight-tested.

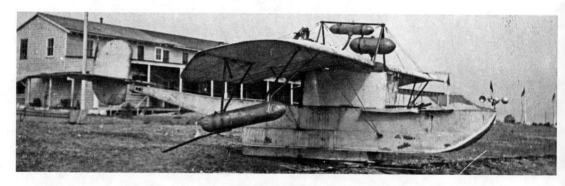

Using a metal speedboat hull and wings from a Blériot monoplane, the Aeroboat was the first flying boat developed by amphibian pioneer Grover C. Loening.

Shaw Flying Boat (1915)

Aerofiles (see www.aerofiles.com) is the only historical source identifying the Shaw Flying Boat, and most of the information about it is derived from five photographs supposedly taken in

Little is known about this flying boat other than photographs thought to have been made in 1915.

1915. Nothing is known of the designer and builder other than the name Shaw. The photographs depict a three-bay biplane having interplane ailerons, joined to a single step hull of planked wooden construction. Its powerplant, identified as a 3-cylinder, two-cycle Johnson engine of 90 hp, was located in the hull in front of the cockpit and drove a single pusher propeller via a sprocket and chain connected to a drive-shaft. General dimensions appear to be similar to that of a Curtiss E Boat. One photograph shows the aircraft in the water and another in flight. No performance data is known.

Stevens Flying boat (1915)

In 1915 or 1916 a firm named B. Stevens and Sons of Woonsocket, Rhode Island, contracted with Fred Chanonhouse to construct a two-place flying boat that appeared to be very similar in design to the late-model Curtiss F Boats having inset ailerons on the upper wing. The aircraft was powered by a 105-hp Sturdevant engine, but no other data is known.

Built for B. Stevens by Fred Chanonhouse of Woonsocket, Rhode Island, this flying boat is thought to have flown in either 1915 or 1916.

THE GOLDEN ERA • 1928–1945

Applegate Amphibian (1937)

Built by Ray Applegate of Lockhaven, Pennsylvania, in 1937, this two-place, metal-hulled amphibian, registered as NX17866, used the wing and possibly other components derived from a Piper

After mating a new metal hull to wings and other components of a J-3 Cub, Applegate sold the design rights to Piper. Never produced.

J-3 Cub. Available data listed a wingspan of 34 feet 5 inches, a length of 22 feet, and a useful load of 650 lbs. Several different powerplants ranging from 55 hp to 145 hp were tested on the prototype. Piper Aircraft Corp. acquired the project from Applegate but never placed it in production.

Argonaut H-20/-24 Pirate (1934)

Argonaut Aircraft, Inc., organized by J. Leroy Sutton in North Tonowanda, New York, tried unsuccessfully to market the H-20 and H-24 Pirate in the civilian market in 1934 and 1935. Both aircraft were three-place, monoplane amphibians powered by a pusher-mounted 125-hp Menasco C-4 inline, air-cooled engine. The main differences between the two were a 35-foot 4-inch span on the H-20 and 42-foot 0-inch on the H-24. Though not revealed, structure appears to be a metal hull with fabric-covered wings and tail surfaces. Available performance data on the H-24 lists a top speed of 104 mph and a cruise of 89 mph, with a useful load of 650 lbs. Argonaut was acquired by White Aircraft Co. in 1938, but there is no record of any more amphibians being produced.

Efforts to market the 2-place Pirate on the civil market in 1934 and 1935 met with no success.

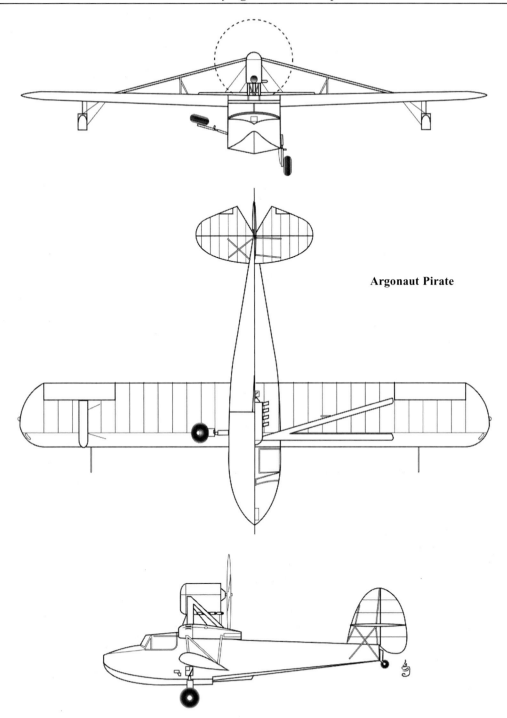

Argonaut Pirate

Booth Flying Boat (1931)

Built sometime in 1931 by H.T. Booth, who lived in Freeport, New York, the two-place Booth flying boat featured a two-bay biplane layout with a tailplane supported by booms running from the wing and hull. A water-cooled engine buried in the hull forward of the cockpit (make and horsepower unknown) used a geared drive-shaft to turn a tractor propeller mounted on the upper wing.

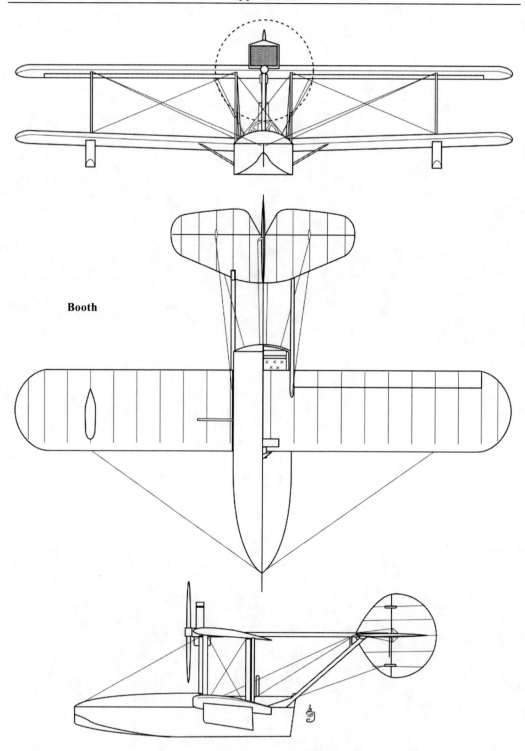

Booth

A separate 32-hp marine outboard motor was also installed to drive a boat propeller mounted beneath the hull. Available data does not mention dimensions, weights, or performance, or whether or not the aircraft was actually ever flown. Booth, an ex-Curtiss employee, is reported to have been involved earlier in the design of the Kirkham Air Yacht.

Cadillac (McCarroll) Duoplane (1929)

The Cadillac Aircraft Co. emerged in 1927 as a spin-off of Inglis M. Uppercu's (founder of Aeromarine) Cadillac dealership in Detroit, Michigan. Its only creation, variously known as the Cadillac amphibian and the McCarroll Duoplane (after its designer, H.G. McCarroll), appeared in 1929 as a four-place, all-metal monoplane powered by two 100-hp Kinner K-5 radial engines mounted in streamlined nacelles above the wings. Specifications listed a wingspan of 46 feet, a length of 32 feet, and a useful load of 1,025 lbs. The sole example built (NX595E) was later modified with a 48-foot wing and two 165-hp Wright R-540 *Whirlwind* engines.

Designed by H.G. McCarroll, this one-off amphibian was built in the late 1920s to the order of Inglis Uppercu's Detroit Cadillac dealership.

Columbia CAL-1 Triad (1929)

The CAL-1 was another hybrid type that seems to have been influenced by the Loening "Shoehorns" (See Loening C-1, -2 Air Yacht in Part I), but with a completely detachable pontoon for land

One of two Triads completed in 1929 and 1930. The pontoon could be completely detached for land-plane operations.

operations. This unusual six-place aircraft employed a monoplane layout with the cockpit situated behind the engine in the upper wing center-section, while the cabin was behind and below. General dimensions were a wingspan of 49 feet and a length of 33 feet, but the weights are unknown. Its 220-hp Wright J-5 engine was mounted high up even with the wing. Available data reported a top speed of 130 mph and a range of 550 miles with a 1,000-lb. useful load. Two CAL-1s (registered as NX306E and NX307E) are known to have been built in 1929 and 1930, and the second was refitted with a 300-hp J-6 engine. Both aircraft were reportedly destroyed in a hangar fire in early 1931.

Fairchild FB-3 (1929)

Fairchild's first effort to offer a flying boat (no FB-1 or -2 reported), the FB-3 appeared in 1929 as a four-place, all-metal monoplane powered by a 410-hp Pratt & Whitney R-1340 mounted as a pusher. The two-step hull was clad in aluminum and the wings and tail surfaces were fabric-covered metal structures. Specifications list a wingspan of 52 feet, a length of 41 feet, and a top speed of 130 mph. Only one prototype (NX7385) is known to have been completed.

Fairchild's first flying boat effort, the FB-3 (NX7385), completed and flown in 1929 but never produced.

Grumman G-65 Tadpole (1944)

Designed by David B. Thurston and Herbert P. Lindbad, who would later form the Colonial Aircraft Corp. (see Part III, page 221), the G-65 was an all-metal, two-place amphibian intended for the post-war civil market. Powered by a 125-hp Continental C-125 six-cylinder engine mounted in a raised pusher nacelle, the prototype, registered as NX41828, flew for the first time in Decem-

Designed by David B. Thurston and Herbert P. Lindbad for the postwar civil market, the Tadpole was never placed into production.

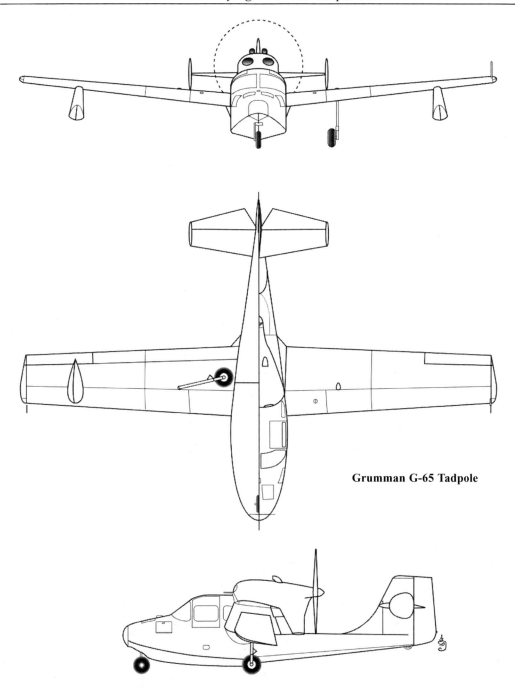

Grumman G-65 Tadpole

ber 1944 with Leroy Grumman at the controls. While Grumman ultimately decided not to undertake production of the G-65, Thurston and Lindbad went on to incorporate many elements of its design into the Colonial C-1 Skimmer.

Issoudun H-23 (1930)

Other than being powered by two 125-hp Warner *Scarab* 7-cyliner radial engines, little is known about this amphibian, built reportedly in 1930 by Issoudun Aircraft Corp. of Northville, Michigan.

The little-known Issoudun H-23, thought to have been built and flown in 1930.

Knoll-Brayton Sachem (1931)

Designed by Felix Knoll and built by Brayton Aeronautical Corp. of Norwich, Connecticut, the "Sachem," named after nearby Sachem Head, appeared in 1931 as a three-place, parasol wing amphibian powered by a 160-hp Menasco B-6 pusher engine enclosed in a streamlined nacelle. The single-step hull was all-metal while wings and tail surfaces were fabric-covered. Strut-mounted sponsons also contained retractable landing gear. Specifications on performance, dimensions, and weights were not published.

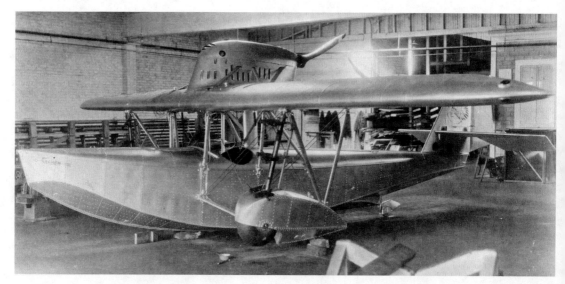

Named after Sachem Head on Long Island Sound east of Hartford, Connecticut, this one-off amphibian was reportedly flown in 1931.

Loening (Keystone) Monoduck (1934)

The four-place Monoduck amphibian, receiving ATC Certification sometime in 1934, was said to have been Grover Loening's final civilian aircraft design. In concept, the amphibian represented a fairly straightforward adaptation of the hull and tail group of a Loening-Keystone K-84 Commuter (see Part II, pages 158–159) to a new monoplane wing. Power was derived from a 300-hp Wright J-6 *Whirlwind*, strut-mounted atop the cockpit area in a tractor configuration. Top speed was listed as 135 mph, about 15 mph faster than the K-84. Only one example was known to have been completed.

The market for the Monoduck as a successor to the biplane Commuter never materialized.

Loening (Keystone) C-5 Monoplane (1934)

The dates and exact origin of this amphibian are not certain, and only one source identifies it as the C-5. It may have originally appeared as the Duckling II with a 110-hp Warner *Scarab* engine at a date earlier than that listed above. In any case, photographic evidence of an aircraft registered as

The similarity between the C-5 and the navy's XSL-1 submarine scout is evident in this photograph.

NX813W shows a two-place monoplane powered a by pusher-mounted Menasco inline engine (probably a 160-hp B-6). The general design was derived almost entirely from Loening's XSL-2 Navy submarine scout (see Part II, page 161), which was modified to include an enclosed cockpit on the forward hull and amphibious landing gear. This aircraft might have been used by Grover Loening as a personal transport.

Miami Aircraft MM-200 and -201 Miami Maid (1929)

A product of the short-lived Miami Aircraft Corp. of Miami, Florida, the five-place MM-200 Miami Maid amphibian, registered as NC619, appeared in either 1928 or 1929 with a 230-hp Menasco-Salmson B-2 radial engine pusher-mounted on top of the wing. Consisting mainly of pre-existing components, the design combined an all-wood Fokker cantilevered wing with the wooden hull of a Curtiss F boat (see Part I, page 32). Specifications on the ATC certificate listed a wingspan of 44 feet, a length of 33 feet, and a useful load of 1,250 lbs. Top speed was reported as 120 mph, with a cruising range of 500 miles at 100 mph. Whether the MM-200 became the MM-201 is not clear, but in any case, a second aircraft, registered as NC178N, was modified in 1930 for installation of a 300-hp Wright R-975 *Whirlwind* engine.

The MM-200 (NC619) as it appeared in 1929. The design reportedly combined a Curtiss hull with a Fokker cantilevered wing.

Spencer-Larsen SL-12 (1939)

Percival H. Spencer (see Spencer S-12 Air Car, Part II, page 208) teamed up with Sikorsky engineer Vincent A. Larsen in 1939 to built the SL-12. This monoplane amphibian, with a reported wingspan of 40 feet and a length of 27 feet 10 inches, was powered by 150-hp Menasco D-4 utiliz-

Prior to the Air Car, Percival Spencer joined with Sikorsky engineer Vincent Larsen to build the SL-12. It reappeared two years later as the Colgate-Larsen CL-15.

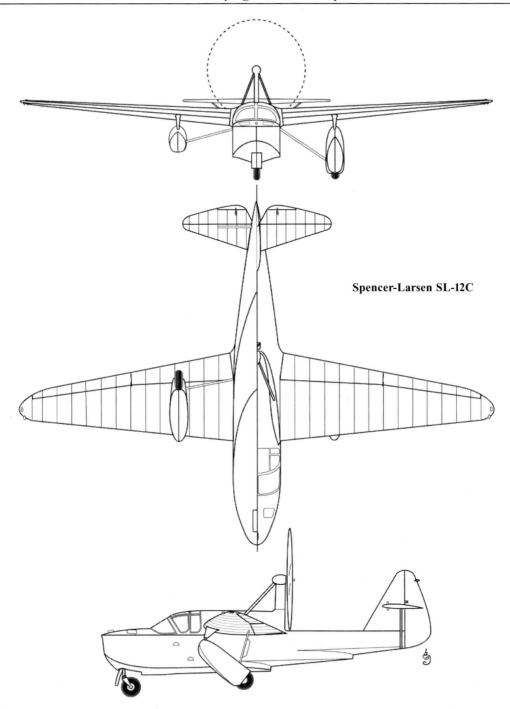

Spencer-Larsen SL-12C

ing a geared extension to drive the pusher prop. Its novel amphibious system featured wheel-equipped stabilizing floats that swiveled-down to act as the main landing gear for land operations. When Spencer left to form his own company, Larsen joined with Gilbert Colgate in 1941 to modify the aircraft as the CL-15 amphibian. While aerodynamically identical to the SL-12C, the CL-15 mounted a 200-hp Ranger engine and featured fixed stabilizing floats and a rearward retracting landing gear that rotated into the wings. It reportedly carried four passengers at a speed of 125 mph over a range of 500 miles. Not a commercial success, only one was built.

Towle WC (TA-1), TA-2, and 3 (1928)

Thomas Towle, formerly employed by Ford Aviation, designed and built at least four twin-engine amphibians between 1928 and 1933. The first, the six-place WC of 1928, featured an all-metal hull and a fabric-covered parasol wing having two 150-hp Comet (R-612) 7-cylinder radial engines mounted above on pylons. General dimensions listed a 52-foot wingspan and a 35-foot length, and reported top speed was 115 mph. The WC is thought to have been followed by at least one TA-1 production version. The larger (56-foot span) TA-2 was flown in 1930 with two pylon-mounted 240-hp Wright J-6 radial engines and introduced an all-metal wing which was reinforced with internal skin stiffeners instead of ribs. Towle's last effort, the TA-3, also appeared in 1930 with two strut-mounted 225-hp Packard DR-980 diesel radials and a twin-fin empennage.

The WC, Towle's first amphibian, as it appeared in 1928. Powered by little-known Comet (R-612) 7-cylinder radial engines.

Towle's larger TA-3, seen here in 1930, was a sophisticated design for its day. Engines were Packard DR-980 diesel radials.

THE POST-WAR ERA • 1945–PRESENT

Aero Gare Sea Hawker and Quickkit Glass Goose (1982)

The Sea Hawker prototype was reportedly flown for the first time in 1982 with a 70-hp Revmaster (Volkswagen conversion) but subsequently redesigned for a 150-hp Lycoming O-320 before any kits were offered. The type's unusual cantilevered biplane layout was achieved with molded fiberglass components utilizing solid core construction. The single-step, molded hull follows a configuration similar to the Seabee but uses sponsons instead of tip floats for lateral water stability. According to the Quickkit website (see http://www.glassgoose.com/sh_ history.html), the original Sea Hawker, as designed, displayed serious structural and stability problems. Efforts to correct the flaws in existing Sea Hawker kits led ultimately to the introduction of the all-new Quickkit Glass Goose kit. Quickkit reports that major engineering changes have been made to the wing structure, control system, and landing gear. A flaperon system has been incorporated to both the upper and lower wings to provide roll control and lower landing speeds to 45-mph range. General specifications given are: wingspan 27 ft., length 19 ft. 8 in., loaded weight 1,800 lbs., max. speed 160 mph and ceiling 12,000 ft.

A recent photograph of a Quickkit Glass Goose, which is currently available as a kit that includes molded airframe parts and other assemblies. The new kit reportedly resolves the problems encountered in the original Sea Hawker design.

Advanced Aeromarine Buccaneer XA (1984)

The single-place Buccaneer XA appeared in 1984 as an "ultralight air vehicle" under FAR Part 103. Marketed as a kit, the XA featured a single-step hull formed from fiberglass, sailcloth-covered flying surfaces made up of preformed aluminum tubing, and three-axis controls that included ailerons. As common with ultralights, the wings and tail group were wire-braced from a kingpost located atop the wing center-section. A pusher-mounted 28-hp Rotax 277 two-cycle engine was standard but could be upgraded to a 35-hp Rotax 377. For water operations, the tailwheel folded upward and the main gear was entirely detached and stowed. Specifications listed a top speed of

The XA, depicted here, was one of the first aircraft offered in the ultralight category possessing a true monohull.

56 mph with a 50-mph cruise. Two improved Buccaneer variants introduced in the late 1980s, the XA and II, will be discussed below under Aero Adventure.

Adventure Air Super Adventurer (1991)

In terms of general design, the two-place Super Adventurer followed the tried and tested hull and aerodynamic arrangement seen on other amphibians like the Colonial Skimmer/Lake LA series as well as homebuilt designs like the Volmer Sportsman, but used new construction methods made possible by airframe components fabricated from composite materials. Although available photographs only depict a Super Adventurer (i.e., N3313) completed in a tailwheel configuration, the builder's information stated that tricycle landing gear may be installed instead. For power, a 160-hp Lycoming O-320 engine was mounted as a pusher in a nacelle on N-struts above the wing center-section. General specifications indicate a wingspan of 35 feet, a gross weight of 3,000 lbs., and a top speed of 150 mph. According to the manufacturer's information, a Super Adventurer kit includes airframe components, control surfaces, and mechanical assemblies, but not engine, propeller, tires, and instrumentation. The Adventure Air website is presently inactive.

The Super Adventurer N3313, date unknown, built from composites and powered by a Lycoming O-320 engine.

Aero Adventure Adventura HP and II (1995)

In 1995 Aero Adventure obtained a license to produce Advanced Aeromarine's Buccaneer kit-plane series, subsequently marketing them under the name "Adventura." The single-place Adventura HP, powered by a 65-hp Rotax two-cycle liquid-cooled engine, comes with a strut-braced wing assembly and landing gear that swings upward for water operations. Specifications list a loaded weight of 545 lbs., a top speed of 63 mph, a cruise of 53 mph, and a range of 250 miles. Since 2004, Adventura builders have the option of licensing the plane a under the new Experimental Light Sport Aircraft (E-LSA) rules. The Adventura II, powered by a 100-hp Rotax 912ULS four-stroke engine, is offered as a two-place amphibian with a cruise speed of 85 mph and a range of 340 miles. According to Aero Adventures' current website (see http://www.sea-plane.com/Product%20Line/Aventura%20II. html) a complete Aventura II kit, including engine and propeller, lists for $44,995.

Although related to the Buccaneer ultralight, the Adventura II is licensed under the kit-built Experimental or E-LSA categories.

Aquaflight W-6 Aqua I and II and Collins W-7 Dipper (1946)

Founded in 1946 by Meredith C. Wartle, this Delaware-based company designed and developed a six-place, twin-engine amphibian initially known as the W-6 but later as the Aqua I and II. The design was characterized by a deep-V, single-step hull having a raised afterbody, high cantilevered wings, retractable tricycle landing gear, and hull sponsons that also housed the main wheels. Listed dimensions were a wingspan of 36 feet, 5 inches and a length of 29 feet, 6 inches.

Aqua II prototype as seen in 1948 with two Lycoming O-435 engines. It reappeared in modified form 34 years later as the Collins W-7.

The W-6/Aqua I (registration number N74141) was flown in 1946 with two 125-hp Lycoming O-290 engines, and two years later, as the Aqua II, with two 215-hp Lycoming O-435s. In 1982, years after the project foundered, the W-6 hull reappeared under the new name Collins W-7 Dipper with a reduced hull afterbody, shorter span wings, and two 180-hp Lycoming O-360 engines. It was flown in August 1982 under civil registration N25WC.

Avid Amphibian/Catalina (1985)

The two-seat Light Aero Amphibian prototype, appearing in mid–1985 under civil registration N47AA, was initially powered by a two-cycle 43-hp Cuyuna 430 but production kits subsequently upgraded to a 65-hp Rotax 532. Except for fiberglass planing surfaces on the hull bottom, the fabric-covered structure of the Amphibian followed the tested Light Aero/Avid formula of a welded, steel tube fuselage with wings built up of sawn wooden ribs and tubular aluminum spars. For water operations, the manual gear retracted upward into recesses on either side of the hull and the tail-wheel remained fixed. One of the interesting features of this kitplane line was full-span, Junkers-type ailerons giving very positive roll control, even if the wing was stalled. The rounded tail group and exposed pusher engine mounted above the wing imparted a nostalgic appearance reminiscent of the Curtiss Duckling of 1931 (see Part II, page 111). In 1992 the improved Catalina entered the kit line, introducing three-seat accommodations and an upgrade to an 80-hp Rotax 912 four-cycle engine, and more recent improvements included molded wingtips that droop to form tip floats, a streamlined engine cowling, and squared-off tail configuration. Specifications list a 36 ft. wingspan, a 19 ft. 4 in. length, a 1,200-lb. gross weight, with a cruise speed of 75 mph over a 325 mi. range.

Recent photograph of Catalina (N1945J) listed for sale on the Barnstormer's website. Trailing edge-type ailerons are clearly visible. The current status of the Avid kit line, including the Catalina, is uncertain.

Commonwealth C-170 Trimmer (1947)

Commonwealth Aircraft of Kansas City, Kansas, successor to the Rearwin Co., attempted to capitalize on the expected postwar lightplane market with a three-place, twin-engine amphibian. Resembling a down-sized Grumman Goose, the general design of the C-170 Trimmer had been adapted from Gilbert Trimmer's smaller Trimcraft of 1938 and was powered by two 85-hp Continental C-85 4-cylinder engines mounted on the leading edges of the wings. Specifications listed a wingspan of 35 feet 8 inches, a hull length of 24 feet 9 inches, and a cruise speed of 118 mph over a 600-mile range. Commonwealth had hoped to market these amphibians for $5,975 each, but orders apparently never materialized. One example (NX41853) was flown in 1947 and a second destroyed in static testing. The company ceased all operations in 1949.

A factory photograph of the Trimmer prototype in 1947. Like so many postwar civil ventures, a market for it never materialized.

Diehls XTC Hydrolight (1982)

The one-place XTC Hydrolight, when it appeared in 1982, was in all likelihood the first amphibious flying boat of any type to fall within the definition of an "ultralight" under FAR Part 103. Originally designed and manufactured as a kitplane by Diehls Aero-Nautical, Inc. of Jenks, Oklahoma, the XTC utilized a strikingly clean canard planform, mounting a two-cycle, two-cylinder 25-hp KFM 107 engine as a pusher at the very aft end of the hull. The hull components were molded from fiberglass using a vacuum-forming process and the wings and tail surfaces made up from a combination of molded fiberglass parts and laminated Kevlar-epoxy structural members, which were then covered with a bonded Mylar film. A three-axis control system used the forward canard for pitch, twin wing-mounted rudders for yaw, and wing spoilers for roll. The spring-type landing gear, which

The XTC was a cutting-edge ultralight design when it appeared in 1982. Sixty-eight kits were produced before Diehls ceased operations.

included a steerable nosewheel, retracted upward against the hull. Although the XTC boasted a 32-foot wingspan having 155 square feet of area, empty weight came to only 247 lbs. Maximum level speed was listed as 62 mph with a cruise of 55 mph. A total of 68 kits were reportedly manufactured before Diehls ceased operations, but the number of XTC's actually built and flown is unknown.

Frenard (Arnoldi) Duck (1949)

Former Curtiss engineer Fred N. Arnoldi designed and built the single-place Duck in the late 1940s to serve as the prototype for a larger four-place amphibian he hoped to ultimately certify and place into production. The term "Frenard" apparently came from a contraction of the designer's name. Completed in 1949 under civil registration N69966, the Duck featured a built-up plywood hull and wood-framed, fabric covered wings and tail surfaces. While following a Seabee-type layout, it departed from convention in having sweepback in the wings and a horizontal stabilizer mounted as a canard on the bow. A 50-hp Continental pusher was used for power and the landing gear had to be removed for water operations. General specifications and flight performance were not published.

The Duck, completed in 1949, featured swept wings and a canard-type horizontal stabilizer.

Goodyear GA-22/-22A Drake (1951)

Using earlier experience gained from the GA-1/-2 Duck (see Part II, above), engineers at Goodyear designed and built the Drake, originally flown as the GA-22 in 1951 with a 190-hp Continental E-185 engine, then reappearing as the GA-22A in 1953, powered by a 225-hp Continental E-225. Though similar in layout and dimensions to the earlier Duck, the Drake differed in having

The GA-22 Drake, though exhibiting excellent performance, was never certificated for production.

four-seat accommodations, metal-skinned wings, and substantially redesigned hull planing surfaces. The new hull was distinguished by a deep pointed step that faired into a smooth afterbody. Testing revealed excellent handling in the water and flight performance indicated a maximum speed of 146 mph and a range of 575 miles at a 135-mph cruise. Goodyear demonstrated the Drake all over the country and also used it for company transportation, but the aircraft was never certificated for production. The sole example was donated to the Experimental Aircraft Association Museum in 1966.

International Duckling (1946)

Little is known about this two-place aircraft other than it was reportedly built in Cleveland, Ohio, by International Aviation Corp. and flown sometime in 1946. The hull configuration, a stream-

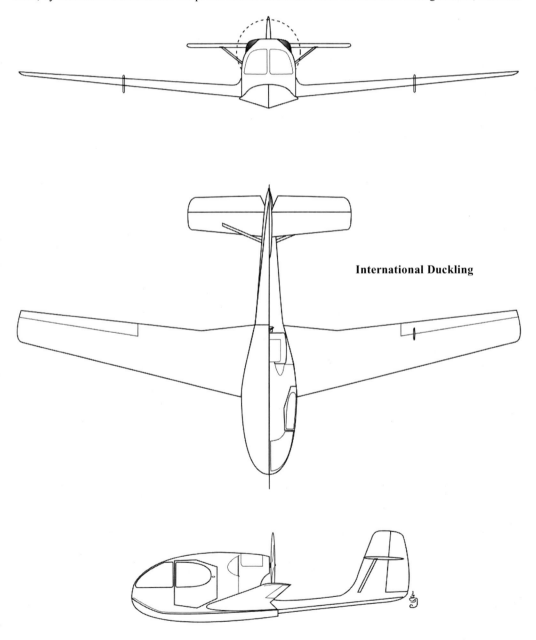

International Duckling

lined cabin pod with a boom-type afterbody supporting the tail, was reminiscent of Percival Spenser's Air Car (see Part II, page 208), except that the wings were mounted low, just above the forward hull chine. Construction appears to have been mostly wood, a semi-monocoque hull structure with fully cantilevered wings, and a horizontal stabilizer braced by struts. Engine make is unknown but was an air-cooled, horizontally opposed type mounted as a pusher. Suggested flight performance was a top speed of 135 mph and a 120-mph cruise.

Island X-199 Spectra (1969)

Designed and built by LeRoy LoPresti, then organized as Island Aircraft Corp., the two-place X-199 amphibian (registered as N9168) was intended to serve as a prototype for a larger and more powerful four-place version that never materialized. The all-metal design was unusual in having its 125-hp Lycoming O-290 engine mounted in a nacelle on top of the vertical tail surfaces and drooping wingtips that also functioned as stabilizing floats. General specifications indicated a 33-foot wingspan and a 27-foot hull length, but no performance data was reported.

Designed by LeRoy LoPresti and flown in 1969, the X-199 was to have formed the basis for a larger production amphibian.

Moyes Microlights Connie (2001)

The one-place "Connie" may be the simplest approach to an amphibian yet seen. Developed and flown in 2001 for Moyes Microlights by ultralight designer Bob Bailey, it is expected to be made available as a kit that can be flown as a "ultralight air vehicle" under FAR Part 103. In the case of an ultralight seaplane, FAR guidelines allow an extra 50 lbs. for the hull and tip floats, plus 24 lbs. for a ballistic parachute, allowing a total empty weight of 328 lbs. Powered by a 39.6-hp Rotax 447UL two-cycle engine mounted as a pusher above the wing, the Connie utilizes the Tempest sailplane wing designed by Bailey and a Cosmos float normally used on a trike (i.e., a weight-shift ultralight). At last report, Bailey was making refinements that included a longer float and a larger wing. For more information, contact Quest Air Soaring Center, 6548 Groveland Airport Road, Groveland, Florida 34736.

Recent photograph of the Connie ultralight piloted by designer Bob Bailey. According to reports, Bailey hopes to offer it in kit form.

Progressive Aerodyne SeaRey—2000

The SeaRey was evidently intended from the outset to be manufactured and assembled only in kit-plane form. The general aerodynamic layout features a strut-braced, pylon-mounted wing with the pusher engine incorporated into the wing's aft center-section. Stabilizing floats are braced into the lift struts. The two-step hull and wing pylon are formed from lightweight carbon graphite material, while the wings and tail surfaces consist of fabric-covered metal tubing. Landing gear configura-

The SeaRey shown here depicts recent improvements made to the hull forebody. Under current FAA rules, kit builders can certificate the amphibian in the new category of Experimental—Light Sport Aircraft.

tion is conventional (tailwheel) with mechanically operated main wheel legs that pivot up to the lift struts for water operations. Wing design includes a formed leading edge with cuffed extensions along with trailing-edge flaps which reduce stall speed to a leisurely 40 mph at gross weight. Provision is also made for the option of installing a ballistic parachute. Water takeoffs at gross weight, as reported by the manufacturer, can be accomplished within 400 feet with an initial climb rate of 700 feet per minute. Whether by accident or design, the SeaRey falls within the new Federal Aviation Administration regulations (2004) allowing seaplanes having a gross weight of 1,430 pounds or less to be certificated under Experimental/Light Sport rules. The first flight of the SeaRey prototype is not published but thought to have occurred sometime in 2000, and a number of completed examples are now flying under civil registrations. Specifications list a 30 ft. 10 in. wingspan, a 22 ft. 5 in. length, a 1,370-lb. gross weight, and an 85-mph cruise speed over a 291 mi. range. For more information, see the SeaRey Builder's Website at http://seareybuilder.com.

Wet Aero M6 Mermaid (2006)

Although designed and originally manufactured in the Czech Republic by CZAW, design and production rights to the two-place Mermaid amphibian are reportedly being acquired by Wet Aero, Inc. of Palm City, Florida, who plans to place the aircraft in production in the light sport category. See Wet Aero's website, http://www.wetaero.com/mermaidm6.html, for more up-to-date information. According to the site, the all-metal Mermaid has been already been certificated by the FAA,

Recent photograph of Czech-built Mermaid on the "step." Wet Aero hopes to have the Rotax-powered American version in production soon.

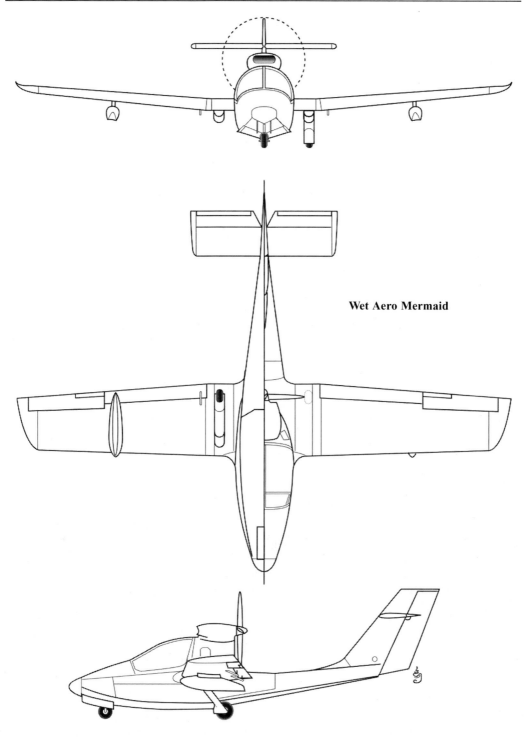

Wet Aero Mermaid

and production was expected to commence in 2009. The Czech prototypes are powered by a 120-hp Jabiru 3300 engine, but the American production version will be built with a 100-hp Rotax 912. General specifications given for the Jabiru-powered prototypes are a wingspan of 33 feet 4 inches, a length of 25 feet, and a gross weight of 1,430 lbs, with a 118-mph cruise speed over a range of 620 miles. Projected price for the Rotax-powered base model is $147,000.

Appendix B: Flying Boat and Amphibian Design Concepts

Naval Aircraft Factory GB-1 Giant Boat (1921)

In order to cover the vast distances of the Pacific Ocean, the Naval Aircraft Factory came up with a scheme in 1920 for a flying boat that would have massed 2.5 times that of Curtiss NC series of 1918 (see Part I, page 47). The GB-1 "Giant Boat," as it was known, was to have been a triplane layout, powered by nine 400-hp Liberty 12 engines grouped in three nacelles, each driving an 18-foot diameter, three-bladed propeller via a clutch arrangement. The hull was of conventional wooden construction, while the wings were metal-framed with fabric covering. Construction of the

Hull of GB-1 under construction at the Naval Aircraft Factory in 1921. The project was cancelled due to lack of funding.

prototype (BuNo A6059) was approximately half complete at the time the project was cancelled in 1921 due to lack of funding. Like the Army's somewhat smaller "Barling Bomber," the Giant Boat probably would have been obsolete by the time it flew. The remnants of the project were reportedly disposed of sometime after 1925.

Bel Geddes Air Liner No. 4 (1929)

Appearing like an apparition out of H.G. Wells' *Things to Come*, this gargantuan twin-hulled flying boat was the brainchild of famed industrial designer Norman Bel Geddes (1893–1958), with the help of an aeronautical engineer named Otto Koller. The craft's 577-foot wing (half again the span of the Hughes H-4 Hercules) would have rested upon a pair of 147-foot-long hulls. The deep wing center-section was to have featured nine decks, including a 200-seat dining room, an enclosed promenade deck, and a solarium. Power would have been derived by twenty engines (type and

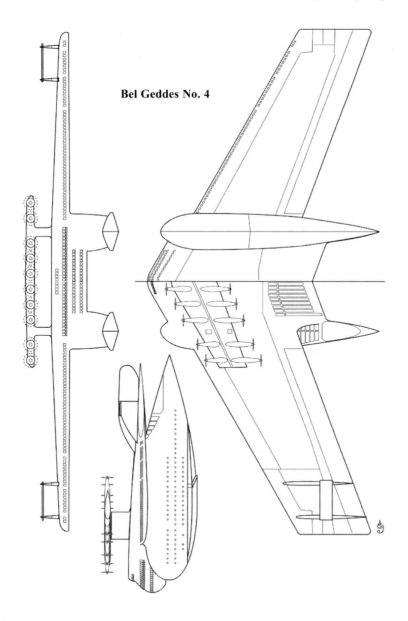

Bel Geddes No. 4

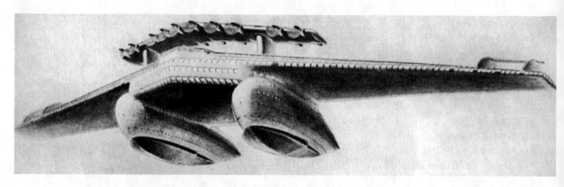

Artist's conception of Bel Geddes' colossal flying boat. Whether it could have flown, given the power needed, is open to speculation.

horsepower not revealed) mounted on an airfoil above the wing. Bel Geddes estimated that the aircraft could be built for $9,000,000, but not too surprisingly, no one ever came forward to finance it.

Grumman G-3 (1930)

For its third in-house design (the G-5, as the Navy FF-1, was the first to actually appear as a completed aircraft), Grumman tendered a design study to the Coast Guard in 1930 for a twin-engine

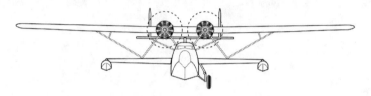

Grumman G-3

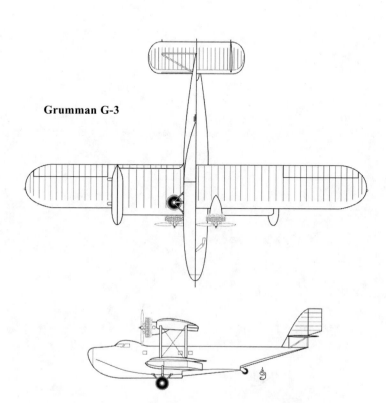

flying boat. Other than its parasol monoplane layout and wing-mounted engines, the general configuration of the G-3 was very similar to the Naval Aircraft Factory PN-11 (see Part II, page 186). Available data does not reveal actual dimensions, engine types, or estimated performance. The Coast Guard considered the proposal, but no aircraft were ordered.

Fairchild SOK (1934)

Designed by Fairchild's Alfred A. Gassner during the same period as the F91 (see Part II, page 126), this single-engine flying boat was ordered by BuAer in September 1934 as the XSOK-1. The naval specification called for a two or three-place monoplane flying boat, to be powered by a single 700-hp Wright R-1510 (a twin-row, 14-cylinder radial never used in a production aircraft). Its size and overall design concept appear to have been similar to Gassner's F91, except for the wing being moved up to meet the engine nacelle and a shallower front hull profile to allow for the lower propeller arc. Interestingly, the glazed observer's position emanated from the back of the engine nacelle. The naval mission intended for this aircraft is not clear, as it seems too large to have been a ship-based scout. Fairchild went as far with the project as to complete a full-scale mockup of the XSOK-1, however, BuAer cancelled the project in August 1935 before a prototype could be built.

Mockup of XSOK-1 in 1934 or 1935. Similar to the F91, it was cancelled before a prototype could be built.

Boeing 320 Navy Patrol Boat (1938)

The model 320, designed in 1938, apparently represented a last ditch effort by Boeing to come up a candidate for the Navy's Flying Dreadnought competition (see Part II, page 79). General specifications indicated a wingspan of 200 feet, a length of 116 feet, and a loaded weight of 134,000 lbs. The eight-place flying boat was to have been powered by six 1,200-hp Wright R-2600 *Twin Cyclone* engines. With the Sikorsly XPBS-1 and Consolidated XPB2Y-1 already flying and the Martin XPB2M-1 forthcoming, BuAer apparently had no interest in adding another project. It is interesting that Boeing proposed something this unorthodox, as opposed to a militarized variant of its model 314, which would have been a more straightforward project.

Sikorsky S-45 (1938)

Originating in 1938 as a proposal for Pan American Airways, the six-engine S-35, if it had been built, would have been the world's largest aircraft of any type. With a projected takeoff weight

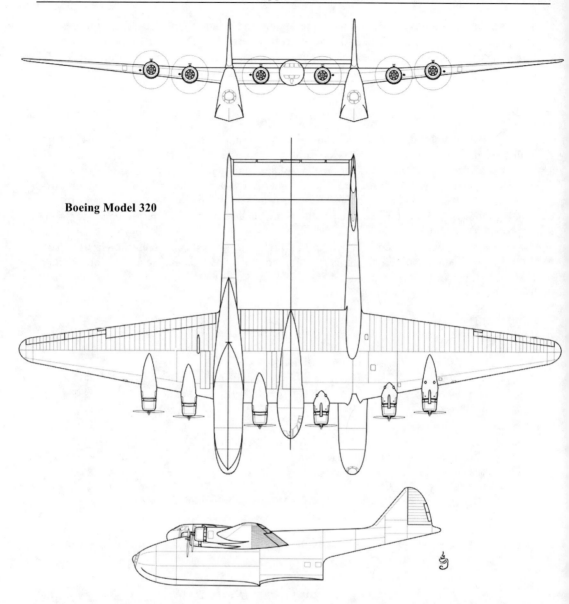

Boeing Model 320

of 280,000 lbs., it comprised five times the mass of the S-44/XPBS-1 and nearly double that of the Martin XPB2M-1. The S-45's specifications called for a hull length of 155 feet with a 236-foot wing encompassing 4,670 square feet of area. Planned power-plants were not listed, but the most powerful American engines available at the time of the design were 2,500-hp Wright R-3350s. The S-45 became Igor Sikorsky's last flying boat design; his next project, the S-46, appeared in 1939 as the VS-300, America's first practical helicopter.

Boeing 326 (1938)

Another six-engine design proposal for Pan American Airways; no dimensions or other specifications are available on Boeing's model 326, but it was very likely similar in size and weight to the Sikorsky S-45.

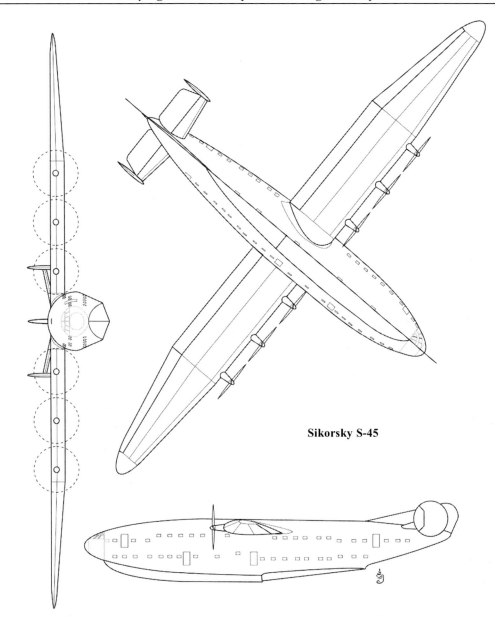

Sikorsky S-45

Consolidated Pan Am Proposal (1938)

The third flying boat proposal made to Pan American Airways in 1938, this time a four-engine aircraft with no model number given. General dimensions were not published, but the layout was similar to the XPB2Y-1 after it was modified to a twin tail configuration. World War II intervened before any of these large airliner proposals could move forward.

Consolidated PB3Y (1940)

Conceived most likely sometime in 1938, the Consolidated model 30 received official BuAer approval in 1940 under the official designation XPB3Y-1. Not to be outdone by Martin's XPB2M-1, apparently, Consolidated's XPB3Y-1 represented an almost fifty percent scale-up of the PB2Y, to

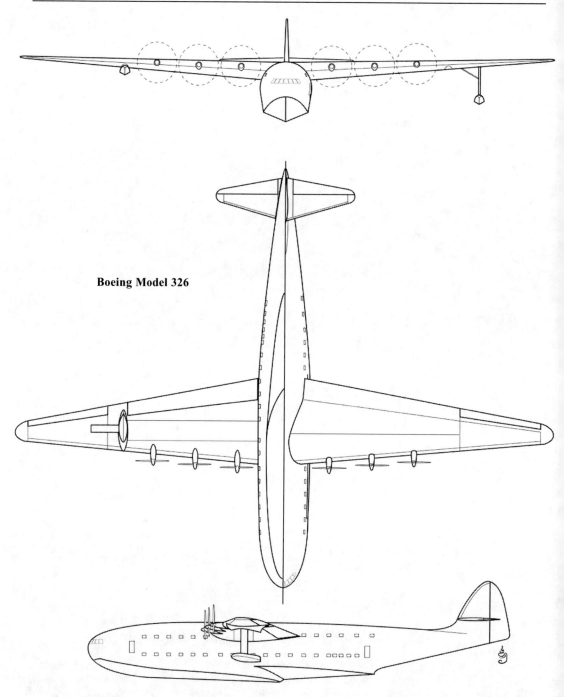

Boeing Model 326

be powered by four 2,000-hp Pratt & Whitney R-2800-18 *Double Wasp* engines. Its design specifications projected a wingspan of 169 feet, a gross weight of 121,500 lbs., and bomb load of 20,000 lbs., twice the mass and load of the PB2Y; estimated top speed was 241 mph. Even though Consolidated obtained authorization to proceed with construction of an XPB3Y-1 prototype in April 1942, the project was cancelled within seven months to facilitate the company's wartime production capacity on existing aircraft such as the B-24, PBY, and PB2Y.

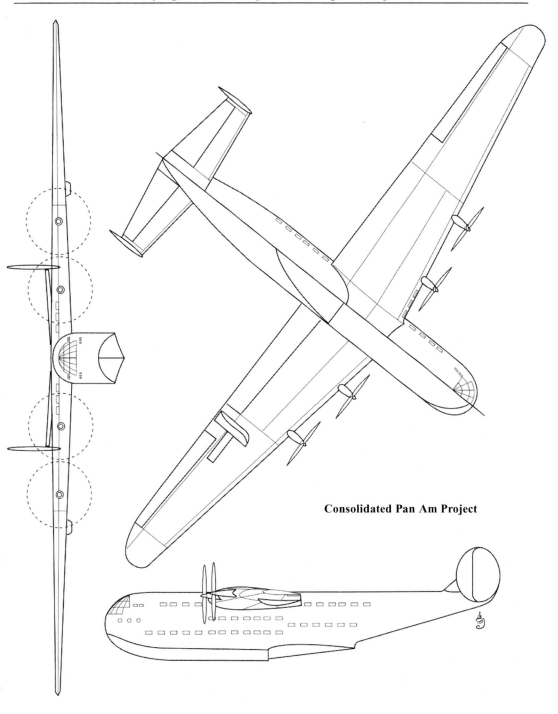

Consolidated Pan Am Project

Martin M193 (1942)

As the "Sky Freighter" concept emerged in response to the U-Boat menace during early World War II, Martin proposed the M193 as a forty percent enlargement of the M170 (see Martin PB2M, Part II, page 182) with a projected takeoff weight of 250,000 lbs. Conceptual drawings of the M193 indicate much similarity to the XPB2M-1, but with a hull and wing stretched span and lengthwise rather than being proportionately scaled-up. While powerplant types were not revealed, to lift the

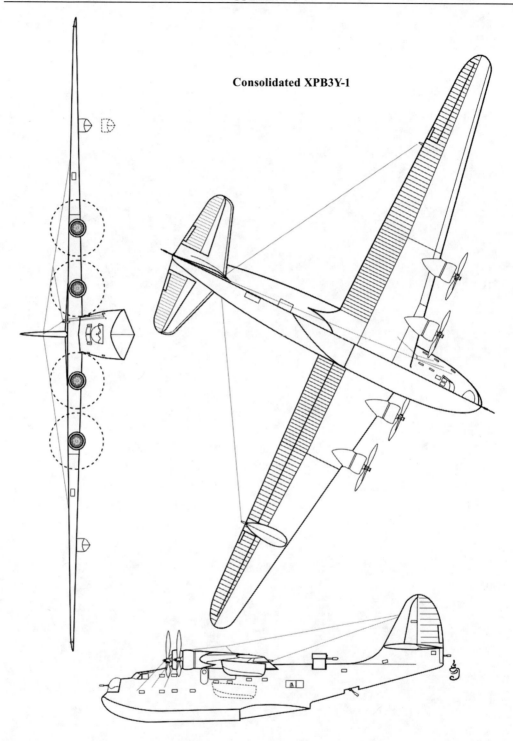

Consolidated XPB3Y-1

weight proposed, they most likely would have been Wright R-3350 *Double Cyclones* or Pratt & Whitney R-4360 *Wasp Majors* (a 3000-hp radial engine that became available during 1944). When the military urgency of Sky Freighters disappeared, Martin tried to develop interest in a commercial version; however, the post-war market for large, passenger-carrying flying boats never came to pass.

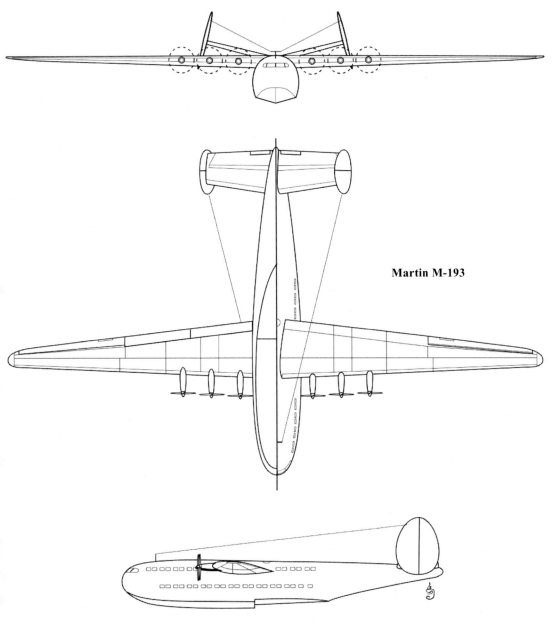

Martin M-193

Consolidated (Convair) 37 (1945)

Toward the end of World War II, as the six-engine XB-36 prototype reached an advanced stage of construction, Convair performed several design studies to develop military cargo and commercial variants that would share the same wing and incorporate other aerodynamic features. The civil model 37 airliner was investigated in landplane (pusher) and flying boat (tractor) configurations, and Pan American Airways is thought to have ordered fifteen of the 204-passenger landplane versions on the premise that turboprop engines would become available by the time construction began. When no engines materialized, the civil project was discontinued. One piston-engine military prototype subsequently appeared as the XC-99 and made its first flight in November 1947. The largest type of piston-engine, land-based transport ever built, the XC-99 boasted a wingspan of 230 feet, a length of 185 feet, and could lift a payload exceeding 100,000 lbs.

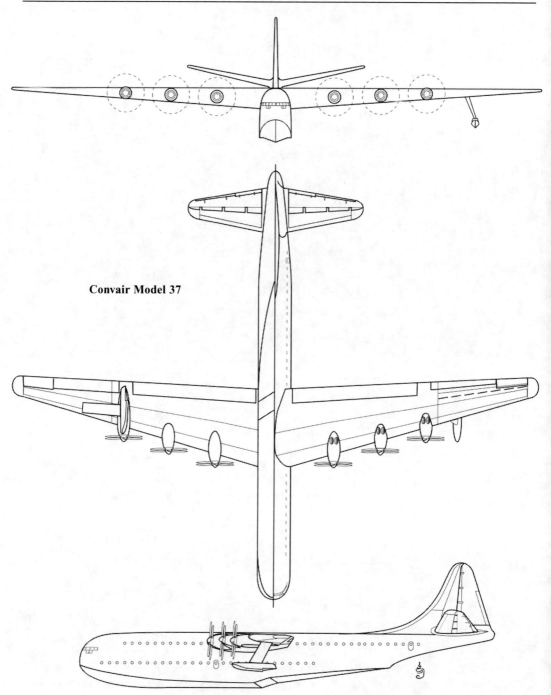

Convair Model 37

Convair Skate (BuAer Spec. OS-116) (1949)

The advent of jet propulsion in 1940s raised the possibility of developing seaplane fighters and attack aircraft that could achieve performance on par with their land-based contemporaries. Among these was a requirement issued by the Navy in 1948 for a two-place night fighter/ attack aircraft capable of operating in sheltered waters and being supported by submarines or seaplane tenders. Convair, a pioneering company in the fields of both flying boat and high-speed jet design, responded

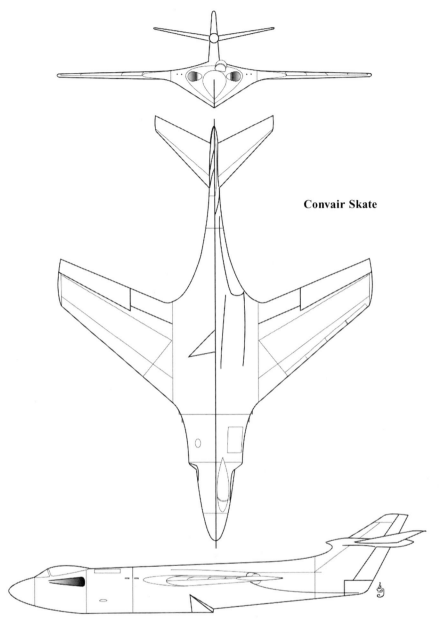

Convair Skate

in early 1949 with a proposal to develop a swept wing flying boat utilizing a blended hull concept in which lower hull and the bottom of the wings merged together to form a buoyant surface. Known under the project name "Skate," the design evolved into a big aircraft that would have been 70 feet long with 67-foot wingspan and a projected takeoff weight of 38,940 lbs. To eliminate the drag normally associated with hull bottoms, the step and spray chines retracted inward to form a smooth fuselage contour. Power derived from two Westinghouse XJ40 engines buried in the hull was expected to enable the Skate to climb to 35,000 feet in two and a half minutes and cruise toward its target at a speed of almost 500 mph. A powerful radar system housed in the nose, manned by a separate crewmember, was intended to allow the aircraft to detect and track targets under all weather conditions. The Skate was never built, and though providing much useful data, the project was concluded in 1951 in favor of Convair's parallel project to develop a single-seat, delta-wing sea fighter which ultimately appeared as the F2Y Sea Dart (see Part III, page 229).

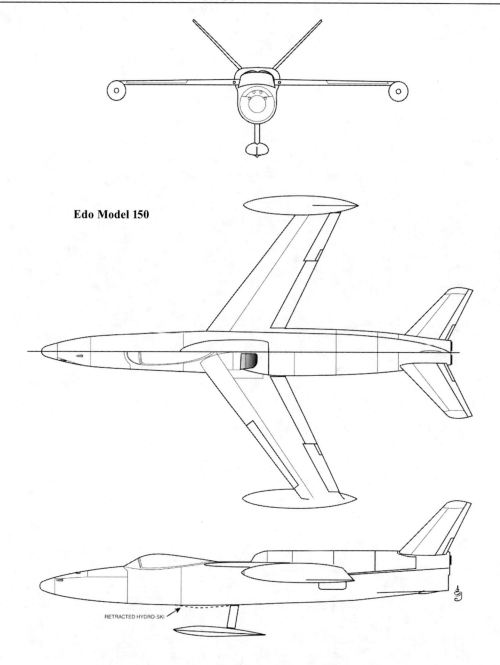

Edo Model 150

RETRACTED HYDRO-SKI

Edo Model 150 and 142 Arctic Fighter (1950)

Among the advanced seaplane concepts that surfaced in the late 1940s, Edo Corp., a well known seaplane float manufacturer, performed a series of design studies for the U.S. Air Force Material Command to determine the feasibility of developing a high-speed fighter-interceptor capable of operating in arctic regions either from snow, ice, or water. The concept was presumably based on the premise that such aircraft could be rapidly scrambled from their arctic bases to engage Soviet bombers approaching North American airspace over the poles. The Edo model 150 appeared in 1950 as a twin-jet design using a retractable hydro-ski that would theoretically enable it to operate from diverse takeoff and landing surfaces. Its aerodynamic design included shoulder-mounted wings having 35 degrees of sweepback, combination tip tanks-stabilizing floats, and a V-tail empennage. Two afterburning General Electric J35 engines, mounted side-by-side in nacelles on the upper hull, were estimated to deliver a top speed of Mach 0.98 (748 mph) at sea level. As laid down, the model 150 would have been a big fighter (e.g., 40 percent larger than a North American F-86)—28,025 lbs. at gross weight with a projected wingspan of 43 feet 3 inches and an overall length of 65 feet. The smaller model 142, a 30 percent scale-down based on the same aerodynamic concept, would have been powered by two Westinghouse J34 engines. The USAF abandoned the arctic fighter project before any aircraft were built, but Edo did successfully test its hydro-ski concept using a modified Grumman Goose.

Convair P6Y (1956)

During the mid–1950s, U.S. Navy planners became interested in procuring a flying boat that could hunt submarines across the open ocean using a dipping-type sonar system. The "Open Ocean Seaplane" requirement, issued by BuAer in early 1956, specified an aircraft capable of landing and taking off in rough sea conditions up to state five (i.e., 12-foot waves). Convair's model 24 design was one of three proposals to be considered (see also Grumman G-132 and Martin P7M). It emerged with a unique tri-motor layout—three 3,700-hp Wright R-3350 engines—characterized by a very high, pylon-mounted wing and a noticeably large vertical tail surface. To achieve the very low touchdown speeds required for rough sea conditions (i.e., 35 to 40 mph), Convair developed a boundary layer control (BLC) system that would be fed by bleed air from two General Electric J85 turbojet engines housed in the central wing nacelle. In BLC mode, the turbojets were ducted to blow air over the flaps and ailerons; while in normal mode, they provided thrust to augment the piston engines. In February 1957, BuAer selected Convair as winner of the competition and authorized two prototypes as the XP6Y-1; however, due to budgetary problems unrelated to the project, funding was cut off before any construction could begin. Although no official cancellation of the P6Y appears on any record, project was clearly overtaken in 1958-1959 by the Navy's decision to commence development of the land-based Lockheed P3V (later P-3A Orion). Interestingly, much of the technology derived from the P6Y was seen years later in the design of the Shinmaywa PS-1 flying boat for the Japan Maritime Defense Force.

Grumman G-132 (1956)

The Grumman G-132 was one of three design proposals (See also Convair P6Y and Martin P7M, page XXX) considered by the U.S. Navy during 1956 and 1957 in response to an "Open Ocean Seaplane" requirement. The specification envisaged an aircraft equipped with a dipping-type sonar that could land and takeoff over large stretches of open ocean in up to 12-foot waves (i.e., state five seas). To make this structurally feasible, normal flying boat touchdown speeds would need to be reduced by half, to about 40 mph. Grumman's G-132, the largest of the three, boasted a takeoff weight of 110,712 lbs. and would have been powered by four 2,300-hp Pratt & Whitney R-2800 engines. Grumman's method of reducing touchdown speed utilized a set of "Carl Configuration" hydrofoils—one foil at the center of gravity and another at the tail—that were expected to keep the main hull clear of the water at speeds above 35 mph. When up on the hydrofoil, the aircraft's retractable tip floats would telescope down to a lower position. Grumman's proposal was not selected and the design never received an official designation.

Martin P7M Submaster (1956)

The P7M was one of three designs (see also Convair P6Y and Grumman G-132) to be considered by the U.S. Navy in the mid–1950s as an "Open Ocean Seaplane." Using a new type of dip-

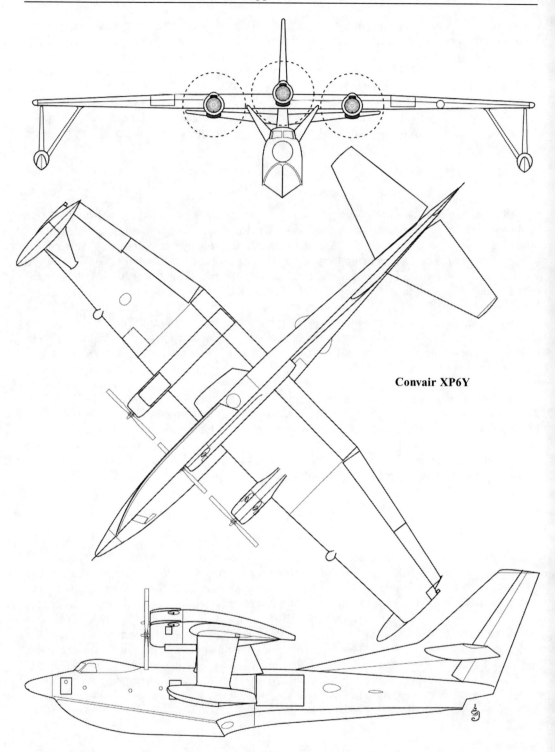

Convair XP6Y

ping sonar system, the aircraft would be expected to detect and track enemy submarines across large areas of open ocean and able to land and takeoff in sea conditions up to state five (i.e., 12-foot waves). In 1955, before BuAer was prepared to issue a formal request for proposals, Martin attempted to get a jump on its competition by tendering a flying boat design billed as the P5M-3. Known inter-

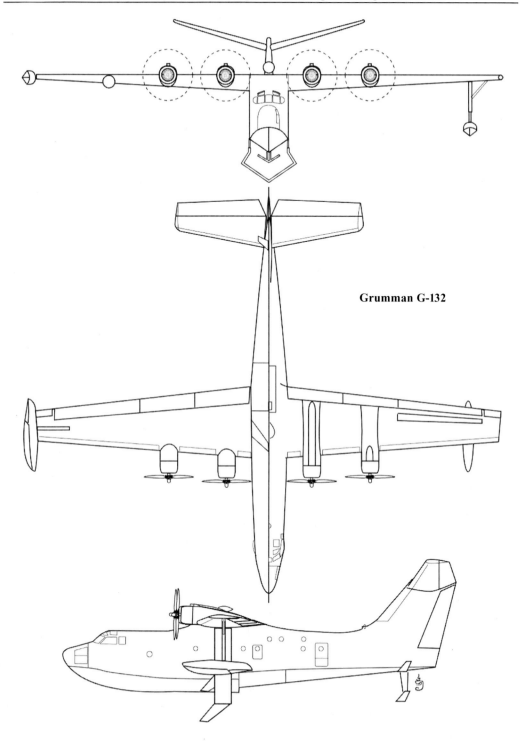

Grumman G-132

nally as the model 313, the P5M-3 was in fact an entirely new airframe incorporating the 15:1 aspect hull and T-tail of the P6M (see Part II, page 264) with a straight wing mounting four 1,525-hp Wright R-1820 engines. To fly at the low touchdown speeds dictated by the sea conditions (i.e., 35 to 40 mph), the aircraft would use a boundary layer control (BLC) system, powered by a fuselage-mounted General Electric J85 turbojet engine that forced air over the flaps and ailerons. In 1956,

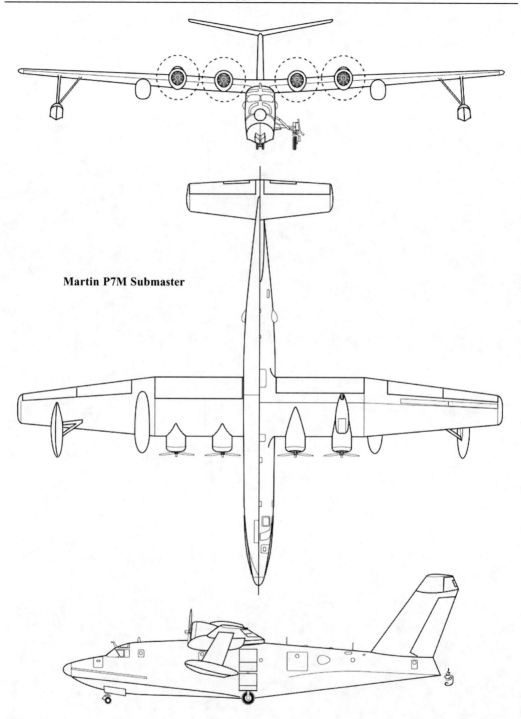

Martin P7M Submaster

apparently at its own expense, Martin took the extra step of building a full-scale mockup under the new name P7M "Submaster," which differed from the P5M-3 in having a BLC system powered by two J85 engines buried in the outboard engine nacelles on the wings. But despite Martin's efforts, BuAer announced Convair's P6Y as the winning entry in early 1957. Although the company still had the P5M-2 in production and the P6M-1 under pre-production development at the time, the P7M would be the last in a long line of Martin flying boat designs.

Mockup of P7M at Martin's plant in 1956. The Navy abandoned the Open Ocean Seaplane concept before any prototypes were built.

Convair Supersonic Attack Seaplane (195?)

Whether this far-fetched idea ever received official consideration is not known. In any case, the drawing suggests that Convair apparently combined certain design elements of its B-58 USAF bomber project with the P6Y open ocean seaplane (see above) to come up with the Supersonic Attack Seaplane. As indicated by the drawing, the wing nacelles rotated upward for takeoffs and landings and lowered for level flight. While actual dates of the study are not reported, it probably coincided with XB-58 development during the mid–1950s.

Acme Anser (1958)

This little known twin-jet amphibious design is mentioned by some sources as a military fighter project; however, data published by Air Craft Marine Engineering Co. (Acme) indicates that it was actually an eight-seat transport intended for civil use. Acme was established in Van Nuys, California, sometime in the mid–1950s, and the name "Anser" was an acronym for Analytical Service, Inc., an organization involved in the project. Roughly similar in size (46-foot wingspan) and weight (9,000 lbs. gross) to a Beechcraft Model 18, the design of the Anser comprised shoulder-mounted straight wings ending in tip tanks, a V-tail empennage, and engine nacelles positioned over the wing's trailing edge. To maximize aerodynamic cleanness, the entire airframe was to have

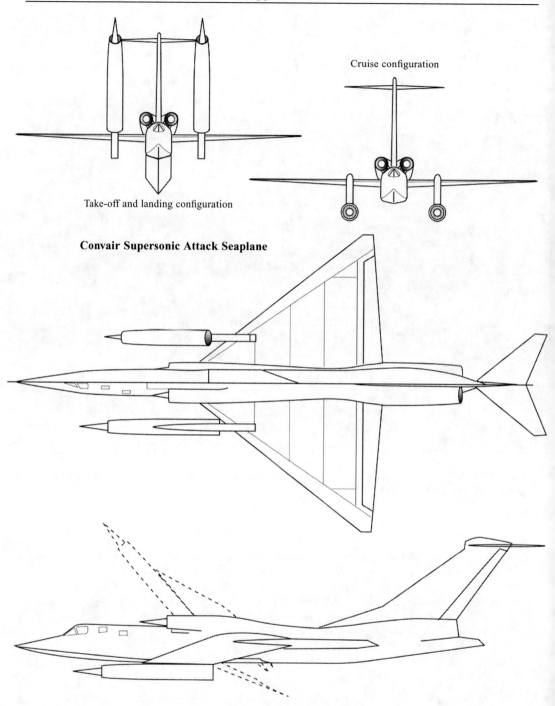

Cruise configuration

Take-off and landing configuration

Convair Supersonic Attack Seaplane

been skinned in fiberglass bonded to a honeycomb core of epoxy resin. Another drag-reducing innovation was retractable fuselage sponsons which also housed the amphibious landing gear. With
the combined 1,580 lbs./s.t. of its two Continental 420 turbofan engines, the Anser's designers pre-
dicted a maximum speed of 471 mph at 25,000 feet. Acme went so far as to build a full-size mockup
and was thought to have had a prototype under construction in 1958, but the aircraft was never
completed.

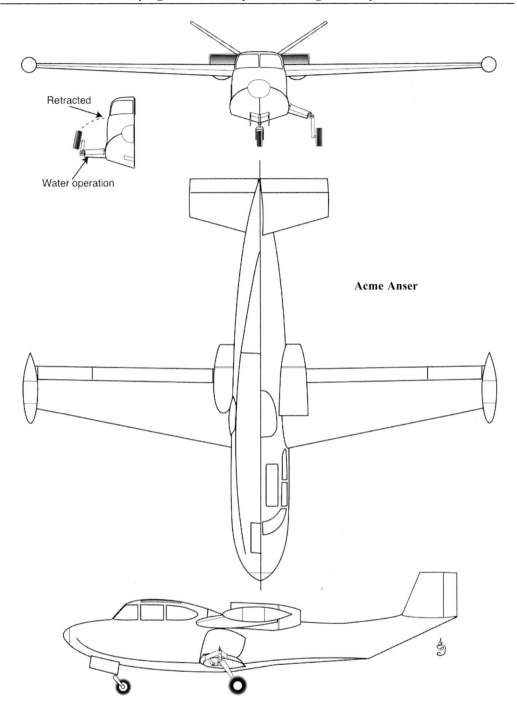

Retracted

Water operation

Acme Anser

Leader Industries Privateer (2008)

Known originally as the 329 Amphibian, the four-seat Privateer is currently being developed by Leader Industries, Inc., at an undisclosed location. Work on the preliminary engineering design was performed by Embry-Riddle Aeronautical University. Exact specifications for the Privateer have yet to be published; however, CATIA drawings on Leader's website (see http://www.329. amphibian.com/sitemap.asp) indicate a twin-hull, twin cockpit concept in either short or long-wing

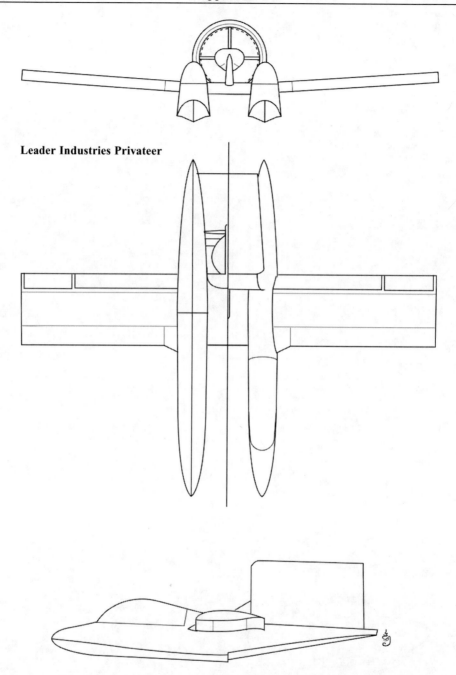

Leader Industries Privateer

variations. The aircraft will be powered by a pusher-mounted 750-hp Walther 601 turboprop engine encased in an annular shroud which also functions as a tail surface. All major airframe components will be constructed of carbon-fiber composites using what is described as a multi-cell configuration. The Privateer's cruise speed is projected to be in excess of 240 mph at 8,000 feet. According to the website, the aircraft is currently under construction, but no completion date has been announced.

Appendix C. Three Glossaries

Aeronautical Terms and Abbreviations

Where a term and an abbreviation are used together, the abbreviation will be expressed in parentheses following the term.

AERODYNAMIC FORCE—A term pertaining to the motion of the air as it acts upon a body (i.e., an aircraft) which is in motion against it.

AERODYNAMIC LIFT—The upward force, perpendicular to the direction of travel, produced by the camber of a wing moving through the air.

AEROMATIC PROPELLER—Aeromatic is a trade name for a self-contained, variable-pitch propeller requiring no control inputs from the cockpit of an aircraft. Changes in pitch—from high RPM to low RPM—are caused by counterweights that vary pitch according to dynamic factors such as centrifugal force and angle of attack.

AFTERBODY—The section of a flying boat or amphibian hull aft of the step.

AFTERBURNER—An annular extension to the exhaust nozzle of a turbojet or turbofan engine (see below) fitted with additional fuel injectors. When engaged, the ignited fuel produces a gas expansion resulting in a steep thrust increase.

AILERONS—Moveable control surfaces on the trailing edge of each wing, which, working in opposition, control the rotational motion of aircraft about its longitudinal axis.

AIR TAXI—An unscheduled commercial air operation using an aircraft with no more than 30 seats and a payload capacity less than 7,500 lbs.

AIRFOIL—The shape of a wing or flying surface as seen in cross-section, sometimes referred to as an airfoil section. Airfoils are designed to produce lift, or in the case of propellers, thrust.

AIRMAN CERTIFICATE—A pilot's license issued by the Federal Aviation Administration. Current regulations recognize seven categories of pilots in the following rank: student, sport, recreational, private, commercial, airline transport, and commercial astronaut. Airman categories are further subdivided by ratings such as airplane—single-engine land, single-engine sea, multi-engine land, and multi-engine sea. A Type Rating is required for an aircraft having a gross weight of 12,500 lbs. or more (e.g., Grumman G-73 Mallard).

AIRSPEED—The measurement of an aircraft's velocity. Airspeed may be calculated using the following methods: (1) Indicated (IAS)—The uncorrected airspeed read directly from an instrument aboard an aircraft (i.e., an airspeed indicator); (2) Calibrated (CAS)—Indicated airspeed corrected for instrument error and position; (3) True (TAS)—Calibrated airspeed corrected for air temperature, density, and pressure.

AIRWORTHINESS CERTIFICATE—A document issued by the Federal Aviation Administration which permits an aircraft to be flown in U.S. airspace. Certificates are issued in two classifications: (1) Standard—Aircraft operating under a Type Certificate or Supplemental Type Certificate (see below); (2) Special—Categories of aircraft possessing no Type Certificate that undergo and receive certification as Experimental, Light Sport, Limited, Primary, Provisional, Restricted, and Special Flight Permit.

ALCLAD—A trademark used by Alcoa Aluminum Company for a high-strength sheet of aluminum consisting of an aluminum alloy core having one or both surfaces metallurgically bonded with a pure aluminum that is electrochemically resistant to corrosion.

ALTITUDE—The height of an aircraft above the ground or water, usually measured in feet. Altitude may be expressed in terms of above-ground-level (AGL) or mean-sea-level (MSL).

AMATUER-BUILT AIRCRAFT—See homebuilt aircraft, below.

AMIDSHIPS—The section of a flying boat or amphibian hull directly behind the wing, corresponding to the "waist" position of a landplane.

AMPHIBIAN, AMPHIBION (old spelling)—As used in this book, an amphibian refers to an aircraft having a boat-type hull or a pontoon forming a permanent part of the fuselage and is equipped with retractable landing gear that permits land operations. It does not include aircraft equipped with detachable floats that are amphibious.

ANGLE OF ATTACK (AOA)—The angle formed by the chord of an airfoil and the direction of the aircraft into the relative wind.

ANGLE OF INCIDENCE—The angle between the chord line of a wing or horizontal stabilizer and the aircraft's longitudinal axis.

ANHEDRAL—A downward angle of the wings or horizontal flying surfaces in relation to the horizontal cross-section of the aircraft. Sometimes referred to as negative dihedral.

ASPECT RATIO—The ratio between the span and the chord width of an aircraft's wing. A high aspect ratio wing is typically long and narrow, while a low aspect ratio wing is short and wide. Aspect ratio is usually expressed as the square of the wingspan divided by total wing area, for example a Consolidated PBY, with a wingspan of 104 feet and wing area of 1,514 square feet, has an aspect ratio of 7.1 $[(104)^2 \div 1,514]$.

BALANCED CONTROL SURFACE—A moveable control surface, such as an aileron or elevator, which incorporates a weight forward of the hinge point to reduce control forces on the stick or yoke.

BEACHING—Pulling a flying boat onto a suitable shore so that its weight is supported by dry ground.

BEACHING GEAR—Detachable wheels and struts fixed to the sides and bottom of a flying boat hull to permit beaching.

BEAUFORT WIND SCALE—A standardized scale from zero to twelve corresponding to the velocity of the wind with predictable surface features of the water. For example, a scale five will generate 18 to 24-mpg winds and wave heights up to 6.6 feet.

BILGE—The lowest point inside a hull, watertight compartment, or float.

BIPLANE—An aircraft having two wings, an upper and lower. Some early aircraft also featured a biplane horizontal stabilizer and elevator.

BLEED AIR—Air at high pressure, usually produced by a gas turbine engine, used for anti-icing, heating, or boundary-layer control.

BLOWN FLAPS—A flap system which uses either engine thrust or a boundary-layer control system (see below) to force air across the flaps.

BOUNDARY-LAYER CONTROL (BLC)—A system in which high-pressure air generated by a gas turbine engine (i.e., bleed air) is forced over the wing or part of a wing to prevent the separation of airflow at lower airspeeds.

BOW—The most forward point or nose of a boat hull or float.

BULKHEAD—A solid partition that divides a hull or float into watertight compartments and provides structural rigidity.

BUOYANCY—The tendency of an object to float when placed in a fluid. In principle, an object has positive buoyancy when its density is less than that of the fluid.

CABANE STRUT—Struts used on a biplane, triplane, or parasol monoplane to attach the wings to the fuselage or hull.

CAMBER—The curvature of the upper and lower surfaces of an airfoil.

CANARD—An aerodynamic configuration in which the horizontal control surfaces are located in front of the wings.

CANTILEVERED—An aircraft wing or flying surface wholly supported by its internal structure without need for external bracing.

CEILING—The maximum height above sea level, normally measured in feet, attainable by aircraft under standard atmospheric conditions.

CENTER OF BUOYANCY—The average point of buoyancy in a floating object. Weight added above this point will cause the object to sit deeper in the water at a level attitude, and vice-versa.

CENTER OF GRAVITY (CG)—The lateral and longitudinal point at which an aircraft balances.

CENTER OF PRESSURE—The aerodynamic point of a wing where the pitching moment (i.e., tendency to pitch nose up or nose down) is constant with the angle of attack.

CHINE—The longitudinal seam joining the sides and bottom of a hull or float. Chines serve a structural purpose, transmitting loads from the bottom to the sides of the hull, along with a hydrodynamic function, directing water away from the hull and providing hydrodynamic lift. The angle between the sides and bottom of a hull or float is referred to as the V-chine.

CHORD—The distance between the leading and trailing edges of a wing. In the case of a tapered or elliptical wing, the distance is expressed as the mean aerodynamic chord. The term is also used in reference to tail surfaces, control surfaces, and flaps.

COMMUTER AIR CARRIER—A scheduled commercial air operation using an aircraft with no more than 30 seats and a payload capacity less than 7,500 lbs.

CONSTANT-SPEED PROPELLER—An electrically or hydraulically controlled propeller equipped with a governor that automatically changes pitch to maintain a constant RPM in response to changes in power settings.

CONTROL STICK—A moveable lever mounted in the cockpit directly in front of the pilot that controls the aircraft's elevators (fore and aft) and ailerons (side to side). Variously known as the joystick or simply the stick.

CONTROL YOKE—A wheel or partial wheel mounted on a shaft or column in the cockpit directly in front of the pilot that controls the aircraft's elevators (pushed and pulled) and ailerons (rotated side to side).

CONVENTIONAL LANDING GEAR—A configuration having the two main landing wheels located in front of the CG and a tailwheel or skid at the rear. Popularly known today as a "taildragger."

COWL FLAP—A moveable flap, usually located at the rear of an engine cowling, that regulates the flow of air through the cowling.

COWLING—A removable fairing around an aircraft engine that improves streamlining and cooling.

DECK—The top section of a flying boat or amphibian hull.

DELTA-WING—A triangular-shaped, low aspect ratio wing characterized by a swept leading edge and a straight or slightly tapered trailing edge.

DIHEDRAL—An upward angle of the wings or horizontal flying surfaces in relation to the horizontal cross-section of the aircraft.

DISPLACEMENT POSITION—The attitude of a flying boat or amphibian when its weight in the water is supported by the buoyancy of the entire hull. The aircraft is in displacement position when at rest or when taxiing at very low speed.

DOLLY—A self-contained system, usually float stabilized, into which a flying boat may simply taxi to accomplish beaching.

DORSAL—A location on the upper section of a hull as in a dorsal turret or dorsal fin.

DRAG—The resistance caused by the motion of an aircraft through the air. There are generally two forms of drag: (1) parasite drag caused by the friction of the outer surfaces of aircraft; and (2) induced drag generated by the lift of the wing and other flying surfaces.

DRAG RING—A cambered ring encircling the cylinders of a radial engine for the purpose of improving streamlining and cooling. Also known as a cowl or speed ring.

DRAG WIRE—A rigging wire in an aircraft's structure designed to resist forward and backward aerodynamic loads.

DURAL—Originally a trade name, now used generically, for any wrought aluminum containing alloys of copper, magnesium, and manganese. Also known under the Alcoa trade name "Duraluminum."

ELEVATOR—A moveable surface at the rear of a horizontal stabilizer controlling the pitch (nose up or nose down) of an aircraft around its lateral axis.

ELEVON—A moveable control surface on the trailing edge of a wing that is interconnected to simultaneously function as an elevator or an aileron. Elevons are typically seen on delta or swept wing aircraft having no horizontal tail surfaces.

EMPENNAGE—The tail group of an aircraft, including the vertical stabilizer and rudder, horizontal stabilizer and elevator, and any supporting structures.

EMPTY WEIGHT—The weight of an aircraft less crew, passengers, cargo, baggage, armament (if military), and usable fuel.

EXPERIMENTAL CATEGORY—The most common category of airworthiness certificate issued for home-built aircraft (see below). The process normally involves two basic steps: (1) inspection of the aircraft by an FAA official, including complete documentation of its construction; and (2) a 25 to 40-hour flight testing program within 25 miles of the home airport, during which time no passengers may be carried. Once certificated, the aircraft is free to be operated in U.S. airspace and may carry passengers.

FAIRING—A non-structural component added to the outside of an aircraft to reduce drag.

FEDERAL AVIATION ADMINISTRATION (FAA)—An agency of the U.S. government having authority to oversee and regulate all aspects of civil aviation.

FEDERAL AVIATION REGULATIONS (FARs)—Regulations issued periodically by the FAA that include certification, registration, and airworthiness of aircraft; operating and maintenance requirements for all commercial air activities; designation of all airspace; licensing of pilots; and general operating and flight rules.

FIN—See vertical stabilizer.

FIREWALL—A fire-resistant bulkhead between the engine compartment and the fuselage/hull or nacelles.

FLAP—A hinged surface on the trailing edge of the wing which changes the camber in order to increase lift and drag. The lowering of flaps has the effect of lowering stall speeds, decreasing angle of attack, and causing the aircraft to fly more slowly. The most common types of flap systems are: (1) Split—A flap consisting of a plate hinged from the bottom surface of the wing; (2) Plain—A flap consisting of a hinged section of the entire trailing edge of the wing; (3) Slotted—A flap in the shape of an airfoil which, when lowered, is positioned to form a slot between the wing and the leading edge of the flap; (4) Fowler Type— A slotted flap, named for engineer Harland D. Fowler, that moves both rearward and downward on a track, thereby increasing camber and effective wing area.

FLAPERON—A hinged surface on the trailing edge of a wing that is interconnected to function as both a flap and an aileron.

FLOATPLANE—An aircraft having one or more detachable floats for its primary buoyancy, as differentiated from a boat-hulled flying boat or amphibian.

FLYING BOAT—An aircraft having a boat-type hull that possesses no type of landing gear, retractable or detachable, for land operations. Some flying boats have been equipped with built-in wheels used only for beaching.

FLYING WIRE—A collective term for all of an aircraft's rigging wires: drag wires, landing wires, and lift wires. Early flying boats were highly dependent on flying wires to support and distribute normal aerodynamic loads.

FORMER—A structural or non-structural internal member of a fuselage or boat-hull that forms its outside shape in cross-section.

FRAME CONSTRUCTION—A type of fuselage or hull construction where most of the structural, hydrodynamic, and aerodynamic loads are supported by an internal framework. In early aircraft such frameworks were usually constructed of wood; later methods use welded steel tubing or riveted aluminum extrusions.

FRISE AILERON—A type of aileron, named after engineer Leslie G. Frise, having a beveled leading edge and mounted forward of its inset hinges. When raised, its nose produces drag and decreases adverse yaw, thus requiring less or no rudder input during a banked turn.

FUSELAGE—The main body of an aircraft housing the cockpit, passenger cabin and/or cargo space and to which the wings and tailplane are attached. In the case of a flying boat or amphibian, the fuselage and hull are normally integrated as one structure. An exception would be a twin-hulled flying boat having the cockpit located in the wing center-section (see American Aeronautical S-55, in Part I, page 15).

GAP—The vertical distance between the upper and lower wings of a biplane or triplane.

GAS TURBINE ENGINE—A type of internal combustion engine using a compressor driven by a turbine mounted on the same shaft. The energy produced by the combustion of the compressed air and fuel (usually kerosene) spins the turbine as the gases are expelled rearward.

GENERAL AVIATION—A generic term describing a branch of civil aviation which includes private or corporate-owned aircraft typically used for training, rental, transportation, or recreation.

GROSS WEIGHT—The design weight of an aircraft when fully loaded with fuel, crew, passengers, cargo, and armaments (if military). The term is sometimes expressed as normal gross, the weight at which the aircraft remains within its airframe operating limitations, and maximum takeoff, which contemplates that the aircraft will reach normal gross following a predictable fuel burn-off.

GROUND EFFECT—A phenomenon caused by the interaction of lift produced by the wing near the ground or water when the aircraft is approximately a wingspan distance above it.

GROUNDSPEED—True airspeed corrected for the direction and velocity of the wind. Traditionally calculated using a dead reckoning computer (i.e., an E-6B), modern navigation systems such as LORAN or GPS provide a continuous groundspeed readout.

HOMEBUILT AIRCRAFT—Known also as amateur-built, homebuilt is a generic term applying to an aircraft operating under a Special Airworthiness Certificate in which at least fifty-one percent of the construction was completed by the person (i.e., the "owner") applying for the certificate. Homebuilt aircraft may be built entirely from plans or from kit components assembled by the owner.

HORIZONTALLY-OPPOSED ENGINE—A type of reciprocating piston engine in which an even number of cylinders (2-4-6-8) are arranged on either side of the crankcase. Most horizontally-opposed aircraft engines are air-cooled.

HORIZONTAL STABILIZER—The fixed portion of the horizontal tailplane to which the elevator is attached.

HORSEPOWER (hp)—A measure of the motive energy required to raise 550 lbs. to a height of one foot in one second.

HYDRODYNAMIC FORCE—A term pertaining to the motion of a fluid (water) as it acts upon a body (i.e., a boat-hull or float) which is in motion against it.

HYDRODYNAMIC LIFT—The upward force generated by the motion of a hull or float through the water. When the aircraft is at rest, there is no lift, but as it moves faster through the water, hydrodynamic lift begin to increasingly support more of the aircraft's weight.

INLINE ENGINE—A type of reciprocating piston engine in which an even (4-6-8-12) number of cylinders are arranged either in a straight line or in a V-type configuration directly above (or below) the crankcase. Most early inline aircraft engines were water-cooled via a radiator system, though air-cooled types began to appear during the 1930s (see Grumman J4F Widgeon, Part II, page 146).

INTERPLANE STRUT—One or more pairs of vertical (or nearly vertical) biplane or triplane struts, located outside of the cabanes, which transmit aerodynamic loads between wing panels and maintain angles of incidence. Some interplane struts, known as "N" struts, feature an additional drag strut between them.

KEEL—A longitudinal extension along the center of a hull bottom that enhances the directional stability of a flying boat or amphibian on the water.

KITPLANE—A homebuilt aircraft (see above) built from manufactured components. Kitplanes are exempt from Standard Airworthiness requirements (i.e., a Type Certificate) and may be certificated under Special Airworthiness requirements as long as fifty-one percent of the construction has been completed by the owner.

KNOT—As a measurement of speed, about 1.15 mph, and of distance (i.e., a nautical mile), about 1.15 statute miles or 6,076 feet.

LANDING WIRE—A rigging wire in a wing or tail structure designed to resist negative (downward) aerodynamic loads.

LEADING EDGE—The forward-most part of an aircraft's wing or flying surfaces.

LIFT WIRE—A rigging wire in a wing or tail structure designed to resist positive aerodynamic (upward) loads.

LIGHT SPORT AIRCRAFT (LSA)—A category of aircraft authorized by fairly recent (2004) FAA rules; in general, a two-place aircraft with fixed landing gear and a fixed propeller, possessing a gross weight not exceeding 1,320 lbs. and a maximum speed not exceeding 120 knots (138 mph). For amphibians, the rule allows retractable landing gear and a gross weight of 1,420 lbs.

LIGHTPLANE—A generic term for a single or multi-engine aircraft having a gross weight of 6,500 lbs. or less and most commonly applied to civil aircraft of the post–World War II era.

LOAD FACTOR (G)—A measurement of the force acting upon an aircraft due to acceleration or gravity, usually expressed in units of G times one.

LONGERON—A main longitudinal structural member in a fuselage or hull.

MACH—A measurement of velocity in ratio to the speed of sound (e.g. 761.6 mph at sea level), usually expressed as a fraction (e.g., 0.85 Mach = 650 mph at sea level).

MAGNETO—An engine-driven aircraft accessory producing high-voltage current to the ignition system of a piston engine. For safety reasons, most aircraft engines are equipped with two magnetos and two spark plugs per cylinder.

MONOCOQUE—A type of fuselage or hull design in which most of the structural and aerodynamic loads are carried by the outer skin rather than internal bracing.

NACELLE—A streamlined structure used to house engines, landing gear, weapons, or in some instances, a cockpit or cabin.

NATIONAL ADVISORY COMMITTEE FOR AERONAUTICS (NACA)—A U.S. government agency established in 1915 to carry out and make available various forms of aeronautical research. It was superceded in 1958 by the National Aeronautics and Space Administration (NASA). Aerodynamic forms tested and developed by the agency, such as airfoils and cowlings, are known by NACA number or type.

PAYLOAD—The proportion of an aircraft's useful load over and above fuel and required crew.

PITCH—The nose up and down motion of an aircraft about its lateral axis.

PITOT TUBE—A tube mounted outside the propeller arc on a wing or strut that measures airspeed by reading the differential between impact pressure and static pressure.

PITOT-STATIC SYSTEM—An aircraft instrument system which takes readings from the outside air, such as the airspeed indicator, altimeter, and vertical speed indicator (VSI).

PLANFORM—The general arrangement of an aircraft as seen directly from above or below.

PLANING POSITION—The attitude of a seaplane when its entire weight is supported by hydrodynamic and aerodynamic lift, as during a high-speed taxi and takeoff. Popularly known as being "on-the-step."

PLANING SURFACE—The bottom portion of a boat-hull or float which is in contact with the water.

PLOWING POSITION—A nose high, powered taxi in which the center of buoyancy shifts aft and causes very little of the aircraft's weight to be supported by hydrodynamic lift.

PORPOISING—A rhythmic pitching motion of a seaplane on the water caused by an incorrect planing attitude during takeoff.

PORT—The left side of a boat or aircraft or the direction to the left of it.

POWER-TO-WEIGHT RATIO—For the aircraft, the rated horsepower or thrust divided by the gross weight; for the powerplant only, the rated horsepower or thrust divided by the weight of the engine and accessories.

PROPELLER PITCH—The angle of a propeller blade in relation to its rotational arc; also, the measurement of the forward distance advanced by a propeller blade in one full arc of rotation.

PUSHER—An engine mounted with its propeller facing aft.

PYLON—A streamlined structural member supporting a wing, tailplane, or engine.

RADIAL ENGINE—A type of reciprocating piston engine in which the cylinders are arranged around the crankcase like the spokes on a wheel. An odd number (5-7-9) of pistons are connected to the crankshaft via a master-and-articulating-rod assembly.

RAMJET—A type of jet engine depending solely upon the forward motion of the aircraft to produce inlet air pressure (as opposed to a rotary compressor).

RAMPING—A process by which an amphibian or flying boat equipped with beaching gear uses its own power to taxi from the water onto the shore.

ROLL—The rotational motion of an aircraft about its longitudinal axis.

ROTARY ENGINE—An early type of reciprocating engine in which the cylinders were arranged around the crankcase similar to a radial, but where the crankshaft was fixed and the entire crankcase, to which the propeller was mounted, rotated around it.

RUDDER—A moveable surface at the rear of a vertical stabilizer controlling the yaw (nose left or nose right) of an aircraft about its vertical axis.

RUDDER PEDALS—Pedals on the floor of a cockpit in front of the pilot that control the aircraft's rudder.

SAILING—When a seaplane on the water uses wind as a motive force.

SEA STATE CONDITION NUMBER—A standard scale from zero to nine indicating the height of waves (e.g., a State 5 Sea = 6–10 foot waves).

SEAPLANE—A generic term for any aircraft capable of taking off from and landing on the water.

SEMI-CANTILEVERED—An aircraft wing or flying surface supported partly by internal structure and partly by external bracing.

SEMI-MONOCOCQUE—A type of fuselage, hull, or nacelle construction where the outside skin is supported by internal formers and stringers that share the structural, hydrodynamic, and aerodynamic loads. It is the most common method used in the fabrication of fuselages and hulls from aluminum.

SESQUIPLANE—A biplane configuration in which the lower wing possesses much less area than the upper wing.

SHAFT HORSEPOWER (shp)—The amount of horsepower delivered to a propeller shaft, corrected for the loss of power caused by a transmission or drive system. Commonly used as a measurement of power in turboprop engines.

SKEG—An extension of the keel behind the step of a boat-hull or float which is designed to prevent the aircraft from tipping back onto the afterbody.

SLAT—A moveable surface on the leading edge of a wing which increases both camber and airflow. Slats can be manual or designed to automatically extend at higher angles of attack.

SLOT—A spanwise gap in the leading edge of a wing which increases airflow over the upper surface at higher angles of attack.

SPAR—The main structural member of an aircraft wing or flying surface running perpendicular to or across its longitudinal axis. Spars are typically designed to resist any structural or aerodynamic loads, i.e., lift, landing, drag, and torsion.

SPOILER—A moveable plate on the upper surface of a wing for the purpose of causing drag or, when used differentially, to induce roll.

SPONSONS—Buoyant extensions to the sides of a boat hull's forebody. Large airfoil-shaped sponsons, located near the center of gravity, have been used in lieu of stabilizing floats under the wings. One-piece stabilizing floats on small amphibians are sometimes referred to as sponsons.

SPORT PILOT—A recent (2004) category of Airman Certificate which may be obtained with as little as

20 hours logged flying time. Pilots holding a Sport Pilot Certificate may only operate a Light Sport Aircraft (see above).

SPRAY RAILS—Metal flanges attached to the chine of a boat-hull or float forebody that are designed to reduce the water spray thrown into a propeller.

STABILIZING FLOATS—Small floats located under the outboard wing panels of a flying boat or amphibian to prevent the wingtips from contacting the water. Also commonly referred to as tip or wing floats.

STAGGER—The relative fore and aft relationship between the leading edges of the upper and lower wings of a biplane or triplane. If the leading edge of the upper wing is forward of that of the lower wing, the aircraft is said to have "positive" stagger. The reverse is true for "negative" stagger.

STALL—An event that causes the wing to lose lift to the extent that it will no longer support the weight of the aircraft. A stall is caused by an increase in angle of attack and resulting loss of airspeed. An "accelerated" stall occurs when the aircraft reaches critical angle of attack while accelerating in excess of one-G.

STARBOARD—The right side of a boat or aircraft or the direction to the right of it.

STEP—A transverse gap between the fore- and afterbodies of a boat-hull or float near or just behind the center of gravity. In principle, the step allows the hydrodynamic lift generated by the forebody to lift the afterbody clear of the water once sufficient forward speed is attained.

STERN—The most rearward point or tail end of a boat hull or float.

STRAKE—A longitudinal member on the outside of a boat-hull or float which adds structural rigidity and directional stability. Sometimes known as a keelson.

STRINGER—A longitudinal member on the inside of a fuselage, boat-hull, or float which adds structural rigidity to the skin. Stingers are also sometimes used for the same purpose in the spanwise construction of wings and flying surfaces.

SUPERSONIC—A velocity exceeding the speed of sound (i.e., 761.6 mph at sea level).

SUPPLEMENTAL TYPE CERTIFICATE (STC)—A certificate of airworthiness issued by the FAA when an aircraft has been modified from its original design.

SWEEPBACK—The rearward angle between the quarter chord line (i.e., the distance between the leading and trailing edges) of an aircraft's wing and its longitudinal centerline.

SWEET SPOT—The smallest section of a hull or float planing surface which is still in contact with the water when a seaplane in planing position reaches a takeoff attitude.

TAILPLANE—See empennage.

TAPER—The angle of a wing or tail surface from root to tip as measured from its leading and/or training edge.

THRUST—An aerodynamic force propelling an aircraft through the air. Thrust may be produced by a propeller or by the expelled gases of a jet or rocket engine. In principle, thrust must exceed drag (aerodynamic and hydrodynamic) in order for an aircraft to achieve flight, and in a level, cruising attitude, thrust and drag are equal.

TORQUE—The rotational force imparted by a turning propeller which causes an aircraft to rotate in the opposite direction, thereby inducing roll and yaw.

TRACTOR—An engine mounted with its propeller facing forward.

TRAILING EDGE—The rear most part of an aircraft's wing or flying surfaces.

TRICYCLE LANDING GEAR—A configuration having the two main landing wheels located aft of the CG and a nosewheel mounted to the front.

TRIM TAB—A small, adjustable or fixed control surface located on or within the trailing edge of a rudder, elevator, or aileron. Adjustable trim tabs, controlled from the cockpit, are used to reduce the aerodynamic forces imposed on flight controls; fixed trim tabs are adjusted on the ground to enable the aircraft to maintain trim in level flight.

TRIPLANE—An aircraft having three wings, an upper, middle, and lower.

TURBOJET ENGINE—A type of gas turbine engine in which thrust is produced by expelling exhaust gases rearward. A turbofan engine is a variation of a turbojet having one or more ducted fans connected to the engine's axial shaft.

TURBOPROP ENGINE—A type of gas turbine engine in which thrust is produced by a propeller connected to the axial shaft through a driveshaft and transmission case.

TYPE CERTIFICATE—A certificate of airworthiness issued by the FAA for an aircraft which meets the criteria for Standard Category. The Type Certificate indicates that the aircraft, its powerplant, and related systems, have fulfilled all the requirements for conduct of safe flight operations under all normally conceivable conditions. Any manufactured, ready-to-fly aircraft must possess a Type Certificate. A Type

Certificate issued for a particular aircraft will remain valid as long as the aircraft meets its approved type design. If modified beyond its approved design, an STC must be obtained.

TWO-CYLE ENGINE—A type of reciprocating piston engine in which the four essential functions (i.e., intake, compression, combustion, and exhaust) are accomplished in two cycles (or strokes) of the piston rather than four. Two-cycle engines characteristically produce greater horsepower for their weight but at much higher RPMs. In aviation applications, two-cycle engines are usually seen on very light or ultra-light aircraft and must use a belt or gear-driven reduction system to drive the propeller.

ULTRALIGHT AIR VEHICLE—A category of aircraft recognized under FAR Part 103 which are exempt from certification and registration. In order to qualify under this rule, the aircraft must be single-place, weigh no more than 254 lbs. empty (274.4 lbs. allowed for seaplanes), carry no more than five gallons of fuel, and have a maximum speed not exceeding 55 mph. Similarly, a pilot operating an ultralight air vehicle is not required to hold a license issued by the FAA.

USEFUL LOAD—The added weight of an aircraft's fuel, crew, passengers, baggage, cargo, and armaments (if military). Armament (i.e., weapons load) may be considered separately.

VERTICAL STABILZER—The fixed portion of the vertical tailplane to which the rudder is attached.

WASH-OUT—A feature of wing design in which a slight amount of 'twist' (as seen from the side) reduces angle of incidence from root to tip. For reasons of stability, an amount of washout is normally incorporated to insure that the wing stalls at the root (which has a higher angle of attack) before reaching the tip. Wash-in, rarely ever seen, is the opposite of wash-out.

WATER RUDDER—A moveable blade at the rear of a boat-hull or float used for maneuvering on the water. Most water rudders are interconnected to the main rudder cables and can be retracted once the aircraft reaches planing position.

WING LOADING—The wing area of an aircraft divided by its gross weight, usually expressed in pounds per square foot.

WING RIB—A chordwise member of a wing structure that forms its airfoil shape and transmits aerodynamic loads from the skin to the spars. Wing ribs may be fabricated from wood, aluminum, or composite material.

YAW—The side-to-side motion of an aircraft about its vertical axis.

Military Terms and Abbreviations

Limited to terms and abbreviations used by the U.S. military services.

AERIAL ATTACK—A branch of warfare using aircraft to attack military objectives such as enemy shipping, shore installations, aircraft (on the ground), bases, supply lines, weapons and munitions, and personnel.

AERIAL BOMBARDMENT—Using aircraft to deliver bombs against tactical or strategic military objectives.

AERIAL REFUELING—The in-flight transfer of fuel by one aircraft (i.e., a tanker) to another aircraft via either a flying boom or probe and drogue system.

AFB (AIR FORCE BASE)—A military base operated by the U.S. Air Force.

ARCTIC FIGHTER CONCEPT—A U.S. Air Force study conducted between 1949 and 1951 to determine the feasibility of developing a hydro-ski equipped, jet-propelled fighter-interceptor that could operate from Arctic waters. (See Edo 150 and 142 in Appendix A).

ARMAMENT—Refers to any type of weapon carried by an aircraft, including machine guns and cannons, bombs, rockets, torpedoes, depth charges, and mines.

ARRESTING GEAR—Equipment fitted to single-engine Navy amphibians enabling them to land aboard aircraft carriers.

ARS (AIR RESCUE SERVICE)—A branch started by the U.S. Army Air Forces and continued by the U.S. Air Force, using landplanes, flying boats, amphibians, and helicopters to rescue downed aircrew.

ASW (ANTISUBMARINE WARFARE)—A branch of warfare using ships or aircraft to detect, track, and/or destroy hostile submarines.

ATOMIC BOMB—See nuclear weapons.

BLACK CAT RAIDERS—The name given during World War II to Consolidated PBYs and Martin PBMs (see Part II, page 102) that were especially equipped to attack enemy convoys at night.

BUAER (U.S. NAVAL BUREAU OF AERONAUTICS)—The military agency having primary responsibility for the development and procurement of U.S. Navy, U.S. Marine Corps, and U.S. Coast Guard aircraft from 1921 to 1962.

CALIBER—The inside diameter of the bore of a gun, expressed either in fractions of an inch (e.g., .50-caliber) or millimeters (e.g., 20-mm).

CGAS (COAST GUARD AIR STATION)—A military base operated by the U.S. Coast Guard.

DEPTH CHARGE—An underwater ASW weapon using an acoustic, hydrostatic (pressure), or magnetic fuse to trigger detonation. The first air-droppable depth charges appeared during World War Two.

ELECTRONIC COUNTERMEASURES (ECM)—A term for the detection, classification, and location of, or interference with, hostile radio signals. Radio signals may include communications, navigation, and radar. The generic term for radio interference is "jamming."

FLB (FLYING LIFE BOAT)—A Coast Guard name originally given to the Fokker PJ (see Part II, page 131), but subsequently applied generally to any flying boat or amphibian used to rescue shipwreck survivors.

GUN MOUNT—The fixed or flexible installation of one or more machine guns or cannons aboard an aircraft for defensive or offensive purposes.

MAD (MAGNETIC ANOMALY DETECTOR)—An ASW system used to detect variations in the earth's magnetic field. The MAD sensor, either pod or boom-mounted on the aircraft, can detect a shallowly submerged submarine.

MARITIME PATROL—An over-water military mission that can include long-range reconnaissance, convoy escort, aerial attack, mine-laying, ASW, and ECM.

MCAS (MARINE CORPS AIR STATION)—A military base operated by the U.S. Marine Corps.

MINE—A self-contained explosive device placed on or below the water to destroy ships or submarines that may be triggered on contact or by magnetic or acoustic exploders. Mines specifically designed to be carried and laid by aircraft first appeared during World War Two.

NAF (NAVAL AIRCRAFT FACTORY)—An aircraft production and development facility established by the U.S. Navy at Philadelphia, Pennsylvania in 1917. NAF was originally created to augment civilian production of Navy aircraft but evolved into a clearinghouse for aircraft design and development during the 1920s and 1930s. It was officially renamed the Naval Air Engineering Facility in 1956.

NAS (NAVAL AIR STATION)—A military base operated by the U.S. Navy.

NATS (NAVAL AIR TRANSPORTATION SERVICE)—Established in 1941 to transport cargo, personnel, and mail to the naval ships and ground forces, especially in advanced areas of operation. Operational control of NATS squadrons was absorbed into MATS (Military Air Transportation Service) in mid–1948.

NUCLEAR WEAPON—An explosive device deriving its destructive force from nuclear (atomic level) reactions, and is generally one of two types: (1) Fission—A chain reaction of fissile material (i.e., enriched uranium or plutonium) that can produce an energy release up to the equivalent of 500 kilotons of TNT. Popularly known as an atomic or A-bomb. (2) Fusion—A chain reaction, termed thermo-nuclear, of fissile material followed by the compression of fusion fuel (i.e., tritium, deuterium, or lithium deuteride) that can produce an energy release up to 50 megatons of TNT. Also known as a hydrogen or H-bomb.

OPEN OCEAN SEAPLANE—A requirement issued by BuAer in 1956 to develop a seaplane that could operate as an ASW platform in the open ocean, specified as state five seas with waves up to 10 feet. (See Convair P6Y, Grumman G-132, and Martin P7M in Appendix A.)

RADAR (Radio Detection and Ranging)—An electronic system that uses electromagnetic waves (radio or microwave) to identify the range, altitude, direction, and speed of moving or stationary objects such as aircraft, ships, weather features, or terrain.

RADOME—A streamlined housing for a radar system.

SAR (SEARCH AND RESCUE)—A branch of the U.S. Navy and U.S. Coast Guard, known as Air-Sea Rescue in the 1940s and 1950s, using flying boats, amphibians, and helicopters to rescue downed aircrew and shipwreck survivors.

SEA FIGHTER—A U.S. Navy program conducted between 1948 and 1957 to develop a jet-propelled fighter capable of operating from the sea. (See Convair F2Y, Part III, page 229.)

SEAPLANE CATAPULT—A shipboard system for launching small flying boats, amphibians, and floatplanes. The first practical turntable catapults, powered first by compressed air and later, gunpowder charges, were placed in service aboard Navy ships during the early 1920s.

SEAPLANE TENDER—A U.S. Navy ship dedicated to the repair and logistical support of flying boats and amphibians and their crews. At the peak of seaplane operations during World War Two, the Navy operated 20 heavy tenders (AV3–AV23) and 47 light tenders (AVP1–AVP57 [hull numbers not in sequence]).

SONAR (SOUND NAVIGATION AND RANGING)—As applied to aircraft, an ASW system that uses underwater sound propagation to detect submarines. Sonar may be (1) active, receiving returns from directed sound waves bounced off solid objects in the water or (2) passive, hearing the sound produced by objects in the water. Airborne systems are generally of two types: (1) Dipping—Sonar equipment lowered into the water while still attached to the aircraft; (2) Sonobuoy—Sonar equipment dropped into the water that transmits information back to the aircraft by radio.

SSF (SEAPLANE STRIKING FORCE)—A U.S. Navy program conducted between 1949 and 1959 to develop a jet-propelled flying boat capable of long-range nuclear strike, conventional bombing, mine-laying, and reconnaissance. (see Martin P6M in Part III, below).

TORPEDO—A self-propelled explosive weapon launched into the water. The first air-droppable torpedoes appeared during World War One and electric-powered ASW types with acoustic homing systems were introduced in 1943.

TURRET—A fully-enclosed, flexible gun mounting that can be powered manually or by a hydraulic or electric system. The first powered systems were introduced just prior to World War Two.

U-BOAT—A submarine serving with the German Navy (Kriegsmarine) during World Wars One and Two.

UTILITY AMPHIBIAN—A type of single or multi-engine amphibian used by all U.S. military branches from 1923 to 1983 for transportation, search and rescue, coastal maritime patrol, ASW, and ship-to-shore duties.

WEAPONS BAY—A fully-enclosed compartment for stowage of aircraft weapons. Weapons bays in flying boats are typically located in the bottoms of the wing nacelles, although some carried weapons within the hull that were launched over the sides via a track system.

WEAPONS RACK—An external rack fitted under the wing of a flying boat or amphibian for the purpose of carrying bombs, mines, depth charges, or torpedoes.

Military Aircraft Nomenclature

The lettering and numbering systems shown below are limited to flying boats and amphibious aircraft in U.S. military service from 1912 to 1983. In the earliest years, before and during World War One, the services used no set system to identify aircraft types and usually relied upon some variation of the manufacturer's model number (e.g., Curtiss H-16, NC-4, etc.).

U.S. Army (USAAS, USAAC, and USAAF) and Air Force (USAF) Designations

A standardized alpha-numeric system for designating different types of Army aircraft first appeared in 1919 and was continued with minor variations by the USAF in 1947. The system is usually expressed in the following order: Type, Sequential Type Number, and Sub-Version. Using the USAAF version of the Consolidated PBY-6A as an example, OA-10B translates to OA = Observation Amphibian, -10 = Tenth Type, and B = Second Version. An "X" preceding the designation generally reflects experimental status and "Y" or "Y1" indicates a pre-production service test model. A tri-service system, adopted for all U.S. military branches in 1962, basically incorporated the USAF system under a new numbering sequence. The following type designations apply to flying boats and amphibians covered in Parts I, II, III, and Appendix A of this book, including U.S. Navy types after 1962:

B = Bomber	O = Observation
C = Cargo and Transport	OA = Observation Amphibian
COA = Corps Observation Amphibian	P = Patrol
HRV = Hydrofoil Amphibian	SA = Search and Rescue Amphibian
HU = Utility Amphibian	SHU = Antisubmarine Utility Amphibian
LU = Cold Weather Utility Amphibian	SP = Antisubmarine Patrol

U.S. Navy (USN), U.S. Marine Corps (USMC), and U.S. Coast Guard (USCG) Designations

A standardized system designating different types of naval aircraft first appeared in 1922 and remained in effect until adoption of the tri-service system in 1962. The pre–1962 system used a combination of identifying letters and numbers in the following order: Type, Sequential Type number, Manufacturer Identifier, Version, and Sub-Version. For example, PB2Y-3R translates to: PB = Patrol Bomber, 2 = Second Type, Y = Consolidated, -3 = Third Version, and R = Transport Sub-Version. An "X" preceding the designation generally reflects experimental status and "Y" indicates a pre-production service test model. The following identifying letters apply to flying boats and amphibians covered in Parts I, II, III, and the Appendix of this book:

Type Designations

F = Fighter	O = Observation	S = Scout
J = Utility	P = Patrol	R = Transport
JR = Utility Transport	PB = Patrol Bomber	U = Utility (after 1948)

Manufacturer Identifiers

B = Boeing	H = Hall	M = Martin
B = Vickers (Canada)	J = General Aviation (Fokker)	N = Naval Aircraft Factory
D = Douglas	K = Fairchild	O = Viking
F = Grumman	K = Keystone	S = Sikorsky
G = Great lakes	L = Loening	

Sub-Versions (suffix)

A = Amphibious	R = Transport
E = Electronic Countermeasures	S = Antisubmarine
G = USCG Equipment	T = Trainer
L = Cold Weather Operations	

Bibliography

BOOKS AND PERIODICALS

"Acme Answer Amphibian." *Aviation Week* magazine. New York: McGraw-Hill, Sept. 1957.

Allward, Maurice. *An Illustrated History of Seaplanes and Flying Boats*. New York: Dorset Press, 1981.

Beech Aero Center. *Private Pilot Manual*. Denver: Jeppeson-Sanderson, 1978.

Bowers Peter M. *Curtiss Aircraft 1907–1946*. Annapolis: Naval Institute Press, 1987.

_____, and Gordon Swanborough. *United States Navy Aircraft since 1911*. Annapolis: Naval Institute Press, 1976.

Bowman. Martin W. *USAAF Handbook 1939–1945*. Mechanicsburg, Pennsylvania: Stackpole Books, 1997.

Breihan, John R. *Martin Aircraft 1909–1960*. Santa Ana, California: Narkiewicz/Thompson, 1995.

Buttler, Tony. *American Secret Projects: Fighters and Interceptors 1945–1978*. Hinckley, England: Midland, 2008.

Casey, Louis S. *Curtiss: The Hamondsport Era 1907–1915*. New York: Crown, 1981.

Cliche, Andre. *Ultralight Aircraft Shopper's Guide*. 12th ed. Richford, Vermont: Cybair, 2005.

Davies, R.E.G. *Airlines of the United States since 1914*. Washington, D.C.: Smithsonian Institution Press, 1972.

English, Dave. *Slipping the Surly Bonds*. New York: McGraw-Hill, 1998.

Fahey, James C., ed. *U.S. Army Aircraft 1908–1946*. New York: Ships and Aircraft, 1946.

_____. *USAF Aircraft 1947–1956*. Wright-Patterson, Ohio: Air Force Museum Foundation, reissued 1978.

Federal Aviation Administration. *Seaplane, Skiplane Operations Handbook*. Pub. No. H-8083-23. Tabernash, Colorado: Aircraft Technical, 2004.

Francillon, Rene J. *Grumman Aircraft since 1929*. Annapolis: Naval Institute Press, 1989.

_____. *McDonnell Douglas Aircraft since 1920*. Annapolis: Naval Institute Press, 1990.

Friedman, Norman. *U.S. Naval Weapons*. Annapolis: Naval Institute Press, 1988.

Green, William. *The Jet Aircraft of the World*. Garden City, New York: Hanover House, 1957.

_____. *War Planes of the Second World War, Flying Boats*, Vol. 5. Garden City, New York: Doubleday, 1962.

Gunston, Bill. *American Warplanes*. New York: Crescent Books, 1986.

_____. *Illustrated Encyclopedia of Propeller Airliners*. London: Phoebus, 1980.

Hoffman, Richard. *The Martin P5M Patrol Seaplane*. Simi Valley, California: Steve Ginter Books, 2007.

Larkins, William T. *Battleship and Cruiser Aircraft of the United States Navy 1910–1949*. Altgen, Pennsylvania: Schiffer, 1996.

_____. *U.S. Marine Corps Aircraft 1914–1959*. Concord, California: Aviation History, 1959.

_____. *U.S. Navy Aircraft 1921–1941*. Concord, California: Aviation History, 1961.

Lawson, Robert R., ed. *The History of U.S. Naval Airpower*. New York: The Military Press, 1985.

Lofkin, Laurence K. *Quest for Performance: The Evolution of Modern Aircraft*. Washington, D.C.: Technical Information Branch, National Aeronautics and Space Administration, 1985 (available online: http://www.hq.nasa.gov/office/pao/History/SP-468/contents.htm).

Pearcy, Arthur. *U.S. Coast Guard Aircraft Since 1916*. Annapolis: Naval Institute Press, 1991.

Reep, Steve. *Go to Hull*. Grand Forks, North Dakota: Eastern Dakota, 1996.

Smith, Hershel. *A History of Aircraft Piston Engines*. Manhattan, Kansas: Sunflower University Press, 1986.

Smith, Myron J. *Passenger Airliners of the United States 1926–1986*. Missoula, Montana: Pictorial Histories, 1987.

Trimble, William F. *Attack from the Sea: A History of the U.S. Navy's Seaplane Striking Force*. Annapolis: Naval Institute Press, 2005.

_____. *Wings for the Navy: A History of the Naval Aircraft Factory 1917–1956*. Annapolis: Naval Institute Press, 1990.

Underwood, John, and George Collinge. *The Lightplane since 1909*. Glendale, California: Heritage Press, 1975.

Wagner, Ray. *American Combat Planes*. 3d ed. Garden City, New York: Doubleday, 1982.

Wainwright, Marshall. "The Mystery Flying Boat from Douglas." *Air Classics* magazine, November 2005. Challenge Publications, Chatsworth, California.

Wegg, John. *General Dynamics Aircraft and Their Predecessors Since 1912*. London: Brassey's, 1990.

Wilson, Steward. *The Light Aircraft Guide*. Moorebank, Australia: Dyowl Pty. Ltd., 1987.

Woodring, Frank, and Suanne Woodring. *Fairchild Aircraft*. Mount Pleasant, South Carolina: Arcadia Publishing, 2007.

WEBSITES

Aero Adventure, Inc. "Product Line." Adventura Kitplane Website, http://www.sea-plane.com/Product%20Line/Aventura%20II.html.

Aeromarine Aircraft, Inc. "Seafire TA16 Amphibian." Seafire Home Page, http://www.nelsonillustration.com/Seafire.htm.

"Airworthiness Certificate Overview." Federal Aviation Administration Website, http://www.faa.gov/aircraft/air_cert/airworthiness_certification/aw_overview/.

"Airworthiness Certification Process." Federal Aviation Administration Website, http://www.faa.gov/aircraft/air_cert/airworthiness_certification/aw_cert_proc/.

Aviation Enthusiast Corner. "Pereira X-28A Osprey I." Aircraft Reference Website, http://aeroweb.brooklyn.cuny.edu/specs/pereira/x-28a.htm.

Dannysoar. "The Bel Geddes #4, A Fine Road Not Taken." Free Flight Website, http://home.att.net/~dannysoar/BelGeddes.htm.

Eckland, K.O., ed. "Aircraft A-Z." Aerofiles Website, http://www.aerofiles.com/aircraft.html.

Flavell, Aird. "Adventure Air Super Adventurer." World Flying Boats Website, http://www.msacomputer.com/FlyingBoats-old/homebuild/Super-Adventurer.htm, as of 2000.

_____. "Flying Boats of the World, A Complete Reference." World Flying Boat Website, http://www.msacomputer.com/FlyingBoats-old/.

"Fleetwings Sea Bird." Wikipedia, The Free Encyclopedia, http://en.wikipedia.org/wiki/Fleetwings_Sea_Bird, 2008.

"Goodyear Duck." Wikipedia, The Free Encyclopedia, http://en.wikipedia.org/wiki/Goodyear_Duck, 2008.

Icon Aircraft. "Icon A5 Information." Icon Aircraft Website, http://www.iconaircraft.com/Experience-ICON.html?id=album-1&num=1#id=album-1&num=1.

Igor I. Sikorsky Historical Archives, Inc. "S-38, S-39, S-42, and S-44." Sikorsky Historical Archives Website, http://www.sikorskyarchives.com/.

Larsson, Björn, ed. "Aeromarine Airways." The Aeromarine Website, http://www.timetableimages.com/ttimages/aerom.htm.

Leader Industries, Inc. "329 Concept." Leader Industries Website, http://www.329amphibian.com/concept.asp.

"Martin Aircraft." The Glenn L. Martin Maryland Aviation Museum Website, http://www.marylandaviationmuseum.org/history/index.html.

Naval Aviation History Branch. "Dictionary of American Naval Aviation Squadrons, Vol. 2." Naval Historical Center Website, PDF download, http://www.history.navy.mil/branches/dictvol2.htm.

Osprey Aircraft. "Osprey II." Osprey Aircraft Website, http://www.ospreyaircraft.com/osprey-2.

Paul Garber NASM Facility. "Ecker Flying Boat." The Aviation History Online Museum, http://www.aviation-history.com/garber/vg-bldgecker_boat-1_f.html.

Pilotfriend Experimental Aircraft. "Specifications." Experimental Aircraft Database, http://www.pilotfriend.com/experimental/experimental_aircraft.htm.

Rainbow Flyers, Inc., QuickKit Division. "The All New Glass Goose." Glass Goose Website, http://www.glassgoose.com/g_goose.html.

"Regulatory and Certification Policy, Sport Pilot and Light Sport Aircraft." AOPA Online, http://www.aopa.org/sportpilot/.

Roos, Frederick W. "Benoist Paper." NASM Website, http://www.airandspacemuseum.org/BenoistPaper.htm, 2005.

Ruzakowski, Henry, and Brian VanWagnen. "About Seabees." International Seabee Owner's Club Website, http://republicseabee.com/about.html, as of 2003.

Saevdal, Steinar. "The Colonial Skimmer and Lake LA-4 Story." Steinar's Hangar Website, http://home.c2i.net/otter32/colonial/colonial_index.htm.

_____. "The Thurston Teal Amphibian." Steinar's Hangar Website, http://www.seabee.info/teal.htm.

Seawind LLC. "Seawind News." Seawind Official Website, http://www.seawind.net/Seawind%20 News.html.

Seawind/SNA, Inc. "General Kit Information." Seawind Kit Website, http://www.seawindsna. com/.

Sportair USA. "SeaRey Performance." Searey Homepage, http://www.searey.aero/performance. htm. See also, Progressive Aerodyne, Inc., http://www.searey.com/index.html.

Strauss, Gary. "Anderson Kingfisher." EAA Members Website, http://members.eaa.org/asplogin. asp?asplReq=%2Fhome%2Fhomebuilders%2Fse lecting%2Fkits%2FKingfisher.html%3F.

Steeves, Richard, ed. "Coot Information." Coot Builders Website, http://www.coot-builders.com /Coot_Information.htm.

Ultralight News. "Moyes Microlites Connie Amphibious Ultralight Aircraft." Ultralight Buyer's Website, http://www.ultralightnews.com/ssulbg/ connie-moyes_microlites.htm.

"Ultralight Vehicle Federal Regulations." U.S. Ultralight Association Website, http://www.ultra lightflying.com/ultralight-vehicle-regulations/ ultralight-vehicle-regulations.html.

Unofficial Home of Avid Flyer. "Avid Aircraft Spec Sheet." Avid Flyer Builder's Website, http://www. avidflyeraircraft.com/avidblog/?page_id=18.

Volmer Club of America. "Volmer VJ-22." Volmer Aircraft Website, http://www.volmeraircraft.com/ Information.html.

Index